WEBSTER'S
CROSSWORD PUZZLE
DICTIONARY

Compiled by:
Patricia Fox-Sheinwold

CHARTWELL BOOKS INC.

A Division of
BOOK SALES, INC.
110 Enterprise Avenue
Secaucus, N.J. 07094

Helpful Hints On How To Use This Dictionary

This handy book for the avid crossword puzzler is not meant to replace the standard dictionary, but in many instances it can lead you to the correct word, which you may or may not have to look up in a larger volume. For example: *file:* row, enter, rape, cabinet. All four are accurate though different definitions. So, if the word you are seeking does not fit into the *row* category then switch your thinking to the *cabinet*-type definition. Prepositions, pronouns, and adverbs are included along with the often used opposites, prefixes, suffixes, slang, combining forms, and pertaining to — these will be found under the entry. Sometimes it may be necessary to check both words for the definition. For example: *at odds*. If you do not find the word under *odds* then check under *at*. A defined word which is derived from the main entry will be listed in the subtitles and will appear with a hyphen followed by the additional letter or suffix. For example: *wall*: parapet, barrier
-ed town: burg

There is a heavy concentration on historical names, book titles, authors, musicians, mythology, heraldry, poetical and musical references — you know, the ones that are so difficult to find. As you become more familiar with this book you will continue to find many more of those elusive words and odd definitions. Plus, the Special Section contains concise and alphabetized information that usually takes hours to track down if you don't happen to have it filed away in your memory bank. If you do not find what you are looking for in the Special Section, always go back and check the entries. For example: *Pennsylvania*: Sect, *Amish,* will be under the entry, not in the Special Section as the listings there are uniform.

Good luck — Happy word hunting. Enjoy.

Patricia Fox-Sheinwold

To my son, John,
who has a way with words.

Special thanks to: Evelyn Lee Jones
Barbara Lea
Jeanne Schapiro

ABBREVIATIONS

Am.	American
Afr.	African
Ar.	Arabic
Austral.	Australian
Brit.	British
comb. form	combining form
colloq.	colloquial
Dut.	Dutch
Eng.	English
Eur.	European
Fr.	French
Ger.	German
Gr.	Greek
instr.	instrument
It.	Italian
Jap.	Japanese
Lat.	Latin
Mex.	Mexican
myth.	mythology
mus.	music
N.	North
N.A.	North American
pert. to	pertaining to
poet.	poetic
Russ.	Russian
S.	South
S.A.	South American
S. Afr.	South African
Scot.	Scottish
Sl.	Slang
Sp.	Spanish

A

a: an, ay, per, each
aa: lava
aal, al: mulberry
Aaron: associate: Hur
 " brother: Moses
 " burial place: Hor
 " rod: mullein
 " sister: Miriam
 " son: Nadab, Abihu
aba: robe, garment
abaca: hemp, lupis, linaga
abacus: slab, calculator
Abaddon: hell, abyss, satan
 " angel: Apollyon
Abadite, Ibidite: Muslim
abaft: aft, astern, rearward
abalone: ear, ormer, mollusk
abash: cow, shame, confound
abatis: obstacle, barricade
abb: wool, yarn
abba: title, father
abbe: cleric, priest, ecclesiastic
 " domain: abbacy, monas-
tery

abbess: amma, prelatess
 " domain: convent, nun-
nery
abbot: abbas, coarb, hegumen
 " assistant: prior
 " hero: rollo
abbreviate: cut, prune, curtail, truncate
abdomen: pleon, paunch,
venter
abduct: kidnap, snatch,
shanghai
Abdul the Bul Bul: Amir
abecederium: book, primer
Abel: brother: Cain, Seth
 " parent: Adam, Eve
Abelard's love: (H)Eloise
abele: pine, poplar
aberrant: wild, abnormal
abettor: fautor, promoter,
auxiliary
abies: firs, evergreens
Abigail: maid
Abigail's husband: David,

7

Nabal

Abijah's son: Asa

abject: base, pitiful, servile

abjectly afraid: craven

ablegate: envoy

abluent: soap, detergent

ablution: bath, lotion, baptism

abnegate: deny, abjure, disclaim

aboard: onto, athwart

aboma: boa, bom, serpent

abominable: vile, odious, loathsome

Abominable Snowman: Bigfoot, yeti

aboriginal: natal, first, primitive, indigenous

aborigine: native, autochthon

abortion: failure, feticide, misconception

abound: flow, swarm, exuberate

about: re, near, anent, circa, circiter, approximately

above: o'er, atop, overhead, supra

  " **board:** open, legit

  " **the ear:** epiotic

  " **poetic:** o'er

  " **reproach:** pure, innocent

abra: pass, defile

abrade: rub, bark, chafe, grind, excoriate

abrading: tool: file, rasp

  " **material:** emery, sand(paper), corundum

Abraham's: birthplace: Ur

  " **brother:** Nahor

  " **concubine: Hagar**

  " **father:** Terah

  " **grandfather:** Nahor

  " **grandson:** Esau

  " **nephew:** Lot

  " **son:** Isaac, Medan, Shuah, Midian, Zimran, Ishmael

  " **wife:** Sara(h), Hagar, Sarai, Keturah

abramis: carp, fish, bream

abrasion: scar, attrition, bruise

abraxas: gem, stone, charm

abret: bread, wafer

abri: shed, cavity, dugout

abrini: licorice, Abrus

abrogate: annul, quash, revoke, nullify

abrupt: curt, blunt, terse, craggy, unceremonious

Absalom: cousin/captain: Amasa

  " **father:** David

  " **slayer:** Joab

  " **sister:** Tamar

abscess: moro, ulcer, lesion, gathering

  " **on gums:** gumboil

abscond: flee, escape, decamp, levant

absence: leave of exeat, furlough

  " **of feeling:** insensate, numb

  " **of hair:** acomia, atopecia

  " **of motion:** rest, inertia

  " **of shame:** brazen

  " **of taste:** ageusia

absentee: truant, malingerer

absinthe: genipi, wormwood, liqueur

absolute: mear, plat, total, plenary, explicit, unconditional

  " **independence:** alod

" **rule:** autarchy

absolve: free, acquit, shrive, dispense, exculpate

" **in law:** vested

" **in sin:** shrive

absorb: sop, unite, occupy, engross, occlude

absorbent: fomes, bibulous

" **material:** sponge, blotter

abstain: deny, spurn, eschew, forbear, teetotal

" **from eating:** fast

abstemious: ascetic, temperate

absterge: wipe, purge, rinse

abstruse: deep, mystic, acroamatic, recondite

abundance: flow, mort, foison, amplitude, exuberance

abuse: mar, tax, defile, vilify, yatter, traduce, invective

abut: join, rest, border, project

abutment: pier, alette

abyss: pit, gulf, chasm, vorago, gehenna

" **Babylonian mythology:** Apsu

" **below Hades:** tartarus

Abyssinia, Abyssinian: Kaffa, Ethiopian

" **coin:** talari

" **drink:** mese, bousa

" **fly:** zimb

" **herb:** ramtil

" **weight:** aket, alada, kasm, natr

acacia: gum, babul, siris, arabic

acaleph: jellyfish, sea nettle

acantha: fin, spine, prickle

acarus: mite, tick, insect

acaudal: bobbed, anurous, ecaudate

accede: let, allow, yield, comply, acquiesce

accented: marcato, stressed

" **syllable:** arsis

accept: fang, agree, honor, espouse, acknowledge

access: adit, accost, portal, paroxysm, passageway

accession: enter, addition, inaugural, enlargement

accessorius: nerve

acclaim: clap, eclat, extol, plaudit

acclimate: inure, season, accustom

acclivity: bank, hill, slope, incline

accolade: sign, award, token, symbol

accompaniment: descant, obligato

accomplice: ally, crony, confederate

accordant: even, attuned, suitable, harmonious

accost: hail, greet, halloo, approach

accouter: arm, rig, gird, equip, furnish

accredit: vouch, depute, certify

accretion: gain, deposit, increase, enlargement

accrue: earn, ensue, mature, acquire, increase

accursed: fey, damned, doomed, execrable

accustom: haft, enure, train, season

ace: jot, pip, hero, basto, adept, topnotcher

acetic: sour, sharp
" **acid:** vinegar
" **salt:** acetate
acetylene: gas, tolan, ethin(e)
Achilles: advisor: Nestor
" **captive:** Briseis
" **father:** Peleus
" **friend:** Patroclus
" **horse:** Xanthus
" **mother:** Thetis
" **slayer:** Paris
" **soldiers:** Myrmidons
" **teacher:** Chiron
" **victim:** Hector
" **vulnerable part:** heel
achiote: tree, arnatta(o)
achira: canna, handless
achromatic substance: linin
acid: keen, amino, ulmic, oleate
" **base indicator:** litmus
" **etching:** mordant
" **nicotinic:** niacin
" **slang:** LSD
" **tanning:** catechin
acinus: raspberry
acle: ironwood
acme: cap, apex, apogee, zenith, pinnacle
acolyte: helper, satellite, altar boy
" **garb:** cotta
acomia: baldness
aconite: bik(h), remedy, wolfsbane
acor: acidity
acorn: nut, mast, orest
" **barnacle:** scuta
" **cup:** valonia
" **dried:** camata
" **edible:** ballote, bellote
" **shaped:** balanoid

acoustic: equipment: sirene
" **vase:** echea
acre: arpent, farmhold
" **¼ of:** rood
" **1/100 of:** hectare
acrobat: zany, gymnast, schoenobatist
" **garment:** leotard, fleshings (tights)
" **high wire:** aerialist
" **net:** trampoline
" **of India:** nat
acrogen: fern
acrolith: caryatid, statue
acropolis: cadmea, Larissa, hill
act: deed, actu, emote, bestir
" **according to rules:** conform
" **like:** simulate
" **of prudence:** caution
" **silly:** clown
" **up:** priss
" **with exaggeration:** ham
" **(ing) by turns:** altern
actor: thespian, player
" **aid:** teleprompter
" **part:** function, role
" **poor:** ham, barnstormer
" **(s) in a play:** cast
acuity: wit, edge
Adam: and Eve: plant, putty root
" **grandson:** Enos
" **needle:** yucca
" **other wife:** Lilith
" **rib:** Eve
" **son:** Abel, Cain, Seth
adda: lizard, skink
adder: viper, whorl, snake
addition: augend, eke, also, too

" **contract:** rider
" **math:** addends
" **sound ending of word:** paracoge
addled: putrid, asea
adherent: votary, disciple
adherents: ists, ites, sequelae
adipose: fat, squab, pursy
adjudicate: act, try, judge, hear
adjunct: helper, ally, auxiliary
ad lib: improvise, offhand
adman: huckster
Admetus' wife: Alcestis
admixture: blend, alloy, tinge
Adonis' slayer: Ares
ad patres: dead
Adriatic: island in: Lagosta, Lastovo
" **river to:** Po, Kerka
" **wind:** bora
adult: grown-up, grown
" **insect:** imago
" **pike:** luce
" **steer:** beeve
aduncuous: hooked, bent
adventitious: casual, episodic
advice: rede, avis, lore
" **contain:** mentorial
adytum: shrine, sanctuary
Aegean Sea: ancient people: Samian
" " **arm of:** Saros
" " **islands:** Ios, Nio, Samos
Aegeon's wife: Aemilia
aeger: sick, ill, excuse
Aegir's wife: Ran
aelurophile: cat lover
Aeneas: father: Anchises

" **follower:** Achates
" **great-grandson:** Brut
" **wife:** Creusa
Aeolian lyricist: Sappho
Aeolus' daughter: Halcyone
aeonian: lasting, infinite, eternal
aerolite: meteorite
aerose: brassy, copper
aerugo: patina, rust, verdigris
Aether's father: Erebus
Aetolian prince: Xydeus
afar: off, away, saho, hamite
affeer: assess, confirm
affray: melee, combat, battle
affy: betroth, trust, confide
Afghan, Afghanistan: Pathan, Durani
" **coin:** anania, pul
" **language:** Pashto, Pushto
" **prince:** amir, ameer
" **rug:** blanket, cover(let)
" **tribe:** safi, ulus
aforesaid: prior, ditto, antecedent
Africa, African: negro, black
" **ancient name:** Libya
" **assembly:** raad
" **boss:** baas
" **camp:** boma, lager
" **chief:** kaid
" **coin:** pesa, akey, rupie
" **garment:** haik, tobe
" **hemp:** sisal, ife
" **hill:** Kop
" **house:** tembe
" **language:** taal, bantu, swahili
" **measure:** doti, curba
" **negro:** egba
" **peasant:** Kopi

aftermath: result, rowen, ea-grass
aftersong: epode
ag: silver
Agag: slayer of: Samuel
agalite: talc
agalloch: wood, garoo
agama: guana, lizard, iguana
Agamemnon: **brother:** Menelaus
" **daughter:** Iphigenia, Electra
" **father:** Atreus
" **son:** Orestes
" **wife:** Clytemnestra
agar-agar: gelose
agaric: fungus
agave: aloe, datil, mescal
" **fiber:** istle, pita, sisal
age: mature, eon, olam, ripen
" **grow old:** senesce
" **pert. to:** senile, geriatric
" **same as:** coeval
" **study of:** nostology
agendum: slate, ritual, liturgy
Agenor: daughter: Europa
" **father:** Antenor
" **son:** Cadmus
agent: means, doer, facient
" **act through an:** media
agglomerate: mass, heap, lump
aggrandize: lift, boost, exalt
aglet: lace, tag, spangle
agnate: akin, allied, cognate
Agni: Kali
agnomen: alias, name, epithet
agnus: dei, bell, lamb
Agra tomb: Taj (Mahal)
agrestic: rural, bucolic, unpolished

Agrippina's son: Nero
Ahab's wife: Jezebel
Ahasuerus: minister: Haman
" **wife:** Vashti
Ahaz: son: Hezekiah
" **wife:** Abi
Ahaziah's **sister:** Jehosheba(th)
Ahiam's father: Sacar
Ahinoam: husband: Saul, David
" **son:** Amnon
Ahira's son: Enan
Aholibamah's **husband:** Esau
Ahriman's angel/spirit: div, deev, deva
ahu: heap, mound, gazelle
ahuehuete: sabino, cedar, cypress
ai: sloth, edentate
Aida: composer: Verdi
" **father:** Amonasro
" **lover:** Radames
" **rival:** Amneris
Ailie: Helen
aine: elder, senior
air: aria, mien, sky, pose
" **component:** argon, oxygen, nitrogen
" **current:** thermal
" **filled with:** aerate
" **fresh:** ozone
" **open:** alfresco
" **passage:** flue, vent
" **spirit:** sylph
" **tight:** hermetic
" **upper:** ether
" **warm:** oam
airplane: jet, aero, gyro
" **carrier:** flattop
" **cockpit:** cabin

" **marker:** pylon
" **part:** wing, aileron, fusi-lage
" **runway:** strip, tarmac
" **vapor:** contrail
airn: iron
airy: gay, rare, ethereal
aiseweed: goutweed
ait: isle, holm, eyot, oat
aith: oath
aitu: god, spirit, demon
aizle: spark, ember
ajaja: bird, spoonbill, jabiru
Ajax: father: Telamon
" **tale about:** myth
ajonjoli: sesame
ajuga: herb, bugloss
akia: poison
akin: allied, sib, germane
aku: victorfish
Alabama: (see special sec-tion)
alabarch: magistrate
Aladdin's spirit: genie, genii, jinni
Alamo: tree, fort, battle, shrine
" **hero:** Bowie, Crockett
alan: dog, wolfhound
alar: pteric, winged
alas: ach, heu, oime(e), ochone
" **poetic:** ay
Alaska, Alaskan: (see spe-cial section) Aleut, Eskimo, Dene
" **garment:** parka
" **glacier:** Muir
" **purchaser:** Seward
" **river:** Yukon
alate: ant, aphid, winged, in-sect

alb: camisia, vestment
Albania, Albanian: gheg, cham, tosk
" **coin:** lek, qintar
" **dialect:** tosk, gheghish
" **soldier:** palikar
albertin: coin
Albion: England, Anglia
albula: chiro, fish
alburnum: sapwood
Alcestis: father: Pelias
" **husband:** Admetus
" **rescuer:** Hercules
alchemy: magic, thaumaturgy
" **god:** Hermes
" **iron:** Mars
alcidine bird: auk, puffin, mu-ree
Alcinous: daughter: Nausi-caa
" **wife:** Arete
Alcmene's husband: Amphi-tryon
alcohol: liquor, vinic, ethyl
" **from idose:** idite, iditol
" **radical:** al
" **solid:** sterin, sterol
" **standard:** proof
" **suffix:** ol
Alcoran: Koran
Alcott heroine: Jo, Beth, Amy, Meg
aldehyde derivative: acetal
alder: arn, bush, sagerose
" **genus:** alnus
" **tree: Scot:** arn
ale: bock, flip, stout, porter, mum
" **mug:** toby, stein
" **sweet mixture:** bragget
Alea: light, Athena
alee: ahead

"   **opposed to:** stoss
alembic: cup, vessel, retort
alette: wing, door jamb
Alexander: born: Pella
"   **kingdom:** Macedonia
"   **mistress:** Campaspe
"   **victory:** Issus, Arbela
Alexandria: patriarch: papa
"   **theologian:** Arius
alfa: esparto
alfalfa: fodder, lucern(e)
alforja: bag, wallet, pouch
alga: nori, seaweed, nostoc
"   **genus:** dasya, alaria, padina
"   **one-cell:** diatom
algarroba: tree, carob, calden
Algeria, Algerian: cavalryman: spahi, spahee
"   **commune:** setif
"   **governor:** dey
"   **measure:** pik, tavri
"   **ship:** xebec
"   **weight:** rotl
Algiers' natives' quarters: Casbah
Alhambra site: Granada
Ali: descendant: Fatmid
"   **wife:** Fatima
Ali Baba: brother: Cassim
"   **word:** sesame
Alice in Wonderland: author: Carroll
"   **character:** Queen, Walrus, Mad Hatter, Cheshire cat, White rabbit
alidade: diopter
alien: deed, remote, adverse
"   **Hebrew territory:** ger
alike: akin, uniform, congruent
"   **comb. form:** iso

alkali: reh, lye, soda, usar
alkaloid: caffein(e), atropine
"   **calabar bean:** eserine
"   **hemlock:** conin(e)
"   **mustard:** sinapin(e)
"   **poison:** curare
all: sum, total, whole, everyone, thoroughly
"   **comb. form:** pan, omni
"   **in:** weary
"   **-knowing:** omniscient
"   **Lat.:** toto
"   **right:** yes, okay, agreed
"   **there:** sane
allan: gull
allanite: cerine, silicate
alleged force: od, odyl
allegiance: duty, honor, fealty
"   **violation of:** treason
allegory: myth, tale, fable
"   **religious:** parable
alley: byway, lane, chare, tewer
"   **back:** slum
allice: shad
alligator: lagarto, (S.A.) cayman
"   **pear:** avocado, aguacate
allium: leek, garlic, onion
allowance: fee, edge, bounty, dole, share
"   **short:** ration
"   **traveling:** mileage, per diem
"   **weight:** tare, scalage
allowing for that: if
alloy: mix, garble, amalgamate
"   **black copper:** niello
"   **carbon + iron:** steel
"   **copper + tin:** bronze
"   **copper + zinc:** brass

"   **gold + silver:** asem
"   **Nickel + silver:** alfenide
"   **nonferrous:** tula
"   **pewter:** bidri
"   **yellow:** aich
allspice tree: pimento
alluvial: clay: adobe
"   **deposit:** mud, silt, drift
"   **fan:** delta
"   **matter:** geest
allyene: propyne
almandine: spinel, garnet
almond: nut, amygdala
"   **emulsion:** orgeat
"   **liqueur:** ratafia
"   **oil:** amarin(e)
alms: dole, charity, bounty
"   **box:** arca, reliquary
"   **-house:** poorhouse
"   **-man:** pauper, beggar
almuce: hood, tippet
alnus: tree, birch, alder
aloe: agave, pita, maguey
"   **derivative:** aloin
"   **extract:** orcin
"   **of powder:** picra
alone: lorn, apart, unaided
"   **comb. form:** soli
"   **on stage:** sola, solus
alongside: close, parallel, abreast
"   **prefix:** para
Alonso's son: Ferdinand
alopecia: baldness
alopecoid: vulpine, foxlike
alouatte: monkey
alpaca: paco, (l)lama
"   **like:** guanaco
alphabet: order, letters
"   **early-old:** rune
"   **Hindu:** Sarada
"   **teacher of:** abecedarian

Alpine: hat, stick
"   **dance:** gavot
"   **dwelling:** chalet
"   **pass:** col
"   **shepherd:** senn
"   **wind:** bora
already: now, e'en, before
alsike: clover
also: eke, too, likewise
"   **ran:** loser, candidate
altar: ara, shrine, autere
"   **area:** apse
"   **boy:** acolyte
"   **carpet:** pedale
"   **cloth:** coster
"   **screen:** reredos
"   **vessel:** pyx
alter ego: friend, agent, self
althaea: mallow
Althaea's husband: Oeneus
altiloquence: pomposity, bombast
altitude: apex, peak, elevation
"   **measuring device:** altimeter, orometer
"   **sickness:** soroche
altruism: generosity, philanthropy
alture: height
aludel: pot
alula: wing, lobe
alum: styptic, astringent
"   **rock:** alunite
alumina: argil
aluminum: discoverers: Davy, Wohler
"   **oxide:** alumina
"   **sulphate:** alum
alveary: beehive
alveolate: pitted, honeycombed

ama: cup, diver, vessel
Amadis' beloved: Oriana
amadou: punk, tinder
Amalekite king: Agag
Amalthaea: goat
" **horn:** cornucopia
" **nursling:** Zeus
amanuensis: scribe, typist, recorder
amaryllis: girl, lily, agave
Amasa's father: Jether
amate: tree, match, daunt
amative: fond, loving, passionate
Amazon: river, women, warrior
" **discoverer:** Orellana
" **estuary:** para
" **mat:** yapa
" **rain forest:** selva, silvas
ambari: hemp, fiber
ambassador: envoy, nuncio, diplomat
" **pert. to:** legatine
amber: gris, resin, electrum
" **colored:** resinous
amber fish: medregal
ambiance: milieu
ambit: scope, limit
ambo: pulpit, desk
Amboina: button: yaws
" **pine:** galagala
Ambos: incus
ambrosia: nectar, honey
" **genus:** ragweed
ambry: niche, closet, pantry
Amen-Ra's wife: Mut
ament: idiot, catkin, imbecile
amerce: fine, punish
America, American: New World, continent, Yank
" **balsam:** tolu

" **bear:** musquaw
" **butterfly:** viceroy
" **buzzard:** buteo, vulture
" **deer:** wapiti
" **elm:** ulmus
" **flag:** Old Glory
" **imaginary town:** Podunk
" **Mexican:** gringo
" **moth:** io
" **plains:** pampas, prairie
" **soldier:** doughboy, Sammy
" **wind:** pampero
Amerind: native, Indian, Eskimo
" **clan symbol:** totem
memorial post: xat
Amfortas' father: Titurel
amice: cape, hood, vestment
amino: acid: protein
" **compound:** diamide, triamine
amit: lose
amm: mother, abbess
ammonia: refrigerant, hartshorn
" **derivative:** amin(e), anilid(e)
" **plant:** oshac
ammoniac plant: oshac
Ammonite king: Uzziah, Hanun
ammunition: arms, material, bombs
" **case:** bandolier
" **depot:** arsenal
" **holder:** tray, gun
" **wagon:** caisson
amnesia: lapse, blackout
amnesty: pardon
amnion: sac, membrane

amoeba: olm, porteus
amole: salt, soap, plant
among: in, amid, midst
  " **prefix:** epi
Amon's son: Josiah
amora: rabbi
Amorc member: Rosicrucian
Amorite king: Og, Sihon
amorphous: vague, shape-less
amort: dejected, inanimate
amount: gob, feck, ream, whole, total
  " **fixed:** rate
  " **indefinite:** some, any
  " **made:** lot, batch
  " **relative:** ratio, degree
  " **smallest:** iota, jot, whit, grain
ampere unit: watt, volt
amphibian: eft, olm, newt, proteus
  " **extinct:** eryop
  " **young:** tadpole
Amphion: father: Zeus, Iasus
  " **mother:** Antiope
  " **twin brother:** Zethus
  " **wife:** Niobe
Amphitrite: father: Nereus
  " **husband:** Poseidon
  " **mother:** Doris
Amphitryon's wife: Alcmene
amphora: urn, jar, cadus
amplify: pad, swell, expand
  " **factor:** mu
ampyx: plate, fillet, headdress
amula: ama
amulet: gem, mojo, scroll, to-ken, periapt
Amulius' brother: Numitor
Amycus: enemy: Lycus
  " **father:** Poseidon

  " " **friend:** Hercules
  " " **mother:** Melie
amygdala: tonsil, almond
amyl: starch, alcohol, pentyl
anabasis: expedition
Anacreon's birthplace: Teos
anadem: crown, wreath
anagogic: occult, abstruse
analgesic: opium, aspirin, codein(e)
ananas: pineapple
Ananias: liar
  " **wife:** Sapphira
anaqua: tree, anama
anarchist: rebel, nihilist
anathema: ban, oath, curse
Anatolia: Armenia
  " **goddess:** Ma, Cybele
  " **rug:** tuzla
anatomy: body, skeleton
  " **animal:** zootomy
  " **quick:** vivisection
  " **microscopic:** histology
Anaximander's principle: apeiron
ancestor: sire, stock, elder
  " **common:** sept
  " **remote:** atavus
ancestral: avital
  " **spirits:** manes, lares
anchor: bind, affix, support, moor
  " **hoist:** capstan, cat
  " **position:** atrip
  " **ring:** tore
anchorite: monk, hermit
anchovy: sprat
  " **sauce:** alec
ancient: eld, hoary, primal, archaic
  " **comb. form:** paleo, arche

"   **country:** Gaul, Canaan
"   **flute:** tibia
"   **sign:** rune
"   **weight:** mina
ancilla: helper, servant
ancon: elbow, console
Andes, Andean: Peruvian, Peru
"   **animal:** llama
"   **bird:** condor
"   **deer:** pudu, vanada
"   **grass:** ichu
"   **tribe:** anti, campa
android: robot
Andromache's husband: Hector
Andromeda: plant, heath
"   **father:** Cepheus
"   **husband:** Perseus
"   **mother:** Cassiopeia
anecdote: joke, tale, sketch
"   **collection:** ana
anemone: buttercup, windflower
angel: dera, backer, seraph
"   **biblical:** Gabriel, Raphael
"   **of death:** Azrael, Sammuel
"   **of resurrection:** Israfil
"   **worship:** dulia
angle: fish, fork, scheme
"   **acute:** akimbo
"   **forty-five degree:** octant
"   **having none:** agonic
"   **of stem:** axil
Anglo-Saxon: armor: hauberk
"   **coin:** ora, mancus, sceat
"   **freeman:** thane
"   **slave:** esne
"   **tax:** geld

Angola coin: macuta, angolar
aniline dye: benzol(e), magenta
animal: creature, brute, carnal
"   **anatomy of:** zootomy
"   **body of:** soma
"   **carrying young:** marsupial
"   **cross-bred:** mule, hybrid
"   **fat:** suet, lard, tallow
"   **footless:** apod(a)
"   **myth:** faun, dragon, griffin, unicorn
"   **pert. to:** zoic
"   **plant life:** biota
anion: ion
"   **opposed to:** cation
Anius' daughter: Elais
ankle: tarsus, coot, talus, tarsus, hock
"   **comb. form:** tar(so)
"   **pert. to:** tarsal, talaric
ann: stipend
anna: coin, hoa(c)tzin
Annam: boat: gayyou
"   **measure:** con, dam, ngu, sao, vai, phan
"   **money:** quan
"   **tribe:** Moi
"   **weight:** li, can, hao, yen, binh
Annapolis: student: plebe
annatto: dye, urucu, salmon
"   **derivative:** orellin
annelid: worm
"   **freshwater:** naid
"   **marine:** lurg
anniversary: fete, mass, annual
"   **1st:** paper
"   **5th:** wooden
"   **10th:** tin

" **15th:** crystal
" **20th:** china
" **25th:** silver
" **30th:** pearl
" **40th:** emerald, ruby
announcer of coming events: seer, herald, prophet
annual: yearly
  " **income:** rentes
  " **winds:** etesian
annuity: income, pension
  " **form of:** tontine
annular: round, circular
  " **die:** dod
  " **reinforcement:** hoop, sput
ant: mine, emmet, termite, pismire
  " **bear:** aardvark
  " **comb. form:** myrmec(o)
  " **cero:** aphid
  " **nest:** formicary
  " **nonworker:** drone
  " **stinging:** kelep
  " **white:** anai, termite
  " **worker:** (comb. form) ergate
Antaeus: enemy: Heracles
  " **father:** Poseidon
  " **mother:** Gaea
Antarctic: bird: penguin, skua
  " **explorer:** Ross, Byrd, Cook
  " **icebreaker:** atka
  " **mountain:** Siple
  " **sea:** Ross
anteater: manis, pangolin
antelope: gnu, sus, poku, gazelle, yakin
  " **ancient:** addax

" **female:** doe
" **forest:** bongo
" **genus:** oryx
" **golden:** impala
" **-like:** bovid
" **male:** buck
" **myth:** yale
" **royal:** ipete
" **tawny:** oribi
" **young:** kid
antenna: palp, feeler, aerial
  " **insect:** clava
  " **radar:** scanner
  " **with Nodose:** nodicorn
anthelion: halo, nimbus, anti-sun
anther: tip, pollen, stamen
Anthony Adverse author: Allen
Anthozoan: polyp, coryl
anthracite: inferior: culm
Antigone: mother: Jocasta
  " **sister:** Ismene
Antilles: god: Zeme
  " **native:** Ineri
  " **pearl:** Cuba
antimony: kohl, paradox
  " **pert. to:** stibial
antiseptic: eupad, salol, cresol, iodine
  " **acid:** boric
  " **mercury:** egol, Metaphen
antler: horn
  " **stag's:** attire
  " **unbranched:** dag, spike
Anvil City: Nome
any: all, some, part
  " **dialect:** oni
  " **one:** an
  " **of stars:** deneb
ape: simian, mimic, monkey,

orang, primate
" **long-tailed (India):** kra
" **man:** alalus
apetalous flower: cactus, trema
apex: acme, zenith, apogee
" **belonging to:** apical
" **covering:** epi
" **elbow:** ancon
Aphareus: brother: Lynceus
" **son:** Idas
aphasia: alalia
Aphrodite: Venus, Urania
" **father:** Zeus
" **got apple from:** Paris
" **love of:** Adonis
" **mother:** Dione
" **son:** Eros
" **temple site:** Paphos
apiaceous herb/plant: celery, parsley, nondo, anise
apocarp: etaerio, strawberry
apocryphal book: Tobit, Esdras, Baruck
Apollo: Caster, Mercury
" **birthplace:** Delos
" **instrument:** bow, lute
" **mother:** Leto, Latonia
" **son:** Ion
" **twin:** Artemis, Diana
apoplexy plant: esca
apostle: disciple, follower, apprentice
" **pert. to:** petrine
" **teaching of:** didache
" **to Franks:** Remi
" **to Gauls:** Denis
" **to Goths:** Ulfilas
apothegm: saying, maxim, dictum
appetite: greed, taste, gusto, orexis

" **morbid:** pica, bulimia
" **want of:** asitia
applause: eclat, salvo, plaudits, acclaim
" **reaching for:** esurience, captation
apple: pome, tree, fruit
" **acid:** malic
" **crushed:** pomace
" **genus:** malus
" **immature:** codlin(g)
" **love:** tomato
" **tree:** sorb
" **wild:** crab, deucin
apricot: fruit, mebo(s)
" **cordial:** persico(t)
" **disease:** blight
" **Jap:** ume
" **Korean:** ansu, anzu
apteryx: moa, kiwi, bird
aquamarine: beryl, blue
Aquinas' work: Summa
Arab, Arabian: nomad, wanderer, gamin, Semite
" **abode:** dar, tent
" **ancient country:** Sheba (Saha)
" **cloak:** aba
" **coin:** carat, dinar, kabik
" **people of:** Omani
" **measure:** ardeb, den, covid(o)
" **script:** neski
" **state of bliss:** kef
" **teacher:** ulema
" **title:** sidi
" **wind:** simoon
Arabic acid: arabin
arachnid: mite, tick, spider
" **trap:** web
Aram's children: Uz, Hul, Mash, Gether

Arawakan: language: Taino
   " **tribe:** Guana
arboreal: dendral
   " **animal:** ai, sloth, lemur, dasyure
arc: bow, curve, orbit
   " **chord:** sine
Arcadian: bucolic, rustic, rural
   " **god:** Ladon
   " **king:** Lycaon
   " **princess:** Auge
arch: sly, coy, cunning, prime
   " **angel:** Uriel, Gabriel, Satan
   " **of heaven:** cope
   " **pointed:** ogive, ogee
   " **Roman:** alette
archery target: clout
architectural: order:
   Ionic, Gothic, Greek, Norman
   Roman, Corinthian, Modern **Noric**
   " **pier:** anta
Arctic: polar, frigid, north
   " **base:** etah
   " **dog:** samoyed
   " **gull genus:** xema
   " **jacket:** anorak
   " **plain:** tundra
   " **transportation:** umiak, sled
arctoid: bearlike, ursine
areca: palm, betel
arenose: sandy
Ares: Mars
   " **father:** Zeus
   " **mother:** Enyo
   " **sister:** Eris
Argentina, Argentine: coin: peso, centavo, argentino
   " **measure:** sino, vara, cuadra
   " **plain(s):** pampa(s)
   " **tree:** tala
   " **weight:** grano, quintal
argillaceous: slaty, clayey, spongy
Argonaut: Jason, Acastus
   " **ship:** Argo
arhat: monk, saint, lohan
Arikara: Ree, Indian
Aristotle: birthplace: Stagira, Thrace
   " **school:** lyceum
   " **teacher:** Plato
Arizona: (see special section)
Arkansas: (see special section)
arm: limb, wing, equip, fiord
   " **bone:** ulna, radius
   " **comb. form:** brachi(o)
   " **part:** wrist, elbow, ares
   " **pert. to:** brachial
   " **pit:** ala, oxter, axilla
   " **sleeve hole:** scye, mail
armadillo: peva, poyou, mulita
   " **extinct animal-like:** glyptodon
   " **giant:** tatu, peludo
   " **small:** peba
Armenia, Armenian: Minni, Anatolia
   " **angel devil worshiper:** Yezidi
   " **cap:** calpac
   " **cumin:** caraway
armful: yaffle
armhole: mail, scye
armor: plate, egis, defense
   " **bearer:** squire
   " **head:** sconce
   " **leg:** cuish, tuille, jamb(e)

"   **shoulder:** ailette
"   **thigh:** cuish
armpit: ala, axilla, oxter
"   **pert. to:** axillar
army: host, array, force, legion
"   **ant:** driver
"   **base:** depot
"   **car:** jeep
"   **commission:** brevet
"   **follower:** sutler
"   **mascot:** mule
"   **meal:** chow
"   **pert. to:** martial, military
"   **school:** OCS, OTS, academy
aroid: taro, tanier
aromatic: spicy, balmy, odorous
"   **fruit:** nutmeg
"   **gum:** myrrh
"   **herb:** anise, clary
"   **medicinal leaves:** buchu
around: circa, near
"   **comb. form:** peri
arpeggio: sweep, roulade
arquebus support: croc
arrange: align, plat, scheme
"   **in layers:** tiered, stratose
"   **side-by-side:** appose
arras: drapery, tapestry
arris: angle, peen
arriviste: snob, parvenu
arrogate: usurp, claim, seize
arrow: shaft, missile, dart
"   **end:** nock
"   **feathered:** vire
"   **handle:** stele
"   **maker:** bowyer
"   **-shaped:** beloid
arrowroot: canna, pia, ararao, musa

arsenic: comb. form: arseno
"   **mixture:** speiss
"   **of copper:** erinite
"   **symbol:** A.S.
Artemis: Upis, Delia, Phoebe
"   **twin:** Apollo
"   **victim:** Orion
artery: road, vessel, conduit
"   **large:** aorta
"   **neck:** carotoid
"   **pulse of:** ictus
arthropoda: crab, spider, phyla
Arthur: king
"   **capital:** Camelot
"   **father:** Uther
"   **foster brother:** Kay
"   **lady:** Enid, Elaine
"   **sword:** Excalibur
article: an, the, object, thing, item, clause
   Ar: al
   Fr: la, le, des, les, un, une(s)
   Ger: der, ein, das
   Sp: el, la, las, los
artificial language: Ro, Ido
artistic strewing: seme
arum: taro, plant, cuckoopint
"   **water:** calla
Aryan: Slav, Mede, Caucasian
"   **deity:** Ormazd
"   **fire god:** Ayni
"   **Indian God:** Hindu
as: qua, like, since, while
"   **far as:** to
"   **it stands/written: mus:** sta, sic
"   **usual:** solito
asafetida: hing, laser, ferula
Asa's father: Abia

ascetic: stoic, yogi, friar, nun, austere
"   **ancient:** essene
Asia, Asian: bird: myna, pitta
"   **comb. form:** Indo
"   **cow:** zo(h), zobo
"   **desert:** Gobi
"   **evergreen:** bago
"   **native:** Shan
"   **tree:** acle, asok
"   **weight:** tael, catty
aspect: mien, guise, feature
"   **general:** facies
ass: dolt, burro, fool, donkey
"   **comb. form:** ono
"   **wild:** kulan, onager
Assam: Mongol: Naga
"   **shrub:** tea, tche
"   **silkworm:** eri(a)
"   **tribesman:** aka, Garo, ao
assay: try, prove, analysis
"   **vessel of:** cup, cupel
asse: fox, caama
assembly: mass, unite, gather
"   **full:** plena
"   **hall:** kiva
asseverate: aver, swear, declare
association: guild, cartel, union
"   **merchants':** hanse
"   **secret:** cabal, lodge
assonance: pun, rhyme, paragram
Assyria, Assyrian: Ashur, Assur
"   **king:** Pul
"   **queen:**(myth.)Semiramis
"   **river:** Zab
"   **sky:** anat

"   **weight:** cola
Asterius: argonaut, minotaur
"   **father:** Hyperasius
"   **mother:** Pasiphae
"   **wife:** Europa
asteroid: first: Ceres
"   **nearest earth:** Eros
Astolat, Lily Maid: Elaine
astrakhan: cloth, apple, caracul, karakul
astral: starry, lamp
"   **fluid:** od, odyl(e)
astrological belief: siderism
astronomy, astronomical: far, distant, uranic, huge
"   **cloud:** nebula
"   **cycle:** saros
"   **measure:** apsis
"   **muse:** Urania
at: the, al, to, ab, atlen
"   **all:** ava, any
"   **any time:** ever
"   **home:** here, tea, in, **Fr:** chez
"   **last:** finally, ultimately
"   **no time: poet.,** ne'er
"   **odds:** out
"   **same age:** coeval
ates: sweetsop
Athamas: daughter: Helle
"   **son:** Phrixos, Learchus
"   **wife:** Ino
Athens, Athenian: Attic(a), Greece
"   **assembly:** pnyx, boule
"   **clan:** obe
"   **coin:** chalcus
"   **founder:** Cecrops
"   **harbor:** Piraeus
"   **hill:** Acropolis
"   **of: America:** Boston
"   "   **Ireland:** Belfast

" " **Switzerland:** Zurich
" " **the North:** Edinburgh
" " **the West:** Cordoba
" **pert. to:** Attic
" **rival:** Sparta
" **sculptor:** Phidias
" **temple:** Nike, Zeus
Atlantides: Pleiades, Hesperides
Atlas: atlas: maps, titan, book
" **daughter of:** Calypso, Electra
" **mother of:** Clymene
atmosphere: aura, mood, welkin, nimbus
" **gas:** argon, oxygen, nitrogen
" **phenomenon:** meteor, aurora
" **prefix:** atmo(s)
" **pressure:** barometric
atom, atomic: ion, iota, monad, shade, particle, molecular, minute
" **machine:** betatron, rheotron
" **part:** proton
" **physicist:** Rabi, Buhr, Pauli, Compton
" **pile:** reactor
" **theorist:** Dalton
Atreus: brother: Thyestes
" **father:** Pelops
" **mother:** Hippodamia
" **slayer:** Aegisthus
" **son:** Menelaus, Agamemnon, Pleisthenes
" **wife:** Aerope
atrocha: larva
Atropos: Fate
atrous: ebon, black

Attica: legendary king: Ogyges
" **resident:** metic
" **subdivision:** deme
" **valley:** Icaria
Attila: Hun, Etzel
attire: array, cloth(e), outfit
" **in armor:** panoply
atua: being, demon, spirit
Au: gold
auction: sale, roup, vend, trade
" **famous for:** Parke-Bernet, Christy's
" **hammer:** gavel
" **platform:** block
" **price:** bid, upset
au fait: expert, proper
auric acid salt: aurate
Augie March creator: Bellow
Augustus' death place: Nola
auk: lemot, puffin, loom
" **family:** alcidae
" **genus:** alca, alle
" **razorbill:** falk, murre
aunt: tia (Sp.), tante (Fr.), gossip, bawd
aural appendage: ear
auricle part: earlobe
aurochs: tur, urus, bison, wisent
Aurora: Eos, dawn
Australia, Australian: Aussie
" **apple:** colane
" **bag:** dilli
" **bear:** koala
" **bird:** emu, lory, bittern
" **boomerang:** kiley, kilie
" **cake:** damper
" **call:** cooey
" **cat:** dasyure
" **coin:** dump

" **countryman:** Billijim
" **dog:** dingo, kelpie
" **duckbill:** platypus
" **fruit:** nonda
" **gum tree:** kari, touart
" **hut:** miamia, mimi
" **kangaroo:** joey
" **kiwi:** roa
" **language:** yabber
" **measure:** saum
" **no:** baal, bale
" **ostrich:** emeu
" **palur:** bangalow
" **parrot:** lory, corella
" **petrel:** titi
" **pond:** billabong
" **settler:** Cook
" **shark:** mako
" **spear:** womerah, wommala
" **toy:** weet-weet
" **tree:** belah, gidya, beefwood
" **tulip:** waratah
" **war club:** waddy
" **wilderness:** outback
Austria, Austrian:
" **amphibian:** olm
" **coin:** ducat, gulden, krune
" **measure:** fass, muth
" **weight:** unze
" **writer:** Kafka

austringer: falconer
auto race: drag, derby
Avalon: isle, island
" **tomb:** Arthur
avellane: nut, hazel, filbert
avens: herb, geum
Avesta: division: Yasna, Gathas
" **translation of:** Zend
avocet: bird, godwit
away: prefix: aph, apo
aweto: weri, caterpillar
awl: punch, needle, broach
ax, axe: adz, poleax, hache, cleaver, twibill
" **blade:** bit
" **butt:** poll
" **handle:** helve
" **pickaxe:** gurlet
axillary: alar
axoloti: newt, salamander
ay: champagne
aye-aye: lemur
Azores: port: Horta
" **volcano:** Pico
Aztec: god: Xipe, Meztli
" **hero,** Natu
" **wife of,** Nana
" **language:** Nahautl
" **temple:** Teocalli, Teopan
azym(e): bread
" **opposed to:** enzyme

B

baa: bleat
baahling: lamb
Baal: (sun) god; idol; deity
  "   consort: Baltis
  "   Baalist: idolater
baba: baby, male, child
  "   au rhum: rum cake
babacoote: lemur
babassu: oil, palm, soap
babbitt: Philistine, business-
  man
babblative: talkative, garru-
  lous, loquacious
babel: tower, tumult, confusion
babiche: thong(s), lacing
babillard: bird, whitethroat
babul: acacia, gum
  "   pod: garad
Babylonia,   Babylonian:
  Shinor, Shinar
  "   abode of the dead:
  Aralu
  "   chief god: Anu, Enki
  "   chief goddess: is(h)tar

  "   people: Sumerian
  "   weight: mina
bacalao: murre, grouper
bacca: berry
baccarat: game
  "   player: punter
  "   term: banco
  "   variety of: chemin-de-fer
bacchanal: orgy,   reveler,
  devotee, carouser
  "   cry of: evoe, evohe
bacchante: maenad, priestess
Bacchus: god, Dionysus
  "   devotee: carouser
  "   son: Comus
bacillus: germ, virus, microbe
back: aid, fro, rat, hind, nata,
  abet, again, dorsum, posterior
  "   and fill: zigzag
  "   at the: abaft, astern
  "   backbite: slander
  "   backbone: spine, courage, grit, pluck, mettle, spirit

" **Back Street author:** Hurst

" **call:** revoke

" **comb. form:** notus

" **country:** hinterland

" **down, out:** withdraw

" **entrance:** postern

" **flow:** ebb, recede

" **lower:** loin

" **lying on:** supine

" **off:** ebb, recede

" **out:** funk, crawfish

" **pain:** lumbago, notalgia

" **pert. to:** dorsal, lumbar, tergal

" **prefix:** re, retro

" **scratcher:** toady

" **talk:** (colloq.) lip, sass, insolence

" **toward:** aft, astern, dorsad

backlog: surplus, reserve, accumulation

backward: lax, arrear, dilatory, unfavorable

backwater: ebb, bayou, retract

backwort: comfrey

bacon: pork, rustic, prize

" **bring home the:** win, succeed

" **fat:** speck

" **side:** flitch, gammon

" **slice:** rasher, collop

" **strip:** lardon, lardoon

Bacon work: Novum Organum

bacteria: germ, fungus, aerobe, microbe, bacillus

" **chain:** towla

" **culture:** agar (-agar)

" **dissolver:** Lysin

" **free from harmful:** asepsis, aseptic

" **vaccine:** bacterin

bacteriologist: culture: agar

" **wire:** oese

bactrian: camel

bad: lewd, qued, vile, nasty

" **comb. form:** dys, mal, caco

" **debt:** default

" **habit:** vice

" **luck:** ambsace

" **prefix:** mal, mis

badak: rhino

badderlocks: murlin, seaweed, honeyware

badgerweed: pasqueflower

badinage: banter, raillery, trifling

baff: bang, beat, blow, strike, worthless

bag: sac, pod, womb, poke, purse, udder, bouge, bulse, seize, alforja, reticule, gladstone, portmanteau

" **botanic:** sac, asci, ascus, spore

" **canvas:** musette

" **fishing net:** bunt, fyke

" **floating:** balloon

" **for books, papers, etc.:** briefcase

" **grain:** sack

" **hop:** sarpler

" **kind of:** duffel

" **-making material:** sacking, jute, burlap, flax, hemp

" **muslin:** tillot

" **slang:** woman, capture

" **sleeping:** sack

" **toilette:** musette

" **with perfumed powder:**

sachet
" **traveling:** telescope
bagatelle: trifle
baggage: gear, minx, harlot, valises, viaticals
" **car/wagon:** fourgon
" **carrier:** ham(m)al, porter, redcap
baggie: belly, stomach
Baghdad merchant: Sinbad
bagman: salesman, tramp, collector
bagnio: bagne, brothel, hothouse, bathhouse, prison, cabana
Bagnold: Enid
bagpipe: drone, musette, zampogne, sordellina
" **drone:** bourdon
" **flute:** chanter
" **mouthpiece:** muse
" **music:** pibroch
" **pipe:** drones, chanter
" **play:** skirl
" **player:** piper, doodler
" **tune:** port
Bahama Islands: Abaco, Andros, Eleuthera, Bimini
" **capital:** Nassau
" **premier:** Pindling
Bahia: (Sao) Salvador, bay
baikie: stick
bailiff: tipstaff, reeve
bain: near, direct, supple
bairn: child
bait: chum, fulcrum, gudgeon, lure, hector
" **artificial:** hackle
" **bird-enticing:** shrap(e)
" **drop:** dip, dap
" **fish:** chum, lure
" **salmon-fishing:** baker

" **take:** bite
baize: fabric, drapery, drape, cloth, domett
baked clay/dishes/pot: tile, crockery, olla
baker bird: hornero
baker's: itch: rash, psoriasis
" **kneading trough:** brake
" **shovel/tool:** peel
" **workshop:** yale
bakie: trough, vessel
baking: chamber: oast, oven, kiln
" **dish:** cocotte, ramekin, remequin, casserole, scallop
" **pit:** Hawaiian: imu
" **soda:** saleratus
Bakongo's   goddess: Nyambe, Nzambe
baksheesh: alms, tip, gratuity
bal: tabarin, masque
Balaam's beast: ass, donkey
balance: even, offset, equilibrium
" **crossbar of:** beam
" **of sales:** atry
" **state of:** equipoise
" **weighing:** steelyard
balancing weight: ballast
balata gum: chicle
balate: trepang
balcony: piazza, sollar, mirador, brattice
" **church singer:** cantoria
" **projecting:** gazabo, gazebo
bald: bare, frank, hairless, glabrous
" **-headed man:** pilgarlic
baldachin: brocade, canopy
Balder: father: Odin

" **giant, victim of:** Loke
" **mother:** Frigg
" **murder weapon:** mistle-toe
" **slayer:** Loke, Hoth(r)
" **son:** Forsete
" **wife:** Nanna
baldicoot: coot, monk
baldmoney: gentian, spicknel
baldric, baldrick: belt, zo-diac, support, necklace
Balearic Island: Iviza, Ca-brera, Majorca, Minorca, Menorca, Formentera
" **capital:** Palma
" **language:** Catalan
baleen: whale, whalebone
baleise: flog
baler: bundler, tier
Bali (Indonesia): dance: ardja, kriss, ketjak, djanger
" **holy day:** njepi
" **musical instrument:** gamelan(g)
" **religion:** Hinduism
" **rice field:** sawaii
Balkan: Slav, Serb
" **bandit:** haiduk
" **coin:** novcic
" **instrument:** gusla
Balkh: Bactria
ball: globe, ivory, dance
" **hit for practice:** fungo
" **metal, athletics:** shot-put, hammer
" **of electrical discharge:** corposant
" **of meat/rice:** pinda
" **of perfume mixture:** po-mander
" **of yarn/thread:** clew
" **tiny:** globule

" **wooden:** knur
ballad: lolt, derry, canzone
ballet: dance, masque
" **leap:** jete
" **movement:** brise, glis-sade
" **posture:** arabesque
" **skirt:** tutu
balloon: bag, gasbag, aerostat
" **altitude controller:** bal-last
" **basket:** car, gondola, na-celle
" **covering:** envelope
" **gas:** helium, hydrogen
" **mooring line:** dragrope
" **pilot:** aeronaut
" **shape of:** sausage, round
" **trial:** feeler, test
" **vine:** heartseed
ballista: catapult
ballistic missile: launching: blast-off
" **storage place:** silo
" **warhead:** payload
balm: bito, anodyne
" **horse:** citronella
" **of Gilead:** balsam
Balmoral: petticoat, cap, cas-tle
balneal: bathing
balneary: bathhouse
balsa: wood, raft
" **like wood:** bongo
balsam: resin, tolu, copaiba
" **gum resin:** storax
" **Swiss:** riga
" **tree:** tolu
Balt: Yod, Esth, Lett, Esto-nian, Lithuanian
balteus: belt, baldric

Baltic: barge: praam
  " **city:** Riga, Danzig
  " **gulf:** Riga
  " **island:** Dago, Faro, Os(s)el, Oesel, Alsen, Oland
  " **language:** Lettic
  " **river:** Oder
  " **seaport:** Kiel, Riga, Memel, Reval, Stettin, Talinn, Rostock
Balzac character: Goriot, Nana
bam: sham, wheedle, hoax
bamboo: cane, reed, tree, tonkin
  " **shoots: pickle, sprouts:** achar
  " **stalk:** reed
  " **sugar:** tabasheer
  " **woven:** sawaii
Bana: conqueror: Krishna
  " **daughter:** Usha
banana: musa, ensete, pesang, fei, platano (Sp.), plantain
  " **bunch:** hand, stem
  " **disease:** mosaic
  " **family:** musa, pesang, musaceae
  " **fish:** albula, ladyfish
  " **leaf:** frond
  " **of the:** musaceous
  " **oil:** sl.: nonsense, softsoap
  " **Philippine:** saging, latundan
  " **plant:** musa, pesang
  " **wild:** fei
band: tie, cord, cohort, cincture, fillet, hyphen
  " **armed:** posse

  " **armor:** tonlet
  " **brain:** ligula(e)
  " **clothes fastener:** patte
  " **narrow:** stria, tape
  " **small:** bandelet(te)
bandicoot: rat, badger
bandikai: okra
Bani: son: Uel, Amzi, Amram
bank: river: ripa
banquet: fete, junket, repast, carousal
  " **room:** cenacula (pl.), cenaculum
banshee: fay, fairy, sidhe, goblin
bant: diet, fast, reduce
bantam: cock, diminutive
  " **breed:** Sebright
banteng: ox, tsine
banxring: tana, tupaia
banyan: bur(r), banian
banzai: cry, attack
baobab: tree, tebeldi
bar: bullion: ingot
  " **legally:** estop
  " **millstone:** rynd
  " **supporting:** fid, rod
barb: anchor: flue
  " **feather:** herl, ramus
Barbados: liquor: rum
  " **native:** Bim
barbarian: Hun, Goth, Philistine, brute, vandal
  " **North African:** Berber
Barbary: ape, magot, simian
  " **sheep:** aoudad
barber's itch: ringworm
bard: scop, druid, poet
  " **India:** bhat
Bard of Avon: Shakespeare
barley: grain
  " **ground:** tsamba

31

  " pert. to: hordeaceous
  " steep: malt
  " variety: big, bere, bigg
barmy: foamy, filly, yeasty
barnacle: genus: Lepas
  " plate: terga (pl.), tergum
barnstorm: tour
barometric line: isobar
barraclade: blanket
barracuda: spet, pelon, picuda, guanchepelon
barras: gal(l)ipot
barrator: bully, rowdy, fighter
barrel: keg, runlet, cask, hogshead, kilderkin
  " herring: cade
  " maker: cooper
  " part: side, hoop, stave
  " raising device: parbuckle
  " stopper: bung
  " support: hoop, gantry, gauntry
barren oak: blackjack
barren privet: alatern, houseleek
Barrie character: Wendy, Peter
barrio: slum, ghetto, village
Bartered Bride composer: Smetana
bartizan: turret, lookout
basalt: marble, navite, pottery
base: low, snide, paltry, scullion, ignominious
  " architectural: socle, plinth
  " attached by: sessile
  " structural: plinth
baseball: field: diamond
  " founder: Doubleday (Abner)

  " hit: bunt, single, double
  " on balls: walk, pass
  " team: nine
Bashan king: Og
Bashemath's husband: Esau
basil: herb, plant, royal, fetter
basilica: canopy, church, temple, Lateran
  " part of: apse
basin: ewer, stoup, marina, aspersorium
  " geological: tala
basket: fan, kipe, scull, dorser, hanaper
  " coal mine: corf
  " eel: buck
  " fig: caba, frail, tapnet
  " fire: grate, cresset
  " fish: pot, cawl, maund, gabion
  " fruit: pottle, punnet
  " material: otate
  " twig: wattle
  " watertight: wattape
  " work: caba(s), slath, slarth
bas-relief: plaquette
basswood: lin, bast, tilia, linden
bast: flax, piassava
basta: stop, enough
bastion: defensive: fort
  " shoulder: epaule
batfish: diablo
bath: comb. form: balneo
  " pert. to: balneal
  " public: piscine
  " river: Avon
  " sponge: loofah
bathos: comedown, anticlimax

Bathsheba: husband: Uriah
" **son:** Solomon
batrachian: frog, toad
battery: floating: praam, artillery
" **plate:** grid
battle: fray, conflict
" **area:** arena, sector
" **formation:** herse, deploy
" **line:** front
Battle Hymn of the Republic author: Howe
battologize: repeat, iterate
bauxite derivative: aluminum
Bavaria, Bavarian: community: Passau
" **measure:** fass, rute, metze, morgen
" **weight:** gran, quentchen
bay: cove, roan, fiord, oriel
" **bird:** snipe, curlew, godwit, plover
" **camphor:** laurin
bayardly: blind, stupid
Beaconsfield: Disraeli (Brit. prime minister)
beadle: macer, herald, servitor
beadsman, bedesman: beggar, hermit, petitioner
beak: prow, lorum, master
" **ship's:** bow, ram, prow
" **without:** erostrate
bean: urd, caster, noggin, thrash
" **Asian:** gram, mungo
" **climbing:** lima, pole
" **cluster:** guar
" **eye:** hila, hilum
" **locust:** carob
" **lubricant:** ben
" **Mexican:** frejol, frijol(e)

" **poisonous:** loco, calabar
Bean Town: Boston
bear: bane: wolfsbane
" **bush:** inkberry
" **cat:** paud, binturong
" **-shaped:** ursiform
bearing: air, mien, orient, gestation
" **fine:** belair
" **heraldic:** ente, orle, pheon
beast: bete (Fr.), monster, quadriped
" **myth:** ogre, Rahu, Apepi, giant, hydra, Geryon, Kraken, scylla, triton, centaur, figfaun, griffin, bucentaur, chichevache
" **pert. to:** leonine
beau geste: favor
beaut: (sl.) lulu
beautiful: comb. form: bel, calo, calli
beaver: hat, coin, castor, rodent
" **cloth:** kersey
" **eater:** wolverine
" **skin:** plew
because of that: thereby, therefore
bechance: befall, chance
becken: cymbals
becloud: darken, obscure, overcast
becoming: right, farrant
becuna: barracuda
bed: cot, bunk, doss, matrix, pallet, plancher
" **feather:** tye
" **small:** pallet, truckle, bassinet
" **stay:** slat

" **straw:** shakedown

bedbug: cimex, chinch, cimice (pl.), conenose

bedizen: daub, adorn, over- dress

Bedouin: Arab, Moor, nomad
" **bead cord:** agal
" **official:** cadi, sheik
" **tribe:** Harb

bedrock: nadir, bottom

bedroll: bindle

bee: dor, apis, dingar, hy- menoptera
" **colony of:** swarm, yeast
" **comb. form:** api
" **family:** apina, apidae
" **female:** queen
" **house covering:** hackle
" **male:** drone
" **nose:** lora (pl.), lorum
" **pollen brush:** scopa, scopae (pl.), sarothrum

beech: buck, tree, myrtle
" **genus:** fagus

beef: meat, complain
" **dried:** bucan, vivda, charqui
" **pickled:** bully
" **salted:** junk

beekeeper: apiarist, skeppist

beer: mum, grog, kvass
" **barley:** chang
" **cask:** butt
" **ingredient:** hops, malt
" **maize:** chic(h)a
" **unfermented:** wort
" **vessel:** mug, seidel, schooner

beeswax substitute: ceresin

beet: chard, mangel
" **genus:** beta

beetle: bug, goga, gogo,

hispa, scarab, battledore
" **bark:** borer
" **bright:** ladybug
" **family:** elateridae, clavi- cornes
" **fire:** cucuyo
" **genus:** fidia
" **grain:** cadelle
" **ground:** amara
" **mustard:** blackjack
" **rhinoceros:** uang
" **wing cover:** scarab

beetle-browed: morose, scowling

before: avant (Fr.), coram (Lat.), prior, afore
" **long:** anon
" **now:** ere, over
" **prefix:** pre, pro, prae, ante

beggar: randy, almsman, mendicant
" **saint:** Giles
" **speech:** cant

Beggar's Opera author: Brecht

behemoth: huge, beast, hippo

behoof: profit, advantage

being: ens, entity, mortal
" **abstract:** ens, entia
" **actual:** esse
" **in front:** anteal
" **physiological:** bion
" **science of:** ontology
" **suffix:** ure

Bela: son: Ard, Iri, Uzzi, Ez- bon

Bel: wife: Belit(is)

Belait: Europe

belaying pin: kevel, bollard

Belgium, Belgian: Fleming,

Walloon
" **coin:** belga, franc, centime
" **Gaul tribe:** Remi, Nervii
" **marble:** rance
" **measure:** vat
Belgrade native: Serb
Belial: devil, Satan
believer: ist
" **in all religions:** omnist
" **in God:** deist, theist
" **in reality of matter:** Cartesian
belittle: dwarf, slight, denigrate
bell: gong, codon, corolla
" **alarm:** tocsin
" **axle-bearing:** cod
" **clapper:** tongue
" **pert. to:** campanular
" **ringer:** toller, carilloneur
" **room:** belfry
" **sound:** ding, dong, toll, knell, tinkle
" **tower:** belfry, campanile
belladonna: dwale, narcotic, nightshade
" **extract:** atropin(e)
bellbird: shrike, arapunga
bellware: kelp
bellweed: knapweed
belongings: traps, effects, chattels
belt: gird: cestus, zonnar
bema: pace, step, chancel
bend: ply, sag, flex, crimp
" **backward:** retort
" **in timber:** sny
Benedictine: monk, liqueur
" **title:** dom
benefice: feu, curacy, kindness

" **first fruit:** annat(e)
Bengal: boat: batel, baulea(h)
" **capital:** Dacca
" **caste member:** baidya
" **cotton:** adati, adaty
" **district:** Dacca, Nadia
" **gentlemen:** baboo
" **grass:** millet
" **hemp:** sunn
" **measure:** cotta(h), chattack
" **native:** Ebo(e), Kol, Banian
" **quince:** b(a)el, bhel
" **root:** cassumunar
" **singer:** baul
" **town:** Dacca, Madras, Barisal, Rangoon, Calcutta, Tittacarh
" **tree:** bola
Benjamin: descendant: Aher
" **grandson:** Iri
" **son:** Ehi, Gera, Rosh
benne: sesame
benthonic plant: enalid
benthos: fauna, flora
benzine derivative: phenol
Berber: Moor, Hamite, Kabyle, Haratin
" **chief:** caid, qaid
" **dialect:** Tuareg
" **tribe:** Daza, Riff, Tibu, Tuareg
Berea: Aleppo
" **grit:** sandstone
bergstock: alpenstock
beriberi: kakke
Bermuda: arrowroot: aruru, ararao
" **barracuda:** spet
" **berry:** soapberry

" **capital:** Hamilton
" **catfish:** coelho
" **ceremony:** gombay
" **grass:** doob
berry-like: baccate
bertha: cape, cannon, collar
beryl: gem, jewel, emerald, aquamarine
" **green:** davidsonite
" **yellow:** heliodor
beryx: alfonsin
beseeching: precative
besom: man, sweep, heather
best: comb. form: arist(o)
bet: broker: bookie
" **fail to pay off:** welch
betel: ikmo, itmo, siri
" **leaf:** pan, buyo
Betelgeuse: star
betel palm: areca
" **extract:** catechu
" **seed:** betel nut
Bethesda: pool, chapel
Bethuel's son: Laban
betise: folly, silliness, stupidity
between: amid, betwixt
" **law:** mesne
" **prefix:** dia, meta, inter
between the lines: latent, secret
beverage: ade, pop
" **extract:** kola
" **malted wheat:** zythem, zythum
" **mixed:** negus, punch, smash, bishop
" **mulberry and honey:** morat
" **Oriental:** rak(ee), sake, arrack
" **pepper:** kava

bewitch: charm, fasci, grigri
Beyle's penname: Stendhal
bezel, basil: rim, seal, chaton
bhalu: bear
Bhutan: disease: dha
" **pine:** kail
" **religion:** shamanism
" **robe:** bakkhu
Bible: biblical: angel: Micah, Raphael
" **animal:** reem, daman, hydrax, behemoth
" **ascetic order:** Essene
" **giant:** Anak, Emim, Goliath
" **hunter:** Nimrod
" **money:** beka(h), shekel
" **ornament:** urim, thummin
" **pool:** Siloam
" **region:** Enon, Ophir, Perea, Bashan
" **spice:** myrrh, stacte, frankincense
" **stone:** ezel, ligure
" **weed:** tare
" **witch's home:** Endor
biddy: hen, chicken
bifid: forked
big toe: hallux
bigener: mule, hybrid
bilbie: refuge, shelter
bill: act, note
" **anchor:** pee
" **five dollar:** fin, vee
" **one dollar:** buck, frogskin
" **ten dollar:** sawbuck
billingsgate: abuse, ribaldry
billionaire: nabob
billycock: derby, bowler
bind: jam, confine

"   **comb. form:** desmo
"   **tightly:** frap
"   **to secrecy:** tile, tyle
"   **up in:** absorb
binding, limp: yapp
bindle stiff: hobo, tramp
biological class: genus, species
"   **factor:** id, gene, idant
biose: disaccharid(e)
biotite: mica, anomite
bird: adjutant: stork, argala, hurgila, marabou
"   **Afr.:** taha, umbrette
"   **Am.:** sora, robin, vireo, darter, fulmar, turkey, grackle, tanager, cardinal, bufflehead
"   **Antarctic:** skua, penguin
"   **aquatic:** duck, swan, grebe, penguin
"   **aquiline:** eagle
"   **Arabian Nights:** roc
"   **Arctic:** auk, fulmar
"   **Asiatic:** mine, hill tit, brambling
"   **Attic:** nightingale
"   **Austral.:** emu, boobook, lorikeet
"   **black:** ani, merle, jackdaw
"   **Central Am.:** daw, magpie, jacamar
"   **crane-like:** wader, chunga
"   **crying:** ramage, limpkin
"   **diving:** auk
"   **dressing of feathers:** preen
"   **emu-like:** cassowaries
"   **extinct:** moa, kiwi, offbird

"   **finch-like:** chewink, tanager
"   **fish-catching:** osprey, cormorant
"   **larklike:** pipit
"   **of paradise:** manucode
"   **oldest known:** archaeopteryx
"   **parts of body:** neb, mala, prectn, syrinx
"   **pert. to:** avian, avine, ornithic, volucrine
"   **predatory:** owl, yager, shrike
"   **red-tailed:** koae
"   **sacred:** ibis
"   **S.A.:** guan, mynah, boatbill
"   **tropical:** koae, barbet
"   **web-footed:** duck, avocet
birdcage: pinjira, volary
bird nest: aery, eyry
bird's-eye view: apercu
biri: cigarette
birl: spin, rattle
birma: calaba
birse: temper, bristle
birth: bear, nascency
"   **after:** postnatal
"   **before:** prenatal
"   **help with:** accouche
"   **nobleness:** eugeny
birthmark: mole, nevus, spiloma
"   **pert. to:** naevoid
bishop: pope, pontiff
"   **apron:** gremial
"   **assistant:** verger, coadjutor
"   **buskin:** caliga
"   **cap:** hura, mitre, biretta

" **robe:** chimer(e)
" **throne:** apse
" **title:** abba
" **vestment:** alb, chimer, tunicle
bishop's weed: ammi, goutweed
bismar: steelyard
bison: bovine, aurochs
bisulcate: cloven
bit: iota, morsel, smidgeon
" **by bit:** gradually
" **horse's curb:** pelham
" **Irish:** traneen
" **part:** walk-on
biting dragon: tarragon
biting of nails: phaneromania
bito: balm, tree
" **oil:** zachun
bitter: bask, acrid, caustic
" **apple:** colocynth
" **bush:** snakeroot
" **gentian:** baldmoney
" **grass:** colicroot
" **oak:** cerris
" **spar:** dolomite
" **vetch:** ers, vicia
bitters: tonic, amer (Fr.)
" **pert. to:** amaroidal
bitterwort: felwort, dandelion
bivalve: clam, mollusk, scallop, pandora
" **genus:** pinna, toheroa
bivouac: etape, encamp
biwa: loquat
Bizet opera: Carmen
blab: blart, clack, tattle
black: calo, inky, atrous
" **amoor:** black, Negro
" **-and blue:** livid
" " **spot:** bruise, shiner, ecchymosis

" **and white:** chiaroscuro
" **art:** alchemy, necromancy
" **berry:** agawam, dewberry
" **bird:** ani, merl, ouzel, jackdaw
" **cap:** gull, titmouse, raspberry
" **cod:** beshow
" **comb. form:** atra, atro, mela(n)
" **damp:** chokedamp
" **diamond:** oil, coal, hematite
" **earth:** mold, chernozem
" **-eyed Susan:** ketmia, coneflower
" **fin:** fish, cisco, sesis
" **fish:** whale, tautog, nigrescent
" **grunt:** tripletail
" **head:** comedo
" **horn:** haw, sloe
" **leg:** scab, gambler, strikebreaker
" **school:** grind
" **sheep:** deviate, reprobate
" **smith:** gow, shoer, farrier
" **shop:** anvil, smithy
" **snake:** whip, racer, quirt
Black Sea: city: Batum, Odessa
" **old name:** Euxine
" **peninsula:** Crimea
" **pert. to:** Pontic
bladder: sac, blister, inflate, vesicle
" **comb. form:** asco
blae: blo, bleak, sunless
blague: lie, humbug, raillery

blain: sore, bulla, pustule

blake: wan, pale, yellow, colorless

Blake's symbol: Zoas

blame: twit, revile, inculpate

" **blameless:** innocent, spotless

" **deserving:** culpable

blast furnace: lower part: bosh

" **nozzle:** tuyere

blat: bleat, blurt

blate: dull, prate, sheepish

blaubok: etaac, antelope

bleaching vat: keir, kier

bleb: blob, bubble, vesicle

bleeding heart: dicentra

blemish: mar, mulct, taint, stigma

" **wood:** mote

" **wound:** scar, cicatrix, cicatrice

blended: fondu, merged

blesbok: nunni, antelope, blesbuck

blind: ante, dunch, obscure, insensate

" **as a hawk:** seel

" **alley:** dead end, impasse, cul-de-sac

" **god:** Hoth, Hoder, Hothr

" **part of:** slat

" **pig:** dive, saloon

" **printing for:** braille

" **spot:** hang-up, bigotry

" **staggers:** gid, vertigo

" **worm:** orvet

blindness: bisson, ablepsia, ignorance

" **color:** achromatopsia, monochromatism

" **day:** hemeralopia

" **partial:** meropia, cecutiency

" **snow:** chiona-blepsia

bliss: joy, ecstasy, felicity

" **place of:** Eden, Utopia, Elysium, Paradise

blob: lip, blot, mark, globule

block: bar, check, hamper

" **architectural:** dentil, mutule

" **electrically insulated:** taplet

" **football:** clip

" **for shaping metal objects:** ame

" **ice:** cube, serac

" **mechanical:** pulley

" **metal type:** quad, quod

" **nautical:** deadeye

" **perforated:** nut

" **small:** tessera

blockhead: ass, dolt, tomfool, grouthead

blood: sap, fluid, lineage

" **comb. form:** hema, h(a)emo

" **deficiency:** an(a)emia

" **disease:** leukemia

" **fluid part:** serum, plasma, opsonin

" **of the gods:** ic(h)or

" **particle in:** embolus

" **poisoning:** pyemia, toxemia, septicemia

" **stagnation:** clot, cruor, grume, stasis

" **strain:** race, stock, family

" **testing instrument:** hemabarometer

blood: hound: lyam, lyme

" **money:** cro, breaghe

"   **pudding:** sausage
"   **root:** puccoon, tetterwort
"   **stone:** chalcedony
blood vessel: vein, hemad
"   **comb. form:** vas
"   **rupture:** rhexis
blooper: error, roseate
blossom: bud, blob
"   **small:** floweret
blowze: trull, wench, hoyden
blowzed: red, ruddy, flushed
blubber: cry, foam, swollen
"   **remove:** flense
"   **whale:** fenks, speck muktuk
blue: low, aqua, perse, indigo
"   **asbestos:** crocidolite
"   **boneset:** mistflower
"   **bonnet:** cap, Scot, cornflower
"   **catalpa:** paulownia
"   **dandelion:** chicory
"   **dye herb:** woad
"   **fish:** bass, tuna, saury, weakfish
"   **gill:** sunfish
"   **gray:** merle, pearl, slate, cesious
"   **green:** bice, teal, beryl, calamine
"   **gum:** tree, eucalyptus
"   **-pencil:** edit, delete, redact
"   **peter:** coot, flag, gallinule
"   **red:** smalt, mallow, gridelin, mazarine, gris-de-lin
"   **rocket:** monkshood
"   **sheep:** bharal
"   **throat:** warbler
Bluebeard's wife: Fatima
bluer: anil

bluet: plant, bluebottle, farkleberry
blunt: bald, flat, deaden
"   **mentally:** hebitate
bo, boh: chief, leader, captain
boa: scarf, snake, anaconda
"   **constrictor:** giboia
boar: hog, aper, swine
"   **head:** hure
"   **wound:** gore, ganch
boat: ark, scor, barge, cutter, garvey, watercraft
"   **coal cargo:** collier
"   **comb. form:** scapo
"   **deck:** poop, orlop
"   **engine-driven:** sampan
"   **fishing:** bracozzo
"   **flat-bottomed:** bac, punt
"   **garbage:** hopper
"   **harbor:** tug, barge, bumboat
"   **joint:** jerl
"   **merchant:** argosy, holcad
"   **ornamental:** navicella
"   **power:** tug
"   **round:** gufa, goofa(h)
boatswain: bosun, serang
"   **whistle:** pipe
Boaz: son: Obed
"   **wife:** Ruth
bobac: marmot
bobbin: reel, braid, ratchet
"   **frame:** ereel
"   **pin:** spindle
Boccaccio work: Decameron
bodkin: awl, needle, stiletto
body: bulk, rupa, corpus
"   **anterior part of:** prosoma
"   **armor:** tace, corium
"   **away from center:** distal

" **cavity:** sinus, coelom(e)
" **comb. form:** soma(to)
" **fluid:** blood, lymph, serum
" **heavenly:** sun, moon, star, planet, asteroid
" **joint:** hip, knee, elbow, wrist, shoulder
" **motion:** gesture
" **of men:** posse, authorized
" **of persons:** corps, posse
" **of water:** bay, sea, gulf, lake, pond, pool, ocean, lagoon, sealet, reservoir
" **path:** orbit
" **pert. to:** somal, systemic
" **wall:** paries, septum
bodyguard: thane, trabant
Boeotia: capital: Thebes
" **region:** Ionia
Boer dialect: Taal
bogey: hag, goblin, bugaboo
Bohemian: arty, gypsy
" **dance:** redowa
" **residence:** village
boil: sty, botch, seethe, inflame, simmer
" **almost:** scald
" **down:** decoct
bole: dose, trunk, opening
Bolero composer: Ravel (Maurice)
bolide: meteor, missile
Bolivia, Bolivian: animal: vicuna
" **coin:** tomin, colivar, centavo
" **dried mutton:** chalone
" **Indian:** Uro, Moxo, Charca

" **measure:** league, celemin
" **weight:** libra, macro
boll weevil: picudo
bolus: cud, lump, pill
bomb: dud, egg, shell, pineapple
" **guide:** fin
" **hole:** crater
Bombay: arrowroot: tikor
" **fabric:** rumal
" **hemp:** sunn, ambary
" **native:** Parsi, Parsee
" **vessel:** patamar
bombyx: eri(a), moth, silkworm
bonasus: ox, boson, aurochs
bond: chemical: diene, valence
bone: os, rib, fillet, radius, humerus
" **anvil:** incus, incudes (pl.)
" **breast:** sterna (pl.), sternum
" **cartilage:** ossein
" **comb. form:** os, osteo
" **elbow:** ulna
" **girdle:** sphenethmoid
" **pert. to:** osteal, osseous
" **scraper:** xyster
boneset: comfrey, hempweed, thoroughwort
boniata: see: yam
boniface: landlord, innkeeper
Bonjour Tristesse author: Sagan (Francoise)
bonnet: hat, decoy, slouch
" **brim:** poke
" **monkey:** zati, munga
" **string:** bride
boo: hoot, jeer, decry
boob: ass, goony, neddy

boobook: owl, cuckoo
boojum: snark
book: opus, diary, catalog
  " **accounts:** bilan, ledger
  " **alphabet:** abecedary
  " **Apocrypha:** Tobit
  " **back:** spine
  " **binding material:** cloth, canvas, buckram
  " **church music:** hymnal
  " **collector:** bibliomaniac
  " **cover ornamentation:** tooling
  " **dealer:** bonguiniste
  " **design:** format, layout
  " **destroyer:** biblioclast
  " **Islam:** Kitab, Koran
  " **lover:** bibliophile
  " **of masses:** missal
  " **part:** leaf, cover, binding, section
  " **school:** primer
  " **title page:** rubric
  " **translation:** pony
  " **words of opera:** libretto
  " **Zoroastrian:** Avesta
bookcase: forel(l)
boondocks: sticks, backwoods
boondoggle: trifle, goldbrick
boot: pac, shoe, eject, benefit
  " **half:** buskin, cocker
  " **heavy:** stogy, brogan
  " **high-water:** wader
  " **loose-topped:** Wellington
  " **riding:** jemmy, gambado
  " **small:** bottine, bottekin
bootlick: fawn, toady, flatter
borax: tincal
border: hem, dado, line, braid, forel, margin

  " **fluted:** frill
  " **ornamental:** dado
  " **wall:** dado, ogee, cornice
Border States (Civil War): Arkansas, Delaware, Kentucky, Maryland, Missouri, Virginia, Tennessee, North Carolina
Boreas: wind, norther
  " **son:** Butes, Calais
boric acid salt: borate
boring tool: bit, auger, drill, gimlet, wimble
born: nee (Fr.), innate, nascent, natural, delivered
  " **dead:** stillborn
  " **prematurely:** abortive
  " **well:** free, noble, eugenic
  " **-e by the wind:** eolian
Borneo: ape: orang, orangutan
  " **measure:** ganta(ng)
  " **mountain:** Kini-Balu
  " **native:** D(a)yak, Iban
  " **pepper plant:** ara
  " **pirates:** bajau
  " **snake:** boiga
  " **timbertree:** billian
  " **weight:** para, chapah
boron: borax, boric, ulexite
borracho: drunk(ard)
bosc: pear
boscage: wood, grove, thicket
Bosnian native: Slav, Croat
boss: pad, bully, headman
  " **logging camp:** bully
  " **political:** cacique
  " **shield:** umbo
bot: larva

botany: angle: axil
" **cell:** spore
" **depression:** fovea, variole
both: bo, two, equally
" **handed:** ambidextrous
" **prefix:** bi, ambi
bothy: cot, lodge, harracks
bottle: vial, cruet, carage, preserve
" **sealer:** capper
" **size:** pint, pipe, fifth, quart, magnum, jeroboam
" **small:** ampul, phial, costrel
boulder: rock, stone
" **monument:** magalith
" **transported by ice:** erratic
bound: dap, leap, stend, costive, confined
" **back:** carom, resile
" **by a vow:** votary
boundary: ahu, dool, meer, verge, barrier
" **comb. form:** ori
bounder: cab, snob, roue
Bounty captain: Bligh
" **actor:** Laughton
bourgeois: common, mediocre
bow: arc, beck, archer, depress, rainbow
" **facing sea:** atry
" **of ship:** beak, prow, stem
" **oriental:** salam, salaam
" **toward:** afore
" **wood for:** yew
" **-shaped:** arcate
bowfin: amia, lawyer, mudfish
bowling: tenpins, duckpins, candlepins
" **division:** frame
" **pin:** ninepin, skittle
" **place:** alley
" **score:** spare, strike
box: bin, till, crate, fostell
" **alms:** arca
" **ammunition:** caisson, bandoleer
" **sleigh:** pung
" **tea:** canister
boxer's hand covering: glove, cesti
boxing: blow: jab, feint, punch, KO, TKO
" **contest:** match, bout
" **pert. to:** fistic, pugilistic
brachyuran: crab, crustacean
brack: crag, brine, crack
bract: glume, palea, palet, spadix
Bragi's wife: Idun, Ithunn
Brahma: Hindu, creator
" **first woman created by:** Ahalya
Brahman: zebu, Hindu, Bostonian
" **land grant:** sasan
" **precept:** sutra, sutta
" **title:** aya
braid: cue, tress, sennet, deceitful
" **gold and silver:** orris
" **hemp:** tagal
" **knotted:** lacet
brain: bean, utac, skull
" **box:** pan, skull, cranium
" **comb. form:** cerebro
" **layer:** obex, cortex
" **membrane:** tela, meninges
" **operate on:** trepan

" **orifice:** lura
" **part:** aula, cerebrum, encephalon, pericranium
" **passage:** iter
" **pert. to:** cerebral
" **white matter:** pia, alba, dura
brainstorm: confusion
bran: treat, cereal, chisel
branch: arm, bow, rame, shoot, vimen, stolon
" **angle of:** axil
" **of nerves:** rami (pl.), ramus
" **pert. to:** ramal, remeal
" **-like:** ramose
branchia: gill
brand: birn, flaw, character
" **on stolen cattle:** duff
" **sheep:** smit
brandy: and soda: peg
" **mastic:** raki
" **plum:** slivovitz
brank: caper, mumps, pillory
brassica: cole, rape, turnip
Brave New World author: Huxley
Brazil, Brazilian: ant: tucandera
" **bird:** ara, soco, macaw, tiriba
" **coffee plantation:** fazenda
" **coin:** reis, conto, dobra, milreis, cruziero
" **dance:** samba, maxixe
" **discoverer:** Cabral
" **drink:** assai
" **duck:** muscovy
" **estuary:** Para
" **fiber:** imbe
" **Indian:** Anta, Arana, Carib, Tariana, Botocudo
" **mammal:** tapir
" **measure:** pe, pipa, fanga, covado, tarefa, quartilho
" **monkey:** sai, miriki, belzebuth
" **palm:** jara, inaja, babassu
" **plant:** imbe, para, yage, caroa, ayapana, seringa, jaborandi
" **rubber:** (h)ule, Para, Caucho
" **tree:** apa, brauna, gomavel, barbatimao
" **weight:** bag, onca, libra, oitava, arratel, quilate, tonelada
" **wood:** embuia, kingwood
breach: gap, flaw, scism, violation
" **of etiquette:** gaffe, solecism
" **pin:** tige
bread: bun, aliment, sustenance
" **boiled:** cush, panada
" **browned:** sippet, crouton
" **communion:** azym(e)
" **crust:** rind
" **leavened:** kisra, cocket
" **pert. to:** panary
" **unleavened:** azym(e), matzos, bannock
break: bust, rive, frush, hiatus, fissure, interval, penetrate
" **down:** debacle, failure, collapse, cataclasm, catabolism

44

" **in:** slip, stave, blunder, initiate, interrupt

" **out:** rash, erupt, escape

" **up:** split, disband, disperse, separate

breakbone fever: dengue

breakwater: cob, dike, quay, jetty

" **bream:** tai, fish, scup, broom, sunfish

" **sea:** shad, sargus

breast: crop, bosom, brace, chest, thorax, encounter

" **-bone:** xiphoid, sternum

" " **pert. to:**

" **ornament:** pectoral, sternal

breastplate: armor, urim, lorica

" **ecclesiastical:** urim

breathing: gasping, respiration

" **difficult:** dyspnea

" **harsh:** rale

" **smooth:** lene

" **sound:** rale, shore, stridor

breeding: origin, gestation

" **science:** eugenics

breeze: aura, flaw, gale, pirr, rumor, zephyr, quarrel, whisper, disturbance

" **land:** terral

brevet: confer, promotion, commission

brewer: grain: rye, corn, malt, barley

" **vat:** tun

" **yeast:** barm, leaven

briar: saw, pipe

brick: tile, quarl(e)

" **handler:** baker

" **oven:** kiln

" **sun-baked:** hat, adobe

" **tray:** hod

" **vitrified:** clinker

" **wood:** nog, dook, scutch

bridge: gume, span, trestle

" **forerunner:** auction, whist

" **lever:** bascule

" **of mus. instruments:** magas, ponticello

" **part:** deck, pier, cable, pylon

" **support:** pier, truss

" **type of:** (game) rubber, duplicate

briery: sharp, spiny

brine: sea, pickle

" **preserve in:** corn, cure, salt

" **shrimp:** artemia

brioche: roll, stitch, cushion, pudding, savarin

Briseis' lover: Achilles

British Columbia: Indian: Haida, Shuswap

" **river:** Nicola

Britomartis: Artemis, Dictynna

" **mother:** Carme

Brittany: ancient name: Armorica

" **canvas:** vandelas

" **king:** ban

" **native:** Breton

" **poetry:** soniou

" **saint:** Anne

broad: ample, coarse, obvious, tolerant

" **comb. form:** late

" **-footed:** platypod

" **-minded:** leniant

broadbill: bird, gaya, scaup, shoveler, swordfish

brobdingnagian: huge, giant, colossal

brocard: gibe, rule, maxim, sarcasm, principle

brocket: deer, pita, spitter

brolly: umbrella

Bronte: Anne, Emily, Charlotte

  " **hero:** Rochester, Heathcliff

  " **heroine:** Jane Eyre

  " **pen name:** Bell

bronze: tan, brown, statue

  " **film:** patine

  " **gilded:** ormolu

  " **nickel:** cupronickel

  " **pert. to:** aeneous

broom: fray, besom, sweep

  " **plant:** hirse, heather, deerweed

brown: dun, cook, russet, half-penny sepia, bronze

  " **and white:** roan

  " **Bess:** musket

  " **Betty:** pudding, coneflower

  " **dark:** burnet

  " **dark reddish:** cuba, henna, khaki

  " **light:** fawn, ecru, beige

  " **study:** absorption, abstraction

  " **thrasher:** bird, thrush

brume: fog, vapor

Brython: god: Dea, Ler, Lludd

  " **goddess:** Don, Rhiannon, Arianrhod

bubal: topi, antelope

buck: (sl.) dollar, oppose, ram, fob, wash

  " **first year:** fawn

  " **fourth year:** sore

Buddha: Fo(h), Gautama, Shakyamuni

  " **cause of intinite existence:** nidana, nirvana

  " **center:** Lassa

  " **church:** Tera

  " **column:** lat

  " **disciple:** Ananda

  " **evil spirit:** Mara

  " **fate:** karma

  " **fertility spirit:** Yaksha, Yakshi

  " **festival:** bon

  " **god:** deva

  " **greater:** Mahayana

  " **hell:** Naraka

  " **language:** Pali

  " **prayer:** mani

  " **scripture:** sutra

  " **throne:** asana

  " **tree:** pipal, botree

buffalo: ox, buff, bison, caribao

  " **large:** arna, arni, arnee

  " **meat:** biltong

  " **wild:** seladang

  " **gourd:** calabazilla

  " **tree:** rabbitwood

bufflehead: duck, clown, merrywing

bug: June: dor

  " **lightning:** firefly

  " **needle:** ranatra

bugbane: herb, hellebore, rattleroot

bugle: bead, horn, buffalo, clarion

  " **blare:** tantara

  " **call:** taps, sennet, tattoo,

retreat, reveille
" **note:** not
" **yellow:** iva
build: nest: nidify
" **up:** enhance, strengthen
builder: erector, tectonic
" **labyrinth:** Daedalus
" **of wooden horse:** Epe(i)us
bulbul: bird, kala
Bulgaria; Bulgarian: Slav, Churash
" **coin:** lev, lew, stotinka
" **measure:** oka, oke, krine, lekha
" **weight:** oka, oke, tovar
bull: apis, jest, quadruped
" **angry:** gorer
" **castrated:** stot, steer, bullock
" **half man:** minotaur
" **hornless:** doddy, doddie
" **pert. to:** taurine
" **young:** stirk, bullock
" **-like:** taurine
bulla: bleb, seal, blain, vesicle
bullfinch: alp, monk, hedge
bullion: bar, ingot, metal, billot
Bull Run: battle: Manassas
" **hero:** Lee
bumblebee: dor, insect
bunch: set, fagot, thump, quantity
" **of grapes:** bob
" **pert. to:** comal
buncombe: rot, bunk, drivel, poppycock
bundle: wad, sheaf, bindle, parcel, collection
" **maker:** baler
" **arrows:** sheaf

" **firewood:** bavin
" **grain:** sheaf
" **sticks:** fag(g)ot
" **straw:** bolt
bung: cork, spile, tampeon, bankrupt
Bunyan: see **Paul Bunyan**
bunyip: sham, imposter
buoy: dan, elate, sustain
" **mooring:** dolphin
" **trawling marker:** dan
burbot: cod, ling, eelpout
burden bearer: Amos, Atlas
burgess: citizen, commoner
burgoo, burgout: soup, gruel, porridge
burial: interment, deposition
" **case:** box, casket, coffin
" **litter:** bier
" **mound:** barrow, tumulus
" **pile:** pyre
" **place:** tomb, grave, golgotha
" **preparation for:** cere, pollincture
burin: tool, graver
burl: knot, pimple
" **in mahogany:** roe
Burma, Burmese: canopy: tazaung
" **chief:** bo(h), wun, woon
" **dagger:** dah, dout
" **deer:** thamin, thameng
" **demon:** nat
" **garment:** tamein
" **girl:** mina
" **head hunter:** Naga
" **knife:** dah, dow
" **measure:** dha, byee, dain, teng, palgat
" **musical instrument:** turr

" **robber:** dacoit
" **sash:** tubbeck
" **spirit:** nat
" **tree:** acle, yamani
" **tribesman:** Lai
" **weight:** mat, vis, kait, ti-cul
burning bush: wahoo
burnoose, burnous: cloak, garment, albornoz
burnt work: pyrography
burse: case, bazaar, ex-change
burst: pop, rend, erupt, salvo
" **forth:** erupt, sally, blasted
" **inward:** implode
bus: jitney, vehicle, chara-banc
bustle: fuss, todo, tumult
" **woman's:** bishop
but: lo, ma (It.), sed (Lat.), yet, still, mere, unless
butcher: kill, bungle, vendor, pigstick
" **hook:** gambrel
" **rabbi:** shochtim
" **tool:** saw, knife, steel, cleaver
butcher-bird: shrike
butte: hill, picacho, mountain
butter: shea, spread, blarney
" **comb. form:** butyro
" **pert. to:** butyric
" **shea:** galam, bambuk
" **tree:** shea, fulwa, phulwa

" **tub:** firkin
butterbur: eldin, plant
butterfish: blenny, gunnel
butterfly: kiho, idalya, vice-roy, cecropia
" **expert:** lepidopterist
" **fish:** blenny
" **genus:** melitaea, helico-nius
" **larva:** caterpillar
" **lily:** sego, mariposa
" **peacock:** io
butterwort: steepweed
buy: shop, trade, acquire
" **cheaply:** snup
" **to sell at a profit:** re-grate
buying and selling: nundina-tion
by: ago, per, close, beside
" **-gone:** yore
" **means of:** with, from, through
" **mouth:** oral
" **pass:** shun
Byron character: Lara, Don Juan, Inez
byssin: flax, linen
byssoid: cottony, fiberlike, byssaceous
byword: axiom, proverb, cat-chword
Byzantine: coin: bezant
" **scepter:** ferula
" **works of art:** icons

48

C

C: hundred
  " **-note:** (sl.) 100 dollar bill
Caaba: shrine
  " **site:** Mecca
caama: fox, asse, hartebeest
cabal: plot, secret, faction, tradition
  " **pert. to:** factional
cabala: occultism, mystery
cabbage: chou, bowkail, cole-wort
  " **broth:** kale
  " **daisy:** globeflower
  " **family:** brassicaceae
  " **fermented:** sauerkraut
  " **salad:** slaw, coleslaw
  " **seed:** colza
  " **soup:** kale (Sc.)
  " **tree:** angelin, yaba
  " **variety:** cale, colza, kohlrabi
  " **worm:** looper, cutworm
caber: beam, pole
cable: boom, wire, ganger

  " **car:** telfer, telpher
  " **post:** bitt
cabob: (roast) meat
  " **holder:** spit, skewer
cabotin: actor, charlatan
cacao: bean, arriba, choco-late
  " **seed powder:** broma
  " **shell extract:** martol
cachalot: sperm, whale, phy-seter
cacholong: opal
cachou: lozenge, catechu
cacoethes: itch, desire, ma-nia
cacography: misspelling
cactus: bleo, nopal, cholla
  " **drug:** peyote
  " **fruit:** cochal, fig
  " **plant:** tuna
  " **plantation:** nopalry
  " **plant process:** spine
  " **spineless:** chaute
caddis worm: cadew

caddle: fuss, confuse, disarray

Caddoan Indian: ree, pawnee

caddow: quilt, jackdaw, coverlet

cadet: plebe, embryo, midshipman

cadew: worm

Cadmus: daughter: Ino, Agave, Semele, Autonoe
"   **father:** Agenor
"   **sister:** Europa
"   **wife:** Harmonia

Caesar: tyrant, emporer, salad
"   **assassin:** Brutus, Cassius
"   **augur who warned:** Spurinna
"   **colleague:** Bibulus
"   **fatal day:** Ides
"   **love of:** Servilia
"   **mistress of:** Eunoe, Cleo(patra)
"   **place of victory:** Actium
"   **river crossed by:** Rubicon
"   **sister:** Atia
"   **site of famous message:** Zela
"   **wife:** Cornelia, Calpurnia

cafard: bigot, apathy, hypocrite

cage hawk: mew, meute

caiman: jacare, alligator

Cain: murderer, fratricide
"   **brother:** Pur, Abel, Seth
"   **descendant:** Lamech, Jubal
"   **father:** Adam
"   **land:** Nod

"   **mother:** Eve
"   **son:** Enoch

cairngorm: quartz

caitiff: vile, wicked, cowardly

caique: rowboat, sailboat

cajeput: laurel

cake: bun, wig, nacket, bannock
"   **boiled in honey:** teiglech
"   **corn:** pone, fritter
"   **filled:** flan
"   **fish:** patty
"   **oatmeal:** bannock
"   **plum:** baba
"   **sacrificial:** hallah
"   **seed:** wig, wiff
"   **small:** tart, jimble
"   **tea:** scone
"   **unleavened:** matzo, damper, tortilla (Sp.)

calaba: tree, birma

calabash: gourd, curuba, shell

caladium: taro

calamanco: manco, fabric, garment

calamus: pen, cane, sweetflag, quill

calcar: oven, spur

calcite: animal, skeleton
"   **deposit:** spar, tatar

calcium: tufa
"   **oxide:** quicklime
"   **sulphate:** hepar, gypsum, plaster
"   **crust:** sinter

calculus: (gall) stone, gravel

Calcutta: hemp, jute
"   **river:** Hugli, Hooghly

calderite: garnet

Caleb: son: Hur, Iru

" **companion:** Joshua
Caledonia, Caledonian: Scotland, Pic, Scot
calefy: heat, warm
calendar: diary, register, ephemeris
" **church:** ordo
" **former:** Julian
calenture: fire, ardor, fever
calf: boy, dolt, bovine, fatling
" **cry:** bl(e)at
" **front:** shin
" **jelly:** fisnoga
" **leather:** elk
" **meat:** veal
" **motherless:** dogy(ie), maverick
" **muscle:** plantaris
" **pert. to:** sural
" **skin parchment:** vellum
" **suckling:** bob
" **unbranded:** maverick
Caliban: beast, slave
" **adversary of:** Prospero
" **deity of:** Setebos
" **witch mother:** Sycorax
calibrate: measure, standardize
calico: girl, goldfish, multicolored
" **horse:** pinto
" **mix colors for:** teer
" **pigment:** canarin(e)
" **printing:** teer, fondu, lapis
California: (see special section)
" **bay:** Monterey
" **bulrush:** tule
" **dam:** Shasta
" **desert:** Mohave
" **fan palm:** erythea
" **fish:** reina, sprat
" **gold rusher:** argonaut
" **grape picker:** bracero
" **Indian:** Hupa, Seri, Yurok, Weitspekan
" **laurel:** cajeput
" **oak:** roble, encina
" **peak:** Lassen, Shasta
" **plant:** tarweed
" **shrub:** salal, chamise(o), tarbush, chaparral, manzanita
" **wine area:** Napa
Caligula: bootikin
" **horse:** Incitatus
calix: cup, chalice
calking material: oakum, tar
call: bid, page, rouse, summon
" **back:** revoke, retrieve
" **creditor's:** dun
" **down:** scold, rebuke
" **in question:** impugn
" **off:** end, cancel
" **prayer:** Adan, Azan
Call of the Wild author: London (Jack)
Calliope: muse
" **son:** Orpheus
Callisto: nymph, constellation
" **son:** Arcas
calomel: powder, cathartic
calorie, calory: therm(e)
calotte: coif, summit
calyx: leaf, sepal
" **helmet shaped:** galea
" **of flower:** perianth
cam: cog, askew, trippet
" **wheel projection:** lobe
camail: hood, guard
Cambodia: ancient capital: Angkor

"   **native:** Khmer
"   **ruins:** Angkor
"   **skirt:** samport
cambogia: (gum) resin
cambrai: batiste, linen
cambric: linen, batiste
Cambridge: college official: bedell, don
"   **student:** sizar, spoon, optime
camel: cont, mehari, dromedary
"   **driver:** sarwan, cameleer
"   **female:** naga
"   **fermented milk:** kumys, koumiss
"   **garment:** aba
"   **hair:** aba, cloth
"   **hair cloth:** aba, cashmere
"   **hair robe:** aba
"   **keeper:** obil
"   **load:** fardel
Cameroon: inhabitant of: Sara
"   **river:** Shari
camion: bus, dray, truck
camlet: fabric, poncho
camomile: mayweed
Camorra: Mafia
campanero: arapunga, bellbird
camphol: borneol
camphor: menthol, asarone
campus: quad, field, yard
"   **building:** gym, dorm
Camus work: Rebel, Stranger
Canada, Canadian: Canuck
"   **court decree:** arret
"   **emblem:** maple

"   **gannet:** margot
"   **goose:** brant, honker
"   **lynx:** pishu
"   **measure:** ton, minot, arpent, chainon
"   **peninsula:** Gaspe
"   **policeman:** mountie
"   **poplar:** liard
"   **roddent:** lemming
"   **settler:** sourdough
"   **squaw:** mahala
"   **territory:** Yukon, Northwest
"   **town president:** reeve
canadine: alkaloid
canaille: mob, rabble
canal: cano, duct, drain
"   **bank:** berm(e)
"   **dredging machine:** couloir
"   **ear:** scala
"   **footpath:** towpath
"   **from mouth to anus:** alimentary, enteron
"   **lock gate:** soo
Canal Zone: city: Balboa
"   **lake:** Gatun
canard: hoax, fabrication
canary broom: genista
canary yellow: meline
candle: dip, light, chandelle
"   **holder:** sconce, candelabra
"   **light:** dusk, twilight, nightfall
"   **lighter:** spill, acolyte
"   **material:** carnauba, wax, tallow, wick
"   **part:** wick, snast
"   **place of keeping:** chandlery
"   **wax:** taper, bougie

candy: lolly, sweet, comfit, flatter, sweetmeat
  " **base:** fondant
  " **mixture:** fourre
  " **pulled sugar:** taffy, penide
candytuft: plant, flower, iberis, mustard
cane: rod, flog, reed
  " **dense growth:** cane-brake
  " **knife:** machete
  " **like a:** ferulaceous
  " **metal cap:** shoe, perrule
  " **part:** ferrule
  " **strip:** splint
  " **sugar:** sucrose
  " **walking:** malacca
cangle: dispute, wrangle
cangue-like device: pillory
canine tooth: laniary
cannabis: hemp
  " **drug:** bhang, hashish, marijuana
Cannery Row author: Steinbeck, (John)
cannibal: savage, man-eater, carnivore
  " **human food of:** long pig
cannikin: can, pail
cannon: gun, thief, mortar
  " **breech-end knob:** cascabel
  " **fire:** barrage
  " **firing stick:** linstock
  " **handle:** anse
  " **harness for men:** bricole
  " **muzzle plug:** tampion
  " **old:** drake, aspic, culverin, falcon
  " **part:** bore, breech, muzzle, rimbase
  " **shot:** grape
canoe: pahi, kayak, pitpan
  " **bark:** cascara
  " **large:** pah, bungo
  " **war:** proa
canopy: hood, celure, baldachin, pavillion, baldacchino, baldachin
  " **altar:** ciborium(a), baldachino
  " **bed:** tester, sparver
canorous: clear, sonorous
cantabank: singer, chanter
cantata: mote, serenata
cantharides: itritant, stimulant
cantilena: legato, graceful
canting: atrip, pious
cantoria: balcony, gallery
cantrip: charm, spell, trick
canvas: duck, scrim
  " **like fabric:** wigan
  " **waterproof:** tarpaulin
canyon: cajon, chasm, gulch
  " **mouth:** abra, jaws
  " **small:** canada
  " **wall:** cliff
caoba: quira, mahogany
caoutchouc: rubber
  " **source:** ule, caucho
cap: fez, lid, eton, excel, outdo, beanie
  " **brimless:** pileus, tam, tarboosh
  " **child's:** mutch, toque, biggin
  " **close-fitting:** toque, cloche
  " **covering:** havelock
  " **ecclesiastical:** barret, galerum
  " **hunter's:** montero

" **Jewish priest's:** miter, mitre
" **knitted:** thrum
" **part:** bill, peak, visor
" **sheepskin:** calpac(k)
" **skull:** pileus, yarmulka
" **slang:** lid
" **steel:** cerveliere
" **winter:** tuque
capa: cloak, mantle
capable: apt, fit, competent
" **of being cut:** sectile, scissile
" **of being defended:** tenable
" **of being heard:** audible
" **of endurance:** wiry, tough
" **of extension:** tensile
capacitate: qualify
Capaneus: father: Hipponous
" **mother:** Astynome
" **son:** Sthenelus
" **wife:** Evadne
capatas: boss, overseer
cape: ras, writ, cloak, sagum
" **cod food fish:** cero
" **crocheted:** sontag
" **ecclesiastical:** amice, cope
" **hanging part:** tippet
" **hooded:** amice, almuce, Moz(z)etta
" **lace:** fichu, bertha
Cape elk: eland
Cape polecat: zoril, muishond
capel: rock, horse, quartz
capelin: smelt
capias: writ, process
capilotade: stew, sauce, ra-

gout
capric acid salt: rutate
Capricorn: goat, beetle
" **star inside:** Deneb
capripede: goat, satyr
caprylate: acid, salt, ester
capuche: cowl, hood
Capuchin: friar, monkey, pigeon
capybara: rodent
car: box, coach, hutch, vehicle
" **aerial cable:** telfer, telpher
" **barn:** depot
caraboa: buffalo, tamaraw
caracara: hawk
carapace: crust, shell, lorica
caravan: van, trek, convoy
" **slave:** coffle
caravansary: inn, serai, imaret
carbon: coal, coke, graphite
" **copy: colloq.:** look alike, (spitting) image
" **deposit:** soot
" **castrated:** gib(bed)
" **point:** crayon
carborundum: emery, abrasive
carcajou: lynx, badger, cougar, wolverine
carcanet: chain, collar
carcel: jail
carcoon: clerk, manager
card: map, menu, ticket, pam, fiche
" **spot:** pip
" **widow:** skat
" **wild:** joker
" **wool:** tum, rove, comb
cardialgin: heartburn

cardinal: bird, basic, cleric
" **assembly at Rome:** college
" **meeting room:** conclave
" **notification of elevation:** biglietto
" **office:** hat, datary
" **skullcap of:** zucchetto
" **vestment:** dalmatic
care: cark, mind, auspice, direction, watchfulness
" **for:** tend, foster
" **requiring:** fragile
" **under another's:** ward, protege
careworn: lined, haggard
cargador: porter, carrier, stevedore
cargo: bulk, load, shipment
" **discarded:** jetsam
" **hot:** contraband
" **loader:** stevedore
" **space in ship:** hold
" **stabilizer:** ballast
" **take on:** lade, load
" **wrecked ship:** flotsam
Caribbean: bird: tody
" **gulf:** Darien
" **island:** Cuba, Nassau
caribe: fish, pirana
caribou: deer, reindeer
" **male:** stag
caricature: ape, skit, squib, burlesque
caries: decay, ulceration, saprodontia
cark: worry, annoy
Carmelite: friar, monk
" **barefoot:** Teresian
carmen: poem, song, incantation
Carmen composer: Bizet

carminative seeds: caraway
carnauba: palm
" **product:** wax
carnelian: sard, chalcedony
carnival: gala, festival
" **character:** barker, shill, grifter
" **gambling operator:** grifter
carob: tree, locust, algarroba, pod
Carolinian: tarheel
carotid: artery
carp: criticize, cavil
" **Japanese:** koi
" **like fish:** dace, goldfish, ide
carpal joint: knee
carpel: carpophyl(l), achene
carpenter: ant, framer, woodworker
" **machine:** lathe, planer, shaper
" **ship:** chips
" **tool:** adz(e), awl, level, plane, gimlet, square
carpet: rug, tapet, covering
" **city:** Tournai, Agra
" **material:** drugget, moquette
carplike fish: dace, rudd
carpus: wrist
" **bone:** carpal(e)
carrageen: alga, moss, seaweed
carriage: air, buggy, landau, conduct
" **baby:** pram, stroller
" **covered:** landau, ricksha
" **for hire:** fiacre
" **hood:** capote
" **one-horse:** fly, gig, sulky

" **open:** dos-a-dos
" **portable:** sedan
" **three-horse:** troika
carrion: vile, rotten, corrupt
Carroll: (see Alice in Wonderland)
carrot: root, plant, daucus
" **deadly:** drias
" **family:** ammaicea
" **genus:** carum
" **oil tube:** vitta
" **wild:** hilltrot, laceflower
carry: cart, bear, poise, convey
" **away:** steal, remove
" **on:** rant, perform
" **out:** effect, sustain
" **over:** tide, postpone
cart: dray, haul, trundle
" **farmer:** morfrey
" **freight:** carreton
" **racing:** sulky
" **two-wheeled:** gig, tonga
Carthage, Carthaginian:
" **citadel:** Bursa, Byrsa
" **conqueror:** Hannibal
" **destroyer of:** Romans, Scipio
" **foe:** Cato
" **founder:** Dido
" **god:** Moloch
" **goddess:** Tanit(h)
" **language, pert. to:** Punic
" **queen:** Dido
cartilage: tissue, gristle
" **ossified:** bone
cartridge holder: clip
carving: in stone: cameo, intaglio, engrailing
" **pert. to:** glyphic, glyptic
" **relief:** cameo

carya: pecan, pignut, bitternut
casco: barge, lighter
case: box, deed, crate, lawsuit, instance
" **book holder:** for(r)el
" **cigar:** humidor
" **document:** hanaper
" **explosive:** shell, petard
" **small:** etui, bulla
cask: keg, foist, barrel, cardel, puncheon
" **oil:** rier
" **rim:** chimb, chime
" **stave:** lag
Cassandra: prophet, seeress
" **father:** Priam
cassava: aipi, juca, tapioca
cassena: yaupon
cassia: drug, herb
" **bark:** cinnamon
cassock: gown, gippo, soutane
cassowary: emu, bird, murup
caster: vial, wheel, pitcher
castle: morro, bastile, citadel
" **part:** bawn, moat, drawbridge, portcullis
" **tower:** keep
" **wall:** bailey
" **warden:** disdar, dizdar
Castor: twin, Gemini, Dioscuri
" **brother:** Pollux
" **father:** Zeus, Tyndareus
" **horse:** Cyllaros
" **mother:** Leda
" **slayer:** Idas
castor-bean poison: ricin
casus: case, event, occasion
cat: flog, feline, mawkin
" **breed:** Manx, Angora, Maltese, Persian, Siamese
" **castrated:** gib(bed)

"   **civetlike:** genet, zibet(h)
"   **comb. form:** aelur(o)
"   **epithet:** baudrons
"   **female:** grimalkin
"   **genusfelis, felidae** (pl.)
"   **musk-yielding:** civet
"   **ring-tailed:** serval
catafalque: bier, coffin
cataian: thief, sharper, scoundrel
Catalonia: dance: Sardana
"   **famous person:** Casals
"   **marble:** brocatel(le)
catamount: lynx, puma, cougar
cataplasm: poultice
catbird: mimidae
cate: food, viands, provisions
catena: link, chain, series
caterpillar: muga, aweto, tractor
caterwaul: cry, wail, miaul
cathedral: dom, church
"   **Passage:** slype
catkin: ament, spike
catmint: nep, nip, herb
Catoism: austerity, harshness
Catreus: daughter: Aerope, Clymene, Apemosyne
"   **father:** Minos
"   **mother:** Pasiphae
cat's-cradle: ribwort
cattle: cows, bulls, beasts, steers, bovines
"   **assemblage:** herd, drove
"   **brand:** duff, buist
"   **call:** sook
"   **dehorned:** mul(l)ey
"   **genus:** bos
"   **goddess:** Bubona
"   **plague:** rinderpest

"   **shelter:** byre, barth
"   **yard:** cancha
caudal: rear, posterior
"   **appendage:** tail
caudata: newt, snake, salamander
cauma: heat, fever
cavalry: horses, troops
"   **horse:** lancer
"   **weapon:** lance, saber
cavalryman: spahi, courier, dragoon
cave: den, weem, grotto, spelunk
"   **dweller:** troglodyte
"   **researcher:** spelunker, speleologist
caveat: beware, caution
cavetto: molding
cavity: pit, vein, lumen, antrum, hollow
"   **anatomical:** fossa, antrum
"   **brain:** coelia
"   **heart:** auricle, ventricle
"   **pert. to:** sinal, atrial, geodic
"   **skull:** aula, fossa, sinus
cavy: paca, pony, guinea pig
cawl: trug, basket
caxi: fish, snapper
cayuse: cavy, pony, bronco
cecidium: gall
cedar: toon, savin, waxwing
"   **camphor:** cedrol
"   **green:** cedre (F.), color
"   **moss:** hornwort
cedrat: citron
ceilidh: call, visit, conversation, entertainment
ceiling: lining, soffit, wainscoting

"   **covering:**   calcimine, kalsomine
"   **division:** trave
"   **mine:** astel
"   **wooden:** plancher
Celebes: bovine: ox, anoa
"   **people:** tora(d)ja
celery: family: ammiaceae
"   **wild:** smallage
celestial: holy, uranic, ethereal
"   **being:** angel, cherub, seraph
"   **body:** sun, star, comet, meteor, planet
"   **elevation of mind:** anagoge
"   **matter:** nebula
cell: egg, jail, vault
"   **coloring:** endochrome
"   **colorless:** achroacyte, lymphocyte
"   **connecting:** heterocyst
"   **division:** spireme
"   **group:** ceptor, blastema
"   **layer:** blastula, blastoderm
"   **pert. to:** cytoid
"   **substance:** linin
cella: naos
Celtic: Erse, Scotch
"   **abbot:** coarb
"   **chariot:** essed
"   **chieftain:** tanist
"   **foot soldier:** kern
"   **god:** Ler, Leir, Llyr
"   **peasant:** kern
"   **priest:** Druid
cenchrus: grass, millet
cenobite: nun, monk, monastic
censer: thurible

centaur: bull's head: bucentaur
"   **father:** Ixion
"   **killed by Hercules:** Nessus
centerpiece: epergne
centipede: veri, golach
Central America: agave: sisal
"   **ant:** kelep
"   **canoe:** pitpan
"   **Indian:** Maya, Carib
"   **measure:** cantaro, manzana
"   **monkey:** mono
"   **village:** boma
"   **weight:** libra
centripetal: afferent
century plant: aloe, agave, maguey
"   **fiber:** pita(o)
ceramics: tiles, pottery, stoneware
"   **oven:** kiln
"   **sieve:** laun
cere: wax, sere, embalm
cereal: rye, spelt, wheat, porridge
"   **coating:** bran
"   **seed:** kernel
"   **spike:** ear
cerebrospinal axis: cord, brain, spine
ceremonial fuss: panjandrum
Ceres: Demeter
"   **mother:** Ops
cernuous: nodding, drooping
certificate: bond, voucher, credential
"   **cargo:** navicert
"   **debt:** IOU, debenture
"   **medical, for ill student:**

aegrotat
certiorari: writ, review
cespitose: matted, tufted, tangled
cess: bog, duty, slope, impost
cessation: letup, truce
  " **of being:** desition
cesspool: sump, cistern
cest: belt, cestus, girdle
cetacean: orc, dolphin, grampus
  " **blind:** susu
  " **genus:** inia
Ceylon: aborigine: Toda, Vedda(h)
  " **coin:** cent
  " **garment:** sarong
  " **governor:** disawa
  " **language:** Pali, Tamil
  " **measure:** para(h)
  " **monkey:** maha, langur, wanderoock
  " **oak:** kusam
  " **skirt:** reddha
  " **soldier:** peon
  " **tree:** doon, tala, talipot
chabutra: dais, terrace, platform
chack: bite, clack, wheatear
chacra: farm, milpa, ranch
chaeta: seta, spine, bristle
chaffinch: robinet
chain: guy, tew, bind, catena, manacle
  " **cable:** boom
  " **collar:** tore, torque
  " **grab:** wildcat
  " **key:** chatelaine
  " **like:** catenate
  " **of quotations:** catena
  " **of rocks:** reef
  " **pert. to:** catenary

  " **set precious stones:** sautoir
chair: seat, office
  " **back:** splat
  " **bishop's official:** cathedra
  " **cover:** tidy, antimacassar
  " **folding:** faldstool
chaise: gig, shay, curicle, carriage
chaitya: shrine, monument
Chalcodon: father: Abas
  " **son:** Elephenor
Chaldea: astronomical cycle: saros
  " **city:** Ur
  " **measure:** cane, makuk, ghalva
chalky silicate: talc
chamber: cell, atrium, lochlus
  " **bombproof:** casemate
  " **private:** adyta (pl), sanctum
  " **underwater construction:** caisson
chambray: cloth, fabric, gingham
chameleon: anole, anoli, lizard
chamois: skin, cloth, antelope
  " **male:** gemsbok
champerty: contest, rivalry, conspiracy
chancel: part: bema, altar
  " **screen:** jube
  " **seat:** sedile
chandelier: pharos, fixture
chandelle: lob, climb, candle
chang: beer, noise, uproar
change: move, amend, mutate, deviate

" **appearance:** obvert
" **back:** return, revert
" **character of:** denature
" **color:** allochroous
" **music:** muta
" **pattern:** kaleidoscopic
channel: gat, vein, canal, arroyo, sluice
" **artificial:** drain, flume
" **brain:** iter
" **formed by cutting:** scarf
" **marker:** buoy
" **narrow:** furrow, strait
" **vital:** artery
Channel Island: Sark, Guernsey
" **measure:** cade, cabot
" **seaweed:** vraic
channels: media, striae
chantage: extortion, blackmailing
chaos: mess, jumble
" **Babylonian:** Apsu
" **daughter:** Nox, Nyx
" **Maori:** kore
" **primeval fluid of:** Nu
" **son:** Erebus
chaparral: buckthorn
chapel: cage, shrine, sanctuary
" **private:** oratory
" **sailor's:** bethel
chaps: jaws, breeches, overalls
charabanc: bus, coach, vehicle
charact: emblem
character: bent, mold, mettle, quality
" **assumed:** role
" **group:** ethos
" **vein:** streak

" **word-representing:** logogram, logograph
characteristic: cast, mark, symbolic
" **individual:** idiopathy
charco: pool, puddle, spring
charcoal: carbo, fusain, pencil
" **animal:** boneblack
chard: beet, thistle, artichoke
chariot: car, esseda, carriage
" **for carrying image of God:** rath(a)
" **Greek:** quadriga
" **Roman:** essed(e), esseda
" **two-horse:** biga
charivari: babel, shivaree
chark: cup, coal, noggin
Charlemagne: brother of: Carloman
" **conquest:** Avars
" **father:** Pepin
" **sword:** Joyeuse
Charlie Chan creator: Biggers
Charlotte Corday's victim: Marat
charnel: ghastly, cemetery, sepulchral
" **house:** ossuary, mortuary
charpoy: bed, cot
charqui: beef, meat, jerky
Charybdis rock: Scylla
chase: hunt, score, engrave
" **away:** rout, drive
" **goddess:** Dian, Diana
chat: mag, ament, babble, samara
chatelaine: pin, clasp, mistress

chatta: umbrella
chattels: gear, slaves
  " **distraint:** naam
  " **tenant's:** farleu, farley
  " **to recover:** detinue
chatter: gab, prate, yammer, nashgob
  " **box:** jay, gossip
Chaucer: inn: Tabard
  " **pilgrim:** reeve
  " **title:** Dan
chauvinism: jingoism, patriotism
chavel: gnaw, mumble, nibble
chawbacon: chaw, rustic, bumpkin
cheat: do, con, dupe, chisel, skelder, prestidigitator
checkers: game, draughts
  " **move:** dyke, fife, huff, cross, bristol
  " **opening:** souter
  " **term:** king, block, crown
checkerwork: tessera(e)(pl.)
  " **inlay:** mosaic
checkrein: curb, saccade
cheek: gall, jowl, temerity
  " **bone:** malar, zygoma
  " **comb. form:** bucco
  " **muscle:** buccinator
  " **pert. to:** genal, malar, buccal
cheese: Mysost, Stilton, Sapsago
  " **basis of:** casein
  " **cake:** dessert, photograph
  " **curdy:** trip
  " **drying frame:** hack
  " **maggot:** skipper
  " **milk whey:** ziega, zieger
  " **pert. to:** caseic, caseous

chela: claw, slave
chelicera: mandible, appendage
chemical: acid, alkalai
  " **agent:** catalyst
  " **catalyst:** reagent
  " **comb. capacity:** valence
  " **compound:** imin, azine, boride
  " **element:** argon, halogen
  " **element 43:** masurium
  " **measure:** dram, gram, liter, titer
  " **prefix:** oxa, amido, aceto, amino
  " **salt:** sal, borate
  " **suffix:** ane, ine, ose, olic
  " **substance:** linin
chemisette: sham, guimpe
chequeen: basket, sequin, zecchino
cherry: duke, morel, oxheart
  " **acid:** cerasin
  " **color:** red, cerise
  " **disease:** blackknot
  " **extract:** cerasein
  " **finch:** hawfinch
  " **holly:** islay
  " **laurel:** cerasus
  " **orange:** kumquat
  " **sour:** amarelle
  " **sweet:** bing, lambert, oxheart
  " **wild:** gean, marasca, mazzard
chest: box, arca thorax, fund, bosom
  " **animal:** brisket
  " **cavity membrane:** pleura
  " **comb. form:** steth(o)

" **located on the:** pectoral
" **of sacred utensils:** cist
" **sound:** rale
" **vibration:** fremitus
chestnut: horse, tree, mast, oldie
" **colloquial:** joke, cliche
" **tree:** chincapin, chinquapin
chevet: apse, termination
chevisance: booty, remedy, resource
chevrotain: napu, deerlet, kanchil
chevy: hunt, chase, fret
chew: cud, gnaw, munch, ruminate
" **inability to:** amasesis
chewing: gum ingredient: chicle, mastic
" **gum tree:** sapodilla
" **tobacco piece:** plug
chewink: bird, finch, joree, towhee
Chicago: windy city
chicalote: poppy
chick: peeper, child, sheila
chick-pea: gram, herb, garbanzo
chicken: fowl, biddy, manoc
" **castrated:** capon
" **chaser:** catcgpole
" **feed: sl.:** coins, cheap, negligible, piddling, dimes, peanuts
" **five-toed:** houdan
" **pox:** varicella
" **raising device:** brooder
" **snake:** boba
" **young:** pullet, fryer, chick, peeper
chicken out: quit, renege

chickweed genus: alsine
chicle: gum, latex
chicory: bunk, root
" **family:** cichoriaceae
chief: bo, aga, main, titan
chigoe: flea, chigger
chilblain: sore, kibe
child: imp, baba, tike, tad, product, babe. moppet
" **advancement:** precocity
" **bad-tempered:** changeling
" **bastard:** by-blow
" **bib:** dickey
" **comb. form:** ped(o)
" **homeless:** waif
" **killer:** infanticide
" **murder of:** prolicide, filicide
" **of light and day, so called:** Eros
" **of the street:** arab, waif, gamin
" **of the Sun:** inca
" **patron Saint:** Nicholas
" **pert. to:** filial
" **Scot.:** bairn
" **unweaned:** suckling
childlike: meek, docile, submissive
children: progeny, offspring
" **dislike of:** misopedia
" **medical science:** pediatrics
" **study:** pedology
" **tender of:** amah, sitter, nursemaid
Chile, Chilean:
" **aborgine:** Inca
" **beech tree:** roble
" **coastal wind:** sures
" **coin:** colon, centavo, es-

cudo
" **deer:** pudu
" **measure:** vara, legua, linea, cuadra, fanega
" **monetary unit:** escudo
" **money:** condor
" **national police:** carabineros
" **rodent:** chinchilla
" **saltpeter:** niter
" **volcano:** Antuco, Calbuco
" **weight:** grano, libra, quintal
" **workman:** roto
chills and fever: ague, malaria
chilver: lamb
chimaera: ratfish
chimera: fancy, mirage
chin: jaw, chat, mentum
" **comb. form:** genio
" **double:** fold, buccula
China, Chinese: sinic, oriental, miao, seric
" **aborigine:** Yao, Mans, Miao, Mantzu, Yao-min, Miaotse, Miaotze
" **ancient name:** Tsao, Seres, Cathay
" **aromatic root:** ginseng
" **bamboo stick:** whangee
" **bean:** adsuki
" **black tea:** oolong
" **boat:** junk, sampan, tongkang, bark
" **Buddha:** Fo, Foh
" **Buddhist paradise:** Chingtu
" **card game:** fan tan
" **cloth:** sha, moxa, pulo, nankin

" **coat:** mandarin
" **coin:** pu, neu, sen, tael, lliang
" **coin with hole:** cash
" **comb. form:** Sino, Sinic
" **dynasty:** Fo, Ming, Tang
" **dynasty, first:** Hsia
" **dynasty, last:** Manchu
" **festival:** Ching Ming
" **god:** Ghos, Joss, Shen, Kuant
" **idol:** joss, pagoda
" **incense:** joss stick
" **invention:** gunpowder
" **mile:** li
" **porcelain:** Celadon, Nankeen
" **servant:** amah
" **silkworm:** sina, tasar, tussah, ailanthus
" **spring:** Ch'un
" **temple:** taa, pagoda
" **treaty port:** Amoy, Shanghai
" **wormwood:** moxa
chinch: bedbug
Chinook: wind, indian, Flathead, salmon
" **god:** tamanoas
" **lily/bulb:** quamash
" **powwow:** wawa
" **state:** Washington
chinse: calk, seam, close
chip: bit, clip, nip, piece, scrap, flake
" **of stone:** spall, gallet
chipmunk: squirrel, chippy, trackee
" **cheek pouch:** alforja
chirk: lively, cheerful
chirm: din, croon
chiro, as comb. form: hand

chiropter(a): aliped, bat
chisel: cut, pare, gouge, engrave, broach
" **ancient stone:** celt
" **bar:** spudder
" **broad-faced:** drove
" **engraving:** scooper
" **mason's:** pommel
" **part:** tang
" **stonemason's:** drove
chit: note, shoot
" **of a kind:** voucher, memo
chiton: mollusk, garment, limpet
chlamys: mantle, cloak
chloride: muriate
chlorophyll: etiolin
chobdar: usher, attendant
chocolate: cocoa
" **family:** sterculiaceae
" **machine:** conche
" **seed:** cacao
" **tree:** cola, cacao
choir: boy's collar: eton
" **leader:** choragus
" **vestment:** cotta, surplice
choke: gag, quar, impede
choke coil: reactor
chokedamp: blackdamp
cholecyst: (gall) bladder
choler: bile, rage, wrath
cholla: cactus
choosing, right of: option
chop: hew, dice, mince
" **down:** fell, raze
" **eye of:** noisette
" **off:** lop, prune
chopine: shoe, pattern
chopping block: hacklog
chord: tone, triad
" **harplike:** arpeggio

" **musical:** major, minor
" **succession:** cadence
Chorda filum: sealace
chorister's garment: cassock
choroid membrane: tapetum
chorten: stupa, monument
chose: chattel
chough: bird, crow
chowk: bazaar, market
Christian, Christianity: Gentile, Nazarene, decent, human
" **abbrev.:** Xtian
" **early:** Galilean
" **Egyptian:** Copt
" **love feast:** agape
" **persecuted:** matyr
" **pulpit:** ambo
" **symbol:** cross, orant, lehthus
" **unity:** irenics
Christian Science founder: Eddy (Mary Baker)
Christmas Carol author: Dickens
" **character:** Tim, Scrooge
Christmas rose: hellebore
chromium: element, mineral
" **group element:** uranium, tungsten
" **symbol:** Cr.
chromosome load: genes
chrysalis: pupa, cocoon
chthonian: infernal
chuff: fat, cross, rustic
church: denomination, edifice, sanctuary, sect
" **altar end:** apse
" **altar offerings:** altarage
" **balcony:** cantoria
" **basin:** lavabo, font

"   **bell ringer:** sexton
"   **bell tower:** belfry
"   **body of:** nave
"   **building:** ecclesia
"   **contribution to:** tithe
"   **cup:** chalice
"   **deputy:** vicar, curate
"   **doorkeeper:** ostiary
"   **law:** canon
"   **loft:** jube
"   **reader:** lector
"   **seat for clergy:** sedilia
"   **stand:** ambo
churchgoer: communicant
churchyard: parvis
churl: cad, lout, miser, boor, hind
chute: rush, flume, hopper
cibarious: edible
cibol: onion, shallot
ciborium: cup, pyx, canopy
cicada: locust
"   **vibrating membrane of:** timbal
cicala: locust, grasshopper
cid: Ruy, hero, chief, Bivar
"   **sword of:** colada, tizona
cilium: hair, eyelash
cimarron: slave, maroon
cimbia: band: fillet
cimex: bedbug, insect
cinch: belt, snap, girth
cinchona: bark, tree
"   **extract:** quinine
cinnabar: ore, vermillion
"   **derivative:** quicksilver
cinnamon: tree, spice, cassia
"   **apple:** sweetsop
"   **oak:** bluejack
"   **stone:** garnet, essonite
Cipango: Japan, Nippon
cipo: vine, liana

Circe: siren, sorceress
"   **brother:** Aeetes
"   **father:** Helios
"   **island:** Aeaea
circle: disk, hoop, swirl, spiral
"   **around sun or moon:** corona
"   **great:** equator
"   **heraldry:** annulet
circular: motion: eddy, gyre
"   **plate:** disc
circumference: arc, border, limits
circumstantial: exact, precise
circus: arena, spectacle
"   **arena wall:** spina
"   **column:** meta
"   **gear:** tent, rings, trapeze
cirrus: cloud, tendril
cisco: blackfin, whitefin
citadel: arx, tower, fortification
citrine: color, rhubarb
citrus:
"   **belt:** Florida, California
"   **disease:** buckskin
city: celestial: Zion
"   **eternal:** Rome
"   **holy:** Mecca, Medina, Jerusalem
"   **oldest inhabited:** Damascus
"   **pert. to:** civic, urban
"   **wicked:** Sodom, Gomorrah
City of: Bells: Strasb(o)urg
"   **Bridges:** Bruges
"   **Brotherly Love:** Philadelphia
"   **Churches:** Brooklyn
"   **Kings:** Lima
"   **Lilies:** Florence

"   **Masts:** London
"   **Rams:** Canton
"   **Saints:** Montreal
"   **Seven Hills:** Rome
"   **Victory:** Cairo
civet-like animal: genet
civil wrong: tort
civilian dress: mufti
clabber: mud, curdle
cladose: ramose, branched
claggum: taffy, molasses
clam: base, hush, mollusk
"   **genus of:** mya
clan: set, cult, horde
"   **pert. to:** tribal
clarinet: reed, instrument
"   **mouthpiece:** birn
"   **snake charmer's:** been
class: ilk, race, genus
"   **pert. to:** generic
classical: pure, Attic, Greek, Latin, Roman
Claudia's husband: Pilate
claut: hand, rake, scrape
clavecin: harpsichord
claver: prate, gossip
clavicle: bone, collarbone
clay: marl, earth, inanimate
"   **box:** saggar
"   **building:** adobe, tapia
"   **comb. form:** pel, argillo
"   **covered with:** lutose
"   **made of:** fictile
"   **pert. to:** bolar
clayey: bolar, heavy, lutose
clear: rid, open, acquit, candid
"   **as crystal:** evident, obvious
"   **away:** fey, dispel
"   **out:** decamp, desert
"   **profit:** net

"   **the way!:** gangway
"   **to the mind:** palpable
"   **up:** solve, settle
clear-cut: lucid, sharp
clear-sighted: discerning, perspicacious
clearing: in woods: glade, tract
"   **of land:** sart, assart
cleat: bitt, kevel, wedge
cleaver: ax, axe, froe, frow
cleek: club, crook
clef: key, character
"   **bass:** eff
"   **treble:** gee
Cleite: father: Merops
"   **husband:** Cyzicus
Clemens' pen name: (Mark) Twain
Cleopatra:
"   **attendant:** Iras, Charmian
"   **killer:** asp
"   **lover:** Antony, Caesar, Mark Antony
"   **needle:** obelisk
"   **river:** Nile
"   **sister:** Arsinoe
"   **son:** Caesarion
clepsydra: clock, waterglass
clergyman: curate, abbe
"   **church service vestment:** canonicals
"   **degree of:** STB
"   **position/garment:** cassock, frock
"   **residence of:** manse, rectory
"   **salary of:** prebend
"   **with the military:** chaplain, padre
clerisy: intellectuals

cleuch: cleft, descent
clever: adept, smart
" **as a fox:** vulpine
" **remark: sl.:** nifty, crack
" **retort:** repartee, sally, bon mot, ripost(e), witticism
clevis: hake, copse
click beetle: elater
cliff: precipice
" **debris:** talus
" **edge:** brow
" **fissure for climbing:** chimney
clinch: fasten, grip
" **argument:** settle
" **breaker:** referee
" **nautical:** noose, clench
" **slang:** embrace
clingfish: remora, testar
clique: circle, faction
cloaca: sewer, privy
cloak: disguise, garment
" **blanket-like:** poncho, serape
" **fur-lined:** pelisse
" **hood of:** cowl
cloam: crockery
clock: time(piece)
" **face of:** dial
" **part:** chime, pendulum, hand, pallet, click
" **water:** clepsydra
clodpate: blockhead, fool
close: shut(in), conclude, finale
" **conclusively:** clinch
" **hermetically:** seal
" **in music:** coda
" **mouthed:** taciturn
" **poetic:** anear, nigh
" **to the wind:** luff
clot: coagulate, jell

" **preventing substance:** heparin
cloth: fabric, goods
" **altar:** pall, vesperal
" **bark:** tapa
" **dealer:** draper, mercer
" **finisher:** beetler
" **measure:** ell, nail
clothesmoth: tinea
cloud: haze, befog, stigma
" **comb. form:** nepho
" **morning:** velo
" **pert. to:** nebular
" **study of:** nephology
clour: blow, dint
cloven: cleft, split, bisulcate
cloven-footed: fissiped
clown: buffoon, zany, mime
" **garment of:** motley
" **woman:** buffa
clubfoot: talipes
clump: mass, cluster
" **of bushes:** shaw
" **of earth:** clod
" **of ivy, etc.:** tod
" **of trees:** bosk, mott(e)
clupeid: herring, sardine, shad
cluster: bunch, clump
" **banana:** hand
" **fruits:** bunch
" **leaves:** fascicle
" **of seven stars:** pleiades
Clytemnestra's: husband: Agamemnon
" **lover:** Aegisthus
" **mother:** Leda
" **son:** Orestes
cnemis: shin, tibia, legging
coach: carriage, tutor
" **for hire:** hack, fiacre
" **for state occasions:**

caroche
coal: fuel, cinder
    agent: fitter
    bed: seam
    bin: bunker
    comb. form: anthrac(o)
    distillate: tar
    miner: collier
    wagon: corb, tram
coast: bank, ripa, border
    dweller: oarian
   to: coastal, orarian
coat: jacket, garment
    formal: cutaway, tails
    leather: jack
    neck: george
    sleeveless: jack
coat of arms: crest
coati: nasua, animal, narica
coaxial: conterminous
cobia: fish, bonito
cobra: snake, viper
    genus: naja
    tree: mamba
cochleate: spiral
cock: rooster, crow
    -and bull story: canard, hoax, yarn
    fighting: heeler
    young: cockerel
cockateel: parrot
cockatrice: serpent, basilisk
cockfight: spar
cocklebur: burdock, ragweed
cockspur: (haw)thorn
cocoa: chocolate, broma
    bean, crushed: nibs
coconut: palm
    husk fiber: coir
    liquid: milk
    meat, dried: copra(h)
cocoon: pod, case, theca

    fiber: silk
    in zoology: follicle
    silkworm: clew
code: salic, law
    church: canon
    message in: cryptogram
    moral: ethics
    of a kind: password
coelenterate: hydra, jellyfish, anemone, acaleph(e)
    larva of: planula
coercion: compulsion, duress
coffee: java
    bean: nibs
    cup stand: zarf
    plantation: chicory finca
    substitute: chicory, succory
    tree: chicot
coffer: chest, strongbox
cognate: related, akin
cognomen: (sur)name, nickname
cogon: grass
cohort: ally, band
    one third of: maniple
coin: cash, mint, shape, token, devise
    ancient: obol, obolus
    box: pyx, meter
    collector: numismatist
    counterfeit: brummagem
    front: head, obverse
    reverse side: tail, verso
    weight: shekel
coin new words: neologize
col: pass, gap
Colchis: king: Aeetes
    princess: Medea
cold: bleak, rheum
    blooded: callous

" **congeal by:** freeze
" **extremely:** gelid
coleopter: beetle, weevil
Coleridge's sacred river: Alph
colewort: kale, cabbage, collard
collar: neckware, capture
" **bird's:** flange
" **bone:** clavicle
" **clerical:** rabato
" **high:** fraise
collection: group, repertory
" **anecdotes:** ana
" **commentaries:** glossary
" **essays:** symposium
" **facts:** ana, data
" **miscellaneous:** olio, fardel
" **opinions:** symposium
" **precious:** treasure
collector of: art: virtuoso
" **books:** bibliophile
" **gems:** lapidary
" **items:** curio, relic
" **jokes:** Cerf
" **plants:** herbalist
" **shells:** conchologist
" **stamps:** philatelist
colleen: lass, belle, damsel
collegiate: varsity
colliery: (coal)mine
" **tunnel:** adit
collop: piece, slice
colly: blacken, soot, grime
Colombia, Colombian:
" **coin:** peso, condor
" **measure:** vara, celemin
" **plant:** yocco
colonial teak: flindosa
Colorado: (see special section)

colossus: statue, giant
" **sculptor of the:** Chares
columbine: aquilegia
Columbus: birthplace: Genoa
" **burial place:** Seville
" **navigator of:** Pinzon
" **son:** Diego
" **starting point:** Palos
column: pillar, shaft
" **base:** plinth
" **designating a:** ionic, doric
" **figure, female:** caryatid
" **figure, male:** Telamon, Atlantes
" **ornament:** griffe
" **support of:** base, pedestal, plinth
comatose: torpid
comb: caruncle
" **horse:** curry
combining form for:
alike: iso
among: inter
bad: cac(o), mal
below: infero
between: inter
death: necr(o)
different: heter(o)
double: dipl(o)
end: tel(o)
far: tele
feet: ped(e), pedi
hatred: mis(o)
hundred: centi, hect(o)
many: poly
people: ethn(o)
self: auto
small: micr(o)
sun: heli(o)
universe: cosm(o)

water: hydr(o)
weight: baro
come: arrive, occur
 " **around:** revive
 " **back:** return, recur
 " **down:** alight, land
 " **forward:** volunteer, advance
 " **out even:** draw, tie
 " **to grips with:** tangle
 " **upon:** chance, meet
comensal: inquiline
comeuppance: (sl.) punishment
comma: pause, mark
 " **shaped organism:** vibrio
Commandments, the Ten: Decalogue
comment: annotation, remark
 " **adverse:** criticism
 " **at bottom of page:** footnote
 " **derisive:** jeer
 " **marginal:** margent
comminate: curse, ban
commit: consign, entrust
 " **in mind:** memorize
 " **perjury:** forswear
common: public, usual, low
 " **people:** masses
 " **people, of the:** grass roots
 " **saying:** saw, adage
 " **to both sexes:** epicene
commonplace: ordinary, prosaic
commune: converse, mir, kibbutz
communicate: impart, transmit
communications: satellite: telstar

communion: sharing
 " **cloth:** corporal
 " **cup:** ama
 " **Holy:** Eucharist, sacrament
 " **plate:** paten
 " **table:** credence
Communist: curtain: iron, bamboo
 " **Party member:** comrade
 " **policy body:** Politburo
 " **youth league:** comsomol
commutator: rheotrope
compact: brief, solid, agreement
 " **between nations:** treaty
 " **mass:** wad
companion: comrade, associate
 " **colloq.:** sidekick
 " **constant:** alter ego, shadow
 " **of cease:** desist
company: society, band
 " **of hunters:** safari
 " **of ten soldiers:** decurion
 " **of travelers:** caravan, caravansary
compare: contrast, liken
 " **beyond:** peerless
 " **critically:** collate
compass: understand, scope
 " **beam:** trammel
 " **case:** binnacle
 " **dial:** card
compend: breviary
compendium: summary, digest
compilation: collection, selection

" **of anecdotes:** memoirs
" **of stories, poems:** anthology
complete: full, entire, intact
" **attendance:** plenary
" **entity:** integer
" **not:** partial
complex: intricate, mixed up
" **kind of:** inferiority, oedipus
complication: mess, nodus, snag
compline: hour, prayers, service
compo: plaster, mortar
component: part, element, ingredient, constituent, unit
" **of atom:** proton
composition: essay, theme
" **for organ:** toccata
" **for practice:** etude
" **musical:** opus, suite
" **operatic:** scena
" **sacred:** motet
compound: combine, mix, concoct
" **carbon:** carbide
" **of silica:** glass
" **raceme:** panicle
" **words' separation of parts:** tmesis
compound interest: anatocism
comprehension: grasp
" **thru intellect:** noesis
compulsive: craze, obsession, etc.: mania
" **petty thievery:** kleptomania
computer: univac, machine
" **information:** data, input, output

" **inventor:** Babbage
" **symbol system:** code
" **type of:** analog, digital, IBM
conative state: nisus
concatenate: link(ed)
conceal: hide, secrete
" **goods:** cache, hoard
" **in law:** eloin
concertina kin: accordion
conclude: close, end, deduce, finish
" **a speech:** perorate
concoct: devise, hatch, compound
concomitant: attendant
concubinage: hetaerism
concubine in harem: odalisk, odalisque
concuss: jar, jolt, force
condensed form: moisture: dew
condenser: cric, aludel
condition: if, provision, status
" **contract:** stipulation, proviso
" **of decline:** decadence
" **of great vitality:** sthenia
" **of oblivion:** limbo
" **of stupor:** coma, narcosis
conditional surrender: capitulation
conductor: guide, maestro
" **platform of:** podium
" **stick:** baton
" **woman:** quach
cone: strobile
" **shaped:** conoid, pineal, conic(al), turbinate
" **shaped yarn roll:** cop
" **spiral:** helix

conepate: skunk

Confederacy: banknote: bluejack

" **general:** Lee, Bragg, Jackson

" **guerilla:** bushwacker

" **president:** Davis

" **soldier:** reb

conference: meeting, confab

" **site of 1945:** Yalta

" **site of 1943:** Cairo, Teheran

confine: restrict, limit

" **to a place:** localize

confined: ill, bound, cloistered

" **to select group:** esoteric

confluence: crowd

confrere: fellow, comrade, colleague

conge: dismissal, farewell

congenital: inborn, innate

" **mark:** mole

Congo: eel, tea, dye, river

" **language:** Bantu, Swahili, Lingala

congou: tea

congress: meeting, assembly, legislature

" **attendant:** page

" **congressman not reelected:** lameduck

" **time off:** recess

conjum: hemlock

Connecticut: (see special section)

connective: syndetic

" **tissue:** tendon, fascia

connoisseur: (a)esthete

" **art:** virtuoso

" **fine food/drinks:** go(u)rmand, gourmet, epicure

conscientious objector: conchy

consciousness: awareness

" **loss of:** coma, apoplexy

consign: entrust, relegate, deliver

" **to hell:** damn, condem

console: comfort, cheer

" **like bracket:** corbel

" **the bereaved:** condole

consonant: aspirated: surd

" **hard:** fortis

" **unaspirated:** lene

" **voiceless:** atonic

constellation: cluster, gathering

" **altar:** ara

" **brightest star: cor**

" **cross:** crux

" **dog:** canis

" **equatorial:** cetus, orion

" **stern:** puppis

" **veil:** vela

constitution: structure, basic law, charter

" **addition to:** amendment

" **composition of:** articles, by-laws, preamble

consuetude: habit, usage

contagion: pox, taint

container: tin, crate, basket

" **cardboard:** carton

" **dose of medicine:** capsule

" **documents:** hanafer

" **glass:** carboy

" **wine:** ampulla

conte: tale, short story

contest: tournament, dispute, fight

"   **endurance:** marathon
"   **in court:** litigation
"   **with lances:** joust, tilt
contiguous: next, adjacent, touching
continent: temperate, Africa, Asia, Australia, Europe, North America, South America
"   **icy:** Antarctica
"   **legendary:** Atlantis
continual: constant, incessant
"   **movement:** flux
contort: twist, deform, warp
contract: incur, agreement
"   **illegal labor:** yellow dog
"   **of agency:** mandate
"   **work:** indenture
contradiction: denial, inconsistency
"   **in terms:** antilogy
contravene: oppose
contrition: penitence, remorse
controversial: debatable, moot
"   **theorist:** Darwin
"   **theory:** evolution
controversialist: eristic
contumacious: unruly, riotous, stubborn, insubordinate
conundrum: riddle, puzzle, enigma
convent: nunnery, monastery
"   **dining hall:** refectory
"   **head:** superior
"   **inmate:** cenobite, nun, monk
"   **member, new:** neophyte
conversational: comeback:

retort, riposte
"   **style/writing in:** causerie
convert: turn, alter, proselyte
"   **fat into soap:** saponize
"   **into money:** realize, liquidate
"   **new:** novice, neophyte
convex: curve: camber
"   **molding:** ovolo, torus, tore, astragal
convey: cede, carry, transmit
conveying: away from center: efferent
"   **toward center:** afferent
convict: felon, condemn, prisoner
"   **privileged:** trusty
"   **sl.:** termer, lifer
convivial: gay, sociable, jolly
"   **drinking:** bowl, wassail
convolute: coil
convolvulus: vine
cony: daman, hyrax, pika, das(sie), ganam
cooing sound: curr
cooking: art: cuisine, magirics
"   **odor:** nidor
cooled: frappe
coolie: changar
coom, coomb: smut, soot, refuse
coop: cote, hutch, pen
coorie: cower, stoop, crouch
coot: scoter, simpleton, fowl
copacetic: fine, snappy
copaiba: tree, balsam, oleoresin
copal: resin, anime
copper: coin, metal
"   **allow:** aroide, tombak

"   **coating:** patina, verdigris, verd, antique
"   **comb. form:** chalco
"   **engraving:** mezzotint
"   **zinc alloy:** pinchbeck
coppice: copse, thicket
copula: band, link
copy: model, imitate, ape
"   **closely:** mimic
"   **court record:** estreat
"   **of original:** replica
coquina: limestone
cora: gazelle
coral: pink, skeleton, stalactite
"   **division:** aporosa
"   **formation:** palus
"   **island:** key, reef, atoll
cord: string, rope, twine
"   **braided:** sennit
"   **drapery:** torsade
"   **rope end's:** marline
"   **trimming:** chenille
Cordelia: father: Lear
"   **sister:** Regan
cordelle: tassel
corduroy: fustian
"   **ridge:** wale
corf: basket, truck
cork: tap, plug
"   **barrel's:** bung
"   **like:** suberose
corn: kernel, maize, papilloma
"   **bin:** crib
"   **husk:** shuck
"   **meal:** masa, samp
corner: bight, trap, nook
"   **chimney/fireplace:** inglenook
"   **of building:** cant, quoin
cornice: molding

"   **projection:** drip, corona
"   **support:** ancon
corolla: petals, ligule
"   **cuplike part:** corona
"   **heraldic:** galea
corpse: cadaver, carcass
"   **animated:** zombi(e)
"   **dissection:** necrotomy
"   **embalmed:** mummy
"   **sl.:** stiff
corpuscle: cell, leucocyte
"   **lack of red:** anemia
correspondent: kind of: penpal, stringer, foreign
corrida cry: ole
corroded: carious
corrupt: rotten, venal, infect
"   **morally:** putrid
"   **official:** grafter
cortex: bark, rind
corvine bird: raven, crow, rook
cosmic: grandiose, vast
"   **cycle:** eon
"   **ray particle:** meson
cosset: pet, pamper, lamb
costard: head, apple
costrel: dress, habit, get-up
cot: bed, charpoy
"   **poet.:** cottage
cotta: surplice
cotton: thread, cloth
"   **canvaslike:** wigan
"   **measure:** hank, lea
"   **tuft:** lock
"   **twilled:** jean, denim, chino
"   **twisted:** rove
coulee: ravine, gulch, lava
council: board, junta
"   **chamber:** camarilla
"   **church:** synod

counterbalance: equipoise
counterfeit: false, postiche, sham
  " **coin:** slug
countersign: password
countless: myriad
country: region, land, realm
  " **fellow:** corydon
  " **house:** villa, casino, hacienda
  " **in law:** pais
  " **live in the:** rusticate
  " **man:** rustic, compatriot
  " **of the:** rural
  " **poet.:** clime
  " **side, of the:** bucolic
coup: blow, (master)stroke
  " **d'** : etat
  " **de grace:** death blow
  " **de grace dagger:** misericord(e)
  " **reporter's:** scoop, beat
couplet: distich
courage: nerve, mettle
  " **loss of:** cold feet
  " **pretended:** bravado
  " **symbol of:** bulldog
courlan: limpkin
court: woo, bench, tribunal
  " **action:** suit
  " **case:** cause
  " **decree:** arret
  " **entrance:** atrium
  " **equity:** chancery
  " **hearing:** oyer
  " **jurisdiction:** soke
  " **messenger:** beadle
  " **minutes:** acta
  " **of law:** forum
  " **order extract:** estreat
  " **pert. to:** aulic
  " **writ:** oyer, subpoena, summons
cousin: cos
cover: top, roof, whelm
  " **detachable:** binder
  " **leg:** puttee, chausses, legging
  " **nipa:** thatch
  " **ornamental:** sham
  " **with feathers:** fledge
  " **with jewels:** begem
  " **with trappings:** caparison
covet: desire, crave, envy
cow: daunt, bovine, bully
  " **breed:** angus, kerry, jersey
  " **cud:** rumen
  " **fat:** tallow, suet
  " **genus:** bos
  " **hornless:** mul(l)ey
  " **unbranded:** maverick
  " **young:** heifer, calf, stirk
cowbird: troupial
cowboy: buckaroo, herder, wrangler
  " **Austral.:** stockman, ringer
  " **breeches:** chaps
  " **rope:** lasso, riata, lariat
  " **saddlebag:** alforja
  " **S.A.:** gaucho
cowfish: toro, manatee, dugong, grampus
coxa: hip
coyo: avocado
coypu: rodent, nutria
crab: shellfish, nag
  " **apple:** scrab
  " **feeler:** antenna
  " **like a:** cancroid
crack: break, chink, joke
  " **deep/glacier:** crevasse

"   **filler:** grout
"   **seal:** ca(u)lk
crackerjack: nailer
cracklings: scraps, greaves
crampfish: torpedo
cranberry disease: scald
crane: heron, stork
"   **arm:** jib
"   **genus:** grus
"   **pert. to:** gruine
"   **relative:** bustard
cranial nerve: vagus
crappie: sunfish
crater: pit, cavity
"   **lunar:** linne
"   **one with:** volcano
cravat: (neck)tie, ascot
"   **handman's:** noose
crawler: baby, worm, reptile
crayfish: egg: berry
creation: invention, cosmos, genesis
creche figure: Joseph, Mary, infant, lamb, magi, shepherd
crecopia: myth
credenza: buffet
credit: believe, attribute, honor, rebate
"   **for achievement:** kudos
credo: belief, creed, tenet
creed: one such: nicene
"   **political:** ism, doxy
creeping: repent, reptant
"   **charlie, for one:** weed
"   **plant:** vine, bine, liana
crenate: scalloped, notched
creosol: antiseptic
crescent: semilunar, demilune, meniscus
"   **moons:** menisci
"   **of a:** bicorn, horn

"   **point of:** cusp
"   **shaped:** lunate, lune
crest: cap, top, ridge
"   **mountain:** arete
"   **of bird/fowl:** comb, caruncle
"   **wave's:** comb
Crete: Candia
"   **mythical beast:** minotaur
cretonne: toile
crew: gang, team
"   **of ship:** complement
"   **relief:** relay
crier: muezzin
crime: sin, guilt, misdeed
"   **high:** treason
"   **major:** felony
"   **where committed:** venue
criminal: convict, felon, outlaw
"   **act:** job
"   **habitual:** recidivist
crimson: red, carmine, bloody, madder
crinoid: sea lily
cripples: (the)halt
"   **patron saint of:** (St.) Giles
crisper: curler
critical: captious, exigent
"   **analysis:** exegesis
"   **mark:** obelus
criticism: review, descant
"   **abusive:** diatribe
"   **adverse: colloq.:** pan
Croat: Slav
cromlech: tomb, monument
Cronus: Titan, Saturn
"   **parent:** Uranus, Gaea
"   **sister of:** Tethys

"   **son of:** Zeus
crooked: curved, askew, bent
"   **sl.:** cockeyed
cross: rood, edgy, crucifix
"   **bar:** rung
"   **breed:** hybridize
"   **current:** rip(tide)
"   **Egyptian:** Ankh
"   **in heraldry:** crux
"   **river:** ford
crossbill genus: loxia
crotchet: hook, caprice
"   **half of a:** quaver
croton bug: cockroach
crouton: sippet
crown: diadem, top, crest
"   **bottle:** cap
"   **sl.:** conk
"   **small:** coronet
crucial: severe, critical
"   **point:** crux, crisis
cruet: vial, ampulla, castor
cruor: blood, gore
crus: shank
crush: grind, bruise, squash
"   **to softness:** mash
"   **underfoot:** trample
"   **with mortar/pestle:** bruise
crustacean: lobster, crab, isopod
"   **burrowing:** squilla, mantis crab
"   **eggs:** roe, coral
"   **segment:** somite, telson
"   **walking and swimming:** amphipod, sandflea, shrimp
crystalline: pellucid
"   **biblical:** bdellium
"   **resin:** cannabin
"   **salt:** borax
Cuba, Cuban: habanero

"   **bird:** tocororo
"   **castle:** Morro
"   **coin:** peso
"   **drink:** pina
"   **tree:** culla
"   **weight:** libra, tercio
cubeb: berry, cigarette
cuckoopoint: arum
cucullate: cowled, hooded
cucurbit: gourd, flask
cudbear: dye, lichen
cudgel: club, drub, truncheon
cul-de-sac: blind alley
culex pipiens: mosquito
cull: select, pick out, glean
culmination: acme, zenith
culpa: fault, guilt
"   **"non mea":** I am not guilty
culver: dove, pigeon
culvert: waterway, drain
"   **opening:** inlet
cumin: anise
cumshaw: gratuity, tip
cup: bowl, calix
"   **assaying:** cupel, test
"   **ceremonial:** ama
"   **drinking:** goblet, tankard, stoup, cylix
"   **flower:** calyx
"   **holder:** zarf
"   **metal:** pannikin
cupbearer of the Gods: Hebe, Ganymede
Cupid: Eros, Amor
"   **infant:** amoretto, amorino
"   **mother of:** Venus
"   **sweetheart of:** Psyche
"   **title of:** Dan
cupola: dome
"   **battleship's:** turret

curbing inward: adunc
curculio: beetle
curdled milk: clabber
curio(s): bibelot, virtu
current: going(on), tide, stream
" **air:** draft
" **beneath surf:** undertow
" **comb. form:** rheo
curse: damn, anathema, oath, bane
" **colloq.:** cuss
curt: bluff, terse, blunt
" **dismissal:** conge
curtain: drape, screen, valance
" **behind stage:** backdrop
" **of gun fire:** barrage
" **rod band:** cornice
curve: arc, ogee, hyperbola
" **double:** ess
" **mark over vowel:** breve
" **of a column:** entasis
" **path of missile:** trajectory
" **plane:** parabola
curved: arcuate, arched, falcate
" **in:** concave
" **molding:** ogee
" **out:** convex
" **surface of arch:** extrados
" **sword:** scimitar
curving inward: adunc
custodian: caretaker, keeper
" **museum:** curator
customs: mores

" **charge:** impost, duty
" **collector, biblical:** Matthew
" **municipal:** octroi
" **official:** surveyor
cut: shear, saw, snip, hew
" **across:** transect, intersect
" **down:** fell, mow
" **horse's tail:** dock
" **in half:** bisect, halve
" **into:** incise, lance
" **out:** excise, elide
" **out disk:** trepan
cutter: vessel, yacht, sleigh
" **of precious stones:** lapidary
cutting: edged, incisive, keen
" **off last letter of word:** apocope
" **off vowel:** elision
" **part of tool:** bit
cyanotype: blueprint
cylinder: tube, barrel
" **part:** piston
" **spiral:** helix
cylindrical: torose, terete
cynic: look of: sneer, cold
" **of sorts:** skeptic
cynosure: polestar, lodestar, north star
Czechoslavakia, Czechoslavakian: Slovak, Bohemian
" **coin:** ducat, kronen, heller, koruna
" **dance:** polka, redowa
" **monetary unit:** koruna

D

D: dee, delta
dabchick: grebe
Dacian: avar
dactyl: adonic, finger, toe, piddock
dactylic hexameter: epos
daddy longlegs: spinner, stilt, curlew
dado: solidum, die, groove
Daedalus: nephew/slayer: Talos
  " **son:** Icarus
Dagda: son: Aengus
dagger: dirk, bayonet, poniard
  " **handle:** hilt
  " **short:** katar
  " **stroke:** stab, stoccado
  " **tapering:** anlace
Dahomey people: Fon(g)
dairy: lactarium
  " **tool:** separator
daisy: shasta, gerbera, gowan, morgan, oxeye

dak: post
Daksha's father: Brahma
dalles: rapids
dam: mare, parent, clog, obstruct, weir, impede
  " **Arizona-Nevada:** Davis, Hoover
  " **Australia:** Hume
  " **California:** Shasta
  " **Canal Zone:** Gatun
  " **Egypt:** Aswan
  " **Missouri:** Osage
  " **S. Carolina:** Saluda
  " **S. Dakota:** Oahe
  " **Tennessee:** Norris
  " **Virginia:** Kerr
dama: gazelle
damage: loss, scathe, mar, deterioration
  " **pert. to:** noxal
daman: hyrax
Damascus: king: Aretas
  " **people:** Syrian
dame: lady

" **correlative:** sire
damourite: mica, muscovite
Danae's Kin: Zeus, Perseus, Acrisius
dance: boh, hoof, tap, ballet, stomp, waltz, twist, disco, minuet
" **art of:** orchesis
" **ceremonial:** areito
" **college:** prom, hop
" **country:** hay, auresca
" **English:** morris, althea
" **Gr.:** belly
" **gypsy:** farruca, zingaresca
" **Hawaiian:** hula
" **Hebrew:** hora
" **masked:** ridotto, ball
" **Muse:** Terpsichore
" **pert. to:** gestic
dancer: artist, hoofer, gypsy
" **Biblical:** Salome
" **clothing:** leotard, tutu, legwarmers
dandelion stalk: scape
dandify: adonize, spruce
dandiprat: pygmy, urchin, dwarf
dandruff: scurf
dandy: fop, buck, dude, dildo, coxcomb, sailboat
" **female:** dandisette
danta: tapir
Dante: circle of Hell: Caina
" **love:** Beatrice
" **patron:** Scala
" **verse form:** sestina
Danube: Ister
" **fish:** huch(o), huchen
" **town:** Ulm
Danzig: coin: gulden, pfennig
" **liqueur:** ratafia

Daphne: Mezereon
" **father:** Ladon (Peneus)
" **mother:** Ge. Creusa
Daphnis' lover: Chloe
dapple: fleck, spot, pied, variegated
darbies: handcuffs, manacles
Dardanelles: Hellespont
dariole: shell, cup, pastry
dark: unlit, dismal, dim, mum, ebon(y), black, cloud
" **complexion:** swarthy
" **horse:** candidate, contestant
darkness: murk, umbra, ignorance
" **place of:** Erebus, Po
" **prince of:** Ahriman, devil, satan
dart: scud, hurl, arrow, missile
" **shooter:** Cupid, Amor, Eros, bow
" **-like:** spicular
D'Artagnan: companion: Athos, Aramis, Porthos
" **creator:** Dumas
Darwin: boat: Beagle
" **theory:** evolution
das: badger, dassie
Das Kapital author: Marx, (Karl)
dasheen: taro
dashes: obeli
dashing: gay, natty, precipitate, impetuous
" **as of waves:** plangent
dastard: craven, coward, milksop
date: day, tryst, era, fruit
" **erroneous:** anachronism
" **on coin:** exergue
daughter: filly, bint,

alumna(e)
" **pert. to:** filial
" **Moon:** Nokomis
dauphin: guigo, heir, delphinium
daut, dawt: caress, fondle
David: captain: Joab
" **cave:** Adullam
" **commander:** Amasa
" **daughter:** Tamar
" **father:** Jesse
" **man of:** Ira, Igal
" **musician:** Asaph
" **son:** Ammon, Absalom
davit: crane, spar, hoist
Davy: lamp
dawn: aurora, dew, origin, precursor
" **comb. form:** eo
" **goddess of:** Eos, Aurora
" **pert. to:** eoan, auroral
" **symbol:** dew
" **toward the:** eastward
day: time, epoch, period
" **before:** eve
" **father:** Erebus
" **god:** Horus
" **judgment:** doomsday
" **pert. to:** ferial
daysman: umpire, arbiter, mediator
dax: spa
deacon: cleric, doctor, master, adept
" **stole:** orarion
" **prayers:** ectene
dead: deceased, amort, lifeless, inactive, napoo
" **abode of:** Hades, Sheol
" **city of:** Necropolis
" **duck:** (sl.) goner
" **house of:** ossuarium,

ossuary, mortuary
" **mass for:** black
" **relating:** mortuary
Dead Sea: city: Sodom
" **territory:** Moab
deadly: fatal, lethal, malign, noxious
deaf and dumb person: surdomute
deaf: dunch
" **make:** surd
deafness: amusia, baryecola
" **cause:** stun
dean: dell, doyen, vale
" **pert. to:** decanal
dearth: famine, want, paucity
death: mort, demise, end
" **Angel of:** Azrael
" **black:** plague
" **bringing:** funest
" **mercy:** euthanasia
" **notice:** obit
" **rattle:** rale
deave: din, stun, bother, deafen, stupefy
debar: estop, hinder
debased: vile, corrupt
debate: argue, moot, rebut,argument
" **pert. to:** forensic, quodlibetary
" **stopping of:** cloture
debauchee: rake, roue, satyr, libertine
Deborah's husband: Lapidoth
debtor: note: IOU
" **proceed against:** excuss
decade: decennium
decamp: flee, bolt, abscond, vamoose
decanter: carafe, croft, ewer

decapod: crab, prawn, squid, shrimp, lobster, crustacean
" **crustacean genus:** homarus
decay: rot, conk, spoil, caries
" **comb. form:** sapro
" **in fruit:** blet
" **process of:** doty
deceive: mislead, sile, hocus, cozen
decibels: ten: bel
decimal: ten, tenth
" **circulating:** repetend
decimate: slaughter, slay, destroy
decision: sudden: whim
deck: array, enrich, cards
" **cards:** pack
" **lower:** orlop
" **post** bitt
" **raised border:** coaming
" **ship:** main, lower, poop, promenade, orlop
declivity: slope, descent, grade
decoction: tisane, opozem(a), sapa, drink
decorate: adorn, (be)deck, scrimshaw
" **garishly:** bedizen
" **with letters:** miniate
" **with raised patterns:** brocade
decorated: nielled, cited
" **wall part:** dado
decoration: niello, trophy, trim
" **metal ware:** tole
" **military:** medal, ribbon, dsc, dsm, dsq
" **mineral:** tinsel, purfle
" **pert. to:** medallic

decorticate: strip, peel, flay, debark
decorum: propriety, convention
decoy: lure, trap, snare, inveigle
" **gambling:** capper, ringer
decree: ordain, canon, mandate
" **imperial:** irade, fiat, arret, ukase
" **papal:** bull
decuman: huge, large
decussation: chiasma, intersection
deer: elk, cervid, moose ·
" **antler:** dag, trestine, horn, bez
" **axis:** chital
" **cry:** bell
" **fallow:** dama
" **family:** cervidae
" **genus:** cervus, dama, rusa, pudu
" **grass:** rhexia
" **male:** buck, stag, hart
" **pert. to:** cervine, damine
" **tail:** scut
" **three year old:** sorrel
" **track:** slot
" **two year old:** brock(et)
" **unbranched antler:** dag
" **young:** fawn, spitter, pricket
defect: bug, flaw, want, foible
" **in cloth:** scob, snag
" **timber:** lag, knot
defendant: reus
defense: alibi, bulwark, plea
" **in law:** answer
" **making a salient angle:** ravelin

"   **means of:** abatis

deference: fealty, esteem, honor

defile: taint, moil, debauch, tarnish

Defoe character: Moll, Crusoe, Friday, Xury

defray: pay, expend, prepay, satisfy

degenerate: rot, debase, degrade, deprave

degree: step, rank, extent, stage

"   **conferral:** laureation

"   **equal:** as

"   **kind of:** nth, third

degust, degustate: savor, taste, relish

dehisce: gape, burst, yawn

dehydrate: dry, parch, desiccate, bake

deiform: divine, Godlike

deify: exalt, apotheosize, honor, idolize

deign: stoop, condescend

dejeuner: lunch, breakfast, collation

dekko: look, peep

delate: accuse, report, denounce

Delaware: (see special section)

delay: linger, dally, laten, loiter

"   **law:** mora, continuance

"   **unjustifiable:** mora

dele: delete, remove, cancel, blot

deletion: last letter of word: apocope

"   **restore:** stet

Delian god: Apollo

delibate: sip, taste, dabble

delicacy: tact, finesse, cate

delict: offense, violation, crime, tort

Delilah's paramour: Samson

deliquesce: dissolve, melt, thaw, liquefy, ramify

delitescent: latent, hidden

dell: vale, glen, ravine

Delphi: shrine, oracle

"   **priestess:** Pythia

"   **modern name:** Kastri

delusion: mirage, phantasm, artifice, cheat

"   **Buddhist:** Moha

"   **partner of:** snare

demagogue: ochlocrat

Demeter: Ceres

"   **daughter:** Kore

"   **mother:** Rhea

demigod: hero, satyr, idol, godling

"   **pert. to:** satyric

demon: imp, fiend, devil, daemon

"   **assembly of:** Sabbat

"   **cunning:** daedal, ogre, imp

"   **female:** empusa, succubus

"   **King:** Asmodeus

"   **worship of:** demonolatry

"   **Zoroastrian:** daeva

demos: district, people, populace, deme

Demosthenes: orator

"   **follower:** Bryan

"   **oration:** Philippic

demulcent: balm, soothing, sedative

den: dive, lair, retreat

"   **wild animal's:** (Rome):

cavea

denary: ten, decimal

dendrophilous: arboreal

dene: vale, mound, dell

denizen: inhabitant, cit, dweller

"   **of Hell:** Hellion, Satan

Denmark, Danish: coin: krone, ore, horse, fyrk

"   **comb. form:** Dano

"   **fjord:** ise

"   **measure:** fod, landmill, favn, fuder, linie, pflug, tomme

"   **mus. instru.:** lure

"   **sand ridge:** scaw, skagi

"   **speech:** stod

"   **weight:** centner, ort, lod, pund, vog, kvint, quint, tonde, waag

dennet: gig, carriage

de novo: afresh, again, newly

dental tool: scaler, drill, forceps

dentine: ivory

deodar: cedar, tree

depilate: strip, pluck, shave

depilatory: rusma

depone: attest, swear, depose

deposit: hoard, ooze, marl, cache, sediment

"   **alluvial:** delta, geest

"   **black tissue:** melanosis

"   **clay:** marl

"   **teeth:** tartar, calculus

"   **wine cask:** tartar

depravity: vice, disgrace, infamy, license, iniquity

depression: trough, blues, cavity

"   **between mountains:** col

"   **pert. to:** bathic

depth: abyss, acumen, midst

deputation: mission, delegation

deputies: posse, agents

deracinate: eradicate, extirpate

derelict: tramp, forsaken, castaway

derf: bold, daring

deride: scoff, fleer, tease

dermal filament: hair

derrick: crane, rig

"   **part of:** boom, gin, leg

derrier: final, last

"   **-ori:** noodty, fashion

derring-do: geste

dervish: fakir, yogi, agib, mendicant, ascetic

"   **headgear:** taj

descendants: progeny, litter

descended: alit, fell, stooped, sank

"   **from same ancestor:** agnate, consanguineous

"   **source:** root, stirps

descent: birth, origin, lurch, decline, lineage

"   **line(s) of:** phyla, phylum

Desdemona: husband: Othello

"   **slanderer:** Iago

desert: renege, waste, abandon, barren

"   **Afr.:** Sahara, Libyan, (el) Erg

"   **Asia:** Gobi

"   **India:** Thar

"   **pert. to:** eremic, sere

"   **plant:** alhagi, cactus, agave

"   **Russ.:** Tundra

" **watering spot:** oasis

desiccated: arid, sere, parched

design: plot, decor, ettle, invent

" **of scattered objects:** seme

" **on skin:** tattoo

" **perforated:** stencil

desipience: folly, conceit, trifling

desmanthus: acuan, herb, shrub

desmid: alga

desolated area: desert, waste

Despoina: Kore

despot: autocrat, tsar, tyrant, dictator

despumate: scum, skim, foam, froth

destiny: lot, fate, goal

" **oriental:** Kismet

" **goddess:** Fate, Norn, Atripos

destroyed: kaput

destroying angel: fungus: amanita

" **Mormon:** Danite

destruction: perdition, havoc, tala

" **god:** Siva

" **goddess:** Ara

" **of species:** genocide

detain in wartime: intern

detect: espy, descry, discover

detecting device: radar, sonar

detectives: Bond, James
Chan, Charlie
Holmes, Sherlock
Hornet, Green

Mason, Perry
Queen, Ellery
Spade, Sam
Saint, the
Templar, Simon
Vance, Philo
Wolfe, Nero

detonator: cap. exploder

detritus: debris, tuff, chaff, garbage

Dev's land: Eire

Deraki's son: Krishna

develop: grow, dilate, evolve

" **rapidly:** boom

development: full: maturity

" **incomplete:** aplasia

Devi: beneficient: Gauri

" **consort:** Siva

" **light:** uma

" **of parentage:** haimavati

deviate: miss, stray, warp, diverge

" **suddenly:** mutate

" **vertically:** hade

device: mot, tool, vehicle

" **holding:** vise, clamp

devil: demon, fiend, Lucifer

" **female:** demoness

" **fish:** manta, octopus, ray, whale

" **pert. to:** satanic

" **of bottomless pit:** Apollyon

" **tree:** Dita, Abroma

devilkin: imp

devil's bones: dice, die

devoir: duty

Devonshire boat: mumble-bee

devotion: fealty, adoration, fervor, novena

" **object of:** idol, fetish

devotional: exercise: Aves, worship
" **period:** Novena, Lent
devouring: vorant, voracious, edacious
dew: moisten, bloom
" **congealed:** frost, rime
dewlap: wattle, fold
dextrose: sugar
diabetic remedy: insulin, orinase
diablerie: devilry, sorcery, demology, mischief
diacope: wound, incision, tmesis
diadem: crown, tiara, fillet
diagram: scheme, plan, sketch
" **illustrative:** icon(ograph)
diameter: caliber, module, breadth, bore, width, chord
diametrically opposite: antipodal
diamond: gem, field, carbon
" **blue:** Hope
" **coarse:** bort
" **crystal:** glassie
" **cup for cutting:** dop
" **face of:** facet, bezel
" **geometrical:** rhomb, lozenge
" **holder:** dop, ring
" **native:** carbon
" **wheel:** skive
" **with true luster of:** naif
Diana: Artemis, Delia, Cynthia, moon
" **mother:** Latona
" **parent:** Jupiter, Latona
" **sacred grove:** Nemus
" **twin:** Apollo
diana monkey: roloway

dianthus plumarius: pink, flower, carnation
diaphragm: midriff
" **pert. to:** phrenic
diaskeuast: editor, redactor, reviser
diaspora: golah, galuth
Diaz de Bivar's title: (El) Cid
dibs: syrup
dichotomy: division, split, cleft
Dickens: Boz
" **characters:** Fagin, Dorritt, Cattle, Uriah Heep, Nell, Dora, Tim
dickey: collar, jacket, mate
dictionary: onomasticon, calepin, vocabulary
" **poet's:** gradus
dictum: saying, apothegm, opinion
didactic: instructive, preceptive
dido: antic, caper, trick
Dido: father: Belus
" **founder of:** Carthage
" **husband:** Acerbas
" **sister:** Anna
" **wooer:** Aeneas
die-hard: Tory
difficult prefix: dys
difficulty: cavil, dilemma, plight, trial
" **pert. to:** spiny, crucial
" **opposed to:** easily
diffuse: pervade, disperse, circulate, copious
diffusion (through membrane): osmosis
digestion: eupepsia, absorption
" **having good:** eupeptic

digging: tool: loy, spade, slick, shovel, pick

dight: dab, rub, adorn, manage, repair

digit: integer, phalange
" **manual:** thumb, finger
" **podal:** toe

diglot: bilingual

digraph: AE, EA, OA, OE, SH, TH

dike: ditch, bank, jetty
" **military:** estacade

diked land: polder

dilation: expansion

dill: anise, anet, herb

diminutive: small, runty, puny, petite
" **suffix:** ule, ette, ita, el, cle

dimmet: dusk, twilight

dining: room: cenade
" **science of:** aristology

dinner: meal, feast, repast
" **pert. to:** prandial

diocese: center, bishopric, episcopate

Dione: consort: Zeus
" **daughter:** Aphrodite

Dionysus: Bacchus
" **festival:** Agrania
" **mother:** Semele
" **pert. to:** Bromian

diopter: alidade, level

Dioscuri: twins, Pollux, Castor, Gemini, Anaces
" **father:** Zeus
" **mother:** Leda
" **sister:** Helen

dipody: syzygy

dipper: piet, scoop, piggin

dipsacus plant: teasel

diptera: flies, gnats, mosquitos
" **lobe of wing:** alula

dipthong: AE, OE, OU

direction: bearing, aim, course
" **musical:** soli
" **pole to pole:** axial
" **without fixed:** astatic

dirigible: blimp, airship
" **famous:** Zeppelin, Hindenburg
" **part:** fin, nacelle

dirk: dagger, snee, sword
" **Roman:** sica

dirl: ring, thrill, pierce

Dis: Pluto

disavow: recant, abjure, deny

disc: medallion, harrow
" **plate:** paten

discarded: shed, castoff
" **place:** limbo

discernment: sagacity, insight, acumen

disciple: apostle, scholar, votary
" **Biblical:** James, John, Peter, Judas
" **chief:** Peter

discolored: ustulate, molded

discord: war, variance, rancor
" **goddess of:** Eris

discordant: ajar, harsh, contrary
" **musically:** scordato
" **serenade:** charivari

Discordia: Eris

discourse: talk, dissertation, confer
" **art of:** rhetoric
" **long:** tirade, descant

discus: disk, quoit, plate

" **thrower:** Discobolus
discussion: talk, conference
" **group:** panel, forum, seminar, class
" **open to:** moot
disease: illness, malady, infirmity
" **animals:** nenta, distemper, mange, surra
" **declining stage of:** catabasis
" **diver's:** bends
" **pert. to:** clinic, loimic
" **producing:** zymotic
" **science of classification:** nosology
" **suffix:** itis, osis, oma
Dishan's son: uz, Aran
disjaskit: jaded
disjune: breakfast
disk: dial, plate
" **hockey:** puck
" **like:** discoid, discal
" **metal:** tag
" **solar:** aten
dislike: antipathy, odium
" **comb. form:** mis(o)
" **object of:** anathema
dislocate: luxate, splay, disjoint
disorder: snafu, chaos, touse, mess
" **visual:** strabismus
disposition: bent, spirit, proclivity
" **toward work:** ergasia
disputations: sassy, eristic, quarrelsome
disseminate: diffuse, disperse, teach
dissenter: heretic, nonconformist

dissolute: fast, corrupt, loose
" **person:** rake, roue
dissolved: substance: solute
distal angle: axil
distant: (a)far, foreign, aloof, away
" **comb. form:** tele
distended: patulous, bloated
distich: couplet
distilling: device: alembic, still
" **tube:** matrass
distinctive: air: cachet
" **mark:** badge
distortion: twist, warp, deformity, falsehood
" **head to one side:** loxia
distribute: deal, mete, allot
distributee: heir
disyllabic foot: trochee
ditch: canal, trench, relais
" **slope:** scarp
dithyramb: hymn, poetry, ode
dithyrambic: wild, boisterous
diurnal: daily, quotidian, butterfly
dive: crib, leap, resort, swoop
" **kind of:** swan, (half) gainer, back, jacknife
divide: sunder, ration, dole, sever, alienate
" **into feet:** scan
" **into number of parts:** multisect
" **in two parts:** bisect, halve
dividing wall(s): septum, septa, partition
divination: augury, foretelling, presage, omen
" **by dreams:** oneiromancy

“ “ **by figures:** geomancy

divine: predict, holy

“ “ **communication:** oracle

“ “ **gift:** grace

“ “ **messenger:** Apostle

“ “ **spirit:** numen

“ “ **word:** logos

“ “ **work:** theurgy

Divine Comedy author: Dante

divinely inspired: entheal

diving: hazard: bends

“ “ **bird:** auk, grebe, loon

division: schism, portion, segment, part, rift

“ “ **house:** estre

“ “ **poem:** canto

“ “ **primary:** eogaea

“ “ **religious:** schism

“ “ **restricted:** meer

divot: sod, clod, turf

dizzard: fool, jester

dizziness: vertigo, giddiness

“ “ **pert. to:** dinic(al), vestibular

djebel: hill

Dnieper tributary: sula, Psel, Bug

do: bilk, cheat, act, render

“ “ **mus.:** ut

“ “ **poet.:** didst

docent: teacher, lecturer

dock: jetty, pier, curtail

“ “ **post:** bollard, pile

“ “ **ship's:** basin, slip

“ “ **yard:** arsenal

doctor's oath: hippocratic

doctrine: logic, dogma, principle

“ “ **pert. to:** dogmatical

“ “ **secret:** esotary

“ “ **single principle:**

henism, monism

document: record, deed, certificate

“ “ **file:** dossier

“ “ **provisional:** script, note, draft, memo

“ “ **true copy:** estreat

dod: sulk, huff, fit

Dodecanese island: Cos, Kos, Coo, Rhodes, Rodi, Patmo(s)

dodo: genus: didus

doe: teg, roe, hind, faun

doer: suffix: er, or, eer, ier, ist, ast, ator, euse, ster

dog: cur, canine, shadow, rascal

“ “ **Arctic:** husky, malemute

“ “ **Austral. wild:** dingo

“ “ **comb. form:** cyn(o)

“ “ **duck hunting:** toller, retriever

“ “ **extinct breed:** talbot

“ “ **fire:** andiron

“ “ **genus:** canis

“ “ **India:** dhole

“ “ **like:** jackal, hyena, wolf

“ “ **short-eared:** alan

“ “ **short-legged:** beagle

“ “ **star:** sirius, canicula

“ “ **tropical:** alco

“ “ **underworld:** cerberus

dogbane: fruit: aboli

“ “ **tree:** dita, apocynum

dog days: canicule

dog rose: bucky, canker

“ “ **fruit:** hip

dog salmon: Keta

doggery: barroom, grogshop

dogmatic saying: dictum, levitism

dogwood: cornus, osier, su-

mac, tree
" **genus:** cornus
Doll's House character: Nora
dolorous: dismal, grievous
dolphin: bouto, dorado, wreath
dolt: idot, oaf, simpleton
" **like genus:** inia
dome: cupola, roof, head, tholus
Dominican measure: ona
domino: amice, cloak, dice
" **spot on:** pip
domite: trachyte
dompt: cow, subdue, daunt
Don Juan's mother: Inez
Donar: thor
donkey: fool, ono, auxiliary
" **comb. form:** ono
" **engine:** yarder
Don Quixote: companion: Sancho Panza
" **steed:** Rosinante
doodlesack: bagpipe
doolee: litter
doomed: fey, fatal
door: gate, inlet, avenue
" **back:** postern
" **handle:** knob, ansa
" **knocker:** risp
" **part of:** rail, jam, sill, mullion
dor(r): bee, joke, deceive, beetle
dorcas: gazelle
Dorian festival: Carne(i)a
doric: rustic
" **capital, part of:** Abacus
" **fillet bottom of frieze:** taenia
" **frieze, space between**

triglyphs: metope
dormouse: lerot, glis, rodent
" **pert. to:** myoxine
dorsal: neural, nerve, notal
" **opposed to:** ventral
" **pert. to:** neural, notal, tergal
dosseret: abacus
dossil: tent, spigot, pledget
dot over the letter i: tittle
dotted: piebald, pinto, pied
dotterel: dupe, morinel, bird
double: dual, substitute, two-fold, deceitful
" **cross:** rat, gyp
" **dagger:** diesis
" **faced:** ancipital
" **prefix:** di
" **ripper:** bobsled
doubloon: coin, onza
dough: money, duff, cash, pasta
" **fried:** spud
dove: inca, tumbler, pigeon
" **genus:** columbidae
" **murmur:** coo
" **ring:** cushat
dovekie: auk, rotche, guille-mot
" **genus:** alle
dovetail: tenon, join, intersect
dowel: peg, tenon, pinion
dowitcher: snipe, fowl
down: below, fuzz, eider, sad
" **comb. form:** cat(a), cath
" **facing:** prone, pronate, prostrate
" **poet.:** adown
" **prefix:** de
" **wind:** leeward
" **with:** a bas
dowry: pert. to: dotal

doxy: opinion, paramour
doyen: dean, senior
drachma: coin, dram
 `"` **1/20 or 1/6:** obol
Dracula: vampire, demon
 `"` **home:** Bran, Risnov
draft: protocol, sketch, plot, current, gully
 `"` **architectural:** epure
dragoman: agent, guide
dragon: ogre, duenna, musket
 `"` **Chinese:** lung
 `"` **fly genus:** odonata
 `"` **Norse myth:** Fafner
 `"` **of darkness:** Rahab
 `"` **twolegged, winged:** Wivern, Wyvern
dragon's teeth sower: Cadmus
drama: stage, spectacle, burletta, masque
 `"` **introduction of:** protasis
 `"` **main action:** epitasis
 `"` **pert. to:** histrionic
 `"` **sudden reverse in:** peripetia
drapery: baize, curtain
 `"` **on bed:** pand, tester
Dravidian: Tamil, Hindu
 `"` **demon:** bhut
 `"` **language:** Tamil, Tulu, Toda, Kota
draw: draft, delineate, tug, siphon
 `"` **away:** abduce, divert
 `"` **back:** withdraw, wince, recoil
 `"` **close:** steal, approach
 `"` **forth:** derive, elicit, tug
 `"` **out:** attenuate, protract
 `"` **fight:** frap, pull, bind

 `"` **together:** coul, frap, assemble
 `"` **up:** tuck
dray: cart, wagon, sledge
dreadnaught, dreadnought: tank, fearless, warship
dream: fantasy, delusion, scheme
 `"` **day:** reverie, vision
 `"` **God of:** Oniros
 `"` **pert. to:** oneirotic, oneiric
dregs: sordor, dross, refuse, faex
dress: attire, adorn, bandage, apparel
 `"` **feathers:** preen
 `"` **full armor:** panoply
 `"` **looped part:** pouf
 `"` **riding:** habit, jodhpurs, breeches
 `"` **trimming:** gimp, lace, braid
dressmaker: modiste
 `"` **term:** godet, gusset
dried: arid, sere, desiccated
 `"` **-out:** effete, stale
drink: swallow, quaff, tipple, bracer
 `"` **ancient:** morat
 `"` **Christmas:** nog, wassail
 `"` **habitually:** tope, sot
 `"` **of the Gods:** nectar
 `"` **palm:** Nipa
drinking: bowl: mazer
 `"` **cup:** cyclix, facer, tankard
 `"` **horn:** rhyton
 `"` **pledge in:** propine, toast, prosit
drive: alley, street, actuate, urge, direct

"   **away:** dispel
"   **back:** repel
"   **in:** tamp, nail
"   **public:** esplanade
drivel: dote, fritter, slobber
driver: whip, motorist, pilot, jenu
"   **camel:** sarwan
"   **of golden chariot:** Helios
droll: odd, zany, punch
"   **saying:** gibe, taunt, quip, jest
dromedary: mehari, camel
"   **like:** bactrian
drooping: alop
drop: trickle, globule, descent, pendant
"   **by drop:** guttatim
"   **gently:** flow, dap
"   **like:** guttate
"   **sudden:** hance, plop
dropsical: hydropic, puffy
dropsy: edema
dross: scoria, cinder, trash
"   **of iron:** sinter
drought: need, aridity, dearth
"   **plant:** guar, xerophyte
drowsiness: lethargy, torpor
drugged bliss: kef, kief
drugget: mat, rug, cloth
Druid: priest
"   **lodge:** cove
"   **priestess of opera:** Norma
"   **stone:** sarsen
"   **symbol:** mistletoe
drum: beat, tabor, repeat
"   **ear:** tympanum
"   **oriental:** anacara, tom-tom
"   **roll at sunrise:** dian

"   **tighten:** frap
drunkard: dipsomaniac, sot
drunt: drawl, pet, grumble
drupe: cherry, plum, apricot
drupetum: etaerio, raspberry
druplet: acinus, grain
dry: arid, brut, thirsty, cynical
"   **comb. form:** xero, ser
"   **as a narrative:** jejune
"   **run:** try
"   **shave:** cheat
dryad: nymph
dual: twin, binary
duck: fowl, evade, dodge, cloth
"   **brood:** team
"   **flock of:** sord
"   **genus:** aythya, anas, clangula
"   **large:** muscovy, pato
"   **like:** coot, decoy
"   **male:** drake
"   **pert. to:** anatine
"   **ringed-necked:** bunty
"   **sitting:** decoy
"   **small:** smew
"   **wooden:** decoy
duckbill: platypus, mammal
duckweed: lemna
ductless gland: thymus, pineal, thyroid
dudeen: pipe
duelist's aide: second
dugong: seacow
duke's realm: Duchy, Dukedom
dull: dense, dim, vapid, apathetic
"   **color:** terne, dun, favel, khaki
"   **finish:** mat(te)
"   **statement:** platitude

dulse: seaweed
Dumas: character: Aramis, Athos
  " **heroine:** Camille
dumping ground: toom
dun: ask, solicit
  " **color:** brown, grey, tan, khaki, ecru
dunker: tumbler
dunlin: stib, sandpiper, bird
dupery: ramp
durable: stable, enduring
durance, vile: jail, imprisonment
D'Urberville lass: Tess
durgah: tomb, court
durra: millet, sorghum, grain
dust: pilm, stive, pollen, dirt
  " **reduce to:** mull
  " **speck:** mote
Dutch uncle: oom
Dutchware blue: delft
dux: chief
dwarf: Galar, Pacolet, Cercopes, gnome, elf, belittle
  " **King:** Alberich
  " **pert. to:** nanism
dweller: cave: troglodyte

  " **city:** urbanite
  " **earth:** tellurian
  " **formicary:** ant
  " **monastery:** cenobite
Dyak: knife: parang
  " **Sea:** iban
dye: kino, stain, tinge
  " **base:** aniline
  " **blue:** woad, anil, cyanine, wad(e)
  " **coal tar:** eosin(e)
  " **compound:** azo, diazin(e)
  " **gum:** kino
  " **indigo:** anil
  " **root pigment:** madder
  " **violet:** archil
dyeing: apparatus: ager
  " **chamber:** oven
dyewood tree: tua
dynamite inventor: Hobel
dynamo: generator, motor
  " **part:** limb, coil, pulley
  " **inventor:** Faraday
dynasty: Chinese: Yin, Ming, Isin, Fo
  " **Fr.:** Capet
dysphoria: anxiety, disquiet
dzeren: antelope

E

E: epsilon
ea: river, inlet, diety, each
each: all, every, both
 " **for each:** per
 " **of each:** ana
eagle: bergut, harpy, coin
 " **Biblical:** gier
 " **brood:** aerie
 " **constellation/genus:** aquila
 " **male:** tercel
 " **nest:** eyrie, eyry
 " **relating to:** harpy, Jove's
eaglestone: etite
eaglewood: agalloch, aloes
eagre: (tidal)wave, bore
ear: lug, knob, hearing, auricle
 " **anvil of:** incus, ambos
 " **auricle:** pinna
 " **comb. form:** ot(o), auri
 " **depression:** scapha
 " **lobe:** lug, pinna
 " **wax:** cerumen
earache: otalgia
eared seal: otary
early: soon, seasonable
 " **poet.:** rath(e), betimes
earnest: grave, intent, diligent
 " **comb. form:** serio
 " **money:** arles, hansel
earnestness: unction
earnings: wages, profits, stipend
earth: terra, soil, globe, planet, orb
 " **axis:** hinge
 " **born:** terrigenous, mortal, human
 " **comb. form:** geo, terra
 " **crust:** horst
 " **occur at surface:** epigene
 " **pert. to:** geal, terrene, clayey, temporal, worldly
 " **poet.:** vale
 " **surface:** epigene, crust,

horst
    " **volcanic:** trass, lava, tuff
earthdrake: dragon
earthenware: Delft, porcelain, pottery, crockery
    " **cooking:** casserole
    " **maker:** potter
    " **making material:** pug
    " **pert. to:** ceramic
earthflax: amianthus, asbestos
earthnut: chufa, pod, peanut, tuber
earthquake: temblor, tremor
    " **pert. to:** seismic
earthstar: geaster, fungus
earthwork: agger, dike, fort
earthworm: dewworm, ess, angleworm
earwig: beetle, centipede
east: Asia, Levant, Orient, sunrise
    " **pert. to:** eoan
East Africa, African: See Africa
East Indies, India: Indonesia
    " **arboreal mammal:** colugo
    " **coin:** cash
    " **dancing girl:** dasi
    " **garment:** sarong
    " **vessel:** patamar
    " **weight:** singh
Easter: feast of: Pasch
    " **fruitcake:** Simnel
    " **Island:** Rapanui
    " **of:** Paschal
    " **third Sunday after:** Jubilate
easy: facile, glib, lenient
    " **job:** sinecure, cinch
eat: ingest, feed, erode, devour
    " **greedily:** gorge, bolt, edacity, voracity
    " **immoderately:** glut, sate
    " **in gulps:** lab
Eban: Israeli diplomat: Abba
ebb: recede, decline, abate
    " **and flow:** tide, (a)estus
Eblis: Satan
eboulement: landslide
ebullient: bubbling, boiling, exuberant
ecaudate: tailless
eccentric: odd, bizarre, irregular
    " **piece:** cam
ecclesiastic: prelate, minister, religious
ecclesiastical: attendant: acolyte
    " **banner:** labarum
    " **benefice:** glebe
    " **cap:** biretta, calotte, zucchetto
    " **council:** synod
    " **hood:** amice
    " **widow's office:** viduate
ecdysiast: stripteaser
eche: grow, enlarge, increase
echidna: anteater
echimyine: hutia, cony
echinate: spiny, prickly, bristly
echinoderm: starfish, sea urchin, trepang
eclat: splendor, acclaim, praise
eclectic: liberal
eclipse: cloud, obscure
    " **region of:** penumbra
eclogue: poem, idyl(l), pastoral

ectad: opposed to: entad
ectoparasite: leech, remora
Ecuador: coin: sucre, condor
  "   **measure:** libra, cuadra, fanega
  "   **animal:** vicuna
ecumenical council: Trent, Lyon
eczema: herpes, tetter
edacious: voracious, devouring, ravenous
edaphic: local, autochthonous
eddish: arrish, edgrow, stubble
eddo: taro root
eddy: twirl, gyrate, vortex
edentata: group: sloth, ai, anteater, aardvark
edentate: genus: manis, pangolin
edge: skirt, margin, labrum, arris
  "   **sloping:** basil, bezel
edict: act, mandate, rule, ordinance
  "   **Pope's:** bull(a)
Edison: inventor: Thomas Alva
Edom: chieftain: Iram
edulcorate: sweeten
eel: congo, moray, whip
  "   **genus:** conger
  "   **young:** elver
eelpout: burbot, ling
efface: erase, obliterate
effete: barren, sterile, spent
effigy: likeness, icon
  "   **fate of (sometimes):** burned, hanged
effloresce: flower, blossom(out)

effluvium: aura, flatus, exhalation
effodient: burrowing, fossorial
effulgence: luster, flare, radiance
eft: lizard, newt
  "   **genus:** triturus
egg(s): ovum, ova, nit
  "   **collector of bird's:** oologist
  "   **comb. form:** oo, ovi
  "   **of insect:** nit, larva
  "   **part of:** latebra, yolk, shell, white, albumen
  "   **shell:** shard
  "   **tester:** candler
  "   **white:** glair, albumen
Egil's brother: Volund
ego: jivatma, atman, self, id
egregious: flagrant, gross, precious
egress: vent, exit
egret: heron, plume, bird
Egypt, Egyptian: Nilot, Arab, Copt, Gipsy
  "   **astral body:** Ka
  "   **beetle:** scarab
  "   **chaos:** Nu
  "   **coin:** fodda(h), kees, para, purse, bedidlik, girsh, tallard
  "   **cross of life:** Ankh
  "   **dancing girl:** alma
  "   **evil spirit:** Set, Seth
  "   **heaven:** Aaru
  "   **jar:** canopic
  "   **language:** Coptic
  "   **measure:** ardab, theb, girba
  "   **plant:** cumin
  "   **tomb:** mastaba
  "   **water bottle:** doruck

" **wind:** kamsin
eider: down, wamp, quilt
eidolon: image, apparition
eight: VIII, eta, card
" **comb. form:** octa, octo
" **days of feast:** utas
ejaculation: mystic: Om
eland: elk, impofo
elapine: cobra, mamba
elasmobranch fish: sawfish, chimera, ray, shark
elbow: push, angle, joint
" **bend:** tope, drink
elchee, elchi: envoy, ambassador
elder: prior, dean, ancestor
" **shrub/tree:** sambucus
eldritch: eerie, ghastly, weird
Electra: Pleiad
" **brother:** Orestes
" **father:** Agamemmnon
" **mother:** Klytemnestra
" **son:** Dardanus
electric: atmosphere: aura
" **atom:** electron, ion
" **circuit   regulator:** booster
" **coil:** tesla
" **detective:** radar, sonar
" **ion:** anion, cation
" **terminal:** electrode, pole
" **unit:** volt, ampere, ohm
electrode: cathode, anode, terminal
electronic tube: vacuum, klystron, triode
eleemosynary: charitable, free, gratuitous
elegiac: funereal, poem, plaintive
element: part, constituent
" **chemical:** uranium, sili-

con, iodine, cobalt, xenon
" **earth group:** erbium
" **even valence:** artiad
" **inert gas:** neon, xenon
" **non-volatile:** barium
" **of air:** argon, nitrogen, oxygen
" **similar:** isotype
" **white:** indium, silver
elemi: anime, oleoresin, resin
elephant: pachyderm, mastodon
" **cry:** barr
" **ear:** taro, fern
" **keeper:** mahout
" **pen:** kraal
" **seat on:** howdah
" **young:** calf
elevated: ground: mesa, rideau
elevation of mind: anagoge
elf: fay, nix, pixie, sprite
elfish sprite: drac
Elia: Charles Lamb, essayist
Elijah: prophet, tishbite
elision: syncope, haplology
elixir: arcanum, panacea
elk: sambar, deer, leather
" **bark:** bay, magnolia
ell: annex, measure
elliptical: oval, oblong, ovoid
elm: ulme, tree
" **borer:** lamid
" **genus:** ulmus, celtis, trema, planera
Elman, violinist: Mischa
elutriate: decant, purify
elver: conger, eel
Elysium: Eden, paradise, bliss
emaciated: tabetic
emanation(s): vapor, niton,

aura(e), efflux, exhalation
" **flower:** aroma, scent
" **invisible:** vapor, aura
" **subtle:** aura
embattled: creneled
emblem: badge, symbol, token
" **of authority:** mace, star, stripe
" **of clan:** totem
" **of U.S.:** eagle
embodiment: avatar, epitome, image
" **of Ptah:** Apis
embonpoint: corpulence, stoutness
embrocation: arnica, liniment, poultice
embroider: adorn, embellish
" **frame for:** taboret, hoop
embroidery: brede
embryo: cell, germ
" **developed:** fetus
" **food for:** endosperm
" **outer cells:** epiblast
" **membrane:** amnion
" **middle layer:** mesoderm, mesoblast
embusque: shirker, slacker
emery: corundum, abrasive
emetic: ipecac, mustard
emmer: spelt, wheat
emmet: ant, pismire
emolument: gain, salary, stipend
emotion: pathos, feeling, fear, love, hate, envy, passion, anger
" **seat of:** spleen, liver
" **turn of:** caprice
emperor: autocrat, Caesar, despot

" **decree of:** Rescript
" **Ger.:** Kaiser
" **Jap.:** Midado, Tenno
" **sovereignty of:** empire, empery
empiric: faker, charlatan
empty: barren, vacuous, hollow
" **comb. form:** ken(o)
empyreal: celestial, ethereal, airy
empyrean: sky, ether, firmament
emunctory: lungs, kidneys, skin
emyd: terrapin, turtle
enchantress: Circe, siren, charmer
enchiridion: handbook
enchorial: popular, native
encomiast: eulogist
encore: again, over, recall
" **anti:** boo, hiss, catcall
encumbrance: burden
" **in law:** claim, lien
" **kind of:** mortgage
end: close, goal, expire, purpose, design
" **mus.:** fine, coda
" **result:** product
" **tending to:** telic
endemic: indigenous, native
endless: eternal, limited, immortal
endocrine: gland
" **designating one:** adrenal, thyroid, pituitary
endogamy: inbreeding
endowment: grant, largess(e)
Endymion: shepherd
" **lover of:** Selene
energy: might, power, force

" **pert. to:** actinic
" **potential:** ergal
" **unit of** erg, ergon
enfilade: barrage, rake
engine: motor, machine, locomotive
" **compressed air:** ramjet
" **cylinder:** piston
" **exhaust noise:** chug
" **of war:** onager, catapult, ram, mangonel, trebuchet
England, English: Albion, Anglican
" **coin:** guinea, florin, pence, farthing
" **emblem:** rose
" **hills:** wolds, clee
" **measure:** pin, cran
" **order:** garter
" **party:** tory, whig, labo(u)r
" **patron saint:** George
" **race course:** Epsom, Ascot
" **school:** Eton, Harrow
" **weight:** stone, tod, mast
engrave: chisel, imprint, etch
" **by dots:** stipple
engraving: print, carving
" **act of:** celature, xylography
" **coin, ancient:** carolus
" **stone:** intaglio, cameo
" **tool:** burin
engulf: (over)whelm, swallow
enigma: rebus, puzzle, mystery, conundrum
enigmatic: obscure, baffling, inscrutable
" **person:** sphinx
" **saying:** parable
enisled: alone, isolated

enkerchief: drape
ennead: ninefold
ennui: fatigue, tedium
Enos: father: Seth
" **grandmother:** Eve
" **uncle:** Abel, Cain
ens: being, entity, essence
ensiform: xiphoid, bone
ensilage: fodder, storage
ensorcel: bewitch, charm
entablature: part of: cornice, atlantes, frieze, architrave
" **support:** atlas, column, atlantes
entad: opposed to: ectad
entellus: monkey
entente: pact, agreement
entertainment: show, repast, recreation
" **of strangers:** xenodochy
enthusiast: fan, bigot, zealot, fanatic
enthymeme: argument, syllogism
entire: total, livelong, all, whole, complete
" **comb. form:** holo
" **prefix:** holo
" **range:** gamut
entozoon: parasite, hookworm, tapeworm
entrance: adit, portal, ingress, charm, delight
" **back:** postern
" **court:** atrium
" **hall:** lobby, foyer
" **with evil intent:** entry
entrechat: leap, jump
entrepot: warehouse, depot
entresol: mezzanine
enuresis: urination
environment: surroundings,

milieu
" **comb. form:** eco
envoy: legate, nuncio, pleni-
potentiary
enzyme: diastase, pepsin,
olease
" **leather making:** tannase
" **opposed to:** azyme
eonic: eral
Eos: goddess, Aurora, dawn
eparch: governor, bishop
eparchy: diocese
ephemeris: almanac, diary,
calendar
epic: epos, saga, narrative
" **poem:** epopee, eneid,
aeneid
epicarp: husk, rind, peel
epicedium: dirge
epicene: neuter
epicrisis: critique, review
Epictetus: stoic
epicure: sybarite, gourmet,
glutton
epicurean: luxurious, he-
donist
epidermis: bark, cuticle, skin
epigram: adage, quip, mot,
saying
" **couplet:** distich
epilepsy: catalepsy, fit, sei-
zure
" **attack of:** grand mal,
petit mal
Epimetheus: Titan
" **wife:** Pandora
epimyth: moral
epinephrin(e): adrenalin, hormone
epiphyte: moss, orchid, lichen, fungus
epistaxis: nosebleed

epithet: agnomen, (by)name,
oath, misnomer
" **Alexander:** (the) Great
" **Clemenceau:** Tiger
" **Eric:** (the) Red
" **Ivan:** (the) Terrible
" **Jackson:** Stonewall
" **Pitt:** Ironside
epoch: eon, age, era, period
epode: (lyric) poem, aftersong
epopee: epic (poem), epos
epoptic: mystic
equable: tranquil, even, serene
equal: par, same, tantamount
" **comb. form:** iso, pari
" **quantity:** identic, ana
" **sides:** isosceles
equanimity: poise, composure, sang-froid
equilateral figure: rhomb, triangle
equilibrist: rope walker, ba-
lancer
equilibrium: poise, balance,
composure
" **want of:** astasia
equine: horse
" **water sprite:** kelpy
equiponderant: balanced
equitable: impartial, just, wise
" **Roman law:** Bonitarian
equivocal: cryptic, vague, dubious
eral: epochal
ere: prior, rather, before
Erebus: darkness, Hades
" **father:** Chaos
" **offspring:** Aether, Day
" **sister:** Night, Nox
eremite: hermit, recluse
erewhile: once, ago, hereto-

fore

ergo: hence, therefore, be-cause

ergon: erg, work

ergot: fungus

" **of rye:** spur

eri: silkworm

erica: heath

Erin: Eire, Hibernia, Ireland, Ierne, Old Sod

eristic: disputant, argumenta-tive

Eritrea: (see Ethiopia)

" **measure:** cubi

Eros: Cupid, Amor, love

" **beloved:** Psyche

" **father:** Mercury, Hermes

" **mother:** Venus, Aphro-dite

error(s): errata, slip, boner

" **printing:** typo, erratum

ersatz: substitute

Erse: Gael(ic), Celt(ic), Irish

erubescent: reddish, blushing

erudition: wisdom, lure, scholarship

erysipelas: rose, wildfire, dis-ease (skin)

Esau: Edom

" **brother:** Jacob

" **father:** Isaac

" **wife:** Adah

escarpment: slope, fortifica-tion

eschatology subject: death, resurrection, immortality

escheat: confiscate

escolar: palu, fish

escutcheon: arms, crest

" **band:** fess

" **voided:** orle

Esdras: Apocrypha, Ezra, Ne-

hemiah

" **angel:** Uriel

Eskimo: Alaskan, Aleut

" **Asian:** Yuit, Innuit

" **boat:** umia(c)k, kayak, bidar

" **garment:** parka, temiak

" **house:** igloo, tupik

" **knife:** ulu

esne: slave, serf

esodic: afferent

esophagus: gula, gullet

esoteric: occult, arcane, se-cret

" **doctrine:** cabala

" **knowledge:** gnosis

esparto grass: alfa

Esperanto: ido

" **deviser:** Zamenhof

espy: spy, view, descry

ess: curve, sigmoid, worm

Essene: mystic, ascetic

essential: intrinsic, neces-sary, basic, vital

" **element:** part

" **oil:** essence

" **part:** pith, member

" **thing:** key

estafet: courier

estate: assets, degree, hold-ings, status

" **manager:** steward, guardian, executor

ester: silicate, ether, oleate

Esther: Hadassah

" **festival:** Purim

" **husband:** Xerxes

esthetics: arts

Est(h)onia, Esthonian: Esth

" **measure:** suld, liin

" **weight:** nael, puud

estivate: summer

" **opposed to:** hibernate
estray: waif, dogie
estuary: plata, inlet, creek
estuate: boil
esurient: greedy, hungry
et al: elsewhere, others
etamine: cloth, voile
etape: storehouse, encampment
Eteocles: brother of: Polynices
" **father:** Oedipus
" **kingdom:** Thebes
" **mother:** Jocasta
Eternal City: Rome
etesian: periodical, annual
etheostomoid: darter, fish
ether: air, sky, space
" **compound:** ester
" **use of:** anesthetic, solvent
Ethiopia,   Ethiopian: Abyssinia(n), Seba
" **coin:** besa, girsh, talari, harf, kharaf
" **fly:** zimb
" **measure:** tat, cuba, kuba, ardeb, berri
" **plant:** (herb) teff
" **primate:** abuna
" **tree:** koso, cusso
" **weight** oket, kasm, natr, alada, pek, rot
ethnarch: governor
ethos: opposed to: pathos
ethyl: derivative: ether
" **hydride:** ethane
" **hydroxide:** alcohol
" **symbol:** et, eth
Etna: volcano, lamp
Etruscan: Tursenoi
" **god:** Tinia

" **goddess:** Menfra
ettle: aim, intend
etui: case, reticule, needle-case
etymon: radical, radix, root
eucalypt: yate, bloodwood
eucalyptus: gum: kino
" **leaf deposit:** cerf
" **secretion:** laap, larp
eucharist: box: pix, pyx
" **plate:** paten
" **vessel:** ama, amula
" **wafer:** host
" **wine:** krama
Euclid: philosopher
" **origin:** Megara
eudaemonia: happiness
eugenics: well born
" **pioneer:** Galton
" **subject   of:** races, breeds
eulogy: encomium, panegyric, tribute
euouae: trope
euphonium: tuba
euphorbia: spurge, plant
eureka: aha, triumph
" **red:** puce
euripus: flow, strait
Europa: father: Ogenor
" **lover:** Zeus
Europe and Asia: Eurasia, Scythia
Europe, European: Lapp, Dane, Slav, Lett
" **ancient:** Celt
" **ape:** baboon
" **ash:** sorb
" **bat:** serotine
" **central region:** Banat
" **country (ancient):** Dacia

" **cherry:** gean
" **coal basin:** Saar
" **deer:** roe
" **grape:** muscat
" **hunting dog:** griffun
" **language:** Ugric
" **lavender:** aspic
" **oak:** holm
" **ox:** urus
" **plain:** steppe
" **rabbit:** con(e)y
" **rodent:** erd
" **squirrel:** sisel
" **tree:** sorb
" **worm:** sao
Eurydice's husband: Orpheus
eutectic: fusible
Euterpe: Muse
" **son:** Rhesus
evanesce: fade, vanish
evanescent: ephemeral, fleeting, transient
even: equable, plane, tied, uniform, placid
" **if:** tho(ugh)
" **minded:** placid, equable
evening: eve, dusk, twilight
" **party:** soiree
" **pert. to:** vesper, crepuscular
" **song:** serena
" **star:** hesper, mercury, venus
Everest: mountain peak: Lhotse
" **site of:** Nepal
evergreen: baretta, spruce, pine
" **cedar-like:** deodar
" **genus:** olax, abies, catha
" **shrub:** toyon

everlasting: ageless, constant
" **plant:** orpine
everted: turned, ectopic
evil(s): vice, nefarious, malign
" **doer:** sinner, felon, culprit
" **prefix:** mal
" **spirit:** bugan, demon, devil
eviscerate: gut, devitalize, disembowel
evolution: growth, change
" **doctrine:** biogeny, cosmism
ewe: keb, theave, sheep
" **old:** crone
ewer: pitcher, jug
exacerbate: irk, embitter, annoy
exaggerated: outre
" **comedy:** farce
" **pious feeling:** pietism
" **praise:** flattery, puffery
examine: try, test, explore, scrutinize
" **accounts:** audit
" **by touching:** palpate
excaudate: tailless
excavation: shaft, pit, cavity
" **for ore:** stope, mine
except: unless, besides, save
excerpt: verse, choice, scrap
excessive: undue, extravagant, ultra
" **affection:** dotage
" **comb. form:** hyper
" **in belief:** rabid
" **zeal:** fanaticism
exchange: bandy, trade, shuffle, swap
" **premium:** agio

excise: toll, levy, duty

exclamation: ah(a), ahem, hoy, grr, bah, egad, ow, phew, hey, tch
" **of disgust:** rats, ugh
" **of exhilaration:** evoe

excogitate: contrive, devise, intent

excoriate: abrade, flay, chafe, denounce

excresence: lump, growth, fungus

exculpate: acquit, clear, absolve, exonerate

excuse: acquit, pretext, apology
" **for non-appearance:** plea, essoin
" **for sickness:** aeger

execrable: detestable, bad, abominable

execution: by burning: stake
" **by drowning:** noyade
" **by hanging:** halter, swing, stretch
" **by electricity:** electrocute

exequies: wake, rites, ceremonies

exfoliate: scale, desquamate

exhort: preach, urge, incite

exhume: disinter, dig, grub, disentomb

exigency: pinch, crisis, urgency

exiguous: small, meager, sparse, attenuated

existence: ens, esse, being, status
" **beginning:** nascent, birth
" **having none:** null, void, defunct

exocoetoid fish: ihi

exodus: flight, hegira

exordium: proem, prelude, preamble

exoteric: popular, public, external

expatiate: enlarge, descant, elaborate

expecting: agog, atip, astir

expedient: convenient, advisable

expedition: crusade, safari, speed, dispatch
" **heroic:** quest
" **hunting:** safari
" **military:** anabasis
" **religious:** crusade

experience: feel, undergo
" **trying:** ordeal

expiate: atone, satisfy, repair

explanation: alibi, solution, key
" **marginal notes:** scholia, annotations
" **of a passage:** exegesis

expletive: oath, curse, egad

explicit: definite, express, precise

exploding: meteor: bolide
" **star:** nova

explorer: Eric, Rae, Byrd, Amundsen, Balboa, De Soto, Cortes, Perry, Lewis

explosive: bomb, mine, dynamite
" **isometric mineral:** thorite

exponent: ite, index, symbol

exposition: show, fair, exhibition

expostulate: object, remonstrate, protest

expression: idiom, locution, phrase, utterance
" **hackneyed:** cliche
" **metaphorical:** figure
" **of assent:** placet
" **of contempt:** fie, bah
" **of sorrow:** alas

expunge: erase, cancel, obliterate

expurgate: censor, purge, cleanse, purify

exsanguine: anemic

exscind: excise, extirpate, cut

exsert: protrude, thrust

exsiccate: dry, parch, desiccate

extemporaneous: offhand, impromptu

extension: arm, ell, range

extenuate: weaken, lessen, diminish

exterior: external, cortical, alien
" **covering:** hide, pelt, clothing

external: outer, superficial, exterior
" **comb. form:** ect(o)
" **covering:** hide, pelt, coat
" **cover of flower:** perianth
" **world:** nonego

extinct bird: auk, dodo, moa, roc, mamo

extirpate: erase, raze, uproot

extra: spare, odd, surplus, additional
" **actor:** super, supernumerary
" **pay:** bonus

extract: essence, excerpt, flavoring, pull
" **from a book:** pericope

extraction: lineage, genealogy

extrasensory   perception: ESP

extreme: radical, ultra, drastic
" **limit:** outrance
" **opposed to:** mean
" **unction:** sacrament
" **unction, give:** anele

extricate: release, free

extrinsic: foreign, extraneous, alien

exudate: tar, sudor, gum, excretion

exuviate: molt, cast off

eye: optic, sight, view
" **black pigment of:** melanin
" **cavity:** orbit
" **dropper:** pipette
" **film:** nebula
" **membrane:** retina, conjunctiva
" **opening:** pupil
" **part:** uvea, cornea, iris, sclera
" **pert. to:** optic
" **symbolic:** uta

eyeball: globe, orb
" **covering:** cornea

eyebrow: supercilium, bree

eyelash(es): cilium, cilia
" **loss of:** madarosis

eyelet: grommet, loophole, ocellus
" **making tool:** bodkin, stiletto

eyelid: drop: ptosis
" **pert. to:** palpebral

eyetooth: canine, fang, cuspid

eyot: ait, isle(t)

eyra: wild cat

eyre: journey, circuit

Ezekiel: father: Buzi (Jeremiah)

Ezrahite: Heman, Ethan, Darda

F

F, letter: ef, eff
fabaceous plant: ers
fable: myth, legend, fiction, allegory
  " **teller of:** parabolist, fabulist
fabled: animal: unicorn, centaur, basilisk
  " **being:** ogre, dwarf, giant, troll, mermaid
  " **bird:** roc
  " **fish:** mah
  " **serpent:** basilisk
fabric: felt, web, ras
  " **coarse:** crash, mat
  " **corded:** rep, repp
  " **cotton/worsted:** paramatta
  " **crinkled:** crepe, crape
  " **dealer:** mercer
  " **design with wax coating:** batik
  " **figured:** moreen
  " **lace:** alencon, mechlin, val

  " **shiny:** sateen
  " **striped:** doria, susi
  " **watered silk:** moire
  " **worsted (light):** etamine
fabrico: method of ornamenting: fagoting
facade: face, rear, facia
face: puss, physiognomy, visage, facet
  " **covering:** veil, mask, yashmak
  " **downward:** prone, prostrate
  " **guard:** beaver, mask
  " **-to-face:** vis-a-vis
  " **value:** par
facet: bezel, culet, aspect
  " **star:** pane
facia: tablet, plate
facing: inward: introse
  " **outward:** extrose
fact: datum, deed, actuality
faction: cabal, side, party
facto: ipso
factotum: servant, agent

faddish: ism, ismal
faddist: neo, monomaniac
"Faerie Queene": author: Spenser
   " **character:** Una, Ate, Talus, Amoret
Fafnir: brother: Regin
   " **slayer:** Sigurd
faik: lessen
faineant: otiose, lazy, idle
fair: even, unbiased, blond(e), show, bazaar
   " **pert. to:** nundinal
fairy: sprite, elf, fay, peri, pixie
   " **air:** sylph
   " **ghost:** sprite
   " **king:** Oberon
   " **queen:** Mab, Titania, Una
   " **shoemaker:** leprechaun
   " **spirit of death:** banshee
   " **tricky:** Puck
faith: trust, creed, dogma, tenet
   " **pert. to:** pistic
faithful: loyal, leal, devoted, tried
   " **friend:** Achates
fake: cheat, fraud, spurious
   " **comb. form:** pseud(o)
fakir: yogi, monk, mendicant
falcon, falconry: sorage, kestrel
   " **Arctic:** gyr
   " **bait:** lure
   " **blind:** seel
   " **genus:** falco, raptores
   " **male:** tercel
   " **prairie:** lanner
   " **recorder of:** Pliny, Martial
   " **rel. to:** accipter

   " **ribbon or strap for:** jess
   " **small:** besra, merlin
   " **unfledged bird:** eyas
falconer's summons: wo
fallal: geegaw, finery
fallfish: chub
falling: cadent
   " **sickness:** epilepsy
fallout particles: radiodust
false: unreliable, tale, luke, sham, bogus
   " **comb. form:** pseud(o)
   " **form(s) of thinking:** idola, idolum
   " **items:** spurious
   " **wing:** alula
Falstaff: follower: Nym
   " **lieutenant and crony:** Pistol
   " **prince:** Hal
Fama: rumor
familiar: versant
   " **saying:** saw, adage, mot
family: line, gens, ilk, stirps, tribe
   " **famous Ital.:** Este
   " **pert. to:** nepotic
fan: cool, foment, winnow, devotee
   " **form:** rooter plicate
   " **oriental swinging:** ogi, punka(h)
   " **palm genus:** inodes
   " **stick of:** brin, blade
fanatical: rabid, energumen
fane: temple, sanctuary
fanfaron: bully, hector, swaggerer
fanion: banner, flag
fanning device: punka(h)
fanon: orale, maniple, cape
fantoccini: puppets, shows

fantod (sl): fuss, pet, sulk
far: distant, afar, progressed
" **comb. form:** tele
farinaceous: mealy, starchy
" **drink:** ptisan
" **meal:** sago, salep, cereal
farm: ranch, plow, cultivate
" **building:** barn, solo
" **fee:** manor
" **grazing:** ranch
" **implement:** header, rake, plow, tiller, seeder, disk, tractor, harrow
" **tenant: cropper, cotter**
farming: husbandry
farmyard: barton
Faroe Island: Bordo, Ostero, Sando, Stromo, Vaago
" **duck:** eider, puffin
" **fish:** char(r)
" **whirlwind:** oe
farrow: pig, litter
fascia: band, fillet
fascicle: cluster, group
fast: wild, apace, quick, diet
" **day:** Ember
" **period:** Lent
fasten: moor, link, tack, chain, lace, pin, glue
" **comb. form:** desmo
fastener: peg, clamp, halter
fastigate: conical, pointed
fat: ester, lipa, obese
" **butter:** oleo, caprin
" **comb. form:** steat(o), lip(o), pio
" **constituent:** stearin, cholesterol
" **geese:** axunge
" **of animal:** tallow, lanolin, suet, adeps, lard

" **liquid part of:** globule, olein(e)
" **pert. to:** adipic
" **true:** lipid
" **wool:** tallow, lanolin
fata morgana: mirage
fatbird: guacharo
fate: doom, destiny, kismet, lot
" **Buddhist:** Karma
" **cuts thread of life:** Atropos (Morta)
" **measures threads of life:** Lachesis
" **oriental:** Kismet
Fates, myth: Atropos, Clotho, Moira, Decuma, Morta, Nona, Parca, Lachesis
" **Three:** Moira (Ger.), Parcae (Roman)
father: abba, ama, dad, pere, sire, papa
" **of English learning:** Bede
" **of hydrogen bomb:** Teller
" **of mankind:** Adam, Iapetus
" **of the gods:** Amon, Amen
" **pert. to:** agnate, paternal
" **of Waters:** Mississippi
Fathers of the Oratory: founder: Neri
Fatima: descendant of: Sayid, Seid
" **sister:** Anne
" **step-brother:** Ali
fatty: adipose, greasy
" **acid:** adipic, valeric, lanoceric
" **secretion:** sebum, oil

   " **tumor:** lipoma
faujasite: zeolite
fault: crime, culpa, defect, imperfection
   " **find:** carp, censure, cavil
   " **in mining:** hade
faultfinder: momus, complainer
faun: satyr, deity
   " **of Praxiteles:** marble
fauna: animals
Faunus: grandfather: Saturn
   " **son:** Acis
Faust: author: Goethe
   " **composer:** Gounod
faronian: mild
favoritism: nepotism, bias, predilection
fe: iron
fealty: homage, duty, fidelity
fear: of being buried alive: taphephobia
   " **of darkness:** nyctophobia
   " **of drafts:** aerophobia
   " **of fire:** pyrophobia
   " **of #13:** triakaidekaphobia
   " **of open spaces:** agoraphobia
   " **of pain:** algophobia
   " **of poisons:** toxiphobia
fearful: comb. form: dino
feast: regale, junket, repast
   " **comb. form:** mas
   " **funeral:** wake, arval
   " **of Lanterns:** Bon
   " **of Lots:** Purim
   " **of Weeks:** Pentecost
feather(s): down, sley, pinna
   " **base of bird's wing:** alula
   " **bed:** tye

   " **grass:** stipa
   " **quill:** covert, aigret
   " **scarf:** boa
   " **slot:** spline
   " **yellow:** hulu
feathering: endysis
featherless: callow
feature: mien, story, trait
   " **principal:** plot, motif
feaze: unravel, untwist
feckless: weak, spiritless, ineffective
feed: dine, subsist, nourish
   " **animal:** mash, hay, grain, fodder, oats, chops
   " **pasture cattle:** agist
feeding, forced: gavage
feeler: palpus, inquiry, antenna
feeling: ardor, passion, opinion
   " **capable of:** sentient
   " **loss of:** anesthesia, analgesia
   " **show:** emote
feet: having: pedate
   " **pert. to:** pedary, podal
   " **six:** fathom
   " **two metric:** dipody
   " **verse of two:** dipody
   " **without:** apod, apodal
feign: act, sham, pretend
   " **sickness:** malinger
feint: in fencing: appel
feldspar: albite, leelite, odinite
   " **yield:** kaolin
felid: cat, tiger, lion, ounce
felis: leo: lion
   " **pardus:** leopard
fellow: equal, mate, egg, chap, companion

" **brutish:** yahoo
" **worthless:** bum, cad, scoundrel, spalpeen
felly: craftily, rim
felt, like: pannose
feltwort: plant, herb, mullein
female: woman, dame
" **comb. form:** gyne, gyn(o)
" **figurine:** orant
" **fish:** raun
" **fox:** vixen
" **red deer:** hind
" **warrior:** amazon
feminine name: suffix: ette
femur: thigh(bone)
fen: bog, morass, sump
" **water:** sud(s)
fence: fagin, palisade
" **crossing:** stile
" **fish:** net, weir
" **interwoven:** raddle
" **movable:** hurdle, glance
" **picket:** pale, paling
" **steps over:** stile
" **sunken:** aha
fencing: breastplate: plastron
" **dummy:** pel
" **hit:** punto
" **maneuver:** appel
" **parrying position:** seconde
" **posture:** carte, septime, seconde, guard, octave, tierce, sixte, quinte, quarte, prime
" **sword:** epee, foil, rapier
fennel: anis, plant, azorian
" **genus:** nigella
feral: wild, deadly, savage
feretory: shrine, chapel

ferment: yeast, seethe, leaven
" **active principal:** enzyme
" **agent to induce:** must
" **revive:** stum
fermentative: zymotic
fern: brake, nardoo, bracken, tara
" **climbing:** nito
" **cluster:** sorus
" **edible:** tara, roi
" **genus:** todea, polypody, pteris, osmunda
" **leaf:** frond
" **like plant:** acrogen
" **male:** osmund
" **patches:** sori
" **root stock:** roi
ferret: female: gill
" **male:** hob
ferric oxide powder: rouge
ferry: pont, bac, traject, carrier
fertility god: Frey(r)
fertilizer: guano, marl, manure
ferule: rod, ruler, fennel, punishment
festival: ancient Gr.: Delia
" **of Apollo:** Delia
" **comb. form:** mas
festoon: swag, garland, bucranium
fete: gala, fiesta, bazar
" **rustic:** Ale
feud: fief, quarrel, vendetta
" **blood:** vendetta
feudal: domain: fief
" **land, right of:** feud, feod, fief
" **lord:** liege

" **opposed to:** al(l)odial
" **service:** avera
" **pert. to:** banal
" **tenant:** vassal, leud, socager
" **payment by:** tac, tak
" **tribute:** heriot
" **Fr.:** feod
fever: ardor, enecia
" **affected with:** pyretic
" **chills and:** ague
" **intermittent:** quartan, malaria
" **kind of:** octan, tap, elodes
" **reducer:** defervescent
" **spot(s):** petechia(e)
" **tropical:** malaria, dengue
" **without:** apyretic, afebrile
few: rare, scant
" **comb. form:** olig(o), pauci
fey: dying, dead, timid
fez: cap, turban, shako, tarboosh
fiber: hemp, eruc
" **bark:** olona, terap
" **century plant:** pita, clusters
" **E. Ind. plant:** ramie
" **hat:** datil
" **knot:** nep
" **palm:** agave, raffia
" **wood:** bast, aralac
" **wool:** kemp, staple, nep
fibril: hair, filament
fibula: brooch, clasp, ouch
fico: trifle, fig, snap
fictile: plastic, molded
fictive: imaginary

fiddle: violin, scrape, kit, crowd
" **medieval:** gigue
fidelity: hold, piety, loyalty
" **symbol of:** topaz
field: area, grid, lea
" **Amer. mouse:** vole
" **Biblical:** ager, aner
" **goddess:** Fauna
" **inclosed:** ager, croft, court
" **pert. to:** campestral, agrarian
" **stubble:** rowen
fig(s): fico
" **genus:** ficus
" **Ital.:** fico
" **dried:** carica
" **like:** caricous
" **marigold:** samh
" **not to care a:** fillip
Figaro: barber
fighting fish: betta
figure: shape, image, symbol, motif, effigy
" **archeology:** caryatid, telamon
" **earth:** geoid
" **five-angled:** pentagon
" **four-angled:** tetragon, rhombus, square, rectangle
" **oval:** ellipse
" **round:** circle
" **ten-sided:** decagon
" **three-angled:** triangle
figure of speech: pun, simile, trope, metaphor
figured: faconne, adorned, computed
figurine: statuette, tanagra
Fiji: island: Viti, Lau
" **group:** Ra, Lau

filament: thread, strand, fiber, tendril
" **feather:** dowl(e)
" **flax:** harl(e)
file: row, enter, rape, cabinet
" **comb maker's:** carlet
" **finisher:** ender
" **flat:** quannet
" **half-round:** grail(le)
" **rough:** rasp
filibeg: kilt, skirt
Filipino: (see "Phillippine")
fillet: orle, sola, ribbon
" **bottom of frieze:** regula, taeina
" **for hair:** snood, band
" **jeweled:** diadem, tiara
" **narrow:** listel, reglet
fillip: snap, excite, tonic
film: haze, coating, membrane
" **coated with:** patinate
" **green/old:** patina
" **thin:** pellicle, brat
fimbriate: hem, fringe, hairy
fin: spinous: acantha, dorsal
" **under:** ventral
fin-footed animal: pinniped
finch: spink, redpoll, siskin
" **Afr.:** fink, moro
" **Amer.:** chewink, junco, towhee
" **canarylike:** serin
" **copper:** chaffinch
" **Eur.:** serin, tarin
" **genus:** fringillidae
" **like:** tanager, canary
find: learn, detect, procure
" **fault:** beef, carp, cavil
" **law:** determine, ascertain, hold
fine: small, penalty, exact, tax

" **for killing:** wergild, cro
" **for misdemeanor:** mulct
" **law:** cro
" **record of:** estreat
Fingal: cave island: Staffa
" **kingdom:** Morven
finger: pointer, feel, handle
" **cap:** cot, thimble
" **comb. form:** digiti
" **fore:** index
" **guard:** thimble, stall
" **inflammation of:** felon, whitlow
" **little:** pinky, minimus
" **middle:** medius
" **nail half moon:** lunule, lunula
" **pert. to:** digital
" **ring:** annular
fingerling: parr, thimble, fish
fingerprint: whorl, arch, loop
finial: epi, apex, top
finishing line: tape
fink: spy, scab, bird, informer
Finland, Finnish: Vote, Vod, Suomi
" **bath:** sauna
" **coin:** markka, penni
" **dialect:** karel
" **god:** Jumala
" **measure:** kannor, tunna
" **pert. to:** Suomic, Suomish
Finlandia composer: Sibelius
Finnegan's Wake author: Joyce, James
fin(n)ikin: pigeon
fippenny bit: fip
fir: evergreen
" **genus:** abies
Firbolg queen: Tailte

fire: blaze, conflagration, eject, animate, arouse
" **artillery:** barrage
" **basket:** cresset, grate
" **bullet:** tracer
" **comb. form:** pyr(o), igni
" **drill:** chark
" **miss:** snap, dud
" **pert. to:** igneous
" **sacrificial:** Agni
" **worshipper:** pyrolater
firecracker: petard
firedog: andiron, support
fireplace: ingle, grate, hearth
" **back of:** reredos
" **ledge:** hob, shelf, mantel
firewood bundle: lena, fagot
firmament: heavens, vault, sphere
firn: ice, snow, neve
first: primus, star, maiden, primordial
" **comb. form:** proto
" **class:** A-one, tops, ace
" **day of Roman month:** Calends
" **installment:** earnest, handsel
" **year's revenue:** annat
firth: estuary, kyle, arm
fish: angle, carp, hake, opah, peto, shad, darter, smelt
" **basket:** corf, caul, cawl
" **bat:** diablo
" **bin for salting:** kench, canch
" **bivalve:** scallop, clam, oyster, diatom, mollusk, pandora
" **black:** swart, tautog
" **bright-colored:** opah
" **butter:** gunnel, blenny
" **catch of:** shack, string
" **chopped:** chum
" **like:** ling, hake, gadus, bib
" **colored:** wrasse, opah
" **snapper:** jocu
" **eggs:** roe, caviar
" **fabled, upholding world:** mah
" **flying:** saury, gurnard
" **genus:** mola, perca, elops, amia, lota, apogon
" **half-beak:** ihi
" **hook:** gaff, sproat, fly
" **imperfect:** thoke
" **jew:** mero, grouper
" **largest fresh water:** arapaima
" **little:** minnow, sardine, smelt
" **pen for:** crawl
" **pert. to:** piscatory, finny
" **scale:** ganoid
fisher: wejack, pekan, bird
fisherman: hat of: squam
fishes: raiae
fishhook: barb, angle
" **attach to snell:** gange
" **leader:** snell
fishing: basket: slarth, slath, creel
" **gear:** reel, rod, line, fly, hook, tackle, nets
" **pert. to:** halieutic
" **smack:** dogger
fishlike: ichthyic
" **skin:** ichthyosis
fist: neif, nieve
fitchew: polecat
five: books of Moses: Pentateuch
" **comb. form:** penta, pent

" **dollar bill:** vee
" **fold:** quintuple
" **group of:** pentad
" **year period:** lustrum
five-finger: oxlip, plant, fish, cinquefoil
Five Nations founder: Hiawatha
fixed: firm, stable, intent
" **routine:** rut
" **time:** era, date, appointment
" **star:** Vega
fizgig: fireworks, whirligig
flag: bunting, pennant, streamer, droop, faint
" **corner:** canton
" **flower:** iris, calamus
" **merchant vessel:** burgee
" **military:** fanion, guidon, colors
" **national:** ensign
" **navy:** burgee
" **pirate:** roger
" **signal:** cornet
" **yacht:** burgee
flagellant: whip, tail, scourge
" **religious:** albi
flageolet: pipe, flute, larigot
flambeau: torch, cresset
flame: blaze, gleed, ardor,
" **fire without:** punk
" **movement:** lick, dart
Flaminia: road, way
flap: fly, bangle, flutter
" **furnished with:** lobed
" **membranous:** loma
" **of sails:** slat
flashing: flange, gaudy
flask: canteen, flagon, carafe
" **glass:** matrass

" **leather:** olpe, girba, matara
" **shaped:** lageniform
flat: insipid, stale, prone, smooth
" **comb. form:** plani
" **-nosed:** simous
flatboat: ark, barge, scow
flax: lint, linen
" **bundle:** head
" **capsule:** boll
" **comb:** card, hatchel, hackle
" **disease:** rust
" **dust:** pouce
" **fiber:** tow
" **filament:** harl
" **genus:** linum
" **insect:** dodder, canker
" **place for processing:** rettery
" **seed:** linseed
" **soak:** ret
" **woody portion:** boon
flea: pulicid, insect, pest
" **genus:** pulex
" **water:** cyclops
fleche: broach, spire, parapet
fleer: gibe, scoff, smirk, flaunt
flesh: meat, pulp, stock
" **eating:** carnivorous, sarcophagic
" **like:** carnose
" **pert. to:** sarcous
fleuret: epee, sword, flower
flex: bend, genuflect
flexion of a limb: anaclasis
flight: exodus, hegira, rout, volee
" **of fancy:** sally
" **of steps:** perron
" **pert. to:** volar

flightless bird: emu, ratite, kiwi
  " **genus:** apteryx, notornis
flint: chert, quartz, stone
  " **impure:** chert
flittermouse: bat
floating: adrift, natant
  " **grass:** foxtail
  " **plant:** frogbit, lotus, sudd
  " **wreckage:** flotsam
flock: covey, brood, school, mob, group
  " **pert. to:** gregal
  " **god of:** Pan
floe: berg
flogging: toco, toko
flood: cataract, sea, flow, surplus
  " **gate:** clow, gool, sluice
  " **lights:** klieg
  " **tidal:** eagre
floor: playa, deck, platform
  " **covering:** mat, rug, tapis, carpet
  " **plank:** chess
  " **raised border:** coaming
flora and fauna: biota
floral leaves: perianth
Florence: coin: florin
  " **devotees:** neri
  " **family:** Medici
  " **gallery:** Uffizi, Pitti
floret bracht: palea, palet
florid: ornate, rubicund, flowery, rhetorical
  " **style:** rococo
Florida: (see special Section)
  " **fish:** tarpon
  " **region:** Everglades
Flotow opera: Martha
flour: and butter: roux
  " **sifter:** bolter, sieve

  " **sprinkle with:** dredge
  " **unsorted:** ata, atta
flow: issue, spring, emanate, gush
  " **out:** spill, exude, issue, ooze
  " **tide:** ebb, neap, flux
flower: bloom, posy, unfold, develop
  " **algae genus:** nostoc
  " **apetalus:** trema, cactus
  " **border:** floroon
  " **bud:** knot
  " **center:** eye
  " **cluster:** raceme, umbel, paniculate, cyme
  " **envelope:** perianth
  " **extract:** attar, otto
  " **forgetfulness:** lotus
  " **full bloom:** anthesis
  " **leaf:** sepal, bract, petal
  " **medicinal:** rue, aloe
  " **part of:** anther, bract, pistil, sepal, stamen, carpel, petal, corolla, spur
  " **pistil, part of:** carpel
  " **seed:** ovule
  " **stalk:** peduncle, petiole, scape, stem
  " **grasses genus:** stipa
  " **tree:** catalpa, tulip, mimosa
flowerless plant: acrogen, fern, lichen, moss
flowerlike: anthoid
fluid: steam, juice, gaseous
  " **blood:** serum, plasma
  " **mythological blood:** ichor
  " **pert. to:** humoral
  " **without:** aneroid
fluosilicate of aluminum: to-

paz
flute: pipe, crimp, piccolo
" **ancient:** tibia
" **bagpipe:** chanter
" **Hindu:** pungi, bin
" **player:** fl(a)utist, aulete
" **stop:** ventage
fly: insect, soar, flutter
" **as clouds:** scud
" **block:** pulley
" **catcher:** peewee, kingbird
" **genus:** musca
" **small: gnat, midge**
" **wings of:** elytrum, elytron
flybane: genus: silene
flyblow: larva
flycatcher: bird: peewee, redstart, tody
flying: adder: dragonfly
" **body:** meteor
" **expert:** ace
" **fish:** saury, gurnard
" **mammal:** bat
" **pert. to:** aviatic
Flying Dutchman heroine: Senta
Fo: Buddha
fodder: stover, ensilage, feed
" **storage place:** silo, barn
" **straw:** stover
" **trough for:** manger
foederatus: ally
fold: bend, crease, reef, flock
" **of skin:** plica
foliage: mass of: spray, bouquet, leafage
foliated: lobed, spathic
folletto: imp, spirit, goblin
follicle: crypt
font: laver, source, basin

" **holy water:** stoup
fontanel opening: vacuity
food: bit, chow, diet, cheer, viands
" **comb. form:** troph(o), sito
" **excessive desire for:** bulimia
" **lacking desire:** asitia
" **miracle:** manna
" **pert. to:** cibarian
" **perverted desire for:** pica
" **room for:** spence
" **semi-digested:** chyme
" **soft:** pap
fool: bauble: marotte
" **gold:** pyrites
" **stitch:** tricot
foot: and mouth disease: murrain
" **bone of:** astragalus, cuboid, calcis, scaphoid
" **comb. form:** ped(i), ped(o), pod(o)
" **deformity:** talipes, planus
" **like part:** pes
" **not having:** apod
" **pert. to:** podal, pedal
" **sole:** plantar
" **three-syllable:** anapaest, dactyl
" **two-syllable:** spondee, iambus, trochee
footed: large: megapod
footprint mold: moulage
footrace: double course: diaulos
footstalk: strig, pedicel
for: because, pro, toward
" **aye:** always, ever
" **example:** vide, e.g.

" **fear that:** lest
" **instance:** e.g., as
" **this case alone:** ad hoc
" **this reason:** hence, ergo
foramen: pore, aperture
forbidden city: Lhasa
force: alleged: od, elod
" **brief and sudden:** brunt
" **by:** amain
" **down:** detrude, trample, tamp
" **out:** expel, evict
" **unit of:** staff, dyne
forced feeding: gavage
forearm: antebrachium
" **bone:** ulna, radius
" **pert. to:** ulnar
forefoot: paw
forehead: brow, sinciput, frons
" **pert. to:** metopic, sincipital
foreign: alien, exotic, remote
" **comb. form:** xeno
" **quarter:** barrio, ghetto, enclave
" **to:** dehors
foreshank: shin
forest: wood, grove, sylva
" **fire locater:** alidade
" **glade:** camas(s)
" **god:** Pan, Tapio, Faunus
" **pert. to:** nemoral, sylvan
~ **treeless:** wold
Forest City: Cleveland, Savannah, Portland
foretelling: fatidic, prophetic
forfeit: penalty, fine, mulct
" **to God:** deodand
forfex: shears
forge: fashion, shape, falsify
" **tongs:** tew

" **waste:** sprue, dross
forgetfulness: lethe, oblivion
" **fruit/tree:** lotus
" **river of:** Lethe
form: cast, scheme, invent, mode, compose
" **carved:** statuary
" **into arc:** embow
" **into ball:** conglobe
" **into fabric:** knit
" **pert. to:** modal
" **philosophy:** eidos
formation: battle: herse, column, line
" **cell:** tissue
" **flesh:** sarcosis
" **sand:** dune
former: die, old late, prior, templet
" **prefix:** ex
formicid: ant
formless: chaotic, fluid, shapeless
" **comb. form:** amorph(o)
fortification: redoubt, bastion, ravelin
" **slope:** talus
" **work:** redan
fortune: hap, estate
" **goddess:** Tyche
" **teller:** sibyl, oracle, seer, palmist, prophetess
forty-five: degree angle: octant
" **inches:** ell
forty-third asteroid: Eros
fossil: relic, stone, fogy
" **egg:** ovulite
" **footprint:** ichnite
" **resin:** amber, retinite
" **shell:** dolite, balanite
" **toothlike:** conodont

founder metal: yet(t)er
fountain: well, fons, source
  " **god of:** Fons
  " **nymph:** naiad, Egeria
  " **of youth site:** Bimini
four: comb. form: tetra
  " **footed:** tetrapod, quad-ruped
  " **group of:** tetrad
  " **inches:** hand
fourgon: tumbril, van, car
fourteen pounds: stone
foveated: pitted
fowl: cock, chuck, bird, hen
  " **kinds of:** bantam, poult, malay, snipe, Houdan, Sussex
fox: female: vixen
  " **genus:** vulpes
  " **male:** stag
  " **paw:** pad
foxglove: popdock
  " **leaf:** digitalis
fragrant: balmy, aromatic
  " **ointment:** valerian, nard
  " **wood:** mimosa, aloe, cedar
fram: spear
framb(o)esia: yaws, pian
frame: bin, form, invent, humor
  " **bar of soap:** sess
  " **cloth stretching:** tenter
  " **glass making:** drosser
  " **skin drying:** herse
  " **supporting:** trestle, horse
France, French: art group: Fauves
  " **article:** see: "articles"
  " **assembly:** Senat
  " **beast:** bete

  " **decree:** arret
  " **dialect:** patois
  " **dry:** sec
  " **friend:** ami(e)
  " **God:** Dieu
  " **house:** maison
  " **inn:** Hotel, Auberge
  " **maid:** bonne
  " **measure:** kilo, minot, toise, centiare, kilaire
  " **museum:** musee
  " **noon:** midi
  " **pancake:** crepe
  " **pronoun:** moi, tu, elle(s), il(s), nous, nos, notre, vous, vos
  " **priest:** abbe
  " **railway station:** gare
  " **saying:** dit
  " **sister:** soeur
  " **son:** fils
  " **star:** etoile
  " **street:** rue
  " **water:** eau
  " **weight:** gros, gramme, kilo, livre, once, marc
  " **wood:** bois
Franciscan: Minorite, Capuchin, Cordelier
  " **nun:** Clare
francolin: titar, partridge, bird
frankincense: olibanum, thus, incense, gum
Franklin's nickname: Poor Richard
Franks, Frankish: hero: Roland
  " **king:** Clovis
  " **law:** salic
  " **peasant:** litus, liti
  " **pert. to:** salic
fratch: quarrel, dispute

fraxinus: ash, tree
fream: roar
freckle: spot, lentigo
" **remover:** adarce
Frederick the First: (nickname) Barbarossa
Frederick the Great: Alaric
free: lax, liss, slake, gratis, unbind
" **from bacteria:** sterile
" " **blame:** clear
" " **dirt:** apinoid
" " **discount:** net
" **-for-all:** melee
" **of charge:** buckshee
" **time:** leisure
freebooter: cateran, pirate
freedom: from fraud: bonafides
" " **pain:** aponia
" **of access:** entree
freeholder: yeoman
freemason: templar
freight: cargo, load, burden
" **car:** gondola, six
frese: furl, bend
freshet: spate, flood, inundation
Freudian term: ego, id
Freya's husband: Oder
friar: lister, monk, abbot
" **bird:** pimlico
" **black:** Dominican
" **gray:** Franciscan
" **mendicant:** servite
" **Robin Hood's:** Tuck
" **white:** Carmelite
friend: patron, ally, crony
" **faithful:** Achates, dog
" **false:** Judas, traitor
Friend: Quaker
" **church founder:** George Fox
friendly: amicable, benevolent
" **relations:** amity
" **understanding:** entente
Friendly Island: Tonga
Friendship author: Cicero
frieze: (Scot.) kelt, adorn
" **band:** taenia
frigate bird: iwa
Frigg(a): husband: Odin
" **maid:** Fulla
frill: ruche, jabot, ruffle
frog: polliwog, amphibian, hoarseness
" **comb. form:** batracho(s), rani
" **genus:** anura, rana, hyla
" **like:** ranine
" **pert. to:** batrachian
" **tree genus:** hyla
froise: pancake
from: fro
" **head to foot:** capapie
" **here:** hence
" **that time:** thence
" **the egg:** ab ovo
front: facade, fore, mien, brass, dial
" **extend the:** deploy
" **in:** anteal, forne, ahead
" **toward the:** anterior
frontiersman: Cody, Carson, Boone
frontlet: tiara, band, frontstall
fronton: jai-alai
frostfish: tomcod, smelt, scabbard, whitefish
frozen: iced, frappe, congealed
" **vapor:** frost, rime
fruit: outcome, yield, crop,

berry
" **aggregate:** etaerio, strawberry, raspberry, magnolia
" **blemish:** blet, spot
" **comb. form:** carpo
" **decay:** blet, rot
" **dry:** regma, legume, nut, achene
" **flesh:** pulp, pap
" **goddess:** Pomona
" **hybrid:** pomato
" **peddler:** coster
" **pert. to:** pomonic, pomonal
" **pulp:** pap
" **refuse:** marc
" **science of:** carpology
" **skin:** epicarp, rind, peel
" **tree genus:** olea
Fuegian: Ona
fugue: diatonic, tonal, theme, dorian
" **answer:** comes
" **special passage:** stretta
" **theme:** dux
fulcrum: prop, support, bait
" **oar:** thole, lock
full: replete, sated, mature, rotund
" **house:** SRO
" **of cracks:** rimose
" **sized:** adult, ripe
" **size draft or plan:** epure
" **suffix:** itous, ous, ose
fuller: earth: bole
" **herb:** teasel, teazel
fulmar: malduck, nelly, bird
fundamental: basic, original, primary, vital, elementary
" **trigonometry:** sine, cosine
funeral: exequies, interment

" **attendant:** mute
" **bell:** mortbell
" **oration:** elegy, encomium
" **pile:** pyre
" **song:** dirge, elegy, requiem
fungoid tissue: trama
fungus: mildew, mold, yeast
" **black:** ergot
" **cells or sacs:** asci
" **disease:** tinea, mycosis, framboesia
" **edible:** cepe, morel, truffle, blewits, mushroom
" **genus:** erysibe, amanita, tuber, boletus
" **parasitic:** ergot, aweto, tinea
" **plant:** uredo
fur: pelage, coat, hair, fitch, vair, nutria, sable
" **bearing animal:** marten, genet, mink, seal, otter
" **collection:** pelts
" **regal:** ermine
" **refuse:** kemp
furbelow: finery, ruffle
Furies: Dirae, Eumenides
" **avenging:** Erinyes
" **gracious:** Eumenides
" **the three:** Alecto, Megaera, Tisiphone
furlana: dance
fur-lined tippet: amice
furnace: smelter, kiln, stove
" **flue:** tewel, pipe, chimney
" **nozzle:** tuyere
" **part of:** bosh, grate
furniture style: Empire, Regency, Colonial, Sheraton,

Chippendale, Hepplewhite, Renaissance

furrow: trench, wrinkle, sulcus

" **having:** guttered, grooved, fluted

" **in a plank:** rabbet

" **minute:** stria

" **notch:** score

furrowing mark: feer, scratch

fur seal: ursal

furze: gorse, whin, plant

" **genus:** ulex

fuse: melt, solder, weld, combine

" **partially:** frit

fustanella: petticoat

fyke: net

fylfot: emblem, cross, swastika

G

G: gee
gabel(le): excise, tax, duty
gaberlunzie: beggar
gabion: basket, cage
gaby: fool, dunce
Gad: father: Jacob
  " **son:** Eri, Ozni
  " **tribe of:** Erites
gadoid,a: codfish, hake, haddock
gadus: fish, cod
gadwall: duck, fowl
Gael, Gaelic: Erse, Scot(ch), Manx
  " **clan:** Sept
  " **hero:** Ossian
  " **poem:** Duan
  " **spirit:** banshee, kelpy
  " **warrior:** Dagda
gainsay: deny, impugn, forbid
gait: shamble, lope
  " **of a horse:** canter, gallop, pace, trot
gaiter: puttee, spat

Galam: Shea
Galatea: beloved: Acis
  " **lover:** Pygmalion
Galician river: Styr, San
galimatias: gibberish
galingale: sedge, root
galiot: merchant ship, galley
galipot: barras, resin, sap
galleon: carrack, argosy, boat
  " **cargo:** oro
gallery: salon, museum, piazza
  " **open:** loggia
Gallic chariot: essed(e)
gallimaufry: hash, ragout, medley, hodgepodge
gallinaceous: rasorial
  " **bird:** turkey, pheasant, quail
gallinae: grouse, quails, rasores, peafowls
  " **order:** rasores
gallinipper: mosquito
gallinule: hen, rail, coot

galliwasp: lizard
galloon: lace, trimming
galluses: suspenders, braces
Galway island: Aran
gambler: dicer, blackleg
   " **accomplice:** shill
   " **stake of:** pot, pool
gambling: cube(s): dice, die
   " **pert. to:** aleatory
gamboge tree family: calaba
game: fun, sport, strategy
   " **board:** halma
   " **confidence:** bunko
   " **Gr.:** agon
   " **marbles:** taw
   " **Scot.:** shinty
   " **using fingers:** mora
gamic: sexual
gammon: ham, deceive, dupe, humbug, mislead
ganef: thief, ganov
Ganges River: dolphin: susu
   " **efflorescence:** Reh
   " **vessel:** puteli, putelee
gangrel: beggar
gangue: matrix
gannet: goose, fowl, solan
   " **family:** sula
ganoid fish: gar, bowfin, sturgeon
gapes: rictus
gapeseed: starer
gaping: open, ringent
   " **of plant capsule:** dehiscence
garden: patch, Eden
   " **of golden apples:** Hesperides
   " **protector:** Priapus
Garden City: Chicago
garfish: snook, hornbeak
garibaldi: blouse

garlic: chive, ramp
   " **root:** ramson, bulb
   " **segment:** clove
   " **wild:** moly
garment: wrap, dress, vestment
   " **ancient:** toga, chlamys
   " **bishop's:** cope, rochet, gremial, chimer
   " **fitted:** reefer
   " **knight's:** mail, tabard
   " **priest's:** alb, stole, amice
   " **rain:** poncho, slicker
   " **tuniclike:** tabard
garnet: jewel, pyrope, red
   " **berry:** currant
   " **black:** melanite
garret: loft, attic
garrot: fowl, tourniquet
garruline bird: jay
garth: yard, garden
garvie: sprat, fish
gas: damp, fume, vapor, reek, fuel
   " **charcoal:** oxan(e)
   " **charge with:** aerate
colorless: ketone, ethane, oxan(e)
   " **blue:** ozone
   " **comb. form:** aer, aero
   " **inert:** argon, xenon
   " **marsh:** methane
   " **non-flammable:** helium
   " **poisonous:** arsine, stibine
gasconade: vaunt, boast, bravado
gaseous: tenuous, thin, aeriform
   " **element:** radon, neon
   " **hydrocarbon:** ethane

gastropod: slug, limpet
" **ear-shaped:** abalone
" **genus:** harpa, nerita, oliva
" **marine:** murex, aplysia, tethys
gate: entry, portal
" **flood:** sluice
" **rear:** postern
gather: reap, muster, convene
" **and compare:** collate
gaucho: cowboy
" **knife:** bolo
" **lariat:** bolas
" **weapon:** machete
gaud: finery, trinket, adorn, bauble, ornament
gauffer: pleat, flute, crimp
gauge: size, type
" **pointer:** arm, hand
" **rain:** udometer
Gaul: France, (Lat.) Gallia
" **anc. people:** Remi, Celt
" **chariot:** esseda, esses
" **gods:** (thunder) Taranis, (vegetation) Esus, (river) Belisama
" **people:** Remi
" **priest:** Druid
gaulding: egret, heron, bird
gaum: heed, daub, understand
gauntlet: cuff, glove, challenge
gavial: crocodile
Gawain: brother: Gaheris
" **father:** Lot
" **son:** Lovel
gazelle: corinne, kudu, dama
" **Afr.:** mohr, admi
" **Asian:** ahu

" **four-horned:** chikara
" **Tibetan:** goa
Geb: father: Shu
" **offspring:** Isis, Osiris, Set
" **wife:** Nu, Nut
gecko: lizard, tarente
Gehenna: hell
gelatin: jelly, agar, collin
" **plate (printing):** bat
gem: stone, jewel
" **carved:** cameo
" **face:** bezel, facet
" **imitation:** glass, paste, strass
" **inlaying for:** crusta
" **measure:** carat
gemel: twin
geminate: coupled, paired, double
gemmation: budding
gemsbok: chamois, oryx, goat
gender: beget, sex, instrument
" **common to both:** epicene
general: vague, wide, broad
" **aspect:** facies
" **effect:** ensemble
genesis: nascency, origin, birth
geniculate: bent
genipap: fruit
" **tree dye:** lana
genos: family, clan, gens
genouillere: kneepiece, kneelet
gentle: tame, placid
" **music direction:** amabile
" **slope:** glacis

genu: flexure, bend
genuflect: curtsy, kneel, bend
genus: class, type, order, sort
    " **antelope:** oryx
    " **bear:** ursus
    " **bee:** apis
    " **beech:** fagus
    " **bivalve:** anomia, pinna
    " **cat:** felis
    " **dog:** canis
    " **duck:** aix, anas
    " **elm:** ulmus, celtis
    " **fox:** vulpes
    " **frog:** rana, anura
    " **goat:** capra
    " **hare:** lepus
    " **hog:** sus
    " **horse:** equus
    " **lizard:** uta, agama
    " **monkey:** cebus
    " **spider:** ateles
    " **oyster:** ostrea
    " **pigeon:** goura, columba
    " **sheep:** ovis
    " **spider:** agalena, aranea
    " **swan:** olor
    " **whale:** inia
    " **wolf:** canis
geode: voog, druse, nodule
geological: age: pliocene, cenozoic
    " **division:** eon, era, lias, trias, triassic
    " **epoch:** ecca, miocene, muav
    " **oldest period:** Archean, Jurassic, Lias
    " **stage:** riss
    " **vein angle:** hade
geomancy: divination
geometrical: body: lune, prism, sphere

    " **figure:** ellipse, solid, square
    " **line(s):** loci, locus
    " **point relating to curve:** acnode
    " **theory:** conics
geometry: coordinate: abscissa(s)
    " **rule:** theorem
    " **solid:** cube, cone, sphere
    " **term:** versor
geophagous: pical
geoponic: rural, bucolic, rustic
Georgia (Caucasus) island: Sapelo
    " **people:** Svan(e)
    " **queen:** Tamara
Georgia: (see special section)
Geraint's wife: Enid
gerefa: reeve, bailiff
gerent: manager, ruler
germ: virus, bug, spore
    " **fermenting:** zyme
    " **freedom from:** asepsis
    " **seed:** chit
German, Germany: Almain, Hun, Teuton
    " **about:** etwa
    " **article:** das, der, die, ein
    " **but:** aber
    " **child:** kind
    " **coin:** mark, thaler, krone, albus
    " **day:** tag
    " **dog:** hund
    " **foot:** fuss
    " **fruit:** obst
    " **god:** Wodan (Odin), Donar
    " **hill:** berg

" **lyric poems:** lieder
" **measure:** aam, kette, eimer
" **no:** nein
" **pronoun:** ich, du, sie, uns
" **valley:** tal
" **weight:** loth, tonne
" **woman:** frau
gesso: chalk, gypsum, plaster
get: secure, take, acquire
" **around:** cajole, circumvent
" **away:** scat, shoo, escape
geum: herb, avens, plant
gewgaw: bauble, trifle, bibelot
geyser: hot(spring)
" **mouth of:** crater
geyserite: opal
ghee: butter
Ghent: river: Lys, Schelde
ghost: haunt, daemon, spirit, lemures
" **comb. form:** scio
" **fish:** chiro
giant: jumbo, vast, colossus, gargantua
" **evil:** Loki, Jotun(n), Goliath
" **god (Norse):** Hymir, Hymer
" **Gr. myth:** Cottus, Cyclops, Gyges
" **Hindu:** Bana
" **hundred eyes:** Argus
" **land of:** Utgarthar
" **Old Testament:** Anak, Goliath
" **one-eyed:** Cyclops, Arges, Polyphemus
" **race of:** Anak
" **sea demon:** Wade

" **strong:** Titan
" **thousand-armed:** Bana
giaour: unbeliever, Christian
gibbet: gallows, jib
gibbous: convex, rounded
gibe: heckle, scoff
Gibralter: Cape: Trafalgar
" **founder of:** Gebir
" **point opposite:** Ceuta
gibus: hat
gift: talent, bent, favor, donation
" **conciliatory:** sop
gila monster: lizard
Gileadite judge: Jair
gilsonite: asphalt, uintaite
gimcrack: bauble, toy, trifle
gimmer: clasp, ewe
gin: snare, game, liquor
" **type of:** sloe
ginger: pep, spirit, spice
" **genus:** zingiber
" **pine:** cedar
" **wild:** asarum
gingerbread: cake, money
" **tree:** doom, dum
ginseng: aralia, plant, herb
giraffe: camelopard, piano, spinet
" **like animal:** okapi
girasol(e): opal, artichoke, sunflower
girdle: ring, obi, sash
" **pert. to:** zonal
" **Roman:** cestus
" **saddle:** cinch
" **sash:** cummerband
girl: chit, minx, damsel
" **cover:** model
" **graceful:** nymph, sylph
" **lively:** filly, giglet
gist: essence, nub, heart

give: waive, cede, impart, bestow
   " **back:** remise, remit, restore
   " **forth:** emit, proclaim
   " **law:** remise, devise, bequeath
   " **up:** cede, resign, render, devote
gizz: wig
glabrous: bald, slick
glacial: icy, frigid
   " **chasm:** crevasse
   " **deposit:** moraine, placer
   " **hill:** paha
   " **ice block:** serac
   " **ridge:** eskar, kame, os(ar), esker, as(ar)
   " **snow:** firn, neve
   " **waste deposit:** drift
glacier: erosion: cirque, corrie
   " **facing:** stoss
   " **shafts:** moulins
glad: happy, fain, blithe
   " **tidings:** evangel, gospel
glade: gap, clearing, vale
   " **comb. form:** nemo
gladiator: fencer, athlete, combatant
   " **competitions:** ludi
   " **trainer:** lanista
gland: organ, adrenal
   " **edible:** noix, liver, ris
   " **salivary:** parotid
   " **secretion:** hormone, insulin, saliva, adrenalin
glary: slick, frosty, slippery
glass: pane, goblet, lens
   " **artificial gems:** strass, paste
   " **blue:** smalt

   " **bubble in:** seed, ream
   " **ingredient:** silica, sand, potash
   " **jar:** bocal, mason
   " **make into sheets:** platten
   " **molten:** parison
   " **mosaic:** tessera
   " **scum:** gall
   " **small:** vial, pony
   " **volcanic:** obsidian
glassmaking: frame: drosser
   " **material:** frit(t)
   " **oven:** lehr, tisar
glasswort: kali, jume, plant
Glaucus: father: Sisyphus
   " **son:** Bellerophon
   " **wife:** lone
glazier: glassworker
   " **diamond:** emeril, emery
glazing machine: calender
glebe: sod, clod, soil, benefice
glebe bird: kite
gleed: coal, ember
gleeman: minstrel
gleg: keen, sharp, alert
gliadin: protein, glutin, prolamin
gliding over: labile, eliding
glioma: tumor
globe: earth, sphere
   " **fish:** diodon
   " **like:** orbed, globular
glockenspiel: lyra, carillon, xylophone
glonoin: nitroglycerin
glory: kudos, aureola, honor
   " **cloud of:** nimbus
glot: comb. form: languages
glottal stop: stoss
glove: gauntlet, mitt(en)

" **leather:** napa
" **shape:** trank
glucose: dextrose, honey
glucoside root: gein
glume: chaff, husk, bract
glutin: gelatin, gliadin
glutinous: viscid, sizy, tenacious
gluttony: greed, voracity, edacity
glycolaldehyde: diose, sugar
gnede: miserly, scanty, sparing
gnome: imp, gremlin, dwarf, nis, maxim
" **Ger.:** kobold
" **N.A.:** owl
gnomic: didactic, aphoristic
gnomon of a sundial: pin, style
gnostic: wise, clever
" **representation:** abrasax, abraxas
" **second century:** sethite
gnu: antelope, kokoon
go: sally, quit, proceed
" **about, nautical:** tack, wear
" **astray:** aberrate, err, diverge
" **away:** scram, depart, flee
" **back:** revert, return
" **forth:** fare, mosey, travel
goa: gazelle
goal: tally, end, meta, purpose
" **distant:** thule, reach, destination
goat: kid, billy, victim
" **Angora:** chamal
" **astronomy:** capircorn

" **cloth:** camlet, mohair
" **genus:** capra
" **like:** hircine, caprine, lewd
" **male:** buck, billy
goatfish: mullet
goatsucker: nighthawk, whippoorwill, potoo
gobbet: bit, lump, chunk, mass, fragment
goblet: glass, tallboy
" **constellation:** crater
" **Eucharistic:** chalice
goby: mapo, fish
God: deity, idol
" **false:** idol, Baal, Baalim
" **home of:** Olympus, Asgard
god(s): Aztec: Xipe, Eecati, Meztli
" **Buddhist:** Deva
" **Gr.:** Pan, Ares, Eros, Zeus, Pluto, Apollo, Hermes
" " **beauty:** Apollo, Helios
" " **dream:** Oniros
" " **hurricane:** Otus
" " **marriage:** Hymen
" " **underworld:** Python
" " **wine:** Bacchus
" **Roman:** Picus, Faun, Mars, Cupid, Apollo, Boreas, Neptune, Pan, Lar, Pales
" " **death:** Mors
" " **fire:** Vulcan
" " **night:** Somnus
" " **sleep:** Morpheus, Somnus
goddess(es): Dea
" **Egypt:** Mut, Amen, Iris, Sekhet

" " **heavens:** Nut
" " **joy:** Hathor
" " **life:** Isis
" " **sky:** Nut
" **Gr.:** Alea, Athena, Eris, Artemis, Aphrodite, Nemesis
" " **destiny:** Moera
" " **earth:** Gaea, Ge
" " **fire:** Hestia
" " **love:** Aphrodite
" " **moon:** Artemis, Astarte, Diana, Selene, Selena, Io
" **Hawaiian: fire:** Pele
" **Peru: fertility:** Mama
" **Roman:** Nox, Nyx, Diana, Ceres, Vesta
" " **beauty:** Venus
" " **dawn:** Aurora
" " **death:** Proserpine
" " **earth:** Lua, Tellus
" " **fertility:** Fauna
" " **flowers:** Flora
" " **harvest:** Ops
" " **love:** Venus
" " **night:** Nox, Nyx
" " **plenty:** Ops
" " **war:** Vacuna, Minerva
goddess(es): classification of:
" " **air:** Aura, Hera
" " **arts:** Muse, Athena
" " **birth:** Parca, Lucina
" " **chase:** Artemis, Diana
" " **destiny:** Moera, Norn
" " **faith:** Clotho, Fides
" " **halcyon days:** Alcyone

" " **hope:** Spes
" " **justice:** Astraea, Dice, Maat
" " **life:** Isis
" " **memory:** Mnemosyne
gold: oro, cyme, wealth, au(rum)
" **assaying cup:** cupel
" **black:** oil
" **coating:** gilt, gilding
" **collar:** carcanet
" **deposit:** placer
" **imitation:** ormolu, pinchbeck
" **in alchemy:** sol
" **like:** aureate
" **native:** nugget
" **pert. to:** auric
" **symbol:** au
Gold Coast: colony: Togo
" **language:** Twi, Fanti, Akan
" **negro stock:** Ga
golden: yellow, auric, precious
" **age:** Saturnian
" **fleece: land of:** Colchis
" " **seeker of:** Jason
" " **ship:** Argo
goldeneye: whistler, bird
goldenrod: genus: solidago
golem: dunce, booby, robot
goliard: minstrel, jester
gombeen: usury
gomeral: dolt, fool, simpleton
gomuti: ejoo, areng, palm
gonad: ovary, testis, spermary
gonagra: gout
Goneril: father: Lear
" **sister:** Regan, Cordelia

gonfalon: flag, banner, standard

good: palatable, moral, honest, valid
  " **arrangement:** eutaxie
  " **-for nothing:** shotten, ket
  " **luck cap, newborn:** caul
  " **working order:** kilter

goods: stock, effects
  " **admission of taking:** avowry
  " **cast overboard:** jetsam, flotsam
  " **law:** bona
  " **movable:** chattels
  " **package:** bale, box
  " **sunk at sea:** lagan

gook: Korean, Japanese, Oriental, Vietcong

goose: gannet, dupe, fowl
  " **barnacle:** anatifer
  " **cry:** cackle, honk
  " **flock:** gaggle, raft
  " **genus:** anser, chen
  " **relating to:** anserine
  " **wild:** barnacle
  " **young:** gosling

goosefoot: blite, shrub, plant

gore: pierce, stab
  " **of cloth:** gusset

Gorgon: Medusa, Stheno, Euryale
  " **watchers for:** Graeae, Deino, Enyo, Pephredo

Gorki, novelist: Maxim

gorse: whin, furze

gossip: cat, rumor, tattle, babble, prate, talebearer
  " **tattling:** piet

Gothic: medieval, barbarous
  " **arch:** ogive

  " **bard:** runer
  " **vault's groin:** ogive

gourd: melon, flask
  " **fruit:** pepo
  " **sponge:** loofa, luffa

government: regimen, rule, sway, policy
  " **by ten:** decarchy
  " **by women:** gynarchy, gynecocracy
  " **control:** regie, regimen
  " **form of:** polity
  " **without:** acracy, anarchy

gowan: daisy, flower

gowk: cuckoo, simpleton

Graces: mother of: Aegle
  " **one of:** Thalia, Aglaia, Euphrosyne

gracile: slender, slim, sylphic

gradient: ascent, slope, incline

gradus: dictionary

graft: cion, joint, bribe
  " **taker:** bribee

grafted heraldry: ente

grail: sangreal, bowl, chalice, cup, ama
  " **knight of:** Percivale, Galahad, Bors

grain: seed, atom, iota, particle
  " **black:** urd
  " **husk:** glume, bran
  " **measure:** grist, moy, peck, bushel
  " **pit:** silo
  " **refuse:** pug, chaff
  " **shelter:** hutch, barn
  " **to be ground:** grist

gramary: magic

gramineous: grassy

grammar: logic and/or rhet-

oric: trivia, trivium
grammatical: arrangement: syntax
" **case:** dative
" **construction:** synesis
" **term:** parse, gender
grampus: orc(a), whale, killer
grandchild: oe, oy(e)
" **great:** ieroe
grandfather: patriarch, ancestor, atavus
" **pert. to:** aval, avital
Grandma Moses: Anna
grandmother: granny, beldam(e), (Rus.) babushka
" **Devil's:** Baba
granite: constituent of: mica, quartz, orthoclase, feldspar
" **porphyry:** elvan
grant: admit, confer, bestow
" **of rights:** charter, deed, franchise
grape: fruit, berry
" **bunch of:** bob
" **genus:** vitis, muscadinia
" **like berry:** uva
" **wine disease:** erinose
grappling iron: grapnel
grasp: hent, comprehend, grip, close
grasping: miserly, avid, rapacious
" **adapted for:** prehensile, prehensive
grass: sod, turf
" **bamboolike:** reed
" **blade of:** traneen, leaf, spike
" **bunch:** stipa
" **devil's:** couch
" **dried:** hay, fodder

" **genus:** coix, stipa, poa, avena
" **husk:** glume
" **Kentucky blue:** poa
" **rope-making:** mung
grasshopper: grig, locust, katydid
gratinate: cook, brown, crisp
gratis: free, gratuitous
gratulation: joy
graupel: sleet, hail
gravamen: grievance, complaint
grave: tomb, quiet, carve
" **cloth:** cerement, shroud
" **mound:** barrow, tumulus
gravid: pregnant
gray: old, hoary, ashen, grizzled
" **comb. form:** polio
" **matter:** brains, obex, cortex, intellect
greasewood: chico, chamiso, shrub
great: huge, eminent, titanic
" **artist:** master
" **comb. form:** magni, mega(lo)
greaves: cracklings, armor, cracknel
grebe: dabchick, fowl
gree: good will
Greece, Greek: Crete, Hellene, Achaia
" **abbess:** Amma
" **assembly:** agora, pnyx
" **clan:** Obe
" **coin:** diobol(on), obol(us), drachma, lepta, ducat, nomas, mina, phenix
" **column:** doric, ionic
" **contest:** agon

" **cupid:** Eros
" **dance:** hormos, strophe
" **drama:** mime
" **drinking cup:** holmos, cotyle
" **epic:** Iliad, Odyssey
" **Furies:** Erinyes, Alecto, Megaera, Tisiphone
" **garment:** chiton, peplos, chlamys
" **headband:** taenia
" **huntress:** Atalanta
" **life:** bios
" **market place:** agora
" **measure:** bema, cados, dichas, hektos, stremma
" **note, music:** nete
" **pitcher:** olpe
" **priest:** papa
" **sacred place:** Abaton
" **soothsayer:** Calchas
" **theater:** odeon
" **tunic:** chiton
" **wine pitcher:** olpe
" **word:** logos
green: verd, unripe, unskilled
" **eyed:** jealous
" **sand:** marl
greenfinch: linnet, sparrow, grosbeak
greenheart: bebeeru, wood
greenlet: vireo, songbird
greenroom: foyer, gossip
grego: jacket, cloak
Gregorian doxology: Euouae
gribble: borer
gride: scrape, rasp
grieve: lament, weep, agonize
griffe: mulatto, spur
griffin: monster, vulture

grifter: conman
" **assistant:** shill
grilse: salmon, fish
grimalkin: cat, moll, woman
grinding: stone: metate, mano
" **substance:** emery, abrasive
gringo: Americano, foreigner
gripple: avaricious, miserly
Griqua: mulatto
griskin: loin
grit: sand, pluck, gravel
grith: sanctuary, peace, security
grivet: waag, tota, monkey
grommet: eyelet, ring, loop
groove: rut, score, routine
" **cut in barrel:** rifle, croze
" **in masonry:** raggle
" **minute/pilaster:** stria
grosbeak: finch, cardinal, sparrow
grotto: cave, cavern, grot
ground: base, foundation, pulverized
" **parcel of:** solum, plot
" **rising:** hurst, knoll
ground hog: marmot, woodchuck
" **day:** Candlemas
group: band, squad, cluster, congregation
" **of species:** phylum, genus
" **together:** file, cluster, band, meet
grouse: bird, complain, grumble
" **gathering of:** lek
" **genus:** bonasa
grout: meal, grounds, sedi-

ment, dregs

grove: tope, thicket, copse
" **pert. to:** nemoral

grow: become, wax, develop, augment
" **old:** senesce, age, ripen
" **in couples:** binate
" **out:** enate

growth: shoot, corn, stubble, increase
" **process of nascency:** development
" **retarding:** paratonic

grue: ice, snow

gruff: short, blunt

grugru: palm, larva

grume: clot

grumous: thick, clotted

grunt fish: ronco, croaker

Grus: crane, constellation

guachoncho fish: pelon

guaiac: tonka bean, seed

guanay: cormorant
" **droppings:** guano

guano: manure, fertilizer
" **source of:** bats, guanay

guarapucu: wahoo, shrub

guardian: trustee, warden, angel
" **church relics:** mystago-gue
" **subject of:** ward
" **watchful:** Argus

Guatemalan, Guatemala:
grass: teosinte
" **insect:** kelep
" **money:** que(t)zal
" **plain:** Peten
" **volcano:** Fuego, Atitlan

gudgeon: dupe, gull

guenon: mona, monkey, grivet

guerdon: reward, recom-pense, prize

guiding: polar, dirigent
" **star:** Lodestar, North, Cynosure

guidon: flag, streamer, marker

Guido's scale: note in: ut, e la, e la mi
" **highest note:** e la
" **low note:** ut

guile: fraud, craft, wiles

guillemot: auk, quet, bird

Guinea: coin, fowl
" **corn:** durra, millet
" **fowl:** pintado
" **native:** Susu, Fulani, Malinke
" **pig, animal like:** pika
" **squash:** eggplant

guinea pig: rat, paca, cavy
" **genus:** cavia
" **male:** boar

guitar: tiple
" **India:** vina
" **oriental:** sitar
" **small:** uke

guitguit: bird, honey, creeper

gula: cyma, gullet

gulf: pit, gap, abysm, eddy
" **weed:** sargasso

gull: larid, bird, dupe
" **like:** jaeger, skua, teaser
" **pert. to:** larine

gully: arroyo, gorge

gum: resin, wax
" **Ar. tree:** kikar
" **astringent:** kino
" **boil:** parulis, abscess
" **plant:** ule, hule
" **white:** camphor
" **wood:** xylan

gumma: tumor
gums: uva
gun: rod, arm, weapon
" **caliber:** bore
" **chamber:** gomer
" **handle:** stock
" **lock part:** catch, sear
" **pointer:** device
" **sight:** bead
gunnel: fish, blenny, gunwhale
gunwale pin: thole
gurgitation: surging, whirling
gurnard: rochet, fish
" **genus:** trigla
gusset: gore, insert, bracket
gutta: drop, spot, treenail

" **percha:** balata
guttle: gorge, gormandize
guttural: husky, velar, gruff
gym feat: kip(p)
gymnosophist: nudist
gynoecium: pistil(s)
gypsy: nomad, wanderer
" **devil:** beng
" **fortune:** bahi
" **girl:** chai, chi
" **husband:** rom
" **man:** chal
" **thief:** chor
gyre: ring, vortex, eddy
gyrene: sl: marine, leatherneck
gyves: irons, fetters, shackles

H

H, letter: aitch
habergeon: jacket, hauberk
habile: apt, fit, clever, handy
habit: dress, usage, garb, routine
" prefix: eco
habitually silent: taciturn, reserve
habituate: inure, drill, frequent
" to weather/surroundings: acclimate
hachure: lines
hack: ax, hoe, cough, taxi, stale
" driver: cabbie
" literary: devil, poetaster, scribbler
" worker: jobber
hackbut: harquebus
hackney: fly, fiacre
" driver: jarvey
Hades: pit, hell, orcus, Pluto, aralu, sheol
" abyss below: Tartarus
" guard of: Cerberas
" related to: abyss, limbo
" river: Styx, Lethe, Acheron
" wheel-turner in: ixion
hadj: pilgrimage
hagfish: cyclostome
haha: laugh, wall, fence
haiku: poem
hair: tress, fur, nap, shag, filament
" band: fillet
" braid: cue, pigtail
" coarse: seta
" comb. form: pil(o), tricho, chaet(o)
" covered with: pilose, lanate, shaggy
" disease of: mange, xerasia, plica
" falling out of: psilosis
" mass of: shock
" nostril: vibrissa

  " **pigment:** melanin
  " **prefix:** crini
  " **tuft:** floccus
  " **unruly:** cowlick
hairiness: pilosity, villosity
hairpin: bodkin
Haiti, Haitian: Hispaniola
  " **coin:** gourde
  " **evil spirit:** bako, baka
  " **sweet potato:** batata
  " **voodoo deity:** zombi(e)
hake: gadid, whiting
  " **kin of:** cod
half: demi, semi, hemi, moiety, partial
  " **baked:** sophomoric, amateurish
  " **breed:** mestee, metis(se)
  " **brother:** half-sib(ling)
  " **man, half bull:** bucentaur
  " **man, half dragon:** cecrops
  " **man, half fish:** dagon, mermaid
  " **man, half goat:** Pan, faunus
  " **man, half horse:** centaur
  " **mask:** loup, domino
  " **moon:** arc, lune, crescent
  " **month:** fortnight
  " **turn:** caracole
halibut: sole, butt, flatfish
Halicarnassus' wonder: mausoleum
halite: (rock)salt
halitus: aura, vapor, breath
hall: dorm, atrium, salle, vestibule

  " **concert:** odeum
  " **heroes:** Valhalla
  " **round:** rotunda
halluces: digits
hallux: (big, great) toe
halogen: iodine, bromine, chlorine
  " **compound:** halide
halting place: inn, oasis, etape, caravansary
ham: hock, meat, actor
  " **hog:** gammon
  " **slice:** rasher
Hamite: Berber, Libyan, Masai, Somal(i)
  " **language of:** numidian
Hamlet: beloved: Ophelia
  " **castle:** Elsinore
  " **country:** Denmark
  " **friend:** Horatio
  " **uncle of:** Claudius
hammer: beat, bang, maul, malleate
  " **auctioner's:** gavel
  " **ear:** malleus
  " **head of:** poll, peen
  " **part of:** claw, peen, head
  " **striking part:** tup
hammerhead: bat, bird, fish, shark
hamstring: maim, lame, tendon, cripple
hanaper: basket, hamper
hand: paw, pud, manus, aid, help, deal, applause
  " **by:** manual
  " **cart:** barrow
  " **clap to music:** tal
  " **comb. form:** chiro
  " **jurist:** learned
  " **measure:** span

" **palm of:** loaf, volar, thenar

handbill: flyer, poser, leaf, throwaway

handle: hilt, grip, operate, manage, wield
" **boat's:** tiller
" **cup's:** ear
" **having:** ansate
" **printing press:** raunce
" **roughly:** paw, maul
" **sword:** hilt

handrail: (kind of) manrope

hands: having two: bimanous
" **on hips:** akimbo
" **pert. to:** manual
" **without:** amanous

handsel: token, present, earnest

handwriting: fist, script, penmanship
" **bad:** cacography
" **expert:** chirographer
" **on the wall:** graffiti, tekel, mene
" **pert. to:** graphic
" **style:** character

handwritten: document/will: holograph

hangar: shelter, shed, (air)drome
" **area:** apron

hangbird: oriole

hanging: suspended, unsettled, pendent
" **apparatus:** gibbet, gallows
" **crookedly:** alop
" **downward:** cernous
" **noose of hangman:** halter

hangrail: whitlow

hank: loop, coil, skein

Hannibal: conquered by: Scipio
" **father:** Hamilcar
" **defeat:** Zama
" **victory site:** Cannae

hanse: guild, league

Hansen's disease: leprosy

happen: befall, occur, fare, transpire
" **again:** recur
" **in the end:** eventuate
" **together:** concur, coincide

happening: event, incident, tiding, occasion
" **before due:** premature, rath(e)
" **by chance:** fortuitous

hara-kiri: suicide, seppuku

harbor: haven, cherish, cove, shelter
" **boat:** tug
" **laborer:** stevedore
" **small:** marina
" **wall:** jetty

hard: rigid, dour, solid, adamant, stern
" **bed:** pallet
" **cash:** specie
" **fat:** suet
" **prefix:** dis
" **rubber:** ebonite

hardhack: rose, shrub, spirea

hardhead: sculpin, menhaden

hardtack: wafer, bread, pantile

hardwood: ash, oak, elm, teak, ebony, yakal, hickory, mahogany

hare: cony, pika, malkin, ro-

dent
" **family:** leporid
" **female:** doe
" **genus:** lepus
" **male:** buck
" **tail:** scut
" **young:** leveret
harem: serai, zenana, seraglio
" **room:** oda
" **slave:** odalisk, odalisque
hari-kari: see hara-kiri
haricot: stew, (kidney)bean
harlot: rahab, strumpet
harmattan: wind
harness: gear, rig, equip, draft
" **bull:** cup
" **horse:** tackle, headgear
" **men's:** bricole
" **ring:** terret
" **strap:** crupper
harrier: dog, hawk, falcon
harsh: stern, coarse, rasping, drastic
" **critic:** slater
" **sound:** roar, stridon
" **sounding:** strident
" **taste:** bitter, acerb
hart: stag, deer
hartebeest: tora, asse, antelope, bontebok, lecama
" **kin of:** sassaby
hartshorn: antlers
hartstongue: fern
haruspex: priest, soothsayer
harvest: reap, crop, yield
" **bug:** tick, chigger
" **feast:** Kirn
" **festival:** Lammas
" **man:** daddy-longlegs
hashish: hemp, bhang, can-

nabis
hashmark: stripe
hask: dry, cold, harsh, coarse
hassock: pess, boss, buffet, cushion
hasty pudding: mush, supawn
hat: cap, toque, beret, headgear, sconce
" **brimless:** fez, toque
" **collapsible:** gibus
" **crown:** poll
" **ecclesiastic:** biretta
" **medieval:** abacot, bycoket
" **part:** band, brim, lining
" **sl.:** lid
" **trimming:** vouleau
" **pert. to:** castorial
" **pith:** topi, topee
" **straw:** boater
hatchet: ax(e), tomahawk
" **handle:** helve
" **stone:** mogo
" **type:** claw, lathing
hate: abhor, detest, phobia, malice
" **comb. form:** mis(o)
" **of foreigners:** xenophobia
hatred: enmity, odium, animosity, dislike
" **of change:** misoneism
" **of children:** misopedia
" **of mankind:** misanthropy
" **of marriage:** misogamy
" **of women:** misogyny
haulm: hay, straw, stem, stalk, culm
hautboy: oboe, strawberry
have: own, hold, retain, pos-

sess
" **effect:** tell
" **feet:** pedate
" **limits:** finite
" **offensive smell:** olid
" **scruples:** demur
" **same origin:** cognate
haver: oat, babble, nonsense
Hawaii, Hawaiian: (see special section) Kanaka, Polynesian
" **basket:** ie
" **canoe:** waapa
" **chant:** mele
" **cookout:** luau
" **dance:** hula
" **fiber:** pulu
" **food:** poi, taro, kalo
" **garment:**   holoku, muumuu
" **temple:** heiau
" **woman:** wahine
hawk: cheater, sell, cry, osprey, vulture
" **bill of:** pawl
" **blind:** seel
" **cage:** mew
" **carrier:** cad
" **claw:** talon
" **falconry:** bater
" **fish:** osprey
" **genus:** buteo, accipiter
" **male:** tercel
" **nest:** aery
" **small:** kite, eyas
" **swoop of:** souse
hay: net, bed, fence, grass, hedge
" **bundle:** bale, rick, wisp
" **kind of:** clover, alfalfa, timothy
" **second cutting:** rewen

" **spreader:** tedder
" **storage:** mow, loft
haying job: ted
haze: fog, film, vapor, glin
" **thin:** gauze
hazel: nut, tree, birch, wood, shrub
head, hd.: pate, mind, capita, chief
" **and shoulders:** bust
" **and shoulders cover:** nubia
" **armor:** movion
" **comb. form:** cephal(o)
" **garland:** chaplet
" **membrane covering:** caul, omentum
" **shaved:** tonsure
headband: agal, fillet, taenia
headdress: diadem, wig, tiara
" **bishop:** miter
" **cobra:** uraeus
" **military:** busby, shako
" **nun:** cornet, wimple
headhunter: dayak
headless: etete, acephalous, leaderless
headlong: rashly, pellmell, recklessly
" **fall:** cropper
" **flight:** lam
headspring: origin, source, fountain
headstone: stele, barrow
hearing: oyer, audition, trial
" **instrument:** audiometer, stethoscope
" **keen:** hyperacusia
" **of:** aural, otic
" **organ:** otocyst
heart: spirit, cardia, core, essence

"   **bleeding:** dicentra
"   **(largest) blood vessel:** aorta
"   **part:** auricle, ventricle
"   **point:** fess
heartburn: envy, pyrosis, water brash, jealousy
hearth: ling, home, fireside
"   **goddess of:** Vesta, Hestia
heartsease: pansy, wallflower
heat: fever, calor, anger, zeal, intensity
"   **animal:** rut, estrus
"   **comb. form:** thermo, thermy
"   **decomposition by:** pyrolysis
"   **measuring device:** calorimeter
"   **unit:** calorie, btu, therm(e)
heated: hot, angry
"   **white:** candent
"   **wine:** regus
heath: pipe, moor, erica, azalea
"   **bird:** grouse, blackcock
heather: ling, gorse, bilberry, crowberry
heaven: glory, zion, elysium, firmament
"   **comb. form:** urano
"   **description of:** uranology
"   **belt of:** zodiac
heavenly: celestial, divine, ethereal
"   **being:** angel, cherub, seraph(im)
"   **body:** moon, sun, star, planet, meteor, comet

"   **bread:** manna
"   **path:** orbit
hebdomad: seven, week
hebetate: stupid, blunt, dull
Hebrew, Hebraic: Israelite, Semite
"   **ancestor:** Eber
"   **bible books:** nebiim
"   **canonical book:** talmud
"   **coin:** gerah, shekel
"   **festival:** seder, purim
"   **horn:** shofar
"   **measure:** kab, kor, hin
"   **weight:** omer, gerah
"   **universe:** olam
hecatomb: sacrifice, slaughter
Hecuba: children of: Hector, Paris, Troilus, Cassandra
"   **husband of:** Priam
heddle: caam
hedge: fence, waver, boma, barrier
"   **form a:** plash
"   **part:** privet
"   **trash:** brash
hedgehog: urchin, porcupine
"   **animal like:** tenrec
"   **spine:** quill
heel: tap, cad, list, tilt, louse, calx
"   **bone:** fibula, calcaneus
"   **comb. form:** talo
hegemonic: ruling, leading
hegira: flight, journey, exodus
"   **destination:** medina
hegumen: abbot
height: alt, apex, top, summit, climax
"   **of great:** skyey
"   **of play's action:** catastasis

Hejaz: holy city: Mecca, Medina

held: gripped, detained
" **in music:** tenato
" **in trust:** fiduciary

Helen of Troy: abductor: Paris
" **daughter:** Hermione
" **husband:** Menelaus
" **mother:** Leda
" **son:** Norus
" **suiter:** Ajax

helianthus: sunflower
helico: comb. form: spiral
Helios: sun, god, Apollo
" **daughter of:** Circe
" **father of:** Hyperion
" **sister of:** Artemis

heliotrope: turnsole, bloodstone, sunflower, girasol
helix: snail, spiral, mollusk
helmet: hat, sallet, morion, casque
" **decoration:** panache
" **front:** ventail
" **lower part:** beaver
" **Roman:** Galea
" **visor:** armet

helminth: worm (tape or round), parasite
helot: esne, serf, slave
hem: edge, sew, border, encircle
" **in:** fence, crowd, invest
" **stiffening cloth:** wigan
hemipterous insect: lick, aphid, bedbug
hemlock: yew, weed, poison, kex, abies
" **alkaloid:** conin(e)
" **poison:** bennet
hemp: plant, fiber, tow, pita, ramie
" **Afr.:** ife
" **drug:** hashish
" **E. Indies:** dunn
" **fiber:** tow, sisal
" **Gr.:** kannabis
" **leaves:** kef, bhany
" **shrub:** pua
" **source:** cannabis

hen: layer, pullet, cackler
" **brooding:** sitter
" **extinct:** heath
" **hawk:** redtail
" **house:** coop
" **mud:** rail
" **spayed:** poulard
" **young:** chicken

henbane: nightshade, hyoscyamus
" **content:** hyoscin
henbit: mint, plant
hence: ergo, thus, off, then, so, away, therefore
henna: dye, shrub, alcana
hepatic: liver-shaped, liverwort
Hephaestus: Vulcan
Hera: husband of: Zeus, Jupiter
" **mother of:** Rhea
" **of Romans:** Juno
" **son of:** Ares
" **rival of:** Io, Leda, Themis

heraldic: bay, armorial
" **band:** orle, fillet, tressure
" **cross:** patte, patee
" **design:** seme
" **mastiff:** alan
" **triangle:** giron
" **star:** estoile
" **shield:**

" " **border:** orle, bordure
" " **boss:** umbo
" " **division:** ente, canton
" " **horizontal band:** fess
" " **side segments:** flanch
" " **stripe:** pale
heraldry: ente, armory
" **bar, horizontal:** label
" **bearing:** orle, saltire
" **bend:** cotise
" **bird:** martlet
" **broken:** rompu
" **chaplet:** orle
" **colter:** laver
" **creature:** bisse, lion, cannet, griffon, martlet, pard
" **division:** pale, paly
" **dog:** alant
" **footless bird:** martlet
" **factor:** gene
" **five:** pean
" **headless:** etete
" **pointed:** urde
" **standing:** statant
" **subject of:** armory, coat of arms, genealogy
" **winged:** vol, aile
herb: grass, catnip
" **aromatic:** mint, ginger, anise, dill, basil, anet, rosemary
" **aromatic rout:** nondo
" **aster family:** arnica
" **bean family:** pea, lotus
" **bitter:** rue, aloe, tansy, gentian
" **carrot family:** parsley, lorage, eringo, fennel, dill
" **flowering:** hepatica

" **forage:** sulla
" **fragrant:** balm
" **genus:** ruta, geum, aletris
" **gourd family:** melon, squash
" **laxative:** senna
" **magic:** moly
" **mustard family:** cress
" **pea family:** mimosa, lotus
" **perennial:** sego, sedum
" **pod:** ocra, okra
" **starchy:** pia
" **strong smelling:** rue, yarrow
" **use of:** food, seasoning, medicine
" **wooly:** poly
herbivore: tapir, vegetarian
Hercules: strong man, constellation
" **monster slain by:** Hydra
" **parent of:** Zeus, Alcmene
" **victim of:** Nessus
" **wife of:** Hebe, Deianira
herd: crowd, flock, shoal, corral
" **animals together:** pod
" **of horses:** caviya, harras
" **of whales:** gam, pod
" **grass of:** redtop, timothy
herdsman: drover, cowboy, vaquero, gaucho, wrangler
" **constellation:** bootes
" **god:** Pales
" **stick of:** goad
heredity: line, inheritance
" **factor:** gene
herl: fly, barb

Hermes: Mercury
" **birthplace:** Cyllene
" **father:** Zeus
" **mother:** Maia
" **winged cap:** petasos, petasus
" **winged shoes:** talaria
hermit crab: pagurian
hero: ace, idol, topnotcher, demigod
" **legendary:** Amadis, Roland, Paladin
" **lover of:** leander
Herodias: daughter: Salome
" **husband:** Herod, Antipas
heron: rail, soco, crane, egret
herring: raun, alewife, anchory, cisco, pilcher
" **barrel:** cade, cran
" **catch:** tack
" **canned:** sardine
" **family:** pilchard
" **female:** raun
" **genus:** clupea
" **young:** brit, sprat, sprot
hership: raid, loot, foray
hery: praise, glorify, worship
hesped: oration, eulogy
Hesperia: Italy, Spain, butterfly, Western land
Hesperus: (evening)Star, Venus
" **father:** Astraeus
" **fate of:** wreck
" **mother:** Eos
hessonite: garnet
hest: bid, pledge, promise, injunction
hetero: comb. form: different, (an)other
" **opposed to:** homo

heterogynous insect: bee, ant
hetman: ataman, headman
heu: alas
hexad: sextet
hexapod: six-footed
hexastich: poem, stanza, sestet, strophe
hexose: sugar
Hezekiah: kingdom: Judah
" **mother:** Abi
Hiawatha: bark: canoe
" **grandmother:** Nokomis
" **mother:** Wenonah
hickory: pecan, shellbark, butternut
hidage: tax
hidalgo: nobleman
" **state capital:** Pachuca
hide: bury, skin, cloud, leather, suppress, hoodwink
" **calf/lamb:** kip
" **safe keeping:** cache
" **raw:** shagreen
" **undressed:** pelt, kip
" **worker:** tanner
hiemal: wintry, brumal
hiero: comb. form: holy, sacred
hieroglyphics key: Rosetta
high: tall, chief, sharp, exalted, important
" **-brow:** egghead, intelligentsia
" **comb. form:** alti
" **crime:** treason
" **flying:** icarian, pretentious
" **-mighty:** arrogant
" **priest:** Eli
" **sounding:** sonorous
" **water:** flood

highest: summa, supreme, upmost
" **comb. form:** aero
" **mountain:** Everest
" **note (music):** ela
" **point:** apex, peak, zenith
" **possible:** maximal, maximum
highlander: Scot, Tartan, Gael
" **garment:** kilt
" **pants:** trews
" **pouch:** sporran
" **sword:** claymore
highway: road, avenue, turnpike, freeway
" **Alaska-Canada:** Alcan
" **Ger.:** autobahn
" **Roman:** iter, avian
" **-man:** pad, hijacker, rider
hill: pile, mount, heap, ascent, colline
" **builder:** ant
" **cone-shaped:** brae
" **dugout:** abri
" **flat-topped:** mesa
" **glacial:** kame
" **on a plain:** butte
" **pointed:** tor
" **rounded:** knob, morro
" **sand:** dune
" **small:** mound
" **top:** crest, brow
hillock: tump, hurst, knoll
" **over grave:** tumulus
Himalaya, Himalayan: Nepalese
" **animal:** ounce, Panda
" **antelope:** goral, serow
" **cedar:** deodar
" **herb:** atis
" **teu:** aucuba

hind: back, rear, stag, peasant, posterior
" **animal's leg:** ham
" **brain:** cerebellum
hinddeck: poop
Hindu, Hindustani: Urdu, Babu, Koli, Tamil, Hindoo
" **age of the world:** yuga
" **ancestor:** manu
" **bible:** veda
" **coin:** ana, pie, rupee
" **drink:** soma
" **ejaculation:** om, um
" **garment:** sari, saree
" **guitar:** sitar
" **hymn:** mantra
" **paradise:** Nirvana
" **philosophy:** yoga, tamas
" **prayer rug:** asan, asana
" **social division:** caste
" **tunic:** jama(h)
" **weight:** ser, tola, tael, maund
hinny: mule, neigh, whinny
" **parent of:** horse, donkey
hip: coxa, ilia, fruit, haunch
" **boots:** waders
" **bone:** pelvis, ilium
" **joint disease:** coxalgia
" **pert. to:** iliac, sciatic
hippo: comb. form: horse
Hippocrates: birthplace: Cos, Kos
" **drug of:** mecon (opium)
hippopotamus: seacow, behemoth, pachyderm
hirple: limp, hobble
hirsel: herd, land, flock
hirsute: rough, course, hairy, shaggy
hispid: bristly, spiny, strigose

hiss: sizz, whiz, assibitate
" **sign of:** disapproval, hatred
hist: hark, hush, shush
historical: real, factual, authentic
" **period:** era
" **records:** annals, chronicles
" **muse:** Clio
hit: bop, ace, sock, pommel, success
" **aloft:** lob
" **direct:** bull's-eye
" **hard:** slug
" **lightly:** tap
" **or miss:** aimless, casual
" **sl.:** wed, marry
hitchpost: picket
hitherto: ago, yet, before, until now
Hitler, Adolp(h): aerie: Berchtesgaden
" **chosen race:** Aryan
" **follower of:** Nazi
" **occupation:** house painter
" **rank:** corporal
" **title:** Der fu(e)hrër
" **wife:** Eva Braun
Hittite: Syrian
" **ancestor:** Heth
" **capital:** Pteria
" **storm god:** Teshub
hive: box, gum, skep, swarm, apiary, multitude
hives: uredo, allergy, urticaria
" **cement for:** propolis,
" **remedy for:** benadryl
ho!: whoa, halt, stop, long, desist
hoarfrost: rag, rime

hoarseness: croup, frog, croup
hoactzin: bird
hobbil: dolt, clown, idiot, dunce
hobnail: rustic
hobo: bo, bum, tramp, vagrant, vagabond
" **bedding/bundle:** bindle
" **camp:** jungle
" **food:** mulligan (stew)
Hobson's choice: take-it-or-leave-it
hock: ham, hox, pawn, joint, wine
" **ailment of joint:** spavin
" **of humans:** ankle
hockey: bandy, shinny
" **disk:** puck
" **goal:** cage
" **stick:** caman
" **trophy:** Stanley (Cup)
hod: soil, scuttle, barrow
hodgepodge: ana, mess, stew, cento, medley, gallimaufry
hog: pig, swine, grunter, shilling
" **cholera:** rouget
" **cured side:** flitch
" **fat:** lard, adeps
" **food:** mash, swill
" **genus:** sus
" **female:** sow, gilt
" **male:** boar
" **young:** shoat, shote
hog peanut: earthpea
hog plum: amra
hogback: ridge
hogfish: porpoise, scorpene
hognose: sand viper
hognut: pignut, ouabe,

earthnut

hogo: taint, flavor, stench

hogshead: cask, barrel, vessel

" **content of:** beer

hogtie: truss, clog, fetter

hogwash: draff, swill, refuse

hoi polloi: mob, masses, rabble, populace, common people

hoiden: tomboy

hoist, hoisting: cat, jack, lift, heave, raise, derrick

" **anchor:** weigh

" **device:** crane, winch

" **off bottom:** atrip

" **-man:** engineman, bandsman

" **sail:** swig

hold: bind, grasp, clutch, occupy, adhere

" **a brief for:** defend

" **attention:** interest

" **back:** detain

" **due to war:** intern

" **fast:** grip

" **forth:** offer

" **off:** avert

" **over:** delay

" **out:** endure

" **ship's:** hatch

" **up:** rob, (sl.) heist

" **water:** sound

holder: haven, tenant, payee

" **of a lease:** renter, lessee

holding: asset, tenure, property

" **adapted for:** prehensile

" **device:** vise, tongs, clamp

hole: bay, pit, cove, cavity, opening

" **air:** spiracle

" **animal's:** den, lair, burrow

" **cloth:** eyelet

" **instr. for making:** awl, bore, drill, stiletto

holes, full of: perforated

holia: fish, salmon

holiday: fete, fiesta, festival, outing, recess, vacation

" **kind of:** Roman, Easter, weekend, Mardi Gras

Holland: Dutch, Netherlands, cloth

" **coin:** doit, raps, florin, stiver

" **dialect:** Frisian, Frunkish

" **gin:** geneva, ochnapps

" **merchant's league:** Hanse

" **townhall:** stadhouse

" **weight:** ons, lood, pond, Koorel

hollow: cave, hole, empty, sunken, gaunt, socket

" **boggy:** slak

" **comb. form:** coelo

" **circular:** corrie

" **cylinder:** tuble

" **opposed to:** solid

" **sound:** hoot

" **title:** key

holly: assi, holm, ilex, acebo, yapon

" **pert. to:** ilicic

holm: oak, ait, islet, bottoms

" **oak:** ilex, holly

Holmes, Sherlock: detective

" **alter ego:** Watson

" **creator of:** Conan Doyle

" **expression:** elementary

holobaptist: immersionist

holt: hill, woods, copse, grove, willows

holy: pious, devout, hallow, sacred, inviolate, spiritual

" **city:** Rome, Mecca, Kiev, Zion, Medina, Jerusalem

" **comb. form:** hagio, hiero

" **communion:** eucharist

" **cross:** rood

" **Grail:** chalice, sangraal

" **Grail finder:** Galahad

" **land:** Palestine

" **land visitor:** palmer, pilgrim

" **oil:** chrism

" **picture:** icon

" **water container:** font, stoup

" **water sprinkling:** asperges

homage: honor, tribute, eulogy, respect, manrent

" **to saints:** dulia

homaloidal: flat, even

homard: lobster

home: adobe, domicile, dwelling

" **at:** (Fr.) chez

" **animal's:** den, lair

" **bird's:** nest, aerie

" **for poor/sick:** hospice

" **Indian:** tepee

" **of Gods:** Olympus

" **wheeled:** trailor

Homer, Homeric: Koz, homerun, epic(al)

" **birthplace:** Chios

" **character:** Ajax, Nestor, Achilles, Odysseus

" **enchantress:** Circe

" **poem:** Iliad, Odyssey

homespun: plain, coarse, homely, (Scot.) kelt

" **cloth:** russet

homestead: toft, onstead, messuage

" **out buildings:** steading

homesteader: sooner

homilist: preacher

homily: talk, adage, discourse, lecture

hominy: samp, grits, bran, corn

homo: man, primate

" **comb. form:** like, same, equal

" **sapiens:** man

homonym: namesake, synonym

homopterous insect: aphid, cicada

homunculus: dwarf, manikin

Honduras: capital: Legucigalpa

" **coin:** peso, centavo, lempira

" **weight:** caja

honewort: parsley

honey: mel, dear, sweet, nectar, precious

" **bear:** Kinkajou

" **bee:** apis, dingar, deseret

" **comb. form:** melli

" **fermented:** mead, metheglin

honeycombed: pitted, favose, alveolar

honeysuckle: widbin, azalea, vine, clover

Hong Kong: bay: Mirs

" **coin:** cent, dollar, British/Hongkong/H.K. dol-

lar
  " **peninsula:** Kewloon

honor: glory, fame, esteem, homage
  " **mark of:** laurel, chaplet
  " **pledge:** parole

honorarium: tip, fee, reward, salary, gratuity

honorary military commission: brevet

hood: cap, bonnet, canopy, tippet, biggin
  " **academic:** liripipe, liripoop
  " **airplane's:** nacelle
  " **bird's:** crest, calot(te)
  " **carriage/cloak:** capote
  " **monk's:** amice, cowl, atis
  " **part:** camail

hooded: cowled, cucullate, capistrate
  " **garment:** cape, parka
  " **seal:** bladdernose
  " **snake:** adder, cobra, puffing
  " **woman's cloak:** capuchin

hoof: paw, foot, clee, cloaf, dance
  " **paring tool:** butteris
  " **shaped:** ungulate
  " **sl.:** walk, tramp

hook: gaff, hold, hitch, capture
  " **and loop:** gemel
  " **engine:** gab
  " **like mark:** cedilla
  " **money:** larin
  " **part:** barb
  " **shaped:** uncinal
  " **stretcher:** tenter

hooka, hookah: pipe, nargile, nargileh

hooked: hamate, aquiline, falcate

hooklike: uncinate, falcate, hamate
  " **process:** uncus

hooper: swan, cooper

hooly: slow, soft, wary

Hoover: dam, Herbert, John
  " **blankets:** newspapers
  " **lake/dam:** Mead
  " **flag:** (empty) pocket

hop: dance, leap, vine, bound, gambol
  " **back:** vat
  " **-bush:** akeake
  " **kiln:** oast
  " **of ball/stone:** dap
  " **o'-my-thumb:** dwarf
  " **plant:** lupulus
  " **stem:** bine

hope: deem, wish, expect, prospect
  " **goddess of:** Spes
  " **lack of:** despair
  " **symbol of:** opal

hophead: addict

Hophni: brother: Phinehas
  " **father:** Eli

Hopi Indian: Moki, Moqui
  " **god of:** Kachina, Katc(h)ina
  " **room of:** Kiva

hoplite: soldier
  " **weapon:** spear

hoppet: yard, bucket, basket

hopple: fetter, hobble, entangle

hoprine: bine

hopscotch: pallall
  " **stone:** potsy, peever

Horae: hours, Dike, Eirene
horehound: henbit
horizon: rim, edge, goal, sky-line
  "   **arc of:** azimuth
  "   **kinds of:** true, visible, celestial
horizontal: flat, level, flush, plane
  "   **band: heraldic:** frieze
  "   **position:** prone
hormigo: quira, ant tree
horn: scur, brass, siren, cornet, oliphant
  "   **bell-like part:** flare
  "   **bird's beak:** epithema
  "   **comb. form:** kera
  "   **deer's:** antler, prong, tine
  "   **drinking:** rhyton
  "   **Hebrew:** shofar
  "   **like:** cornu
  "   **of plenty:** cornucopia
  "   **snail's:** tentacle
  "   **tissue:** scur, keratin
  "   **unbranched:** dag
hornbeam: ironwood
hornbill: tock, bird, homari
  "   **genus:** buceros
horned: gored, corniculate
  "   **animals:** ram, gnu, deer, stag, bull, ibex, rhino, buffalo
  "   **animal fabled:** unicorn
  "   **toad:** lizard
  "   **viper:** asp, cerastes
hornless: polled, acerous
  "   **cow:** mulley
horologe: clock, watch, sundial, hourglass
  "   **studier of:** horologist, watch maker

horse: gee, nay, mount, beast, steed
  "   **Achilles':** Xanthus
  "   **Alexander the Great's:** Bucephalus
  "   **ankle:** hock
  "   **armor:** bard(e)
  "   **back of:** withers
  "   **backward movement:** passade
  "   **belly band:** girth
  "   **blinder:** winker
  "   **breastplate:** poitrel, peytrel
  "   **breed:** Arab, Barb, Shire, hunter, Morgan, Belgian, Suffolk, trotter, harness, Shetland, Clydesdale
  "   **brown:** bay, sorrel, chestnut
  "   **calico:** pinto
  "   **comb. form:** hipp(o), kerat(o)
  "   **dappled:** pinto, roan, piebald
  "   **dark:** zain
  "   **female:** filly, mare, yaud, dam
  "   **foot:** hoof, frog, fetlock, pastern
  "   **forehead:** chanfrin
  "   **gait:** run, lope, rack, pace, walk, trot, canter, gallop, winding
  "   **genus:** eguus
  "   **golden:** palomino
  "   **gray:** schimmel
  "   **lover of:** hippophile
  "   **male:** stud, entire, gelding, stallion, colt, steed
  "   **mane:** crest
  "   **measure:** hand

" **pack:** drudge, sumpter, bidet
" **piebald:** calico, pinto
" **prehistoric:** Eohippus
" **rearing:** pesade
" **saddle:** cob, mount, palfrey
" **small:** cob, nag, tit, pony, genet, Shetland
" **winged:** Pegasus
horsefly: botfly, gadfly, tabanid, cleg
horsehair: snell, seton, mane
horseman: canter, cowboy, rider, equestrian, caballero
" **armed:** cavalier
" **bullfighter's:** picador
horsemanship: manege, equitation
" **herd of:** harras
" **pert. to:** equine
" **rearing:** pesade
" **sidewalk:** volt
" **turn:** caracole
horsemint: monarda
horseshoe: ringer
" **gripper/spur:** calk
" **point:** sponge
" **rim:** web
" **one who applies:** farrier, blacksmith
Horus: Ra, Re, sun, god
" **brother:** Anubis
" **father:** Osiris
" **head of:** hawk
" **mother:** Isis
Hosea: Osse
" **wife of:** Gomer
hospital: refuge, spital, infirmary
" **attendant:** nurse, orderly
" **for foundlings:** creche

" **mobile:** ambulance
" **for the poor:** lazarette
hospitality, to strangers: xenodoehy
host: horde, army, bread, throng
" **heavenly:** angel
" **receptacle for:** pyx, paten, ciborium
hostel, hostelry: inn, hotel, tavern
hot: fiery, hectic, ardent, thermal
" **baths:** therme
" **cargo:** contraband
" **rod race:** drag
" **spring:** geyser
" **wind:** sirocco
hothead: raver, inciter, reactionary
hothouse: bagnio, greenery, vivarium
hot-tempered: iracund, choleric, irascible
Hottentut: Nama, Negro, Bushman
" **garment:** kaross
" **instr.:** gora(h)
" **village:** kraal
" **war club:** knobkerrie
hound: dog, hunt, harry, addict, talbot
" **female:** brach
" **hunting:** basset, beagle, setter
" **tail:** stern
" **wolf:** alan
hour: matin
" **canonical:** sext, none
" **class:** period
" **lights out:** taps, curfew
houri: nymph

house: cot, hut, nest, hovel, manor, domicile
  " **cluster:** dorp, hamlet
  " **comb. form:** eco
  " **bees:** hive
  " **birds:** nest, aerie
  " **fortified:** peel
  " **instant:** prefab
  " **mud:** tembe
  " **pert. to:** domal
  " **pidgeon:** cote
  " **outbuildings of:** messuage
  " **Eskimo:** igloo
  " **French:** maison
  " **Newfoundland:** tilt
  " **Oriental** serai
  " **Russian:** isba, dacha
  " **Spanish:** casa
  " **Upper:** Senate
housefly: pest, insect
  " **genus:** musca, fannia
  " **of the:** muscid
household: meiny, common, menage
  " **gods:** Lares, Penates
  " **linen:** napery
  " **mallet:** beetle
  " **sprite:** kobold
housel: Eucharist
houseleek: sengreen
houses, buyers of old: knacker
housesite: toft
housing: pad, box, cowl, cover, shelter
  " **engine:** nacelle
  " **horses:** blanket, trappings
howe: deep, empty, hollow
howling monkey: araba

hoy: barge
hoyden: tomboy
hr., part of: sec, min
Hreidmar's sons: Regin, Otter, Fafnir
huaca: idol, tomb, holy, shrine
hub: nave, core, center
  " **the:** Boston
hubris: insolence, arrogance, vanity
huckle: hip, haunch
huckleberry: blueberry
  " **family:** ericaceae
Huckleberry Finn: author: Mark Twain (pen name), Samuel Clemens
hucklebone: talus, hipbone, anklebone
hud: husk, shell, hall
huff: dod, pet, blow, puff, peeve
huffcap: bully, heady, strong blusterer
hug: coll, clasp, embrace, cherish
  " **kind of:** bear, bunny
  " **me-tight:** vest
hugger-mugger: sly, secret, confused, jumble
Hugo, Victor: novelist
Huguenot: Protestant
  " **leader:** Adrets, Conde
hui: firm, guild, society
huisache: wabi, aromo, shrub, cassie, popinac
huitain: stanza, octave
huke: cape, dress, cloak
hulled grain: samp, groat, bran
hulver: holly
human: man, mortal, person, biped, Adamite

" **body:** corpus, carcass
" **body model:** manikin
" **comb. form:** anthrop(o)
" **soul:** psyche
" **trunk:** torso
humble: low, mean, meek, abase, plain, stoop
" **pie:** crow, numbles
humbug: hoax, sham, fraud, dupe, bosh, flax, cajole
humdinger: (a)oner, corker, lulu
humect: wet, moisten
humerus: bone
humidity measuring device: hygrometer
humming: brisk, active, brool
" **bird:** ava, carib, sheartail, froufrou
" " **genus of:** Sappho
" **sound:** chirm, drone, whir(r)
hummock: knoll, hump, mound, hill
humor: pet, wit, mood, whim
" **bad:** tiff
" **body:** bile
" **quaint:** drollery
" **sl.:** corn
humorist: wag, joker, wit
" **famous:** Cobb, Rogers, Nash, Benchley, Rabelais
hump: bile, hunk, bulge, ridge
" **animal with:** camel, zebu, dromedary
" **-backed:** gibbous
" **of a humpback:** Kyphos
" **the:** Himalayas
humus: soil, mold, mulch
Hun: vandal, savage, barbarian
" **leader:** Etzel, Attila

Hunchback of Notre Dame: Quasimodo
" **actor/movie:** Lon Chaney
hundred: cantred, centum, cantref
" **comb. form:** centi, hecto
" **division into:** centuriation
" **dollar bill: sl.:** c-note
" **lacs:** crone
hundred-eyed-being: Argus
hundredweight: cwt, cental, quintal
Hundred Years' War battle: Cressy
Hung Wu: Ming
Hungary, Hungarian: Magyar
" **cavalryman:** Hussar
" **chocolate party:** Dobos
" **coin:** gara, balas, pengo, filler
" **dance:** czardas
" **dog:** puli
" **dynasty:** Arpad
" **gypsy:** tzigane
" **measure:** ako, joch, antal, metze
" **weight:** vamfont
" **wine:** tokay
hunger: pine, yen, starve
" **abnormal:** bulimia, polyphagia
" **greedy:** ravenous
hunks: miser, tightwad
hunt: seek, quest, ferret, trail
" **god of:** Apollo, Ninip
" **goddess of:** Diana, Artemis
" **illegally:** poach
hunter: yager, trapper, chaser, nimrod

" **assistant:** jager, gilly
" **bait of:** decoy
" **cap of:** montero, deerstalker
" **myth:** Orion
" **Golden Fleece:** Jason
" **patron saint:** Hubert
hunting: art of: chase, venery
" **bird:** falcon
" **call:** yoick, toho, tallyhoo
" **dog:** beagle, hound, basset
" " **chase:** bake
" " **cry:** tongue
" " **stance:** point, deadset
" **pert. to:** venatic(al)
huntsman, changed into stag: Actaeon
hurdies: hips, rump, buttocks
hurds: tow
hurlbat: javelin, harpoon
huron: grison
hurried: sped, hasty, raced, urged
" **music:** agitato
hurtful: malefic
husband: eke, rom, chap, mate, partner
" **authority of:** manus
" **more than one:** polyandry
" **one:** monandry
husbandry: thrift, economy, farming, geoponics
" **God of:** Faunus
husks: chaff, bhoosa
hussar: soldier, cavalryman
" **headdress:** busby
" **jacket:** dolman
" **monkey:** patas

hussy: minx, tart, doxy, slut, madam, sewing kit
hut: cabin, shanty, hovel, lodge
" **army:** quenset
" **fisherman's:** skeo
" **leanto:** shed
" **mining:** coe
" **shepherd's:** bothy
hyacinth: greggle, bluebell, harebell, stone
" **gem:** topaz, garnet, zircon
" **wild:** camas
hyalite: opal
hyaloid: glassy, vitreous
hybrid: bovine: catalo
" **citrus tree:** tangelo
" **horse and ass:** mule, hinny
" **horse and zebra:** zebrula, zebrinny
" **language:** jargon
" **zebra and donkey:** zebrass
hydra: polyp, serpent, constellation
hydrocarbon: butane, retene, benzene, octane
" **compound:** imine
" **gaseous:** ethane, ethene
" **liquid:** toluene
" **wax:** montan
hydromedusa: jellyfish
hydromel: (fermented) mead, aloja
hydrometer: spindle
" **scale:** baume
hydrophobia: rabies, lyssa
hydrous: watery
" **silicate:** talc

" **wool fat:** lanolin
hymenopteron: bee, ant, wasp, sawfly
hymn: following psalm: sticheron
" **for the dead:** requiem
" **funeral:** dirge
" **of praise:** anthem
" **victory:** epinicion
hyperbole: elas, auxesis, exaggeration
hyperborean: cold, gelid, frigid
Hyperion: Titan
" **daughter of:** Eos, Selene
" **parent of:** Gaea, Uranus
" **son of:** Helios
hyperpnea: panting
hypethral: roofless
hypnotic: (condition) coma, trance, lethargy
" **compound:** amytal
" **force:** od(yle)
hypnotism: sleep, mesmerism
" **founder of:** Mesmer
hypnum: moss
hypochondria: hyp, megrim,
anxiety, melancholy
" **victim of:** nosomania, valetudinarian
hypocrisy: cant, simulation, pharisaism, pretense, deceit
hypocrite: sham, pretender, Levite, Tartuf(f)e
hypostasis: deposit, essence, sediment
hypostatic: basic, elemental
hypotenuse: slant
hypothesis: ism, theory, system
hypothetical being: ens, entity
hyrax: procavia, rabbit, cony, hyracoid
Hyrtacus' son: Nisus
hyson: tea
hyssop: mint, thistle, aspergillum
hysteria: tarassis, panic, frenzy, fit, jitters
" **symptom of:** aura, aerophagia
hystricomorphic animal: cavy, rodent, agouti, porcupine

I

I: ego, self
  " **am to blame:** mea culpa
  " **am not to blame:** non mea culpa
  " **enlarged:** ego
  " **excessive use of:** iota-cism
  " **do not wish to contend: Lat.:** nolo contendere
  " **have found it:** eureka
  " **understand:** roger
Iago: master: Othello
  " **wife:** Emilia
iamb: foot (metrical)
Iasi: jassy
  " **coin:** leu
Iasion's father: Zeus
Iberia: Pict (see Spain)
ibex: goat, zac, kail, tur, walie
  " **habitat:** alps, pyrenees, mountains
ibis: jabiru, heron, stork
Icarian: rash, daring, foolhardy

Icarius: daughters of: Erigone, Penelope
  " **father of:** Daedalus
ICBM: weapon, missile, Atlas
ice: chill, geal, freeze, dessert, sherbet
  " **breaking up in water:** debacle
  " **coat:** rim
  " **floe:** pan, pack
  " **mass:** berg, serac, glacier
  " **pinnacle:** serac
icecap: calotte
Iceland: coin: krona, eyrir, aurar
  " **giant:** Atli
  " **God:** Loki, Thor, Aesir, Odin
  " **measure:** fet, alen, korntunna
  " **weight:** pund, pound, tunna smjors
ichneumon: fly, mongoose

ichnolite: fossil, footprint
icicle: shoggle
    " **limestone:** stalactite, stalagmite
icon, ikon: image, figure, symbol
ictus: fit, blew, attack, stroke
Idaho: (see special section)
    " **state gem:** garnet
idant: chromosome
idea: fancy, ideal, archetype, impression
    " **comb. form:** ideo
    " **main:** motif
    " **worthless:** bilge, chimera
ideal state: Eden, Utopia, Oceana
ideologist: dreamer, theorist, visionary
idiocy: fatuity, anoesia
idiosyncrasy: way, manner, idiasm
idle talk: rumor, gossip
Idmon: father: Apollo
    " **killer:** boar
    " **mother:** Cyrene
    " **ship:** Argo
idol: icon, image, satyr, fetish
    " **Chinese:** Joss
    " **household:** Teraphim
    " **social:** lion
idolatrous: pagan
idyl, idyll: poem, eclogue
idyllic: bucolic, pastoral
i.e.: that is, id est (Lat.)
Ieperen: Ypres
if: si (Fr., It., Lat.), provided, granting
    " **not:** else, unless, nisi
igneous rock: trap, basalt, periodot

ignition cap: fuse, fure
ignoble: low, mean, base, humble
ignoramus: dolt, nitwit, dunce
ignorance: agnosy, tamas
Igorot, Igorrote: Bontok, Nabaloi, Kankanai
    " **chief:** Apo
iguana: lizard, tuatara
ihi: fish, skipper, halfbeak
ikary: caviar
ileus: colic
    " **cause of:** constipation
ilex: holly, oak
Iliad: epic, poem
    " **ascribed author of:** Homer
    " **characters:** Ajax, Priam, Hector, Achilles, Agamemnon, Cassandra
Ilium, Ilion: Troy
ill: sick, evil, adverse, ailing, noxious
    " **at ease:** awkward
    " **prefix:** mal
    " **smelling:** fetid
    " **will:** enmity, spite, animus
illative word: therefore
illegal: foul, illicit, contraband
    " **in boxing:** foul (blow)
    " **liquor:** bootleg
Illinois: (see special section)
illness: colic, malady, disorder
    " **feign:** malinger
illude: mock, bilk, cheat, deride
illuminant: ligroin(e), gas, petroleum
illumination: light, instruction
    " **device:** torch, lamp

"   **in eclipse:** penumbra
"   **measure:** phot
"   **unit:** lux
illy: badly
ilvaite: yenite
image: copy, form, effigy, likeness
"   **deceptive:** chimera
"   **destroyer:** iconoclast
"   **good luck:** alraun
"   **maker:** iconoplast
"   **mental:** idea, concept
"   **pert. to:** iconic, simulacral
"   **rainbowlike:** spectrum
"   **stone:** herma
"   **wooden:** tiki
"   **worship:** arati
imago: bee
imam: calif, caliph, priest
"   **last:** Mahdi
imaret: inn, serai, hospice
imbosom: cherish, shelter, embrace
imbricate: overlap
imbroglio: plot, confusion, disagreement
imbrue: wet, soak, tinge, steep
imidogen compound: imid(e), imin(e)
imitation: copy, bogus, echo, sham
"   **derisive:** mockery, mimicry
"   **fantastic:** travesty, caricature
"   **gem:** glass, paste
"   **gold:** oroide
"   **gold leaf:** clinquant
"   **pearl:** olivet
"   **of speech/behavior:** mimesis

immaterial: spiritual
immaturity: period of: nonage, youth, infancy
immersion: baptism
immigrant: alien, comeling, stranger
"   **illegal:** wetback
"   **Israel:** chalutz, halutz
"   **newly arrived:** griffin, greenhorn
immolate: sacrifice
immortality: athanasia, deathlessness
"   **Hindu:** amrita
immortelle: everlasting
immunity: freedom, exemption
"   **kind of:** diplomatic, congressional
"   **method for:** inoculation
"   **producing substance:** serum, toxoid
Imogen's mother: Cymbeline
imp: elf, brat, demon, scamp, sprite
impact: slam, freeze, whang, force
"   **main:** brunt
impala: rooibok, rooyebok
impar: odd, unequal
imparting motion: kinetic
impasse: stalemate, (Fr.) cul-de-sac, deadlock
impasto: painting
imparid: fearless
impede: clog, block, check, delay
"   **legally:** bar, estop, debar
impedimenta: baggage, emcumbrance

impelling force: impetus, momentum

impend: hang, loom, approach

impennate bird: penguin

imperceptible: unseen, invisible

imperfect: cull, poor, faulty, defective

  " **prefix:** mal, atelo

imperial: royal, regal, august, kingly

  " **cap:** crown

  " **color:** purple

  " **decree:** rescript

  " **domain:** empire, empery

  " **officer:** palatine

imperial woodpecker: ivory-bill

imphee: plant, sorghum

impi: zulu, kaffir, warriors, soldiers

impignorate: pledged, pawned

implement: gear, kit, tool, accomplish, fulfill

  " **ancient:** celt, eolith

  " **baker's:** peel

  " **barbed:** harpoon

  " **enlarging:** reamer, dilator

  " **furcate:** fork

  " **hand printing:** roller, brayer

  " **hay spreading:** mulcher

  " **household:** appliance

  " **kitchen:** utensil

  " **lifting:** pry, tongs, lever

  " **logging:** tode, peevey

  " **pounding:** maul, pestle

  " **printer's:** biron, press

  " **threshing:** flail

  " **war:** petard

impone: stake, wager

impose: inflict, entail, burden

  " **by fraud:** foist

  " **upon:** fob, dupe

impost: duty, levy, tax, tariff

  " **salt:** gabelle

imposture: sham, fraud, artifice

impound: store, seize, poind

impouring: influx

imprecation: oath, curse, blasphemy

impresa: motto, device, maxim, proverb

impressed dearly: graven

impression: dent, mark, stamp, signet

  " **on coin:** mintage

  " **printing:** macule

  " **trial:** proof

imprest: loan, lent, advance (cash)

imprevu: unforeseen

imprimatur: license, sanction, approval

improperly: amiss, unduly

improvise: contrive, invent, devise

  " **in mus.:** ride, vamp

  " **on stage:** aside, ad lib

impulse: urge, motive, impetus

  " **characterized by:** sensory

  " **divine:** afflatus

  " **to steal:** kleptomania

  " **to travel:** wanderlust

in: at, among, amid, nook, corner

  " **a chamber:** incamera

  " **a flutter:** pitapat

" **a frenzy:** amuck
" **a row:** alined, serial
" **a series:** en suite
" **a standing position:** statant
" **a vertical line:** apeak
" **abeyance:** pending
" **accord:** en rapport
" **accordance:** pursuant
" **any event:** notwithstanding
" **capacity of:** qua
" **concert:** together
" **contact:** attingent
" **existence:** extant
" **fact:** de facto
" **favor of:** pro
" **great need:** straits
" **hoc signo:** vinces
" **manner of:** a la
" **name only:** nominal, titular
" **prefix:** il, en
" **same place:** ibid
" **the whole:** in toto
" **truth:** certes, indeed
" **year of:** anno
inability: incapacity, impotence
" **to articulate:** anaudia
" **to chew:** amasesis
" **to read:** alexia
" **to speak:** anepia
" **to swallow:** aphagia
" **to understand:** acatalepsia
" " " **(speech):** aphasia
Inachus' daughter: Io
inamorata: mistress, sweetheart
inarch: graft

inarm: embrace
inasmuch: as, for, since, because
inbeing: essence
inborn: innate, connate, natural
" **desire:** conatus
inbreeding: endogamy
Inca: Atahualpa
" **empire:** Peru
" **god:** Inti, Chasca, Choun
" **king:** Atabalipa
" **priests:** Amauta
incarnadine: red, rosy
incarnation: avatar, advent, Christ
" **of Vishnu:** Rama
incasement: emboitement
incendiary: firebug, arsonist, goon, pyromaniac
" **bomb material:** thermit(e)
incense: anger, arouse, odor, perfume
" **burner:** censer, thurible
" **Chinese:** joss stick
" **spice:** stacte, balsam
" **vessel:** censer, navette (Fr.)
inch: uneia
" **along:** worm
" **forward:** edge
" **one-thousandth:** mil
" **three-quarters:** digit
inches: eighteen: cubit
" **forty-five:** ell
" **four:** hand
" **nine:** span
" **two and one-quarter:** nail
inchpin: sweetbread
incidental: minor, odd,

chance, random
" **muse:** grace note
" **opinion:** obiter dictum
incidentally: obiter, byhand, apropos
incise: cut, etch, rase, carve
" **narrowly:** laciniate
incisor: tooth, cutter, fore-tooth
inclusive: generic
incognito: disguise
income: gain, profit, revenue, rente
" **pert. to:** tontine
incondite: crude, unpolished
incorporeal right: patent, copyright
incorrect: untrue, faulty, erroneous
" **epithet/naming:** misnomer
increase: wax, eche, swell, flourish
" **comb. form:** auxo
" **in sound:** crescendo
" **possessions:** amass
incubus: demon, spirit, burden
incunabulum, incunabula: infancy, cocoon, origin, cradle
incus: anvil, ambos
indefinite: loose, vague, neutral
" **amount:** any, some
" **article:** an
" **pronoun:** any, one
indehiscent fruit: uva
index: file, list, catalog(ue), exponent
India, Indian: Tamil, Bharat, Hindustan(i)

" **aborigine:** Bengali
" **alcoholic drink:** arrack
" **astrologer:** joshi
" **attendant:** peon, ayah
" **bazaar:** chawk
" **bear:** baloo
" **bearer:** sirdar
" **bird:** jacana, balu
" **British founder:** Clive
" **buck:** sasin
" **building:** mahal
" **bush:** kanher
" **canoe:** tanee
" **carpet:** agra
" **caste:** Jat, Mal, Gaddi, Rajput
" **caste mark:** tilka
" **cedar:** deodar
" **cigarette:** biri
" **coin:** hoon, anna, pice, fels, rupee
" **comb. form:** Indo
" **condiment:** curcuma
" **dancing girl:** bayadeer
" **diamond, famous:** Kohinoor
" **falcon:** basara, shashin
" **festival:** dewali
" **garment:** kurta, dhoti, banian
" **greeting:** namaste
" **harem:** zenana
" **hat:** topi
" **headman:** patel
" **hemp drug:** hashish
" **hut:** bari
" **kingdom:** Nepal
" **laborer:** palli
" **lady:** begum, memsahib
" **lady's maid:** ayah
" **language:** sanskrit, bengali, bihari

" **learned man:** pundit
" **litter bearer:** sirdar
" **low class:** bhat
" **master:** sahib, mian
" **measure of distance:** kos, guz
" **military caste:** rajput
" **Moslem:** Swat
" **musical instrument:** vina, ruana
" **nurse:** amah, ayah, dhai
" **ox:** zebu
" **peasant:** ryot
" **pipe:** hookah
" **Punjabi caste:** Sansi
" **rainy season:** varsha, monsoon
" **rice:** boro
" **rule:** raj
" **silkworm:** eri
" **snake:** krait
" **song:** raga
" **turban:** seerband
" **vessel:** lota(h)
" **weight:** tola, pice, ser
" **wine:** shrab
Indian: (see special section for all Indian tribes) aborigine, redskin, indic
" **arrow poison:** curare
" **ax:** tomahawk
" **baby:** papoose
" **bead money:** wampum
" **blanket:** stroud, mackinaw
" **brave, young:** tenderfoot
" **bread:** tuckahoe
" **ceremonial chamber:** kiva
" " " **pipe:** calumet
" **ceremony:** powwow

" **chief:** sachem, sagamore
" **corn:** zea, maize, samp
" **daughter of moon:** Nakomis
" **female:** mahala, squaw
" **festival:** potlatch
" **game:** canute
" **Great Spirit:** manito
" **guardian spirit:** totem
" **headdress:** topknot
" **man:** buck, brave, sannup
" **moccasin:** pac
" **pillar:** xat, lat
" **pony:** cayuse
" **prayer stick:** paho
" **sorcery:** obe, obi
" **village:** pueblo
" **white person:** paleface
Indiana: (see special section)
Indic dialect: Pali
indicating: marking, signing, showing
" **chemical group:** azo
" **literal transcript:** sic
" **succession:** ordinal
indices: files, tables, pointers
indigent: poor, needy, destitute
indigene: native
indigestion: apepsy, dyspepsia
indign: unworthy, disgraceful
indigo: dye, anil, blue
" **artificial source:** isatin
" **bale of:** seroon
" **berry:** randia
" **Chinese:** isatis
" **derivative:** ketole, indol(e)
" **wild genus:** baptisia

indigo bunting: bird, finch
indirect: devious, circular, oblique
  ‘‘ **expense:** overhead
  ‘‘ **expression:** ambage, periphrase
indiscrete: compact
individual: one, unit, sole, self
  ‘‘ **biological development:** ontogeny
  ‘‘ **comb. form:** indio
  ‘‘ **of compound animal:** zoon
  ‘‘ **performance:** solo
  ‘‘ **physiological:** bion
  ‘‘ **selfish:** egoist
  ‘‘ **smug:** prig
individuality: oneness
  ‘‘ **rare:** seity
Indo-Aryan: Jat, Rajput
  ‘‘ **god:** Indra
Indo-China: dialect: ao
  ‘‘ **former kingdom:** Anam
  ‘‘ **part of:** Burma, Malaya, Thailand, Laos, Vietnam, Cambodia
  ‘‘ **tree:** mee, eng
Indo-European: Slav, Serb, Lett, Croat, Czech, Aryan
Indo-Portugese: halfcaste Christian: Topaz, Topas(s)
Indonesia, Indonesian: East Indies
  ‘‘ **bird:** bulbul, peafowl
  ‘‘ **coin:** rupiah
  ‘‘ **Indian:** Ata
  ‘‘ **law:** adat
  ‘‘ **measure:** depa, depoh
  ‘‘ **priest caste:** brahmana
  ‘‘ **pyramid:** stupa
  ‘‘ **shop:** toko

  ‘‘ **weight:** soekoe
  ‘‘ **wind:** brubu
Indra: Sakra, Sakka
  ‘‘ **dragon:** Vritra
  ‘‘ **elephant:** Airavata
  ‘‘ **food:** soma
indri: lemur
inductance, measure of: henry
inductile: inflexible, unyielding
indulge: pet, baby, pamper, coddle
  ‘‘ **in antics:** skylark
  ‘‘ **in fault finding:** cavil
  ‘‘ **in revelry:** roist
Indus: constellation
  ‘‘ **tribesman:** Gor
indweller: denizen, sojourner
inearth: bury, inter
inelastic: rigid, stiff, limp
inert: lazy, dull, stupid, torpid
inertia: sloth, idleness
inesculant: inedible
inexorability: rigor
infant: babe, chrisom, bantling, bairn
  ‘‘ **doctor of:** pediatrist
  ‘‘ **in law:** minor
  ‘‘ **murder of:** infanticide
infanta: princess
infante: prince
infare: housewarming
infection: malady, disease, plague
  ‘‘ **freedom from:** asepsis
infecund: barren
inferal: stygian
inferno: fire, hell, Hades, gehenna
  ‘‘ **Hebrew:** sheol
infest: vex, haunt, torment

infix: inset, instill, engrave
inflammation: itis, fire, combustion
   "   **bone:** osteitis
   "   **bone marrow:** myelitis
   "   **eyelid:** sty
   "   **intestinal:** colitis
   "   **throat:** catarrh
inflated: blew, turgid, bloated
   "   **condition:** tympany
inflection: tone, cadence
   "   **of words:** paradigm
inflict: deal, impose
   "   **great pain:** torture
   "   **vengeance:** wreak
inflorescence: raceme, flowering
   "   **axial circle of:** whorl
influence: coax, impel, induce, power
   "   **by electricity:** induction
   "   **by fixed ideas:** obsess
   "   **by reward:** bribe
   "   **region of:** orbit
inform: tell, alert, warn, advise
   "   **against:** delate, betray
   "   **sl.:** rat, sing, squeal
information: data, aviso, notice, facts
   "   **bit of:** item
   "   **condensed:** digest
   "   **detailed:** dossier
infortune: Mars, Mercury, Saturn, misfortune
infusion: tea, tincture, admixture
   "   **malt:** wort
infusoria: vorticella, protozoa
ingang: porch, intestines, entrance
ingluvies: crop, craw

ingot: metal: pig, gad, bullion
   "   **silver:** sycee
   "   **worker:** barman
   "   **zinc:** spelter
ingredient: element, compound
   "   **baking:** soda, alum, yeast
   "   **incense:** stacte
   "   **ink:** tannin
   "   **varnish:** lac, rosin
ingrowing nail: acronyx
inhabitant: dweller, inmate, ite
   "   **desert:** nomad
   "   **early:** aborigine
   "   **foreign:** alien
   "   **local:** native
   "   **moon:** selenite
   "   **suffix:** ese, ite
inhabiting: caves: spelean
   "   **ground:** terricolous
   "   **island:** nesiote
   "   **lake:** lacustral
   "   **sea:** pelagic
inhere: stick, cleave, belong
inheritance: legacy, bequest, parcenary
   "   **by first-born:** primogeniture
   "   **law:** salic
   "   **portion:** legitime
   "   **restricted:** entailment
   "   **seizer:** abator
inhume: bury, inter, entomb
inimical: frosty, averse, hostile
initial: first, letter, elementary
   "   **design of:** monogram
   "   **ornamental:** paraph
   "   **payment of:** ante, deposit

injure: mar, scathe, harm, spoil
" **by bruising:** contuse
" **by scorching:** char, singe
injury: damage, wound, mar, ill, loss
" **causing:** malefic, traumatic
" **compensation for:** damages, solatium
" **pert. to:** noxal
" **retaliation to:** reprisal
" **sense of:** umbrage
ink: blacken, millrynd, color, daub
" **berry:** pokeweed
" **fish:** cuttle, squid
" **ingredient:** tannin
" **pad of printer:** dabber
" **pert. to:** atramental
inkle: tape, yarn, thread
inlaid: mosaic, champleve, bahl
inlay: insert, filling, adorn
" **material:** tile, niello
inlet: oe, cay, gio, slew, zee, fjord
" **coastline:** strait, bight
inmate of harem: oda
inn: pub, hospice, fonda, tambo
" **worker:** barmaid, potboy, tapster
inner: ben, interior, esoteric
" **bark:** bast
" **comb. form:** ent(o), ental
" **parts:** innards
" **sole:** rand
Innisfail: Erin, Eire, Ireland
Ino's grandfather: Agenor

innocence: symbol of: diamond
inorganic: mineral
insane: daft, batty, senseless, manic
" **asylum:** bedlam, madhouse
" **to make:** derange, dement
" **person:** lunatic
insanity: temporary: amentia
inscription: rune, graffito, epigram, legend
" **appropriate:** motto
" **end of book:** colophon
" **explanatory:** titulus
" **on book:** envoy
" **on coins:** sigla
" **tomb:** epitaph
inscrutable: secret, enigmatic, inexplorable
" **expression:** deadpan, pokerface
" **one:** sphinx
insect: ant, bug, mite, emmet
" **adult:** imago
" **antenna:** palp, feeler
" **back of:** notum
" **blood-sucking:** conenose
" **burrow of:** mine
" **comb. form:** entomo
" **egg:** nit
" **female:** gyne
" **genus of:** nepa, acarus, termes
" **long-legged:** emesa
" **limb:** prolog
" **nest:** nidus
" **order of:** locust, acarid
" **poison:** venom
" **resin:** lac

"   **stinger of:** dart
"   **wingless:** aptera
"   **young:** nit
insee: foretell
inside: inner, lining, within, secret
"   **comb. form:** intra
"   **out:** evert
"   **toward:** entad
insignificant: trivial, paltry, minor
"   **part:** bit, iota, tithe
"   **person:** snip, shrimp
insolation: sunstroke
inspan: yoke, harness
instar: pupa, larva, imago, maggot
instruction: lesson, order, advice
"   **art of:** didactics, pedagogy
"   **period of:** term, year, quarter, session
"   **place of:** conservatoire
instrument: deed, writ, means, medium, utensil
"   **altitude:** aba, altimeter
"   **copying:** hectograph
"   **cutting:** razor, knife, scythe
"   **measuring:** octant
"   **nautical:** sectant
"   **sacred:** urim
"   **surveying:** transit, theodolite
"   **to study motion:** stroboscope
instruments: for all: tutti
insulin: discover: Best, Banting
"   **used for disease:** diabetes

insurance: warranty, guaranty
"   **agent:** underwriter
"   **computer:** actuary
"   **contract:** policy
"   **payee:** beneficiary
"   **system:** tontine
intaglio: die, gem, engrave
"   **opposed to:** cameo
intarsia: mosiac
integer: whole, entity
"   **odd:** gnomen
intellect: brain, inwit, nous, reason
"   **limited in:** moronic
"   **of the:** noetic
intellectual: mental, ideal, sophic
"   **identification:** empathy
"   **liking:** palate
"   **(s) collectively:** clerisy, intelligentsia
intelligentsia: intellectuals
intemerate: pure
inter: bury, entomb, inhume
"   **companion of:** alia, alios
intercalary: inserted
"   **month:** Veadar
interconnection: nexus
interest: fetch, good, behalf, attract
"   **exorbitant:** usury
"   **in law:** title, right
"   **lose:** tire
"   **rate:** yield
"   **without:** jejeune
interfacing: dineric
interference: static
interferometer: etalon
interlaced: complex
interlude: truce, episode, in-

terval
" **short:** verset
international: world-wide, pact, entente
" **business:** cartel
" **exhibition:** exposition
" **language:** ro, ido, esperanto
" **sports:** Olympics
" **writers' group:** pen
" **organizations:** UN, NATO, SEATO, UNESCO
internecine: deadly
interpret: explain, construe, render
" **dreams:** rede
" **falsely:** gloss
interpretation: gloss, oracle, sense
" **of science:** exegesis, hermeneutics
interrogation: quiz, probe, query
" **mark:** eroteme
intersection: secant, chiasma
interstice: pore, mesh, space, crevice, cranny
" **pert. to:** areolar
interval: gap, hiatus, lacuna, break, interim
" **irregular:** sporadically
" **mus.:** second, third, fourth, fifth, sixth, seventh, octave, ninth, tenth
intestinal: enteric
intestine: gut, inner, viscera, domestic
" **comb. form:** entero
" **part:** ile, ileum
" **pert. to:** enteric
into: unto, until, inside, among

" **prefix:** en
" **that:** thereinto
intolerance: misoneism
intort: twist, curl
intracellular: histonal
intrada: prelude, introduction
intricate: Daedalian, Knotty, Gordian, difficult
intrinsically: per se
introduction: debut, intrada, preface, exordium
" **of new word:** neology
" **to treatise:** isagoge
inulase: enzyme
inunction: oitment, anointing
" **pert. to:** aliptic
inundation: alluvion
invader: raider, intruder, Hun, Pict
inveigle: lure, coax, entrap, snare
inventor: creator, discoverer, engineer
" **airplane:** Wright, Fokker
" **baseball:** Doubleday
" **cotton gin:** Whitney
" **dynamite:** Nobel
" **electric light:** Edison
" " **motor:** Davenport
" **elevator:** Otis
" **gun:** Colt, Remington
" **photography:** Niepce, Talbot
" **printing:** Gutenberg
" **radio:** de Forest, Marconi
" **right of:** patent
" **sewing machine:** Lester, Howe
" **steamboat:** Fulton, Fitch, Rumsey
" **telegraph:** Morse

"   **telephone:** Bell
"   **television:** Nipkow
invertebrate: polyp, insect, sponge, worm, mollusk
investigator: tracer, prober, detective, P.I.
"   **body of:** panel, jury
investment list: portfolio
Invisible Empire: Klan
invitation initials: R.S.V.P.
involucre: whorl, rosette, envelope
Io: father: Inachus
"   **guard:** Argus
"   **son:** Epaphus
iodine: comb. form: iod(o)
"   **salt:** iodate
"   **source:** kelp
"   **substitute:** aristal
Iolcus King: Pelias
ion: negative: anion
"   **positive:** cation, kation
Ion: father: Apollo
"   **mother:** Creusa
Ionia, Ionian: city: Teos, Myus
"   **coin:** obol(o)
"   **gulf:** Arta
"   **island:** Corfu, Zante, Paxos, Ithica
"   **monk:** Aidan
iota: ace, jot, bit, whit, atom
Iowa: (see special section)
ipecac: **genus:**   evea, cephaelis
"   **substance:** emetine
Iphicles: brother of: Hercules
"   **mother of:** Alcmene
"   **son of:** Iolaus
iracund: choleric, irascible
Irak: see Iraq

Iran, Iranian: Persia, Kurd, Lur
"   **angel:** Mah
"   **bird:** bulbul
"   **caste:** magi
"   **chief:** Mir
"   **coin:** pal, cran, dinar, toman, rupee
"   **dynasty, founder of:** Agha (present), Cyrus (former)
"   **garment:** chedar
"   **hat:** fez, turban
"   **measure:** guz, mou, zar, zer, artaba, jerib
"   **nomad:** Luri
"   **saint:** Safari
"   **tent-maker:** Omar
"   **title:** mir, azam, shah
"   **vessel:** aftaba
"   **weight:** dram, ser, abbas, pinar
"   **writings:** Avesta
Iraq: ancient: Kish
"   **city:** Hilla, Mosul, Bagdad
"   **coin:** dinar
"   **district:** Basra
Ireland, Irish: Eire, Erin, Irena, Celt, Innisfail
"   **accent:** blas, brogue
"   **basket:** skeough
"   **boat:** pook(h)aun
"   **cattle:** kerry
"   **church:** kil
"   **clan:** sept, Cinel, siol
"   **coin:** rap, real, turney
"   **dagger:** skean
"   **dance:** rinkafadda
"   **exclamation:**   och, arra(h)
"   **fairy:** banshee, lepre-

chaun, sidhe
" **garment:** inar
" **goblin:** pooka
" **holiday:** Whitmonday
" **liquor:** pot(h)een
" **measure:** bandle
" **national   emblem:** shamrock
" **no!:** sorra
" **pert. to:** Gaelic, Celtic
" **saint:** Aidan, Patrick
" **servant:** biddy
" **song:** rann
" **sweetheart:** gra
iridium: pert. to: iridic
" **symbol:** ir
iris: lis, sedge, ixia, Florentine
" **comb. form:** irid
" **family:** tileroot
" **part:** uvea, argola
" **pert. to:** irian
iron: hard, fetter, yetlin, goose, robust
" **comb. form:** sidero
" **compound:** steel
" **magnet:** armature
" **pert. to:** ferric
" **sand:** iserin
" **sulphate:** ilesite
" **symbol:** Fe
Iron City: Pittsburgh
ironwork: ferament
" **tool of:** lifter
Iroquois: (see special section)
irrational number: surd
irregular: erose, ataxic, cursory, sporadic, anomalous
irreligious: pagan, impious, profane
is: exists, personifies, represents

is not: nys, nis
Isaac: kin: Esau, Jacob, Abraham
isagoge: intro(duction)
Iseult: beloved: Tristan, Tristam
" **husband:** Mark
Ishmael: pariah, outcast, rover
" **kin of:** Hagar, Abraham, Nebaioth
" **son:** Kedar
Ishtar's lover: Tammuz
isinglass: mica, kanten
Isis: brother/husband: Osiris
" **mother:** Nut
" **shrine:** Iseum
" **son:** Sept
Islam: (see Mohammedan)
island(s): oe, ait, cay, key, eyot, isle
" **channel:** Sark
" **China:** Amoy, Quemoy
" **comb. form:** neso
" **coral:** Atoll
" **Cuba:** Pines
" **enchanted:** Bali
" **friendly:** tonga
" **Great Barrier:** Otea
" **group:** Faroe, Samoa, Antilles, Caroline, Marshall, archipelago
" **legendary/mythical:** Avalon, Utopia, Meru, Bimini, Atlantis
" **low:** Key
" **Mediterranean:** Capri, Crete, Gozo, Sicily, Malta
" **pert. to:** insular
" **snake-free:** Erin
Isle of Man: city: Peel, Ram-

sey, Douglas
" **division:** Treen
" **measure:** kishon
" **part:** Ayre
" **pert. to:** Manx

ism: ology, belief, tenet, doctrine
" **follower of:** ite, ist

Isolde's lover: Tristan

isomeric hydrocarbon: octane, terpene

isometric: same, cubic, parallel

Israel, Israeli: Zion, Sion, Jacob
" **anthem:** Hatikva
" **child:** sabra
" **dance:** hora
" **land of plenty:** Goshen
" **lawgiver:** Moses
" **measure:** cor, hin, bath, omer, kaneh
" **settlement:** kibbutz, moshav

ist: devotee, disciple, follower

Istanbul: Byzantine, Constantinople
" **foreign quarter:** Pera
" **Gr. quarter:** Fanar
" **inn:** imaret

isthmus: neck, strait, land, peninsula
" **Malay /Siam:** Kra

istle fiber: pito, pita

isurus: shark

it may be: haply

Italy, Italian: Sabine, Roman, Picene, Oscan, Volsci
" **article:** et, il
" **art center:** Siena
" **astronomer:** Galileo
" **cathedral:** duomo

" **coin:** lira, tari, paoli, ducato, zecchino, centisimo
" **dance:** volta, rigoletto, tarantella
" **diety:** faun
" **food:** pizza, ravioli, zabaglione
" **grape:** verdea
" **holiday:** festa
" **house:** casa, casino
" **inlay work:** tarsia
" **innkeeper /landlord:** padrone
" **marble:** carrara
" **measure:** orna, canna, palma, tavola, braccio
" **monk:** padre
" **opera:** Aida, Tosca, Norma
" **opera house:** (La) Scala
" **poetic name:** Ausonia
" **policeman:** shirro, carabiniere
" **pottery:** majolica
" **priest:** fra
" **secret society:** Mafia, Comorra
" **song:** villanella
" **soup:** minestrone
" **street:** via, strada
" **violin maker:** Amati
" **weight:** carat, ottava, libra
" **wind:** sirocco

itch: barber's: sycosis

item: bit, scrap, topic, detail
" **curious:** ana

Ithunn's husband: Bragi

Ithaca king: Odysseus

itineration: tour, eyre, circuit

Ivan the Terrible: Tsar
" **wife:** Anastasia

Ivanhoe: author: Scott
" character: Tuck, Cedric, Isaac, Rowena, Beowulf
" clown: Wamba
ivories: dice, teeth, keys (piano)
ivorine: smooth, white
ivory: dentin, creamy, ribzuba
" bone black: abaiser
" carving art: toreutics
" dust/cement: eburine
" Latin for: ebur
" nut: anta, tagua
" rasping: scobs
" source: tusk
" synthetic: ivoride
ivy: vine, laurel, gill, tod
" crowned with: hederated
" ground: hove, alehoof
" pert. to: hederic
" poison genus: sumac, rhus
Ixion's descendants: Centaurs
ixtle: pita, fiber, istle
Izmir: Smyrna
izzat: credit, honor, prestige

J

jaal: ibex, goat, beden
Jabal's father: Lamech
jabberwocky: tune, brillig, nonsense, rigmarole
jabiru: stork, ibis
jabot: frill
jacare: caiman
jacent: prone
jack: flag, ensign, pump, tree, boor, pike, coin, toy, mule, rabbit, carnation
" in cards: knave
" of clubs: pam
" group of 4: quatorze
" in-the-pulpit: plant, herb, figwort
" of-all-trades: tinker
" tree: jaca
jackal: kola, diebs
jackanapes: fop, ape, dandy, beau, coxcomb, monkey
jackass: fool, dolt, dunce, nitwit, blockhead
" comb. form: ono
jackdaw: daw, coe, kae,

(black)bird, grackle
" genus: corvus
jacket: bajo, grego, blazer, hietle, reefer, wampus
" Artic: parka, anorak, temiak
" armor: acton
" short: Eton, jerkin, spencer
" sleeveless: vest, bolero
jackknife: barlow
jackpot: all, award, windfall
jackrabbit: hare
jackstay: rope, horse, staff
jackstones: dibs
Jacob: Israel (new name)
" brother: Esau, Edom
" daughter: Dinah
" descendant: Levite, Israelite
" father-in-law: Laban
" ladder: phlox, flower
" parent: Isaac, Rebekah
" retreat: Haran
" son: Pan, Gad, Levi,

175

Asher, Reuben, Judah, Simeon, Joseph, Benjamin, Isaachar, Zebulun, Naphtali
" **vision:** Bethel
" **wife:** Leah, Rachel, Bilhah
jade: nag, fag, plug, tire, hussy, green, tremolite, cloy, pall, yu, weary
jaeger: bird, gull, skua, allan, shooi, diamond
jag: barb, load, tooth, prick, scrap, indent, quantity
Jagannath: place of worship: Puri
jaguar: ounce, tiger, cat, car, panther
jaguarundi: cat, eyra
jai alai: pelota, game
" **court:** fronton
" **racket:** cesta
jail: can, jug, brig, stir, pokey, cooler, hoosgow, calaboose
" **fever:** typhus
Jairite: Ira
jako: parrot
jalousie: shutter, blind
Jamaica: bitter drug: quassia
" **dogwood:** barbasco
" **ginger alcohol:** jake
James' father: Zebedee
Jamshid: Yima
" **realm of:** Peris
Janizarian chief: dey
japan: varnish, lacquer
Japan, Japanese: Nip(p)on
" **alcoholic beverage:** saki
" **art design:** notan
" **battle cry:** banzai
" **Buddha:** Amita, Amida

" **Buddhist sect:** Zen, Jodo-shu, Shin-shu
" **button:** netsuke
" **cherry:** fuji
" **church:** tera
" **clan:** Satsuma
" **coin:** rin, yen, koban, ichibu, tempo
" **dancing girl:** geisha
" **dish:** tempura, sukiyaki
" **drama:** no(h)
" **drink:** sake, mate, saki
" **fan:** ogi
" **festival:** Bon, Matsuri
" **fish:** tai, aya, fugu
" **garment:** haori, kimono, mumpei
" **girdle:** obi
" **girl:** mousme(e)
" **harp:** koto
" **lacquer:** urushi
" **magnolia:** yulan
" **measure:** bu, jo, cho, hiro, tsubo
" **money:** mo, ro
" **outcast:** eta, ronin
" **pire:** matsu
" **plum:** kelsey
" **quince:** japonica
" **religion (early):** Shinto
" **rice cake:** ame
" **ruler:** shogun
" **samurai:** ronin
" **seaweed:** nori
" **shoes:** geta, zori
" **song:** uta
" **storm:** monsoon, tyhoon
" **street:** Ginza
" **suicide:** hari-kari, seppuku
" **sword:** catan
" **untouchable:** eta

" **volcano:** fuyi, aso(san)
" **weight:** kin, fun, rin, momme, rjoo
" **wisteria:** fuji
" **wooden shoes:** geta
" **writing system:** kana
" **zither:** koto
Japanese-American: Nesei, Kib(b)ei, Sansei
jape: joke, quip, gag, fool, mock
japery: buffoonery
Japeth: father: Noah
" **son:** Tubal, Magog, Meshech
japonica: bush, shrub, camellia, quince
jar: ola, urn, vase, banga, krater, discord, croppa, clash
" **coarse earthen:** crock, terrine
" **fruit:** mason
" **Gr.:** pelike
" **rubber:** lute
" **Sp.:** olla
" **two-handled:** amphora
" **very large:** cadus
" **wide-mouthed:** ewer
jardiniere: urn, jug, stand, flowerpot, pot
jargon: argot, lingo, slang, zircon, gibberish, balderdash, chinook
jarl: headman, chieftain, earl
jasmine: bela, papaw, shrub, flower, jessamy, jessamine
Jason: father of: Aeson
" **love/wife of:** Medea
" **rival of:** Creusa
" **ship:** Argo
" **teacher of:** Cheiron
" **uncle of:** Pelias

jasper: morlop, ruby, quartz, bloodstone
jauk: trifle, dally
jaundice: icterus, envy, bias, prejudice, gulsach
jaunt: sally, trek, tour, jounce, ramble, excursion
jaunty: perky, airy, easy, chic, cocky, stylish, finical
Java, Javanese: coffee, Sudanese, Madurese
" **almond:** talisay
" **berry:** Cubeb
" **carriage:** sado(o)
" **cotton:** kapok
" **dancers:** bedoyo
" **fig tree:** gondang
" **island:** Bali
" **measure:** palen, paal
" **ox:** bantens
" **plum:** duhal, lomboy
" **rice field:** sawah
" **speech:** ngoko, krama
" **temple:** c(h)andi, tjandi
" **weight:** pond, tali, amat
" **wild dog:** adjag
javelin: spear, lance, assagai, dart, harpoon
" **cord:** amentum
" **game:** jerrid
jaw: vise, maw, chop, scold, chatter
" **comb. form:** gnath(o)
" **lower:** mandible
" **muscle:** masseter
" **part:** chin
" **pert. to:** malar, gnathic
" **upper:** maxilla
jawab: reply, answer, building, balance
jawless: agnathic, agnathous
jayhawker: bird of prey, guer-

rilla, fighter

jaylike bird: piet, magpie

jazz: hot, cool, third-stream, west coast, funky, progressive, ragtime

jeer: gibe, hoot, jabe, boo, taunt, scoff, sneer

jeering: sarcasm, glaiks

Jefferson's home: Monticello

Jehiada's wife: Jehosheba

Jehiel's son: Ner

Jehouhaz's mother: Hamutal

Jehoiachin's successor: Salathiel

Jehoshaphat: father of: Asa
" **son of:** Jehu

Jehovah: Ja(h)ve, Jah, Yhwa, God, Yhva

jehu: driver

Jehu's father: Jehoshaphat

jejune: arid, flat, trite, vapid, insipid, sterile

jelly: jam, conserve, colloid, preserve
" **animal:** gelatin(e)
" **base:** pectin
" **grape:** sapa
" **like:** gelatinous, gel (material)
" **meat:** aspic

jellyfish: acaleph, medusa
" **group:** discophora
" **part:** exumbrella

Jena: glass objective: unar

jennet: ass, horse, donkey

jeofail: mistake, oversight

jequirity: licorice

Jerahmeel: son: Oren, Achia

jeremiad: tirade, lament, complaint, tale

jerez: sherry

Jericho: publican: Zaccheus

" **woman:** Rahab

jerk: tic, bob, dolt, flip, tweak, hike, shog

jerked beef: charqui, biltong

jeroboam: bowl, bottle, goblet

jersey: sweater, gansey
" **tea:** wintergreen, checkerberry

Jerusalem: Zion, Salem, Jebus
" **captor:** Omar
" **corn:** kafir, durra
" **mountain:** Olivet, Zion, Moriah
" **oak:** ambrose
" **region:** Perea

Jerusalem artichoke: tuber, girasol(e), topinambou

Jespersen's language: ido

jess: thong, strap, binding, ribbon

jessamy: fop, dandy

Jesse: father of: Obed
" **son of:** David

jessur: snake, viper, daboia

jester: fool, mime, clown, buffoon
" **roving student:** goliard

Jesuit: " **bark:** cinchona
" **founder:** Loyola
" **motto:** A.M.D.G.
" **saint:** Regis

jet: gush, ebon, ladle, spurt, plane
" **-assisted takeoff:** JATO

Jethro's daughter: Zipporah

jetty: pier, mole, groin, wharf

Jew: Essene, Semite, Hebrew
" **dispersion of:** diaspora
" **harp:** quimbard, trump, (Sp.) bijuela
" **horn:** shofar

jewel: gem, stone, loupe, bijou, joy, treasure, darling
" **box:** casket
" **case:** tye
" **connoisseur:** lapidarist
" **setting:** bezel, ouch, pave, dop
" **weight:** tola
jeweler: gemmary
" **cup:** dop(p)
" **glass:** loupe
" **weight:** carat
jewelry: gems, beads, trinkets, bijouterie
" **adorn with:** begem
" **alloy:** oroide
" **artificial:** paste, strass
" **facet:** quoin, bezel
" **setting:** pave
Jezebel: virago, fury, gorgon
" **husband of:** Ahab
" **victim:** Naboth
jib: balk, crane, arm, gib, sail
" **boom:** spar
Jimsonweed: datura
jinnee: eblis
jinni: genie, spirit, demon, Alukah, Yaksha
jinx: hex, jonah, voodoo
jivatma: ego, atman, soul
Joan of Arc: Pucelle
" **counselors:** voices
" **victory:** Orleans
Joan's spouse: Darby
job: char, stint, berth, position, task
" **soft:** snap, sinecure
Job: comforter: Bildad, Elihu, Boil
" **daughter:** Kezia, Jemima
" **home:** Uz

" **tears:** coix, adlay, grass, plant
Jocasta: daughter: Antigone, Ismene
" **husband:** Oedipus
" **son:** Eteocles, Oedipus, Polynices
jocose: merry, droll, dry
John: Gaelic: Ian
" **Irish:** Sean
" **Rus.:** Ivan
" **Sp.:** Juan
John Brown's Body: author: Bonet
John of Gaunt: Lancaster
John the Baptist: father: Zachary
" **mother:** Elizabeth
johnnycake: pone, hoecake
joiner: splicer, carpenter
joint: hip, butt, seam, link, junction
" **articulated:** hinge
" **grass:** stem, culm
" **lubricator:** synovia
" **pert. to:** nodal, articular
" **plant stem:** phyton
" **put out of:** dislocate
" **right angle:** tee, ell
" **sac:** bursa
" **turn outward:** valgus
" **without:** acondylose
" **wooden:** tenon
Joktan: father: Eber
" **son:** Ophir
joll: lurch
jolly boat: yawl
Joloano: moro, sulu
Jonah: jinx, crab, prophet
" **deliverer:** whale
Jonathan's father: Saul
Jordan: Petra: **part of:** Moab

" **region:** Basham
" **valley:** Ghor
joree: chewink
Joseph: brother: Dan, Gad, Asher, Levi, Reuben, Judah
" **buyer:** Potiphar
" **father:** Jacob
" **mother:** Rachel
" **son:** Igal, Ephraim
Joshua: associate: Caleb
" **burial place:** Gaash
" **father:** Nun
" **important place:** Aijalon
" **tree:** yucca, redbud
Josiah: father: Amon
" **mother:** Jedidah
" **son:** Jehoahaz
Josip Broz: Tito
joss: idol, image, crowd, master
jouk: duck, dart, hide, stulk, fawn
joule: part of: erg
journey: expedition, passage, hadj, trek, travel, roam, hike
" **course:** itinerary
" **division of:** lap, leg
" **in circuit:** eyre
" **pert. to:** viatic, peripatetic
" **up:** anabasis
journeying: errant
joust: combat, spar, bout, tilt
" **field:** list
" **ready to:** atilt
Jove: Jupiter
joy: muse of: Tara
Judah: (see also, **Judea**) Aman, Hazor, Shema, Ain
" **brother:** Levi, Reuben, Simeon, Joseph
" **daughter-in-law:** Tamar

" **father:** Jacob
" **first born:** Er
" **king:** Ahaz, Urziah
" **mother:** Leah
" **queen:** Athaliah
" **son:** Onan
Judaism: (see also **Hebrew, Israel**)
" **abode of the dead:** Sheol
" **alphabet:** (see special section)
" **ascetic:** essene
" **Bible:** Tora(h); " **text of:** miqra
" **Book of Psalms:** Tehillim
" **bread:** matzo(s), hallah
" **calendar:** (see special section)
" **convert to:** ger
" **dispersion of:** golah, diaspora
" **doctrine:** Mishna(h), Kodashim
" **garment:** talis, shawl
" **harp:** nebel
" **healer:** Asa
" **holidays:** (see special section)
" **horn:** shofar
" **immigrant:** oleb, halutz
" **judge:** shopet
" **lawgiver:** Moses
" **lyre:** asor
" **marriage broker:** shadchen
" " **custom:** levirate
" **miter:** petalon
" **Old Testament division:** Hagiographa
" **patriot family:** Macca-

bee
" **poems:** yigdal, Azharoth
" **prayer book:** siddur, mahzor
" **prophet:** Amos, Ezra, Hosea, Elias, Micah, Jonah, Daniel, Naham, Elijah, Elisha, Haggai, Habakkuk, Jeremiah, Zechariah
" **prophetess:** Huldah
" **sabbath:** Saturday
" **sacred objects:** urim
" **scroll:** Sepher Torah
" **skullcap:** kippah, yarmulka
" **song:** hat(t)ikvah
" **synagogue:** schul, temple
" **tassel:** zizith
" **teacher:** rabbi
" **temple precentor:** cantor
" **vestment:** ephod
Judas: traitor, betrayer
" **suicide place:** Aceldama
Judea: (see also, **Judah**)
" **ancient name:** Judah
" **governor:** Pilate
" **king:** Asa, Herod
" **place:** Berea
judge: try, deem, opine, critic, edile, arbiter, umpire, sentence
" **bench:** banc
" **chamber:** camera
" **circuit:** iter, eyre
" **entry of, after verdict:** postea
" **gavel:** mace
" **group:** bench
" **of dead:** Osiris

" **of Hades:** Minos
" **rigorous:** rhadamanthus
" **robe:** toga
" **subordinate:** puisne, junior
judgment: arret, award, wisdom, censure, verdict
" **lack of:** acrisy
" **use one's:** discretionary, discretion
judicial: assembly: court
" **journey:** eyre
judiciary: bench
" **document:** writ, decision
Judith: husband of: Manasses
" **victim of:** Holofernes
jug: olla, gaol, jail, cruse, flagon, prison, pitcher
" **man-shaped:** toby
Juggernaut: Vishnu
juice: sap, broo, resin, gasoline, electricity
" **apple:** cider
" **fruit:** must, wine, stum, vinegar
jujitsu: judo
juju: fetish, charm, amulet
jujube: elb, ber
Juliana's house: Orange
Juliet: betrothed: Paris
" **father:** Capulet
" **lover:** Romeo
"Julius Caesar": (see, **Caesar**)
jump: in Gr. game: halma
" **stick for:** pole, pogo
jumping: rodent: jerboa
" **sickness:** palmus, lata(h)
junco: finch, snowbird
June bug: dor(r)

June grass: poa
Jungfrau: peak, mountain
   " **location:** Alps
jungle: shola
   " **dweller:** snake, beast, savage
juniper: ezel, cade, gorse, savin(e), evergreen
junker: noble, German, conservative
Juno: Hera
   " **consort:** Jupiter
   " **messenger:** Iris
junto: cabal, coterie, faction
jupe: coat, skirt, shirt, tunic, stays, bodice
Jupiter: Zeus, Jove, planet
   " **angel:** Zadkiel
   " **consort:** Juno, Hera
   " **daughter:** Bura, Minerva
   " **epithet:** Stator
   " **lover:** Io
   " **Roman temple:** Capitol
   " **satellite:** Io, Callisto, Europa
   " **son:** Pollux, Castor, Arcas
Jupiter Pluvius: rain

jural: legal, juristic
Jurassic division: Lias
jurema: tree, acacia
jurisdiction: law, soc, soke, venue, diocese, control, dominion
   " **ecclesiastical:** see, parish, deanery
   " **of an emir:** emirate
juror: assizer, talesman
   " **group:** panel, jury
jury: panel, peers, dicasts
   " **attempt to influence:** embracery
   " **summons:** verrire
justice: law, equity, due, doom, validity
   " **god:** Forsete, Forsite
   " **goddess:** Maat
   " **pert. to:** juridical
   " **seat of:** court, banc(us), tribunal
jute: desi, burlap, sacking, gunny, tat, plant
Jutlander: Dane, German
jutting: salient, rock, crag, tor
Juventas: Hebe

K

K: kay, kappa

kaama: hartebeest

kaddish: prayer, doxology, hymn

kae: jackdaw

kaffeeklatsch: social, gathering

Kaf(f)ir: Bantu, Zulu, Tembu, Xosa, fondo
" **body of warriors:** Impi
" **corn:** sorghum
" **language:** Xosa
" **servant:** umfaan
" **weapon:** keri, knobkeroie

Kafka character: Olga

kago: litter, palanquin

kah: carpet, plant, saltwort

kaka, kakapo: parrot
" **genus:** nestor

kaki: bird, stilt, persimmon

kakkak: bittern

kale: collard, green, cabbage, colewort
" **sea:** cole

Kali's husband: S(h)iva

kalinite: alum

Kalmu(c)k: Mongol, Eleut

Kamchatka: **codfish:** wachna
" **salmon:** mykiss

kamias: bilimbi

kanae: fish, mullet

Kanaka: Hawaiian, Polynesian, Melanesian, Micronesian

kanari: almond

Kandh language: Kui

kangaroo: bilbi, turatt, bettong, marsupial, paddymelon
" **female:** rov, gin, doe
" **male:** boomer
" **rat:** potoroo
" **young:** joey

Kansas: (see special section)

Kant's category: relation, quality, quantity, modelity

kapok: oil, ceiba, tree, fiber

karakul: sheep, lamb, far, as-

trakhan
Karelian lake: Seg
karma: fate, destiny, duty, rite
Kartrelian: Svan(e)
kasha: cereal, grain, mush
Kashmir: alphabet: sarada
  " **deer:** hangal
  " **official:** pundit
  " **river:** Jhelum
kat shrub: kafta
katchung: peanut, oil
Kate: Shakespeare's shrew
kava: awa, ava, drink, pepper
  " **bowl:** tanoa
kayak: canoe, kaiak
kazoo: gazoo
kea: parrot
Keats poem: Lamia
Keb: see **Geb**
Kebbie: stick, club, cudgel
ked: tick
kedge: anchor
keek: spy, peep, look
keel: timber, capsize, ship, vat, careen, fowl, upset, ocher
  " **part:** skag, skeg
  " **right angles to:** abeam
  " **shaped:** carinate
  " **wedge:** templet
  " **without:** ratite
keelbill: ani, ano, bird
keeling: codfish
keenly: dearly
keenness: acumen, talent, genius, edge
keep: fend, guard, arrest, husband, preserve
  " **back:** bar, hap, detain, reserve
  " **going:** sustain
  " **in:** retain

  " **in view:** regard
  " **on:** continue
  " **on course:** cape, head
  " **out:** bar, exclude, save, withhold, except
keeper: guard, alcade, curator, custos
  " **door lock:** nab, stang, risp
  " **Masonic door:** tiler
  " **of golden apples:** Ithun
  " **of marches:** margrave
  " **of park:** ranger
keest: sap, manew, substance
keeve: kier, tub, vat, basin
kef: tobacco, euphoria, dreaminess
keg: cask, tun, firkin
  " **open:** unhead
kegler: bowler
kelly: green, color, derby, hat
kelp: ware, seaweed, varec(h)
kench: bin
Kenilworth author: Scott
Kent, Kentish: district: Penge
  " **Iceman:** laet
  " **sheep:** romney
  " **tribal law:** laes
Kentucky: (see special section)
  " **coffee tree:** bonduc, chicot
Kenya: native/reserve: Masai
kercheo: sneeze
  " **answer to:** gesundheit
Keresan Indian: Sia
kerf: notch, slit, groove, cut
kermis: fair, carnival

kernel: core, bunt, pith, acinus, gist, seed
  " **having:** nucleated
kestrel: falcon, hawk, stannel
ketch: saic, boat, ship
kethib: kere
ketone: carone, acetone, camphor
kettle: vat, cazo (Sp.), caldron, pail
kettledrum: naker, tabor, timpani
  " **cavalry:** anacra, timbal
  " **Moorish:** atabal
kevel: peg, bolt, cleat, bit
key: reef, opener, pitch, solution, quay
  " **chain:** chatelaine
  " **false:** glut
  " **fruit:** samara
  " **instr.:** clavis, manual
  " **notch:** ward
  " **part:** bit
  " **pert. to:** tonic, tonal
  " **telegraph:** tapper
  " **skeleton:** giet, screw
keynote: theme, tonic, feature
  " **sign, Gr. music:** ison
keystone: sagitta, wedge, voussoir, principle
khan: title, inn, resthouse, caravansary
Khedive's estate: daira
Khnemu's consort: Anukit
Khyber Pass: tribe: Afridi
Kiang: ass, onager
kibble: bucket, grind
kibe: chap, sore, ulcer, chilblain
kibitzer: meddler, spectator
kickshaw: toy, bauble, food, gadget

kid: banter, hoax, child, leather
  " **undressed:** suede
kidcote: prison
kidney: organ, ilk, neer, stripe, nature
  " **comb. form:** reni
  " **Lat.:** ren
  " **pert. to:** renal
  " **-shaped:** reniform
  " **stone:** jade, nephrite, calculus
Kilauea goddess: Pele
kilderkin: cask, measure, barrel
Kilimanjaro peak: Kibo
kill: fake, slay, deaden, achieve, poniard, slaughter, cancel
  " **by stoning:** lapidate
  " **by strangling:** gar(r)otte
killer whale: orc(a), grampus
killing: of: brother/sister: fratricide
  " " **father:** patricide
  " " **king:** regicide
  " " **mother:** matricide
  " " **self:** suicide
  " " **small child:** infanticide
  " " **wolf:** lupicide
Kilmer poem: Trees
kiloliter: stere
kilt: pleat, filibag, fasten
  " **pouch for:** sporran
kilter: order, condition
kimmer: witch, girl
kimono sash: obi
kin: (see **kinship**) germane
kind: ilk, genre, good, benign species
  " **comb. form:** geno

" **same:** homogeneal

kine: cows, cattle, beasts

kinetic: active

king: rex (Lat.), rey (Sp.), roi (Fr.), ruler, sovereign
" **chamber:** camarilla
" **family:** dynasty
" **legendary:** Lud, Hogni, Sesha, Oberon, Prestes
" **symbol:** scepter

King Arthur: abode: Avalon
" **birthplace:** Tintagel
" **court site:** Camelot
" **death place:** Camlan
" **father:** Uther
" **forest:** Calydon
" **hound:** Cavall
" **knight:** Galahad, Lancelot, Percivale
" **lady:** Enid
" **magician:** Merlin
" **mother:** Igraine
" **queen:** Guinever(e)
" **sword:** Excalibur

King Canute's consort: Emma

king clover: melilot

king crab: limulus

King Henry IV character: Blunt, Percy, Scroop, Henry (Hal), Poins

King Lear: daughter: Regan, Goneril, Cordelia
" **dog:** Tray

kinglet: wren, bird, lionet

King of: Bath: Nash
" " **Beggars:** Carew
" " **Dwarfs:** Alberich
" " **Fairies:** Oberon
" " **Fomorians:** Balor
" " **Golden Touch:** Midas

" " **Judea:** Herod
" " **Serpents:** Shesha
" " **waters:** Amazon

King's: bodyguard: thane
" **evil:** scrofula
" **letter:** brief
" **topper:** (cards) ace
" **yellow:** orpiment

kingfish: haku, opah, bagara

kingfisher: halcyon

kink: loop, chink, caprice, spasm
" **in thread:** burl

kinkajou: potto, mammal

kinship: blood, clan, race, related, family, connection
" **father's side:** agnat(e),
" **Mohammedan law:** nasab
" **mother's side:** enate

kiosk: newsstand, pavilion

kipe: basket

Kipling: hero/novel: Kim
" **poem:** L'Envoi
" **Shere Khan:** tiger

kirtle: coat, gown, cover, tunic

Kish: father: Ner
" **son:** Saul

kiss: buss, caress, salute, peck
" **-me quick:** bonnet
" **of peace:** pax
" **science of:** philematology
" **sculptor of Kiss:** Rodin

kist: cist, box, locker

kitchen: ben (Sc.), chil (Ind.), cuisine, scullery
" **garden:** olitory
" **pert. to:** culinary
" **ship's:** galley
" **tool:** corer, ricer, beater,

grater, sifter, spatula, colander, opener

kite: fly, soar, rascal, bird, hawk, raise
" **Europe:** glede
" **genus:** elanus

kittiwake: gull, waeg, annet, bird

kitty: pool, stakes, ante, cat

kiwi: moa, roa, bird
" **genus:** Apteryx

kloof: glen, gorge, ravine

knabe: boy, piano

knapweed: bluet, hardhead, bellweed

knave: rogue, jack, cheat, miscreant
" **in clubs:** pam
" **in cribbage:** nob

knee: joint, supplicate, bow
" **armor:** genouille
" **bend:** kneel, genuflect
" **bone:** cap, patella, rotula
" **breeches:** knickers

kneeling desk: prie-dieu

knell: omen, summon, bell

knife: cut, blade, wound, dirk, bowie
" **Burmese:** dah
" **case:** sheath
" **dealer/maker:** cutler
" **Dyak:** parang
" **Hindu:** kukri
" **Irish:** skean
" **large:** snee, bolo
" **Malay:** kris, creese
" **Maori:** patu
" **one-bladed:** barlow
" **Philippine:** bolo, machet(t)e
" **plaster/paint:** spatula
" **sharpener:** hone, stone

" **Spanish:** machet(t)e
" **surgical:** catlin, scalpel, fleam

knight: gallant, templar, lover, eques
" **attendant:** page, squire
" **banner:** gonfonon
" **champion:** paladin
" **cloak:** tabard
" **ensign/flag:** pennon
" **famous:** Caradoc, Lohengrin, Galahad
" **fight:** joust
" **horse:** palfrey, charger
" **rank above:** baronet
" **rank next:** armiger
" **(of the) road:** tramp, hobo
" **Round Table:** (see King Arthur)
" **servant:** varlet
" **wife:** lady, dame
" **wreath:** orle

knighthood: chivalry
" **confer:** dub

knitting: craft, union, network
" **of a blanket:** afghan
" **machine guide:** sley
" **rod:** needle
" **stitch in:** purl
" **term:** castoff

knob: lump, boss, bunch, stud, umbo, handle
" **like:** nodal
" **ornamental:** boss, knop, stud
" **pointed:** finial
" **wood:** burl, knur

knobkerrie: club, stick, kiri, weapon

knobstick: club, cane, blackleg, scab

knock: rap, hit, strike, decry, blame
" **-about:** sloop, actor, handyman
" **down:** fell, floor, prostrate
" **-kneed:** valgus
" **off:** rob, stop, kill, overcome
" **out:** kayo, bash, beaut, dilly, daze
knot: snag, tuft, problem, sandpiper, joint, nodule
" **fibrous:** nep, noil
" **free from:** unravel, enode
" **in wood:** knag
" **pert. to:** nodal
" **running:** noose, slip
" **thread:** burl
" **tree:** gnarl, knur
knotted lace: tatting
know: realize, discern, see, ken, wist
" **-it-all:** wiseacre, smarty
" **-nothing:** agnostic, ignoramus
knowing: scient, informed, cunning, epistemonic, acute, sharp, artful
knowledge: lore, wisdom, ology, ken, sapience, erudition
" **highest, Plato:** noesis
" **instrument:** organon
" **lack of:** nescience, atechnic
" **object of:** scibile, cognitum
" **pert. to:** gnostic
" **seeker:** philonoist
" **slight:** smatter, inkling
" **summary:** encyclopaedia
" **systematized:** science
" **universal:** pantology
knuckle: submit, joint, strike
" **bone:** dib
kobird: cuckoo
kobold: gnome, goblin, nisse, spirit, brownie
koel: bird, cuckoo
kohinoor: diamond
kohl: antimony
" **used in:** mascara, eye make-up
kohlrabi: turnip
koklas: fowl, pukras, pheasant
kokoon: gnu
kokopu: para, fish
Kol: dialect: Ho, Mundari
kola: nut, jackal
kopje: hill, mound
Koran: Alcoran
" **chapter:** Sura
" **compiler's son:** Ali
" **interpreter:** ulema, alfaquin
" **pert. to:** alcoranic
" **register:** sijil(l)
" **scholars, body of:** Ulema
Korea, Korean: Chosen
" **money:** won, hwan
" **soldier:** Rok
" **weight:** kon
kosher: pure, clean, proper, Kashruth
" **meat maker:** porger
" **opposite of:** tref
kra: ape, macaque
kraal: crawl, pen, hut, enclosure

krimmer: fur, (lamb) skin
Krishna: Vishnu, Juggernaut
  " **grandson:** Aniruddha
  " **mother:** Devaki
  " **paradise:** Goloka
Kornus' wife: Rhea
kudo: glory, fame, praise
kudu: antelope
kulak: farmer, peasant
Kulanapan: Indian, pomo
kumiss: drink
Kuomintang: council: Yuan

Kurd: Persian
  " **ancestors:** Gordyaean
Kurile island: Iturup, Chishima
Kurland Peninsula inhabitant: Lett
kurrajong: tree, shrub
kurtosis: arc, curvature
Kwantung seaport: Dairen
kyphosis: humpback, hunchback
Kyushu volcano: Aso

L

L, letter: ell, el
La Rochefoucauld's forte: maxims
laager: camp
Laban: daughter: Leah, Rachel
labellum: lip, petal
labia: lips
  " **minora:** nympha(e)
labor: work, toil, strive, childbirth
  " **group:** union
  " **omnia**   : vincit
  " **union negotiation:** collective bargaining
laboratory: burner: etna, bunsen
  " **need:** acids, oleates, test tubes
laborer: prole, worker, serf
  " **Chinese:** coolie, cooly
  " **Egyptian:** fellah
  " **Indian:** toty
  " **Mex.:** peon, bracero

  " **migratory:** okie
  " **Sp.:** obrero, peon
  " **underground:** sandhog
  " **unskilled:** navvy, bohunk
labra: lips
Labrador: peninsula
labroid fish: wrass
laburnum: pea tree, shrub, sandalwood
labyrinth: maze
  " **builder of:** Daedalus
  " **dweller, legendary:** minotaur
lace: weave, whip, string, intertwine
  " **cape:** mantilla
  " **collar:** bertha
  " **edging:** frill
  " **frilled:** r(o)uche
  " **loop(s):** purl
  " **pattern:** toile
  " **three-cornered:** fichu
Lacedaemon: Sparta

lacert(il)ian: chameleon, lizard, gecko
Lachesis: goddess, fate, weird
lachrymose: teary, mournful
lack: need, dearth, shortage
 " **desire:** inappetence
 " **of stress:** atony
lacking: void, short, deficient
 " **brightness:** lackluster
 " **grace:** clumsy
 " **reverence:** impious
Laconia: capitol: Sparta
lacs, 100: crore
lactase: enzyme
lactescent: milky
lacuna: gap, hiatus, space
ladder: stee, scale
 " **part:** rung, stave, step, round, spoke, rundle
ladle: dip, scooop, dipper
 " **dip/pour with:** lave
 " **spout:** geat
lady: of the Lake: Ellen, Nimue, Vivian
ladybird: beetle, vedalia
Laertes: sister: Ophelia
 " **son:** Odysseus
lagan: jetsam, flotsam
laggard: loiterer, backward
lagomorph: pika, hare, rabbit, rodent
lagoon: pond, lake
 " **island:** Ellice
 " **site of:** coral reef, atoll
lair: den, cave
 " **hare's:** form
Laius: son: Oedipus
lake: pool, loch, lagoon
 " **artificial:** reservoir
 " **basin:** playa
 " **bird:** loon

 " **fish:** pollan
 " **herring:** cisco
 " **island in a:** holm
 " **outlet:** bayou
 " **study of:** limnology
 " **world's lowest:** Dead Sea
laky: dark-red
lalique: glass
lamb: child, sheep, fatling
 " **breast:** carre
 " **fur:** karakul
 " **hide:** kip
 " **holy:** agnus
 " **mother of:** ewe
 " **pet:** cade, cosset
 " **skin:** budge
lambent: glowing, flickering
lambrequin: drapery
Lamech: son of: Jabal, Jubal, Noah
 " **wife of:** Adah
lamelli: as prefix: plate, scale, leaf
lamellibranch: oyster, clam, mollusk
lamellirostral bird: swan, goose, duck
lamentation: jeremiad, wailing, plaint
lamia: vampire, sorceress, demon(ess)
lamiaceous plant: mint, rosemary, bergamot
lamina: flake, scale, layer
 " **brain:** obex
laminated: layered, sheeted
 " **material:** plywood
 " **rock:** shale
lammergeier: vulture, ossifrage
lamp: torch, gooseneck, lumi-

naire
" **decorative:** lampion
" **holder:** cresset
" **miner's:** davy
" **part of:** wick, burner, cresset
" **waving:** arati
lamprey: eel, cyclostome
lanate: wool(l)y
lance: javelin, spear, cut
" **barb:** fluke
" **part:** rest, morne
lancelet: amphioxus
Lancelot: knight
" **liege of:** Arthur
" **love of:** Elaine
" **mistress of:** Guinevere
" **nephew of:** Bors
lancet: scalpel, (surgical) knife
" **point:** neb
lancewood: yaya
land: country, earth, soil, tract
" **along river:** holm
" **border:** rand
" **close:** garth
" **cultivated:** arado, tillage
" **grant:** homestead
" **holder:** thane
" **marshy:** maremma
" **mine:** claymore
" **owner of adjacent:** abutter
" **pert. to:** geoponic, agrarian
" **pledged as security:** wadset
" **point of low:** spit
" **reclaimed:** polder
landau: carriage
landloper: vagabond
landowner: laird

landscapist: topiarist
landtag: diet, assembly
language: speech, lip, parlance
" **artificial:** esperanto, ido
" **classical:** Lat., Gr.
" **dialect:** lingo, idiom
" **difficulty of understanding:** dysphasia
" **hybrid:** jargon
" **mixed:** pidgin
" **Romance:** Sp., Fr., Catalan, Provencal, It., Romanian, Portugese
langur: monkey, simpai
laniferous: fleecy
lanner(et): falcon
lantana: viburnum, majorana
lantern: lamp, lanthorn, cresset
" **feast:** bon
" **roof:** louver
" **wheel:** trundle
lanugo: down, hair
lanyard: cord, rope, thong
Laomedon: kingdom: Troy
" **son:** Priam
Laos: kingdom
" **monetary unit:** kip
" **language:** French, Laotian
lapactic: laxative, cathartic
lapel: rever(s), facing, flap
" **stiffener:** wigan
lapillus: rock
lapin: rabbit, fur
lapis: stone
" **lazuli:** sapphirus, azure-blue
Laplander: sledge of: pulk(h)a
lappet: flap, lobe, label

lapsus: slip, lapse
laputan: absurd, dreamy, impractical
lapwing: peewee, plover
large: man-size, out-size
   " **prefix:** mega, macro
   " **scale:** extensive
   " **very:** decuman
largess(e): gifts, bounty
lariat: rope, lasso
   " **eye of:** honda, hondo
lark: prank, adventure, wagtail, songbird
   " **genus:** alauda
larrigan: moccasin
larva: maggot, planula
   " **beetle's:** grub
   " **butterfly:** caterpillar
   " **case enclosing:** indusium
   " **final stage of:** chrysalis
   " **fly:** gentle
   " **frog's:** tadpole
   " **moth's:** egger, caterpillar
   " **next form of:** pupa
laryngeal clearing sound: ahem
laser inventor: Townee
lashings: loads
lasso: lariat, reata, rope
last: end, omega, ultimate
   " **chance of   :** Montana
   " **in succession:** lattermost
   " **Mohican:** Uncas
   " **person in a race:** tailender
   " **supper:** Cena
   " **syllable of word:** ultima
latchkey notch: ward

lateen: vessel, dhow
lateral: sidewise, sideways
   " **opposed to:** medial
laterite: clay
latex: Plant's: milk
   " **source of:** poppy, milkweed, rubber tree
lathe: clamp: chuck
   " **operator:** turner
Latin: Roman, Italian, Spaniard, language
   " **always:** semper
   " **and:** et
   " **and others:** et al
   " **before:** ante
   " **being:** esse
   " **book:** liber
   " **brother:** frater
   " **day:** diem, dies
   " **discourse:** sermo
   " **earth:** terra
   " **egg:** ovum, ova
   " **fish:** pisces
   " **head:** caput
   " **highest:** summa
   " **holy:** sanctus
   " **law:** jus, lex
   " **man:** homo
   " **name:** nomen
   " **peace:** pax
   " **star:** stella
   " **this:** hoc
   " **thus:** sic
   " **total:** summa
   " **water:** aqua
   " **we:** nos
   " **without:** sine
   " **year:** anno, annus
latite: lava
latitude: width, breadth, scope, extent
Latona: Leto

" **progeny of:** Apollo, Diana
latrant: barking, snarling, complaining
Latter-day Saint: Mormon
lattice: grille, trellis, espalier
Latvia, Latvian: Lett(ic)
  " **coin:** lat
  " **monetary unit:** lat(u)
laugh: deride, chortle, guffaw, bray
  " **able to:** risible
  " **pert. to:** gelastic
  " **too much:** cachinnate
lauraceous tree: avocado, laurel, nutmeg, camphor
laurel: bay, shrub, cajeput, rhododendron, azalea
  " **bark:** coto
  " **family:** heath, kalmia
  " **mountain:** calico, bush
lava: magma, latite, taxite
  " **cinder:** scoria
  " **pieces of:** scoria, slag
  " **stream of:** coulee
lavender: mint, aspic, purple
  " **product:** perfume, oil
laverock: lark
law: code, canon, statute, ordinance, lex, jus
  " **appendix in:** codicil
  " **break the:** infract
  " **imperial:** ukase
  " **kind of:** statute, common, (un)written
  " **pert. to:** legal, forensic, canonic
  " **written:** statute
lawgiver: Solon, Draco, Minos, Moses
lawsuit: action, case
  " **party to:** suer, litigant, litigator
lawyer: barrister, solicitor, mouthpiece
  " **Bible:** Blackstone
  " **cap of:** coif
  " **patron saint:** Ives
laxative: physic, purgative, cathartic
  " **drug:** aloes
  " **leaf:** senna
  " **pulp:** cassia
lay: ditty, deposit, set, poem
  " **aside:** table
  " **down arms:** surrender, capitulate
  " **open:** expose
  " **siege:** invest
  " **waste:** ravage
layers, form in: stratify
layman: laic, amateur
lazar: leper, beggar
lazy: indolent, sluggish
  " **fellow:** idler, drone
  " **Susan:** tray, turntable
leaching product: lye
lead: guide, minium, bullet, pilot
  " **black:** graphite, plumbago
  " **oxide:** litharge
  " **poisoning:** saturnism, plumbism
  " **red:** minium
  " **white:** ceruse
leader: chief, head, commander
  " **in printing:** dots, dashes
  " **sheep:** bellweather
leaf: page, tendril, petal
  " **bud:** gemma
  " **central vein:** midrib
  " **comb. form:** phyll(o)

" **disease:** mosaic, rust
" **fern:** frond
" **front of:** recto
" **like:** phylloid
" **miner beetle:** hispa
" **part:** stoma, lamina, stipel, vein, stipules, blade, petiole, (mid)rib, stalk
" **point:** mucro
" **pores:** stoma
" **side:** verso, recto
" **tip:** mucro
" **vein:** rib, nervure
leafless: aphyllous
" **plant:** cactus
leafstalk: chard, rhubarb
Leah: father: Laban
" **husband:** Jacob
" **sister:** Rachel
" **son:** Levi
leal: true, loyal
leam: husk
lean: spare, cant, incline
" **to:** shed, shack, roof
leap: loup, dive, bound, spring, vault
" **ballet:** entrechat
" **year:** bissextile
Lear: daughter of: Regan, Goneril, Cordelia
" **dog:** Tray
" **follower:** Kent
learned: erudite, wise, informed
" **man:** pandit(a), pundit, scholar, savant
" **people:** literati, clerisy
learning: lore, education
" **branch of:** ology, science
" **shallow:** sciolism
lease: let, contract, tenure

" **grant:** demise
" **party to a:** lessor, lessee, landlord, tenant
leash: control, curb, rein, lung
" **hound:** limer
" **ring:** terret
leather: suede, calf, kid
" **armor:** gambeson
" **bookbinding:** skiver
" **cutter:** skiver
" **factory:** tannery
" **kind of:** chamois, oxhide, levant, napa
" **like:** coriaceous
" **maker:** tanner
" **saddle:** mochila
leatherback: turtle
leatherfish: lija
leatherneck: marine, gyrene
leatherwood: wicopy
leave: bequeath, forsake, depart, vamo(o)se
" **kind of:** sabbatical
" **military:** furlough
" **out:** omit, elide
" **secretly:** decamp
leaven: barm, yeast, sourdough
leaves: foliage, pages, departs
" **cluster:** rosette
" **having:** foliaceous, foliaged, petaled
" **having two:** bifoliate
" **of:** foliar
Lebanon, Lebanese:
" **dance:** dabkeh
" **monetary unit:** pound
" **people:** Arab
" **seaport:** Tyre, Saida, Tripoli
lebensraum: living space

lebistes: guppy
lectern: ambo, pulpit
Leda: daughter: Helen, Clytemnestra
" **husband:** Tyndareus
" **lover, myth.:** swan, Zeus
" **son:** Castor, Pollux
ledger entry: credit, debit, interest
lee: shelter, protection
" **opposed to:** stoss, windward
leech: annelid, parasite, worm
" **like:** hirudinoid
" **sucker of:** acetabulum
leek: allium, bulb, scallion
leet: court
left: larboard, departed, gone
" **comb. form:** l(a)evo
" **hand of page:** verso, levo
" **handed:** southpaw, dubious, sinistral
" **political:** liveral, radical
" **turn:** haw
leg: limb, pin, shank
" **bone:** fibula, tibia
" **from knee to ankle:** crus, shank
" **in heraldry:** gamb
" **joint:** knee, ankle, hock
" **pert. to:** crural, sural
" **thigh:** femur
" **vein:** saphena
legal: valid, lawful, jural
" **arrest:** caption
" **claim:** lien, demand
" **code:** pandect
" **delay:** mora
" **notice:** monition
" **paper:** deed

" **record:** estreat, acta
" **right:** droit
" **tender:** money
" **warning:** caveat
" **wrong:** tort
legally: competent: sui juris
legend: saga, myth, fable
legendary: bird: roc
legging(s): puttie, gaiter, gambade
Leghorn: Livorno, chicken, hat
legislature: parliament, congress
" **lameduck:** rump
legless amphibian: caecilian
legume: pod, bean, seed, plant, soy, lentil
legumin: globulin
lehua: tree, myrtle
leister: trident, spear
leisure: otiose, ease
leman: lover, mistress
lemma: bract, membrane
lemming: rat, rodent
lemon: fruit, citrus
" **juice squeezer:** reamer
" **juice vitamin:** citrin
" **peel:** relish
lemure: potto, monkey, sifaka
" **arboreal:** loris
" **flying:** galago, colugo
" **kin of:** tarsier
" **nocturnal:** loris
lemuroid: potto
length: extent
" **finger to elbow:** cubit
" **having:** linear
" **of day's march:** etape
lenis: soft, mild, smooth
" **opposed to:** fortis
lenitive: laxative, soothing

leno: fabric, weave
lens: meniscus
" **kind of:** concave, convex
" **shaped:** lentoid, lenticular
lent: imprest
" **observance:** Penitence, fasting
lentigo: freckle
L'envoi: stanza, verse, inscription
leopard: cat, ocelot, ounce, panther
" **young:** whelp
leper: outcast, lazar
" **hospital:** spital
" **patron saint of:** Giles
lepidolite: mica
lepidopteron: moth, butterfly
leporid animal: rabbit, hare
leprechaun: fairy, elf, goblin
leptus: mite, larva
lerot: dormouse
lesbian: Sappho, erotic
less: smaller, minor
" **in music:** meno
lesson: exercise, instruction
" **from fable:** moral
" **music:** etude
let: allow, lease, abandon, assign
" **down:** slacken
" **it be given:** detur
" **it stand:** stet, sta
" **sink:** vail
lethargic: comatose, dull
" **sleep:** sopor
Lethe: river, oblivion
Leto: Latona
" **daughter of:** Artemis, Diana

" **son of:** Apollo
letter: epistle, message, breve
" **cross stroke:** serif
" **cut off last:** apocope
" **main stroke:** stem
" **Papal:** bull
" **representing a word:** logogram
" **short:** memo, note
" **to the:** exactly, literal, precisely
lettuce: minion, romaine, salad, cos, bibb
leucorrhea: whites
Levantine: silk, ship
" **garment:** caftan, grego
" **state:** Syria, Lebanon
level: rase, plane, flat(ten)
" **comb. form:** plani
levulin: carbohydrate
lexicographer: wordman, compiler, Roget
" **lexicographic work:** dictionary, thesaurus
liang: tael, weight
lias: rock
libel: slander, malign, calumny
libido: sex
library: bibliotheca
" **reading place:** carrel(l)
" **supervisor:** curator
libretto: book, text, words
Libya, Libyan: kingdom
" **gulf:** Sidra
" **strongman:** gadaffi
lice: vermin
" **of:** pedicular
licet: legal
lich: corpse
lichen: alga, moss, fungus

" **genus:** evernia, usnea
licorice: abrin, pea
lie: perjure, mendacity, fib, admissable
" **anchored:** moored
" **detector:** polygraph
lied: lyric, song
lierne: rib
life: existence, breath, animation
" **destruction of:** biolysis
" **insurance:** tontine
" **pert. to:** biotic(al)
" **prefix:** bio
" **principle:** atman, spirit, jive, prana
" **without:** azoic, dead, amort
lifting muscle: levator, erector
ligament: taenia, tendon
" **comb. form:** desmo
ligan: flotsam, jetsam
light: illume, neon, glim, illumination, kleig
" **anchor:** kedge
" **around sun:** aureola
" **celestial:** halo, nimbus, corona
" **fuse:** spit
" **giving substance:** phosphor
" **measure:** lumens
" **of reflected:** catoptric
" **pert. to:** photic
" **ring of:** corona
" **science of:** optics, photics
" **without:** aphotic
lighthouse: phare, beacon
lignaloes: aloes
ligneous: woody, xyloid

like: enjoy, similar, choose, akin
" **comb. form:** home(o), ine, oid
" **ladder:** scalar
" **tail:** caudal
" **wing:** pteric
likeness: effigy, similarity, image
" **bad:** caricature
likewise: ditto, also, moreover
lilac: shrub, flower, syringa
lily: lotus, arum, lys, tulip
" **bulb:** squill
" **calla:** arum
" **sand:** soaproot
" **shaped:** crinoid
limacine mollusk: snail, slug
liman: bay, marsh, lagoon, estuary
limb: arm, edge, branch, margin
" **joint:** elbow, knee
" **muscle:** levator, flexor
limbus: border, edging
lime: catch, calx, citron, fruit
" **bush:** snare
" **comb. form:** calci
" **powder:** conite
" **tree:** teil, linden, tupelo, bass(wood)
limen: stimulation, threshold
limestone: tufa, calcite, chalk
" **crystallized:** marble
limicoline bird: plover, sandpiper, snipe, curlew, killdeer
limn: draw, depict, portray
limonene: terpene
limpet: lamprey, shellfish
limpkin: courlan
limulus: king crab
Lincoln: hat: stovepipe

" **sobriquet:** (honest) Abe, railsplitter

" **son:** Willie, Robert

" **wife:** (Mary) Todd

line: route, cord, queue, cordon

" **cutting:** secant

" **hair:** ceriph

" **intersecting:** vector, secant

" **nautical:** earing, marline

" **threadlike:** stria

" **with bricks:** revet

linen: toile, lingerie, napery, batiste

" **cloth for bookbinding:** buckram

" **cloth, mummy's:** byssus

" **fiber:** flax

" **measure:** cut

" **room:** ewery

lines: on map: hachure

" **on optical lens:** reticle

ling: burbot

lingo: jargon, cant, patois

linguist: polyglot

linguistics branch: syntax, semantics, morphology, phonology, philology

link: yoke, nexus, copula, join

linn: cascade, linden, ravine

linnet: finch, songbird, lintwhite

lintwhite: linnet

lion: leo, cat, idol, feline

" **female:** lioness

" **group:** pride

" **mane of:** crest

" **of God:** Ariel

" **young:** cub, whelp, lionet

lip: labium, labial, superficial

" **comb. form:** chil(o)

" **sound:** labial

lipase: enzyme

lips: labia, kisser

" **comb. form:** labio

" **of the:** labial

liquefy: thaw, melt, fuse

" **opposed to:** solidify

liquer: kummel, ratafia, cordial, curacao, cognac

" **glass:** pony

liquid: fluid, transparent, clear

" **body tissue:** lymph

" **fatty oil:** olein

" **measuring device:** jigger, dosimeter

" **opposite:** solid

" **waste:** slops

liquidambar: tree, sweetgum, balsam

liquor: juice, tiff, mead, drink, bitters

" **alcoholic:** lush, mescal

" **bottle:** magnum

" **drink:** tiff, dram

" **glass:** snifter

" **sap:** nipa

liripipe: tippet

list: heel, tip, calendar, careen, roll, index

" **ancestors':** pedigree

" **saints:** canon, hagiology

lister: plow

listing: selvage, table

listlessness: apathy, ennui

litany: prayer

literal: word-for-word, accurate, exact, prosaic

" **translation:** metaphrase

literary: learned, lettered

" **collection:** ana, miscel-

lany
" **composition:** vignette, parody
" **criticism:** review, critique
" **extracts:** analecta
" **form:** poem, essay, verse
" **pseudonym:** Elia, Saki
" **society:** Lyceum
lithograph: chromo, print
lithoid: stonelike
lithomarge: clay, kaolin
Lithuania, Lithuanian: Balt, Lett
" **coin:** lit(as), ruble
" **seaport/territory:** Memel
litotes: meiosis
litter: bier, scatter, mulch, clutter
" **bearer:** cat, dog, pig
" **last-born of:** wallydrag
" **of pigs:** farrow
little: wee, small, puny, paltry, trivial, minute, poco
" **Bear:** Ursa Minor
" **bit:** fig, morsel
" **by little:** piecemeal
" **comb. form:** micr(o)
littleneck: clam, quahog
liturgy: mass, ritual, rite
live: endure, inhabit, subsist, vivid
" **able to:** viable
" **oak:** encina
lively: spry, agile, vivid, vivacious
" **music:** vivo, animato
liver: hepar
" **disease:** cirrhosis, hepatitis, porphyria

" **function of:** metabolism
" **pert. to:** viscera, hepatic
" **secretion:** bile, gall
" **shaped like:** hepatic
liverwort: agrimony, hepatica, bryophyte
" **genus:** riccia
living: being, extant, animate
" **on land/in water:** amphibian
" **prefix:** livi
" **thing:** organism
" **within:** immanent
lizard: basilisk, monitor, gila, reptile
" **amphibious:** salamander, newt
" **chameleon-like:** agama
" **climbing:** iguana
" **comb. form:** sauro, saurus
" **fish:** ulae, saury
" **genus:** uma, agama
" **legless:** blindworm, slowworm
" **wall:** gecko
llama: vicuna, ruminant, alpaca
" **habitat:** Andes
" **hair of:** wool
llanero's weapon: bola
llano: plain, steppe
lo: behold, look, ecce
loa: larva
loach: carp
loadstar: lodestar, polaris
loaf: of white bread: manchet
lobbyist: rainmaker
lobe: lappet, lobule
" **ear:** earlop
lobo: wolf

lobster: crustacean, macruran
  " **claw:** nipper, chela, pincer
  " **feeler of:** antenna, palp(us)
  " **part of a:** chela, telson, thorax
  " **trap for:** pot
local: chapter, branch, topical
  " **relationship:** ubiety
loch: pond, bay, lake
lock: tress, jam, link, confine
  " **mechanism:** detent
locofoco: match, cigar
locomotive: mogul, iron horse, dolly
  " **coal car:** tender
  " **cowcatcher:** fender
locust: cicada, tree, insect
  " **tree:** carob, honey, acacia
lode: ore, vein, deposit
  " **cavity:** vugh
log: timber, diary
  " **measure:** scalage
  " **roller:** decker
  " **splitter:** wedge
loganberry: bramble
loggerhead: dunce, turtle
  " **bird:** shrike
loggia: portico, gallery, arcade
logia: maxims, sayings
  " **singular:** logion
logic: reasoning
  " **deductive:** syllogism
  " **major premise:** sumption
logogriph: word puzzle, anagram
logrolling: birling

lohan: monk, Arhat
loin: rack, chump, beefcut
  " **comb. form:** lumb(o)
  " **muscle:** griskin
loins: hips
  " **pert. to:** lumbar
lomita: hill
London: ancient name: Agusta
  " **bobby's beat:** point
  " **district:** Soho, Mayfair, Lambeth, Chelsea, Limehouse
  " **streetcar:** tram
lone: solitary, solo, sole, isolated
  " **Star State:** Texas
long: crave, hanker, aspire, prolix
  " **ago:** lang syne
  " **discourse:** descant
  " **fish:** eel, gar
  " **knife:** yatagan
  " **winded:** prolix, wordy, verbose
longeron: spar
longspur: finch, bird, sparrow
loo: pam, card game
look: pore, con, glance, search, peer
  " **alike:** ringer
  " **askance:** leer
  " **obliquely:** squint, skew
  " **over: sl:** case
lookout: ship's: conner
  " **turret:** bartizan
loom: weave, appear
  " **frame:** batten
  " **part:** pirn, heddle, treadle, warp, roller, batten
loop: tab, terry, noose
  " **in electricity:** circuit

" **in lace:** picot
" **in lariat:** hondoo
" **like structure:** ansa
looper: larva, (measuring) worm
loose: lewd, free, inexact
" **end:** tagrag
" **set turn:** free, release
loquacious: talkative, voluble
" **bird:** magpie, jay
" **opposite:** reticent, taciturn
lord: liege, peer, earl, nobleman, prince, domineer, master
" **of Hosts:** Jehovah, God
" **priveleged:** Palatine
" **attendant:** thane
lorelei: siren, Lurlei
" **golden possession:** comb
" **victims of:** mariners, sailors
lorgnon: monocle, lorgnette, pincenez
lorikeet: parrot, lory
lorry: wagon, truck
losel: bum, loafer, ne'er-do-well
loss: defeat, forfeiture
" **of consciousness:** syncope, syncopation
" **of feeling:** anesthesia, insensate
" **of hair:** alopecia
" **of memory:** amnesia
" **of mental power:** dementia
" **of sense of smell:** anosmia
" **of voice:** aphonia
lot: fate, share, parcel, grist

" **city of:** Zoar
" **father:** Haran
" **feast:** Purim
" **uncle:** Abraham
" **sister:** Milcah
" **son:** Moab
lottery: chance, game
" **kin:** raffle, Keno, Numbers, Bingo, Lotto
lotus: herb, shrub, water lily
" **tree:** jujube, sadr
Louisiana: (see special section)
" **boat:** bateau
" **land measure:** arpent
" **native:** Creole, Acadian, Caijan
" **tobacco:** perique
louse: aphid, nit, cootie, slater
lovage: parsley
love: liking, affection, dote, enamor
" **apple:** tomato
" **feast:** agape
" **god of:** Eros, Cupid, Amor
" **goddess of:** Venus, Freya
" **knot:** amoret
" **meeting:** tryst
" **potion:** philter, philtre
" **pert. to:** amatory, erotic
loving: erotic, amorous, doting
" **comb. form:** phile
low: deep, vulgar, inferior, menial
" **bow:** curtsy
" **brow:** plebeian
" **necked:** decollete
lowan: mallee, leipoa
lower: demote, debase,

glower, frown, reduce
" **World:** hell, Hades
" **World gods:** Manes
lowest: animal life: am(o)eba
" **point:** nadir
" **point of planet's orbit:** perigee
lox: oxygen, salmon
Loyalite: Jesuit
LSD: source: ergot
luau: feast
" **dish:** poi
lubricant: castor, vaseline, oil, grease, dope
Lucan's work: Pharsalia
luce: pike, fish
luces: lights
" **singular:** lux
Lucifer: devil, Satan, match
" **poetic:** Venus
luck: fortuity, lot, chance
" **of:** aleatory
lucule: sunspot
lugworm: annelid
lumbricoid: roundworm
luminary: sun, moon, star
luminous: bright
" **energy:** light
" **radiation:** aura
lunar: pale, pallid, crescent
" **crater:** linne
" **month:** moon
" **phenomenon:** eclipse
lung: membrane: pleura
" **sound:** rale
lungfish: mudfish, dipnoan
lungi: loincloth
lunule: halfmoon, lune
Lupercus: Faunus
Lupin, thief: Arsene
Lupus: constellation, wolf

lurk: sneak, prowl, skulk
Lusitania, now: Portugal
lustrum: five-year (period), luster
lute: seal, clay, instrument
" **oriental:** tar
" **relative of:** mandolin, guitar
Lutetia: Paris
luthern: window, dormer
luxate: disjoint, dislocate
luxury-lover: sybarite, Lucullus
Luzon: battlesite: Bataan, Manila Bay, Corregidor
lying: false, mendacious, reclining
" **downward:** prone, acumbent
" **flat:** prostrate
" **on one's back:** supine
lymph: humor, serum, spring
" **gland swelling:** bubo
lymphoid tissue of mouth: tonsil
lyncean: keen-eyed
lynx: bobcat, wildcat, constellation
" **fur:** caracal
lyre: harp, trigon, asor
lyrebird: menura
lyric: lied, songlike
" **muse:** Erato
" **poem:** rondeau, sonnet, hymn, elegy, canzone
" **poet:** lyrist, odist
lyrics of opera/oratorio: libretto
lytic: lysin
lytta: worm

M

M, letter: em (ma)
Maas: Meuse
mabolo: plum
macaco: lemur, monkey
macadam: road, stones
  " **material:** tar, asphalt
Macao: coin: avo
  " **island:** Taipa, Coloane
macaroni: dandy
  " **ingredient:** durum, semolina
macaroon: biscuit, cooky, ratafia
maccaboy: snuff
mace: staff, maul, spice
  " **reed:** dod
  " **royal:** sceptre
  " **source of:** nutmeg
macedoine: medley, salad
machete: bolo, knife
Machiavellian: crafty, deceitful
machine: tool, motor, device, mechanism
  " **cutting:** cropper
  " **finishing:** edger
  " **glazing:** calendar
  " **hoisting:** crab, gin
  " **part:** cog, cam, gear, crank, solenoid
  " **threshing:** combine
  " **tool:** lathe
  " **weighing:** trone
machinist's groove: tslot
mackerel: fish, tuna, bonita, albacore
  " **cured:** bloater
  " **net:** spiller
  " **young:** spike, tinker
Mackinaw: coat, blanket, boat
  " **trout:** namaycush
mackle: blur, blot, macule
macrocosm: world, universe
macrural crustacean: shrimp, lobster, prawn
mad: sore, insane, rabid, frenetic
  " **monk:** Rasputin
Madagascar: native: hova
made: invented, constructed

" **of wood:** xyloid
" **up:** invented, cosmetized, fabricated
Madeira: wine, island
" **wine:** Tinta
mademoiselle: abbrev: mlle
madid: wet, moist
madras: cloth, kerchief
" **weight:** pollam
madrigal: song, glee, poem
madwort: shrub, alyssum
maelstrom: whirlpool
maenad: nymph, bacchante
maffle: muddle, mumble, confuse, squander
mage: wizard, magician
magic: obeah, art, wizardry
" **black:** sorcery, voodoo
" **horse:** Bayard
" **potion:** philter
" **sign:** sigil
" **symbol:** pentacle
" **word:** sesame
magistrate: judge, justice
" **civil:** syndic
" **Greek:** Ephor
" **Roman:** Pr(a)etor
magnesium silicate: talc
magnet: loadstone, lodestone
" **alloy:** alnico
" **end:** pole
magnetic: mesmeric, attractive, electric
" **direction:** north, south
" **force:** od, odyl(e)
magnificat: hymn, song, poem
magnitude: size, extent
magnolia: shrub, flower, sweet bay
maguey: aloe, agave, fiber
magus: sorcerer, magician

maharaja's wife: maharani
mahogany: tree, caoba, baywood
" **of the:** meliaceous
" **pine:** totara
Maia: Pleiade, May
maid: lass, virgin, domestic
" **of Astolat:** Elaine
" **of Orleans:** Joan of Arc
maidenhair: fern, ginko
mail: post, dispatch, armor
" **boat:** packet
" **pert. to:** postal
main: chief, duct, power
" **body:** trunk
" **point:** gist, nub, crux
Maine: (see special section)
" **native:** down-easter
maize: corn yellow
" **ground:** samp, grite, hominy
majolica: pottery
majuscule: uncial, capital
make: style, create, devise
" **airtight:** seal, lute
" **black:** negrify
" **choice:** opt
" **cross sign:** sain
" **indistinct:** blur
" **into law:** enact
" **like:** imitate
" **out the meaning:** decipher
" **position secure:** entrench
" **small(er):** minify
" **stupid:** hebetate
" **up:** invent, form
" **watertight:** calk
" **whole:** mend, heal
" **young:** rejuvenate
mako: shark

Malabar monkey: wanderoo
Malacca: cane, strait
malachite: bice, verditer
Malaga: grape, wine
malanders: pustules, eczema
malar: cheekbone
malaria: quartan, paludism
" **carrier:** mosquito
malarial: paludal
Malay, Malayan: apple: ohia
" **ape:** lar, mias
" **bird:** megapod
" **coin:** ora, tra(h), tam-
pang
" **dyeing method:** bat(t)ik
" **measure:** pau
" **weight:** kati, caddy
Malaysia: title for man: tun
" **title for woman:** toh
puan
male: manly, he, virile
" **animal:** ram, stag, boar,
bull
" **bee:** drone
" **castrated human:** eunuch
" **ferret:** hob
" **fish:** milter
" **hog:** boar
" **kangaroo:** boomer
" **plant:** mas
" **salmon:** jack
" **seal:** seecatch
" **sheep:** ram, tup, wether
" **swan:** cob
" **swine:** boar
malefic: harmful, evil
malic acid salt: malate
malicious: vicious, spiteful
" **burning:** arson
malignant: evil, virulent,
harmful

" **opposed to:** benign
Malines: mechlin, lace
malison: curse, malediction
malkin: dowdy, hare, scarecrow
mallard: drake, (wild) duck
" **genus:** anas
malleate: pound
mallee: eucalyptus
mallemuck: fulmar, albatross
mallet: hammer, gavel, pestle
" **presiding officer's:**
gavel
" **striking part of:** tup
Malmo man: Swede
malmsey: wine, grape
" **grape:** malvasia, mal-
voisie
malt: liquor, barley
" **liquor:** ale, beer, stout,
porter
" **liquor's yeast:** barm
" **sugar:** maltose
Malta: wind: gregale
maltha: cement, tar, bitumen
mamba: cobra, elapine,
snake
mammal: primate, suckler
" **egg-laying:** platypus,
duckbill
" **extinct:** mastodon
" **flesh-eating:** mink, otter,
weasel
" **lowest order:** mono-
treme
" **nocturnal:** bat, lemur
" **water:** seal, otter,
seacow, whale
mammary: gland: udder
mammet: idol, doll, puppet
mammilla: nipple, teat
mammoth: enormous, ele-

phant
" **like animal:** mastodon
man: fortify, person, male, biped
" **bald-headed:** pilgarlic
" **Genesis:** Onan
" **handy:** factotum
" **Lat.:** homo
" **lecherous:** satyr
" **like:** android
" **little:** manikin
" **patient:** Job
" **who annoys women:** masher
manager: gerent, director
" **opera:** impressario
manakin: model, dwarf, bird
manatee: halicore, dugong, cowfish
manavelins: orts, leftovers
Manchu: Mongolian, Tungus
" **dynasty:** Ta Ch'ing
manciple: slave, steward
Mandan: indian, Sioux
mandolin strumming piece: plectrum
mandrel: lathe, spindle
maned: jubate, leonine
manes: soul
mange: scab
" **cause of:** mite
" **loss caused by:** hair
mango: fruit, muskmelon
mania: craze, obsession
" **for dancing:** tarantism
manifesto: edict, declaration
Manila: paper, hemp, cigar, city
" **hemp source:** abaca
maniples, three: cohort
manna: food, lerp
manner: air, mien, fashion,

method
" **of dress:** guise
" **of speaking:** diction
" **of walking:** gait, waddle
manners: mores, behavior
" **study of:** ethology
manorial court: leet
mansard: garret, attic, roof
manse: parsonage
manta: cape, shawl, devilfish
manteau: cloak, mantle
mantel: ledge, shelf
" **ornamental band:** frieze
mantis crab/shrimp: squilla
manual: handbook, textbook
" **training:** sloid
manufacturing left-overs: shorts
manuscript: ms., handwritten
" **copier:** scribe
" **leaf of:** folio
" **to be set in type:** copy
manx: cat, celt, gael
many: manifold, numerous, myriad
" **comb. form:** poly, myria
Maori: canoe: waka
" **parrot:** tui
" **weapon:** patu
map: chart, orrery, plat
" **line(s):** hachure, isobar, osocheim
" **maker:** mercator, cartographer
" **maker's abbr.:** isl, rd, rte
maple: tree, wood, sirup
" **leaf land:** Canada
" **seed:** samara
" **tree:** box elder, sycamore
maquis: guerrilla
marabou: stork, argala

marabout: tomb, hermit
maraca: rattle
Maracanda: Samarkand
marasca: cherry
" **product:** liqueur
marble: shooter, carrara, mib, cold, aggie
" **flooring:** terazzo
" **imitation:** scagliola
" **worker's tool:** burin
March: file, advance, border
" **date:** Ides
" **day's:** etape
" **for dead:** dirge
marchen: tale, story
Mardi Gras: carnival, festival
" **day:** Tuesday
" **home of:** New Orleans
" **king:** Rex
mare: yaud, horse, equine, dobbin
" **tail of:** cloud
" **young:** filly
margarite: pearl
margay: cat, ocelot
marginal note: scholium, apostil(le)
marguerite: daisy, chrysanthemum
marijuana: hemp, narcotic, ganza
" **cigarette holder:** roach clip
marine: naval, fleet
" **plant:** seaweed
" **plant group:** benthos
mariner: victim (fictional): albatross
mariposa flower: lily, tulip
mark: vestige, stain, scar, symbol
" **adverse:** demerit

" **black:** stigma
" **critical:** obelus
" **for   identification:** dogtag
" **missile's:** target
" **of bondage:** brand, yoke
" **of disgrace:** stigma, brand
" **of omission:** ellipsis, caret
" **over syllable:** breve
" **proofreader's:** caret, dele, stet
" **Twain:** Clemens
" **with line:** striate
" **with spots:** mottle, speckle
marker: scorer, milestone, liner, peg
" **channel:** buoy
" **grave:** barrow
" **stone:** cairn
market: store, sell, bazaar
" **place:** agora, emporium, plaza
marking instrument: scribe
marlin: spearfish
marmalade: jam, confection
" **material:** rind, peel
" **tree:** sapodilla, mamey, chico
marmoset: monkey, mico, tamarin
marmot: rodent, prairie dog, woodchuck
Marquand's sleuth: Mr. Moto
marriage: hymen, nuptials
" **broker:** schatchen
" **dowry:** dot
" **hater of:** misogamist
" **obstacle annulling:** diriment

" **pert. to:** marital
" **second:** digamy
" **vow:** troth
marrow: pith, medulla
" **bones:** knees
Mars: planet, Ares
" **comb. form:** areo
" **moon of:** Phobos, Deimos
" **sister:** Bellona
" **son:** Remus
marsh: bog, morass, wetland, quag
" **bird:** coot, sora, rail
" **fever:** helodes
" **grass:** sedge, reed
" **hen:** coot, rail
" **plant:** tule, bulrush, cattail
marshy: fenny, boggy
" **inlet/outlet:** bayou
marsupial: tait, koala, wombat, kangaroo
marsupium formation: pouch
marten: mammal, sable
" **fur:** baum
martin: swallow, martlet
martinet: disciplinarian, tyrant
Martinique: music: beguine
" **volcano:** pelee
Maryland: (see special section)
" **founder:** Calvert
mask: vizard, visor, conceal, disguise
" **half:** domino, loup
masker: mummer
mason: stonecutter
" **bench:** banker
" **chisel:** tooler, broach
" **mortar board:** hawk

mass: clot, lump, magnitude, majority, wad, liturgy
" **for the dead:** requiem
" **meeting:** rally
" **of bacteria:** clump
" **solidified:** concretion
Massachusetts: (see special section)
Massacre: carnage
" **organized:** pogrom
mast: acorns, spar, pole
" **platform:** lookout, maintop
" **support:** bibb
master: chief, control, dom, sahib
" **pert. to:** herile
" **stroke:** coup
masterpiece: magnum opus, chef-d'-oeuvre
mastic: resin, cement, liquor
" **tree:** acoma
masticating animal: goat, camel, deer, llama, antelope, giraffe, biscn
mastication product: cud
mat: snarl, matrix, carpet
" **leaf:** yapa
" **sleeping:** petate
matador: bullfighter, toreador, torero
" **queue of:** coleta
" **red cloth used by:** muleta, muletilla
" **sword:** estoque
match: team, vesuvian, equal, fit, contest
" **boxing:** setto, bout
" **stick:** linstock
" **wax/wooden:** vesta
matchmaker: schatchen
" **indefatigable:** Cupid,

Eros
mateless: azygous
maternal: relationship: ena-
tion
matgrass: nard, marram
mathematical: precise, exact,
accurate
" **arc:** radian
" **figure:** cone, diagram,
graph
" **line:** vector
" **ratio:** sine
" **term:** constant, (co)sine
matrass: flask, bolthead
matrimonial: conjugal, nup-
tial, marital
matted: cespitose
matter: copy, pith, content,
affair
" **classification:** animal,
mineral, vegetable, organic
" **in law:** res
Matterhorn: Mont Cervin,
mountain
mattock: pick(ax), hack
mattress: stuffing material:
kapok, ceiba, flock
maturation: meiosis
Mau Mau land: Kenya
maud: wrap, rug, shawl, plaid
" **clothing for:** shepherd
mauler: Manassas: soubriquet. . .(Jack) Dempsey
maumet: idol, puppet
Mauser: pistol, rifle
mavis: bird, thrush
max., opposite of: min
maxilla: jaw bone
maxim: motto, axiom, precept, adage, gnome
" **collection of:** sutra
May: heyday, prime, spring-

time, maiden
" **apple:** plant, mandrake
" **Day folk dance:** Morris
" **fifteen:** Ides
" **tree:** hawthorn
maybe: perhaps, possibly,
perchance
maze: labyrinth, stupefy
" **exit aid:** clew
mazzard: cherry
McCoy, the real: genuine
mdse: merchandise
meadow: lea, grassland
" **barley:** rie
" **grass:** fescue, poa
" **lark:** troupial
" **mouse:** vole
" **poetic:** mead
meal: mess, farina, chow,
flour, repast, agape
" **coarse:** samp, hominy,
corn
" **family:** potluck
meals: board
mean: base, nasty, snide,
poor, humble, vicious
" **person:** caitiff
meaning: purport, sense
" **ambiguous in:** cryptic
means: agency, resources,
riches, method
" **for communicating
knowledge:** organon
" **of defense:** muniment
" **of escape:** loophole
" **of expression:** outlet,
medium
measles: rubeola, roseola
measure: cloth: ell
" **comb. form:** metro
" **depth:** fathom
" **dry:** rotl, bushel

" **equality:** isometry
" **nautical:** knot
" **of:** mensural
" **of earth:** geodesy
" **of energy:** entropy
" **of wood:** cord
" **paper:** ream, quire
" **sound volume:** decibel
" **wine:** butt
" **wire:** mil
" **yarn:** lea, spindle

measurement: meterage, mensuration
" **contents/weight:** metage
" **standard/unit of:** module

meat: food, pork, beef, flesh, steak, veal, mutton, tripe, venison
" **and vegetable dish:** olla, ragout
" **carving board:** trencher
" **eater:** carnivore
" **in gravy:** au jus
" **jelly:** aspic
" **leg/ribs:** cutlet
" **paste:** pem(m)ican
" **slice:** collop
" **spiced:** bologna, sausage, salami
" **strips:** biltong

meatless: maigre

Mecca: pilgramage: Hadj
" **shrine:** Kaaba, Caaba

medal: badge, medallion
" **back:** verso
" **face:** obverse
" **space:** exergue

medals: disk, badge, plaque
" **of:** numismatic

Medea: sorceress

" **husband:** Jason
" **father:** Aeetes
" **rival:** Creusa

Medes' language: Avestan

medical: iatric, curative
" **comb. form:** iatro
" **professional symbol:** Caduceus
" **student:** medic(o), intern(e)
" **suffix:** itis, oma

medicinal: iatric
" **bark:** pereira, cinchona, viburnum
" **gum:** kino
" **herb:** aloe, senna, arnica
" **plant:** rue, tansy, spurge, simple, urena, ipecac, boneset
" **root:** jalap, zedoary, ginseng, artar
" **shrub:** alem

medicine: drug, remedy, cure
" **cure-all:** elixir, panacea
" **dropper:** pipette
" **measure:** dose
" **mock:** placebo
" **science of:** iatrology

medieval: coat: gambeson
" **knight:** Pennon
" **lyric:** alba
" **servant:** sewer
" **shield:** ecu, pavis
" **sport:** joust, tilt
" **tunic:** gipon, jupon
" **vassal:** vavasor
" **weapon:** oncin, mace

Mediterranean: inland, landlocked
" **bush:** caper
" **evergreen:** laurustine
" **fish:** omber

" **grass:** diss
" **pine:** pinaster
" **principality:** Monaco
" **resin:** mastic
" **shrub:** laurustine
" **trading ship:** padrone
" **tree:** carob
" **wind:** mistral, ptesian, solano, levanter, sirocco
medium: mean(s), agency, average
" **response of:** oracle
" **session with:** seance
" **spiritualistic:** psychic
medley: fantasia, mixture, pastiche, melange
medrick: gull, tern
medulla: pith, marrow
Medusa: gorgon, jellyfish
" **hair:** snake(s)
" **sister:** Euryale, Stheno
" **slayer:** Perseus
medusan: jellyfish
meerschaum: pipe, mineral, seafoam
meet: equal, convene, seemly
" **face to face:** confront
meeting: rally, date, huddle, caucus, session, bee, gathering, assembly, symposium, conference, conclave
" **clandestine:** tryst
" **full attendance:** plenary
" **lovers':** tryst, rendezvous
" **place of "Big Three":** Yalta, Potsdam, Casablanca
" **room:** camarilla
" **to elect Pope:** conclave
Megiddo: Armageddon
"Mein Kampf" author: Hitler

mel: honey
melancholic spell: hump
Melanesian:　　language: Santo
" **islands:** Solomon, Fiji, Admiralty
melanin: pigment
melanous, opposed to: xanthous
Melba, soprano: Nellie
Meleager: argonaut
" **mother:** Althea
melicocca: genip
melilot: clover
melli: comb. form: honey
melodic: lyrical, ariose
" **phrase:** ostinato
melody: strain, aria, cavatina
" **counterpoint of:** descant
meloid: beetle
melt: fuse, soften, dissolve, liquefy
" **fat:** render
" **ore:** smelt
melting pot: crucible
Melville, novelist: Herman
" **character:** Moby Dick, whale, Billy Budd
membrane: web, pia, velum, covering, velamen
" **animal eye:** tapetum
" **bird's beak:** cere
" **comb. form:** hymen(o)
" **enclosing:** caul
" **eyeball:** sclera
" **uniting　toes/fingers:** web(bing)
memorabilia: ana
memorable: notable
" **period:** era, epoch
memory: recollection, remi-

niscence, remembrance
" **loss of:** amnesia
" **pert. to:** mnesic
" **science to improve:** mnemonics
Memphis: god: Ptah
" **ruler:** Pharoah
menad: nymph, bacchante
mendel, botanist: Gregor
" **forte of:** heredity, genetics
Menelaus: brother of: Agamemnon
" **daughter of:** Hermione
" **father of:** Atreus
" **wife of:** Helen
meniscus: lens, crescent
Mennonite: Amish
mentally: alert: acute
" **sound:** lucid, sane
mentum: chin
Mephisto(pheles), debtor of: Faust(us)
Mercator: mapmaker
merchant: of Venice character: Antonio, Shylock, Tubal, Portia
merchants, guild of: hanse
mercuric: chloride: calomel
mercury: Azoth, planet, Hermes, messenger, quicksilver
" **shoes:** talaria
" **staff:** caduceus
mercy: killing: euthanasia
mere: nonsense: falderal
" **nothing:** fiddlestick
merganser: harle, smee, smew, sheldrake
meridian: noon, apex, prime, zenith
merino: wool, yarn

meros: surface, thigh
Merrimac: frigate, ironclad
mescal: cactus, liquor, agave
mesmeric: hypnotic, magnetic
" **force:** od
Mesopotamia: Iraq
" **wind:** shamal
messenger: envoy, nuncio, herald
" **of the Gods:** Mercury, Hermes
Messrs.: messieurs, misters
metal: tin, iron, lead, aluminum
" **assaying vessel:** test, cupel
" **coating:** rust, patina
" **cutting tool:** hacksaw
" **dross:** slag
" **fastener:** tnut
" **for coins:** planchet, flan
" **lightest:** lithium
" **marker:** stamp, die
" **mixture:** alloy
" **plate, cut:** trepan
" **purify:** smelt
" **refine:** smelt
" **shaped for coins:** flan
" **suit:** mail, hauberk
metalloid: arsenic, silicon
metalware, enameled: tole
"Metamorphoses": author: Ovid
" **character:** Thisbe, Pyramus
metaphorlike figure of speech: trope, simile
" **mixed:** catachresis
meteor: fireball, leonid, rainbow
" **train of:** tail

meteorologic prefix: strato
metheglin: liquor, mead
  " **material:** honey
Methodism: founder of: Wesley
Methuselah: famous for: age
  " **father:** Enoch
  " **grandson:** Noah
metis: mulatto
metrical: accent/stress: ictus
  " **time unit:** mora
metro: subway
mewl: whimper, whine
Mexico, Mexican: Aztec emporer: Montezuma
  " **bandit:** ladrone, bandido
  " **beverage:** tequila, mescal
  " **bird:** verdin, tinamou
  " **bread:** tortilla
  " **cactus:** peyote, mescal, chaute
  " **coin:** peso, centavo
  " **dance:** raspa
  " **Indian:** Zuni, Otomi, Mayan, Aztec, Lipan
  " **laborer:** bracero, peon
  " **mix-blood:** mestizo
  " **pine:** ocote
  " **poppy:** chicalote
  " **temple:** teocalli
  " **weight:** arroba
Miami county: Dade
Michaelmas daisy: aster
Michigan: (see special section)
  " **river:** Cass
microspores: pollen
Midas: touch: gold
middle: median, center, mid, hub
  " **comb. form:** medi(o)
  " **ear:** drum, tympanum
middy: blouse, plebe
mien: air, bearing, look, appearance, manner
migale: mouse, shrew
miggle: taw, migs
mignon: pretty, dainty
migratory: nomadic, wandering
  " **bird:** tern, wi(d)geon
  " **butterfly:** monarch
  " **creature:** locust, lemming
  " **horde:** swarm
mildew: mold, blight, fungus
mile: nautical: knot
  " **⅛ of:** furlong
  " **⅓ of:** li
military: army, soldiers
  " **cap:** shako, kepi, busby
  " **force:** legion, army, militia
  " **formation:** phalanx
  " **group:** army, division
  " **jail:** brig
  " **messenger:** estafet
  " **movement:** march, deployment
  " **roll:** muster
  " **station:** garrison
  " **storehouse:** arsenal, etape, depot
  " **truck:** camion, amtrac
milk: lac, emulsion, extract, suck
  " **comb. form:** lact(o)
  " **curd:** casein
  " **giving:** milch
  " **pert. to:** lactic, lacteal
  " **sugar:** lactose

" **with:** au lait
" **without:** yeld
milkfish: awa, tarpon, sabalo
milkwort: senega
miller: moth
millet: grain, panic, pearl, grass
" **sorghum-like:** milo
million: times: comb. form: mega
mim: shy, demure, quiet
mimosa: herb, acacia
" **descriptive word for:** shrinking
mind: reason, purpose, nous, psyche
" **bear in:** remember
" **call to:** recollect
" **of the:** mental, phrenic
mine: dig, pit, explosive, tunnel, source
" **car/truck:** hutch
" **entrance:** adit
" **kind:** coal, silver, gold, diamond
" **passage:** stulm, winze
" **safety lamp:** davy
" **vein:** lode
" **worker:** collier, pitman
mineral: talc, ore, fluorite, spinel, barite
" **black:** coal, graphite
" **blue:** iolite, lazulite
" **glassy:** silica
" **hardest:** diamond
" **magnetite:** lodestar
" **mixture:** magma
" **radioactive:** carnotite
" **silicate:** mica
" **softest:** talc
" **truck:** corf
" **vein:** lode

miniature: tree: bonsai
minify: reduce
" **opposed to:** magnify
minister: curate, serve, vizier
" **assistant:** deacon
" **home:** manse, rectory, parsonage
" **to become a:** ordained
Minnehaha's love: Hiawatha
Minnesota: (see special section)
minnow: gudgeon, moonfish
minor: youth, petty, underage
" **details:** minutiae
" **offense:** misdemeanor
" **planet:** Amor, Ceres, Eros, Hermes
minorite: Friar, Franciscan
Minos: kingdom: Crete
" **monster:** minotaur
mint: candy, stamp, fabricate, herb
" **genus:** mentha
" **product:** coin(s)
Minuit's bargain: New York
minute: wee, miniscule, instant, petty
" **comb. form:** micro
" **groove:** stria
minutiae: details
Mira: star
" **constellation:** Cetus
miracle: feat, anomy, wonder
" **scene of:** Cana, Lourdes
Miriam: brother: Moses, Aaron
Miranda's father: Prospero
misanthrope: (man) hater
" **kind of:** cynic
miscellanea: ana
misdeed: sin, fault, crime
miser: niggard, skinflint

"   of   fiction: Marner, Scrooge
misle: drizzle, mist
misogynist: woman-hater
missal: prayerbook
missel: thrush
missile: arrow, projectile, rocket
  "   **detecting device:** radar
  "   **part of:** warhead
  "   **returning:** boomerang
  "   **whaler's:** harpoon
Mississippi: (see special section)
  "   **native:** tadpole
Missouri: (see special section)
misstep: error, faux pas, trip
mistral: wind
misunderstanding: imbroglio
misuse: of words: malapropism
mixed: impure, motley
  "   **language:** pidgin, jargon
  "   **blood, person of:** metis, mulatto
  "   **metaphor:** catachresis
mizzen: sail
mnemonic subject: memory
Mnemosyne: daughters: Muses
moa: ratite
Moab: kingdom
  "   **father of:** Lot
Moby Dick: author of: Melville
mochila: knapsack
mochy: damp, misty, muggy
mock: deride, mimic, scoff, defy, imitate
  "   **attack:** feint
  "   **up:** model, dummy

modal auxiliary verb: may, might, must, would, should
model: pattern, standard, design, exemplar, prototype
  "   **for imitation:** lodestar
  "   **of   perfection:** ideal, paragon
modified leaf: bract
modus: way, means
  "   **operandi:** procedure
  "   **vivendi:** compromise
mogo: hatchet
moha: millet
mohair: fabric, garment
  "   **source of:** angora
Mohammed: mahound
  "   **birthplace:** Mecca
  "   **burial place:** Medina
  "   **flight of:** Hegira
  "   **follower:** Islam, Muslim
  "   **successor:** Calif
  "   **wife:** Aisha
Mohammedan: angel: Azrael
  "   **bible:** Koran, Alcoran
  "   **canonical law:** Sharia
  "   **crusade:** Jehad
  "   **festival:** Bairam
  "   **god:** Allah
  "   **infidel:** Kafir
  "   **law:** Sunna(h)
  "   **noble:** Emir, Amir
  "   **priest:** Imam
  "   **saint:** Pir
  "   **scholars:** Ulema
  "   **sect member:** Sunnite, Shite
  "   **slave:** mameluke
  "   **woman's clothing:** izar
moire: silk, fabric, tabby
moisture: comb.   form: hygr(o)
  "   **condensed:** mist, dew

molasses: treacle
  ‘‘ **source:** sorgo
mold: fen, calm, cast, die, model
  ‘‘ **pert. to:** humic
molded: can be: fictile
molding: shaping, cornice, ogee, fillet
  ‘‘ **cornice:** cyma
  ‘‘ **curved:** nebule
  ‘‘ **edge:** arris
  ‘‘ **material:** ormolu
mole: pier, quay, mammal, platypus
molecule: particle
  ‘‘ **component:** atom
molluscoid: by-product: pearl
mollusk: snail, chiton, abalone, oyster, scallop, helix
  ‘‘ **arm of:** tentacle
  ‘‘ **beaked:** octopus
  ‘‘ **fake:** slug, queer
  ‘‘ **genus:** oliva, murex
  ‘‘ **shell:** conch, cowry
  ‘‘ **teeth:** redula
moly: garlic
moment: flash, sec, point, instant
  ‘‘ **of truth:** crisis
Monday: Black: cold
  ‘‘ **blue:** (colloq.) depressing
  ‘‘ **Easter:** day after Easter
money: fund, tender, lucre
  ‘‘ **box:** till, arca, kist
  ‘‘ **bronze:** aes
  ‘‘ **changer:** cambist, shroff
  ‘‘ **market:** bourse
  ‘‘ **sl.:** boodle, moola, lettuce, scratch

  ‘‘ **substitute:** coupon, scrip
Mongol, Mongolian: Kalmuck, Tungus
  ‘‘ **dynasty:** Yuan
  ‘‘ **coin:** tugrik
  ‘‘ **priest:** Shaman, Lama
  ‘‘ **tribesman:** Buryat
  ‘‘ **weight:** lan
monk: Friar, Lama, Franciscan, Carmelite, Votary, Dominican
  ‘‘ **ever silent:** Trappist
  ‘‘ **head:** Abbot
  ‘‘ **settlement:** Scete
  ‘‘ **title:** Fra
monkey: primate, simian, fool
  ‘‘ **Asiatic:** langur
  ‘‘ **bread:** baobab
  ‘‘ **green:** guenon
  ‘‘ **marmoset:** tamarin
  ‘‘ **red:** patas
  ‘‘ **sacred:** rhesus
  ‘‘ **spider:** ateles, quata
monocotyledon plant: palm, lily, orchid
monolith: column, pillar, obelisk
monostich: poem, verse, epigram
monotreme: duckbill, anteater, echidna
monster: enormous, ogre, freak
  ‘‘ **comb. form:** terat(o)
  ‘‘ **female:** gorgon, Medusa
  ‘‘ **fire-breathing:** dragon, chimera
  ‘‘ **hundred-eyed:** Argus
  ‘‘ **many-headed:** Hydra
  ‘‘ **myth.:** Centaur, Sphinx,

Hippogriff, Griffin
" **snake-haired:** Medusa
" **winged:** Geryon
Montana: (see special section)
Monte Cristo author: Dumas
" **hero:** Dantes
month: by the: permensem
" **first day:** kalends, calend(i)s
" **last:** ult(imo)
monument: honoring the dead: cenotaph
" **of stone(s):** cairn, dolmen
moon: month, satellite, Diana
" **between half and full:** gibbous
" **dark area on:** mare
" **hole:** crater
" **on the wane:** decrescent
" **pert. to:** lunar, selenic
" **poetic:** lamp
" **point farthest from earth:** apogee
" **point nearest earth:** perigee
" **shadow:** umbra
moor rope: painter
Moorish: Moresque, Moriscan
" **coin:** maravedi
" **fabric:** tiraz
" **garment:** jupon
moose: alces, deer, elk
" **male:** bull
" **pouch:** bel
moral: ethical, chaste, decent
" **allegorical story with:** apologue, fable

" **law:** decalog(ue)
morals: pert. to: ethics
moray: eel, conger, elgin
more: plus, again, further
" **cry for:** encore
" **in music:** piu
morello: cherry
moreover: and, else, also, besides, further, likewise
mores: customs
" **singular of:** mos
morganite: beryl
Mormon: Danite
" **church founder:** Smith
" **priest:** elder
" **sacred instrument:** urim
morning: eos, aurora, matin, dawn
" **glory:** sunrise, plant, ipomea
" **of:** matutinal
" **star:** Venus, Saturn
Morocco, Moroccan: Berber, Marrakech, leather
" **coin:** rial
" **dynasty founder:** Ali
" **hat:** fez
" **international zone:** Tangier
" **monetary unit:** dirham
Morpheus, god of: dreams
morphine: addicts' analgesic drug: methadone
mortal: deadly, fatal, human
" **opposed to:** venial
mortar: bowl, cement, cannon
" **mixer:** rab
" **sound-proofing:** pugging
mortise: join, fasten
mosaic: collage, inlay

" **material:** tessera, tile
" **work:** intarsia
Moscow: Moskva
" **citadel:** Kremlin
" **square/writer:** Pushkin
Moses: leader, lawgiver
" **brother:** Aaron
" **death place:** Nebo
" **people led by:** Israelites
" **sister:** Miriam
" **wife:** Zipporah
Moslem (see Muslim): Saracen, Islam(ic), Mohammedan, Berber
" **coin:** dinar
" **converts:** ansar
" **devil:** Eblis
" **holy city:** Mecca, Medina
" **holy man:** Imam
" **idol:** Maumet
" **lady:** begum
" **language:** Urdu
" **measure:** ardeb
" **messiah:** Mahdi
" **monk:** Santon
" **mystic:** Suni
" **nomad:** kurd
" **pilgrimage:** hadj
" **prayer:** salat
" **religious   festival:** Bairam
" **temple:** mosque
" **tomb:** tabut
" **weight:** rotl
mosquito: culex, insect
" **genus:** culex, aedes
" **larva:** w(r)iggler
mot: repartee, witticism
moth: egger, insect, io, browntail, gypsy, luna

" **group of:** tortricid
" **larva:** looper
" **night-flying:** noctuid
motion: gesture, movement
" **pert. to:** motive, kinetic
" **producing:** motile
motorcyclist: Hailwood
mott(e): grove
mottle: dapple, streak, spot, blotch
motto: adage,   maxim, gnome, device, slogan
" **in a book:** epigraph
moulding: (see molding)
mound: pile, heap, dune, knoll, tell, hillock
" **domelike:** stupa
mountain: pile, heap, mound
" **antelope:** klipspringer
" **Apollo's:** Parnassus
" **Asia Minor:** Ida
" **Biblical:** Sinai, Nebo, Horeb, Ararat
" **chain:** Sierra, range
" **climber's aid:** crampon, piton
" **comb. form/prefix:** oro
" **crest:** spur, arete
" **formation:** arete, spur, ridge
" **gap:** col, pass
" **goat:** tahr, ibex
" **highest:** Everest
" **legendary:** Meru
" **movable:** Ossa
" **pass:** col, gap, ghat, defile
" **ridge:** arete, sawback
" **sheep:** bighorn, mouflon
" **sickness:** veta, puna
" **trail marker:** karn

mourning: band: crepe, crape
" **cloak:** butterfly
" **clothes:** weeds
" **song:** dirge
mouth: lips, stoma, orifice, opening
" **comb. form:** stome, ori
" **gaping:** rictus
" **opening:** rictus
" **part:** lip, velum, uvula, tongue
" **pert. to:** buccal, stomatic
" **river:** frith, estuary, delta
" **to pharynx passage:** fauces
" **open:** agape
mouths: ora
move: affect, touch, shift, stir, budge
" **able to:** motile
" **along:** sashay, mosey
" **confusedly:** mill
" **in circles:** eddy, purl, swirl
" **movie camera/TV:** pan
" **on casters:** trundle, truckle
" **sidewise:** edge, sidle
" **sinuously:** snake, writhe
" **slowly:** worm, inch, crawl
" **to and fro:** wag, shuttle, vibrate
" **toward something:** gravitate
movement: action, motion
" **in music:** tempo, rhythm
" **of charged particles:** cataphoresis
" **of organism:** taxis

" **of the sea:** tide
movie: cinema
" **camera platform:** dolly
" **comb. form:** cine
" **film, 1000 ft.:** reel
" **low budget:** quickie
" **script:** scenario
" **shot:** clinch, close-up
" **sound adjustment:** sync
moving: stirring, motile, current
" **about:** ambulant
" **area around body:** periphery
" **comb. form:** kineto
" **in circular path:** gyral
mowing implement: sickle, reaper, scythe
moxa: plant, cautery
Mozambique: native: Bantu, Yao
Mozart's city: Salzburg
much: many, lot
" **in music:** molto
mucilage: glue, adhesive, arabin
mucous: slimy, viscous, blennoid
" **comb. form:** myx(o)
mudfish: bowfin, dipnoan
mudguard: fender
mudworm: ipo
mufti: ulema
muggins: game, fool, domino
mugwump: republican, independent
mulatto: metis, creole
mulberry: tree, sycamine
" **bark:** tapa
" **tree genus:** morus, ce-

cropia
mule: hinny, shavetail
" **driver:** skinner
" **female:** mare
" **young:** foal
mulla(h): teacher, interpreter
multiplied creature: centipede
mumbojumbo: idol, fetish, gibberish
mummy: corpse
" **cloth:** byssus
mundungo: tobacco
Mundy work: Om
muntjac: deer, ratwa
murder: slay, homicide, bump off
" **by drowning:** noyade
" **by suffocation:** burke
murderous frenzy: berserk, amok
murex: whelk
murid: rat, disciple
murmuring sound: sussurus
murre: auk, guillemot
murrelet: (sea)bird
musaceous plant: banana
muscid insect: housefly
muscle: sinew, sphincter, tissue, brawn
" **attachment:** tendon
" **comb. form:** my(o)
" **contraction:** cramps, spasm, tic
" **disease:** myopathy
" **jaw:** masseter
" **loin:** psoas
" **protuberance:** venter
" **tension:** tonus
muscles: brawn, thews, psoas

" **science of:** myology
" **wasting of:** dystrophy
muscovado: sugar
muscular: burly, strong, brawny
" **elasticity:** tonus
" **fatigue:** myasthenia
" **impotence:** ataxia
muse: ponder, meditate, goddess
" **astronomy:** Urania
" **chief:** Calliope
" **comedy:** Thalia
" **dance:** Terpsichore
" **epic poetry:** Calliope
" **history:** Clio
" **love:** Erato
" **poetry:** Erato
" **tragedy:** Melpomene
Muses: domain: Parnassus, Aonia
" **fountain:** Hippocrene
" **home:** Helicon
" **mountain:** Helicon, Parnassus
" **of the:** Pierian
" **one of:** Calliope, Clio, Erato, Euterpe, Melpomene, Polymnia, Urania, Thalia
" **place where worshipped:** Pieria
" **spring of:** Castalia
museum: gallery
" **custodian:** curator
" **part of:** court
mushroom: fungus, agaric, morel, champignon
" **alkaloid:** muscarin(e)
" **cap:** pileus
" **covering:** volva
" **poisonous:** toadstool,

agaric, amanita
" **underground:** truffle
music: tune, air, harmony
" **adapter:** arranger
" **canto:** passus
" **clef:** treble, bass
" **concluding passage:** coda
" **for nine:** nonet
" **for practice:** etude
" **for two:** duet
" **high part:** treble
" **major scale:** gamut
" **measured beat:** pulse, moto, tempo
" **moderately, slow:** andante
" **rate of speed:** andante, allegro, lento, tempo
" **sacred:** choral(e)
" **short song:** ode
" **sign:** presa, segno
musical: melic, melodious, lyric(al), canorous
" **ballad:** derry
" **character:** clef, key, sharp, rest
" **combination:** chord
" **drama:** opera
" **ending:** coda
" **excerpt:** morceau
" **exercise:** etude
" **instrument:** reed, piano, lyre, lute, flute, viol(in), sitar, cornet, guitar
" " **brass wind:** cornet, trumpet, trombone
" " **keyboard:** clavier, piano, organ
" " **string:** chord, catgut
" " **stringed:** vina, lute, dulcimer, bandore, guitar, rebec, rote, lyre, banjo, clavier, asor, citole, zither, cither(n), samisen, samebuke, mandolin, ukelele, viola, viol
" " **trumpet-like:** tuba, clarion
" " **wind:** flute, reed, clarinet, tuba, organ, saxophone
" **instruments, collectively:** strings, traps, brass, winds, percussion
" **interlude, short:** verset
" **introduction:** overture
" **movement:** scherzo
" **note of old:** elk, ut, fe, are
" **passage in fast tempo:** presto
" **pitch:** tone
" **sounds, science of:** harmonics
" **trill:** tremolo
" **vibrato:** trill
" **work:** opus
musicians' patron saint: Cecilia
musk: cat: civet
muskellunge: pike
musket: dragon, firearm, jingal, culverin
" **flintlock:** fusil
muskmelon: atimon, casaba
Muslim (see Moslem): cap: kopia
" **court:** Agama
" **fasting month:** Ramadan
muslin: batiste, adati, mosal,

shela
" **bag:** tillot
" **striped:** doria
mussel: unio, mollusk
" **product:** pearl
must: sapa, alba, mold, essential
mustached sea animal: walrus
mustang: pony, horse, bronco
mustard: weed, condiment, turnip, woad
" **dye:** woad
" **gas:** vesicant
" **plaster:** sinapism
" **pod:** silique
" **wild:** charlock
mustee: mestizo, octoroon
musteline animal: polecat, mink, weasel, otter, wolverine
muster: summon, gather
" **in:** enlist
" **out:** disband
mutant: sport
mutation: change, evolution
" **in linguistics:** umlaut
mutton: flesh, sheep
" **bird:** oii
" **chop:** kabobs
" **fish:** sama
" **stew:** haricot
mutually destructive: intercine

myna(h): bird
myrmicid: ant
Myrmidon: adherent, follower
myrrh: cicely
myrtle: guava, periwinkle, cajeput, shrub
" **berry:** allspice
mystic: essene, occult, sufist, enigmatic
" **art:** cabala, voodoo, alchemy
" **union with God:** theocrasy
" **word:** abraxas, abracadabra
" **writing:** rune
mythical: legendary, imaginary, fabulous
" **animal:** griffin
" **antelope:** yale
" **being:** centaur
" **flyer:** Icarus
" **giant:** Ymir, Cyclops, Ymer, Jotun, Fafnir
" **horse:** Pegasus, unicorn
" **hunter:** Orion
" **island/continent:** Atlantis
" **land:** Lemuria
" **monster:** sphinx, chimera, dragon, minotaur
" **river:** Styx
" **sisters:** Gorgons
" **wolf:** Fenrir

N

N, letter: en, nu
Na: sodium
Nabal: home: Maon
  " **wife:** Abigail
nabob: dives, Midas, viceroy
  " **deputy:** Nawab
Nabokov novel: Lolita, Pnin, PaleFire, Ada
nacelle: chassis, basket, cockpit
nacket: boy, cake
nacre: (mother-of) pearl, shellfish
nacrite: kaolin(e)
nadir: opposed to: zenith
naga: snake
nahoor: bharal, sha, sheep
Nahor: son: Terah
  " **wife:** Milcah
naiad: nymph, mussel, hydriad
nail: tack, stud, talon, plate, clench, trap

" **drive at slant:** toe
" **Fr.:** clou
" **headless:** sprig
" **ingrowing:** acronyx
" **marking on:** lunule
" **shoemaker's:** brad, sparable
" **size:** penny
" **wooden:** peg, fid
nais: nymph
namaycush: trout, fish, togue
name: epithet, agnomen, moniker, alias, christen
" **assumed:** pen, alias, pseudonym
" **bad:** caconym
" **consisting of:** onomastic
" **derived from father:** patronym
" **derived from mother:** matronym
" **family:** cognomen,

agnomen
" **female:**
" " **beautiful:** Bell(a), Belle
" " **beauty:** Ada(h)
" " **beloved:** Amy, Vida
" " **bird:** Ava, Avis
" " **bitter:** Mary, Mara, Moya, Mari(e), Moll(y), Poll(y)
" " **chaste:** Catherine, Karen
" " **clinging:** Ivy
" " **compassionate:** Ruth
" " **destiny:** Carma
" " **eagle:** Arva
" " **felicity:** Naomi
" " **good:** Bonnie
" " **grace:** Ann(a), Nancy, Nina
" " **happy:** Ida
" " **high or holy:** Elga, Olga, Holly
" " **honey:** Millie, Melissa
" " **jewel:** Pearl, Opal, Ruby
" " **life:** Vita, Zoe, Eve
" " **lovable:** Mila
" " **maiden:** Cora
" " **mistress:** Martha
" " **one:** Mona
" " **peace:** Irene, Freda, Olive
" " **poem:** Edda
" " **power:** Dyna
" " **rainbow:** Iris
" " **royal:** Rani
" " **snow:** Neva
" " **sound:** Echo

" " **true:** Vera
" **feminine of:**
" " **David:** Vida
" " **John:** Jean, Jane, Joan, Janet
" " **Joseph:** Josepha, Josephine
" " **Solomon:** Salome
" **first:** praenomen, forename
" **maiden:** nee
" **male:**
" " **amiable:** Elmo
" " **beloved:** David
" " **bitter:** Omar
" " **blind:** Homer
" " **cautious:** Cato
" " **cheerful:** Tate
" " **courageous:** Neil
" " **dove:** Jonas, Jonah
" " **fighter:** Boris
" " **free:** Frank, Francis
" " **God's grace:** Jess(e)
" " **healer or physician:** Asa, Jason
" " **judge:** Dan
" " **laughter:** Isaac
" " **Lord is God:** Joel
" " **love:** Lief
" " **man:** Enos
" " **of the forest:** Silas, Sylvester
" " **peace:** Fritz
" " **red-haired:** Rufus
" " **safe:** Titus
" " **wanderer:** Errol
" " **watchful:** Ira
" **of a thing:** noun
" **of two terms:** dionym
" **written backward:**

ananym
namesake: homonym
Nandu: rhea
Naomi: Mara
  " **daughter-in-law:** Ruth
  " **land settled in:** Moab
naos: temple, cella, shrine
nap: ras, down, fuzz, snooze
  " **long:** shag
  " **raising machine:** gig
  " **to raise:** tease(l)
nape: scruff, niddick
  " **of sheep's neck:** scrag
napery: linen
Naphtali: mother: Bilhah
  " **son:** Jezer, Guni
Naples: Napoli
  " **coin:** carlin(e)
  " **secret society:** Camorra
Napoleon: battle: Waterloo
  " **birthplace:** Corsica
  " **exiled to:** Elba
  " **wife:** Josephine
napu: deerlet
Naraka: hell
narcissus: plant, flower, egoist
  " **loved by:** Echo
narcotic: dose: locus
  " **package:** deck, bindle
  " **plant:** hemp, mandrake, poppy
  " **seller:** pusher
nardoo: clover, plant, nardu
nares: nostrils, nose
narghile: pipe, hooka(h)
nark: spy, informer, tease
narrative: fable, history, recital
  " **poem:** epic, epos
narrow: close, lineal, rigid,

small, confined
  " **comb. form:** sten(o)
  " **inlet:** ria
  " **mindedness:** bigotry, bias
narthex: foyer, porch, hall, portico
nashgab: gossip
nasi: patriarch
nasicorn: rhinoceros
nasutiform: noselike
nat: spirit, demon
Nata's wife: Nana
natatorium: pool, tank
Nathan Hale: spy
native: natal, son, denizen, ite
natterjack: toad
natural: raw, wild, primitive, innate, easy
  " **condition:** norm
  " **group:** race, ethnicism
  " **location:** situs
  " **principle:** guna
naturalist: Muir, animist, biologist
nature: bent, essence, ilk, quality, tenor
  " **pert. to:** cosmo
  " **spirit:** Nat
  " **worship:** physiolatry
  " **god:** Pan
  " **goddess:** Artemis
nauntle: fuss, strut, raise
nautical: marine, maritime, naval
  " **before:** afore
  " **below:** alow
  " **cease:** avast
  " **chain:** tye
  " **fasten:** batten
  " **hook:** becket

"   **stop:** avast
"   **tighten:** frap
"   **tilting:** alist
"   **water's surface:** ryme
nautilus: mollusk
Navaho hut: hogan
nave: center, hub, apse
navel: umbilicus
navigation: cabotage
"   **call:** ahoy
"   **signal:** bell, flag
nawab: ruler
neal: temper
neap: tide
near: close, short, adjacent, stingy
"   **comb. form:** par(a)
"   **sighted:** myopic, purblind
Near East: Levant
"   **native:** Arab, Turk
Nebraska: (see special section)
nebris: fawnskin
nebula: galaxy, vapor
nebulous: hazy, vague, cloudy
"   **envelope:** coma, chevelure
necessity: of life: aliment, food, bread, water
neck: swire, cervix, channel, woo
"   **-and neck:** tie, even, close
"   **armor:** gorget
"   **artery:** carotid
"   **back of:** nape, nucha, scruff
"   **frill:** jabot, ruche
"   **hair:** mane
"   **horse:** withers

"   **part of:** gula, throat
"   **pert. to:** wattled, nuchal
"   **thin:** scrag
necromancy: goety, magic, sorcery
necropsy: autopsy
nectar: drink, honey
"   **bird:** sunbird
"   **of Gods:** ambrosia
neddy: donkey
needle: bodkin, obelisk, pointer, vex
"   **bug genus:** ranatra
"   **comb. form:** acu
"   **finisher:** eyer
"   **medical:** hypo
"   **pointed:** acerate, acerose
"   **shaped:** acicular, spicular, aciform
needlefish: gar, earl, pipefish
neep: turnip
nef: clock
negative: not, film, x-ray, negate
"   **ion:** anion
"   **pole:** cathode
"   **prefix:** non, im, un, dis
negro: Luri, Ethiopian, Hubshi, Hottentot, Bushman
"   **Afr.:** Dahoman, Vei, Vai
"   **dance:** juba
"   **dialect:** Gullah
"   **Egypt:** Nubian
"   **ghost:** Juba
"   **Niger:** Ibo, Nupe
"   **secret society:** Mau, Egbo
"   **Sudan:** Hausa, Egba
"   **white and:** Mustee
negus: beverage

neither right or wrong: adiaphorous
Neleus son: Nestor
nelumbo: lily, lotus
nemoral: sylvan
nema: eelworm
neoplasm: growth, tumor
neoteric: late, new, novel
nep: catnip
Nepal, Nepalese: coin: mohar, anna
" **mongoloid:** Rais
" **native:** Kha
" **peak:** Api
nephelite: mineral, lenad
nephew: nepote (Sc.)
Neptune: sea God
" **Celtic:** Ler
" **emblem:** trident
" **consort:** Salacia
" **son:** Triton
Ner's son: Abner
Nereides' steed: seahorse
Nereus: wife: Doris
nerfling: ide, id, fish
Nero: tyrant, fiddler
" **successor:** Galba
" **victim:** Seneca
" **wife:** Octavia
Nero Wolfe creator: Stout, Rex
nerve: vigor, grit, cheek, energy, sciatic
" **cell:** neuron
" **center:** brain, cortex, plexus
" **comb. form:** neur(o)
" **cranial:** vagus, optic
" **motor:** efferent
" **network:** rete, retia, plexus
" **sensory:** afferent
nerve cell framework: stroma
nervous: jittery, edgy, timorous
" **malady:** tic, aphasia, neuritis
ness: suffix, cape
nest: lair, den, bed, colony
" **build:** aerie, nidify
" **builder:** bird, mouse, ant, wasp, hornet, bee
" **building fish:** acara, stickleback
" **of boxes:** inro
" **squirrel's:** dray, drey
Nestor: sage, counselor
net: fabric, gin, snare, profit
" **bag:** reticule
" **like:** retiary
Netherlands: (see **Holland**)
netop: crony, friend
nettle: plant, vex, offend
" **genus:** urtica
" **rash:** hives, urticaria
network: mesh, web, system, complex
" **arterial:** vas
" **nerve:** rete, plexus
neume: sequence
neural: dorsal
neurite: axone
neuroglia: glia
neutral: indefinite, noncombatant, unbiased
" **equilibrium; having:** astatic, balanced
Nevada: (see special section)
neve: snow, ice, firn
nevus: freckle, mole

new: novel, young, another, original
" **comb. form:** neo
New Caledonia: bird: kagu
Newfoundland: log house: tilt
New Guinea: Papua
" **people/tribesman** Karon
New Hampshire: (see special section)
New Jersey: (see special section)
New Mexico: (see special section)
" **art colony:** Taos
" **turpentine tree:** tarata(h)
New Testament: gospel: Luke, Mark, John, Matthew
" **letter:** epistle
New York: (see special section)
" **city:** Gotham, Olean
New Zealand(er): Maori, Kiwi, Antipodes
" **bell bird:** mako
" **fish:** hiku, ihi
" **shrub:** karo, tutu, kowhai
" **wages:** utu
" **war club:** mere
newel: post
news: word, tidings
" **-boy:** camelot
" **paragraph:** item
" **stand:** kiosk
" **-monger:** gossip
newspaper: article: item
" **file:** morgue
" **hoax:** canard
" **-stand:** stall, kiosk

newt: eft, triton, salamander
next: beside, neist, closest
" **in order, comb. form:** eka
nexus: link, tie, bond
ngaio: tree, kio
Nicaragua: coin: peso, centavo
" **measure:** vara, milla, suerte, manzana
" **weight:** caja, bag
nickel: jit, coin
" **alloy:** monel, invar, konel
" **symbol:** Ni
nickname: form of: prosonomasia
" **Winston Churchill:** Winnie
" **Geo. Clemenceau:** Tiger
" **Thom. Edison:** Wizard of Menlo Park
" **Elizabeth I:** Virgin Queen
" **Ernest Hemingway:** Papa
" **Andrew Jackson:** Old Hickory
" **Pres. Lincoln:** Honest Abe
" **Napolean I:** Little Corporal
" **Richard I:** Lion-Hearted
" **Babe Ruth:** Bambino
nide: nest, brood, litter
nidus: nest
Nigeria, Nigerian: native: Ijo, Ibo, Eboe, Aro, Beni
" **region:** Benin
" **tree:** afara

" **walled city:** Kano
night: bird: nightingale
" **comb. form:** nyct(i)(o)
" **goddess:** Nyx, Hecate
" **pert. to:** nocturnal
nightcap: biggin, drink
nighthawk: pisk
nightingale: philomel, bulbul, Florence
nightjar: potoo, nighthawk
nightshade: belladonna, henbane, herb, pokeweed
nihil: nothing
Nile: river (see also **Egypt**)
" **bird:** ibis
" **boat:** cangia, baris
" **dam:** Aswan
" **houseboat:** dahabeah
" **native:** nilot
" **negro:** Jur, Suk, Luo
nilgai: antelope
nim tree: margosa
nimb: halo
nimbus: aura, gloria, vapor
nimshi: fool
nine: ennead, IX
" **comb. form:** ennea
" **day's devotion:** Novena
" **headed monster:** Hydra
" **inches:** span
" **-eyes:** lamprey
" **-headed monster:** Hydra
" **-killer:** shrike
" **-pins:** skittles
ninth: enneatic, nonus (Lat.)
" **day before ides:** Nones
" **recurring every:** nonan
ninut: magpie
Niobe: brother: Pelops
" **father:** Tantalus

" **husband:** Amphion
nipa: a(t)tap, palm, drink
nis: nix, brownie, kobold, nisse
nisi: unless
nisse: sprite, goblin
Nisus' daughter: Scylla
nit: speck, egg, insect
niter: saltpeter, potash
" **comb. form:** nitro
nithing: coward
niton: radon
nitrogen: gas
" **comb. form:** azo
" **compound:** azin(e)
niveau: level
Njorth: son: Frey(r)
" **wife:** Skathi
no: Baal, none, denial, drama (Jap.)
" **one:** nemo, none, nix, nobody
Noah: dove: Columba
" **father:** Lamech
" **grandson:** Aram
" **great grandson:** Uz
" **pert. to:** Noetic, Noachian
" **son:** Japheth, S(h)em, Ham
nob: jack
nobleman: pert. to: ducal
nobleness of birth: eugeny
noctuid: moth, worm
noctule: bat
nocturnal: carnivore: ratel
" **mammal:** bat, lemur
noddy: fool, noodle, auk
node: knot, tumor, point
" **of a poem:** plot
" **of a stem:** joint

nodule: mass, granule
" **stone:** geode
noel: Christmas (Fr.), carol
noir: black (Fr.)
noisette: hazel
noisily: larum
nom de plume: pen name
noma: ulcer
nomad: gypsy, river, Moor, Arab, Redouin, Saracen
nonage: minority, pupilage, infancy
nonce: occasion, purpose, present
nonconductor: resin
none: nane (Scot.)
nonessential: unneeded, incidental
" **in religion:** adiaphorus
nongypsy: gajo
non-passerine bird: hoopoe, tody, motmot
nonsense: trash, folderol, balderdash, twaddle
" **creature:** goop, snark
nook: herne, cant, cove
nope: bullfinch
Norn: fate, Skuld, Wyrd
Norse: Dane, Scandinavian, Norwegian, Ogier
" **Adam:** Buri, Ask(r)
" **alphabet:** runic
" **collection of songs/epic:** edda
" **deity:** Odin, Ran, Woden
" **giant:** Fafnir, Ymer
" **giantess:** Groa, Natt
" **king, myth.:** Atli
" **poem:** rune
" **queen of underworld:** Hel(a)

" **saint:** Olaf
" **serpent, myth.:** Midgard
" **viking:** Rollo
" **watchdog,   myth.:** Garm(r)
north: arctic, polar
" **Africa:** (see "Africa")
" **pole discoverer:** Peary
" **star:** Lodestar, Polaris, Polestar, Cynosure
" **wind:** boreas
North Carolina: (see special section)
North Dakota: (see special section)
Norway, Norwegian: bird: rype, ptarmigan
" **coin:** krone, ore
" **early ruler:** Haakon
" **measure:** fot, pot
" **weight:** lod, pund
" **writer:** Ibsen
nose: conk, beak, proboscis, scent
" **bee's:** lore
" **cartilage:** septum
" **having flat:** simous
" **having large:** nasute
" **openings:** nares
" **pert. to:** rhinal, narial
" **partition:** vomer, septum
nosebleed: epistaxis
noselite: lenad
Nostradamus: seer, prophet, astrologer
nostril: pert. to: narine
not: in style: passe
" **prefix:** ir, il, im, non, un, in
" **wanted:** superfluous
note: espy, IOU, fame, billet

" **endorsement or guar-antee of:** aval
" **explanatory:** scholium
" **half:** minim
" **marginal:** adversaria, annotation, scholium
" **tail of:** filum
nothing: trifle, blank, bagatelle
" **more than:** mere
not-kosher: tref
notice: book: blurb
" **death:** obit
" **honorable:** citation
" **good:** rave
" **official:** edit, bulletin
notum: back
notus: southwind
noumenal: ontal, real
noun: thing, name
" **common gender form:** epicene
" **form:** case, gender
" **suffix:** ery, et, ier, ion, fer, ise, ist, ana
" **two cases:** dipote
" **verbal:** gerund
nous: mind, reason, we/us (Fr.)
nouveau riche: parvenu, upstart
novelette: conte
Nox: Nyx
" **brother:** Erebus
" **father:** Chaos
noy: harm
nubia: cloud, wrap, scarf
nucha: nape, neck
nuclear: element: proton
" **machine:** betatron
nudibranch: conch, snail, mollusk
nugae: trifles, jests
nuisance: pest, bane, plague, evil
" **remover:** abator
nullah: ravine, gully, gorge
nullo: task, game
number: amount, sum, digit, reckon
" **describable by:** scalar
" **extra:** encore
" **irrational:** surd
" **pure:** scalar
" **suffix:** th, st, eth
" **whole:** integer
numbered: Biblical: mene
numeral style: Roman, Arabic
numerical prefix: tri, uni
Numidia city: Hippo
numinous: awe
nun: recluse, votaress, cloistress
" **bird:** monase, titmouse
" **dress:** habit, wimple
" **hood:** faille
" **moth:** tussock
Nun's son: Joshua
nuncupative: oral, spoken, designative
nunni: antelope, blesbok
nupson: fool
nuque: nape, neck
nur: gnarl
nurse shark: gata
nursery: day or public: creche
nut(s): core, pith, problem, fool
" **bearing:** nuciferous
" **pert. to:** nucal

" **tanning:** bomah

Nut's children: Ra, Isis, Osiris

nuthatch: genus: sitta, bird

nutmeg: spice, tree, calabash

" **husk:** mace

nymph: larva, pupa, houri, sylph, Echo, damsel, kelpie

" **beloved by Pan:** Syrinx

" **changed into laurel:** Daphne

" **fountain:** Naiad, Egeria

" **in love with Narcissus:** Echo

" **laurel/tree:** Daphne

" **mountain:** Oread

" **queen:** Mab

" **sea:** Nereid, Scylla, siren, oceanid

" **water:** Nais, Undine

" **wood:** Dryad

nyssa: genus: tupelo, tree

nystagmus: wink, tic

Nyx, Nox: night

" **daughter:** Eris, Day, light

" **father:** Chaos

" **husband:** Erebus

" **son:** Charon

O

O, letter: Omicron, oh
O. Henry: Porter
oak: tree, brave
  " **bark:** crut
  " **beauty:** moth
  " **fruit:** acorn, mast, camata, bellote
  " **genus:** quercus
  " **holm:** ilex
  " **immature fruit:** camata
  " **types:** barren, white, bur, live, black, pin, post, holly, scrub, chestnut, swamp, red, willow, water, holm
  " **white:** roble
oaky: hard
oam: steam
oar: paddle, scull
  " **blade:** peel, wash
  " **flat part:** palm
  " **part:** palm, loom
  " **shaped:** remiform

oasis: spa, wadi, ojo
oat(s): genus: avena
  " **head:** panicle
obeah: charm, voodoo, fetish
Obed: father: Boaz
  " **mother:** Ruth
  " **son:** Jess(e)
obedient plant: dragonhead
obelisk: pylon, guglia, needle, column
Oberon: poem, opera, fairy, king
  " **wife:** Titania
obi: sash, girdle, charm, fetish
object: goal, cavil, design, aim
  " **lesson:** example
  " **sacred:** urim
  " **to:** mind
objet d'art: curio, vase, figurine, bibelot
oblate: monk, dedicate
  " **opposed to:** prolate

235

oboe: hautboy, reed, musette, shawm

obnok: tax

obsequies: funeral, wake, rites

obsidian: lava, iztle, iztli

obsidian: lapis

obstacle, insurmountable: impasse

obtain, by threat: extort

obtund: blunt, dull, deaden, quell

obvious: clear, visible, liable
" **not:** subtle, hidden, arcane

obvolution: fold, twist

oca: oxalis, sorrel, plant

occident: west, Hesperia

occultism: cabala, magic, mystery

occurring: at eight day intervals: octan
" **at nightfall:** acronical
" **at regular intervals:** horal
" **at twilight:** crepuscular
" **every fourth year:** penteteric
" **every seven days:** hebdomadal

ocean: brine, main, drink, expanse
" **floating matter:** flotsam
" **motion:** tide
" **on the:** asea
" **Oceanid:** nymph

Oceanus: daughter: Doris, Eurynome
" **father:** Uranus
" **mother:** Gaea
" **wife:** Tethys

ocellus: eye(let), stemma

ocher: pigment, ore
" **black:** wadd
" **Ind. or Sp.:** almagra
" **red:** tiver
" **yellow:** sil

ocrea: sheath

octave: eight
" **of a feast:** utas

Octavia: brother: Augustus
" **husband:** Antony

octopus: hee, squid, cuttle
" **arm:** tenacle
" **secretion:** ink
" **ten arms:** decapod

octoroon: mestee, mustee, metis, mestizo

ocuby: rum

odds: edge, chance, variance, discord
" **and ends:** brott, orts, seconds, refuse, fragments, scraps

ode: psalm, lyric, hymn
" **kind of:** pindaric

odic: lyric
" **electric forces:** elod, od

Odin: Woden
" **brother:** Ve, Vili
" **daughter-in-law:** Nanna
" **father:** Bor
" **son:** Balder, Tyr, Vali
" **wife:** Rind(r), Frigg

odor: aroma, fume, scent
" **of cooking:** fumet, nidor

"Odyssey": author: Homer
" **sorceress:** Circe

Oedipus: daughter: Antigone
" **father:** Laius
" **mother:** Jocasta
" **sister:** Creon

" **son:** Eteocles
" **victim:** Sphinx
" **wife:** Jocasta
Oeneus: kingdom: Calydon
" **wife:** Althaea
oestrid: fly, larva, bot
oeuvre: work, opus
of: from, off, de
" **each:** ana, per
offense: pique, onset, affront, umbrage
" **against law:** delict, crime, felony
" **civil:** tort
" **offer:** present
" **up:** oblate
offering: bid, donation, sacrifice
" **as a vow:** corban
" **block:** aloe
" **resistant to force:** renitent, recalcitrant
office: post, wike(n), station
" **divine:** akoluthia
" **paid without work:** sinecure
" **purchase/sale:** barratry
officer: sheriff, agent, functionary
" **assistant to:** aide, deputy
" **Brit. royal guard:** Exon
" **non-commissioned:** chief, corporal, sergeant
" **of king's stables:** avener
official: VIP, Bashaw, approved, authoritative
" **approval:** vise, visa
" **decree:** ukase, writ
" **weights:** sealer

oflete: wafer, offering
Ogier: Norseman, Dane, Prince, hero
ogtiern: son, lord, master
Ohio: (see special section)
oii: muttonbird
oil: grease, lube, smear, smooth, bribe
" **beetle:** meloe
" **bottle:** cruet
" **cask:** rier
" **comb. form: oleo**
" **dry well:** duster
" **fish:** escolar
' **flaxseed:** inseed
" **lamp:** lucigen, lantern
" **made from butter:** ghee
" **orange blossom:** neroli
" **pert. to:** oleic
" **skin:** sebum
" **tree:** tung, eboe, mahwa, poon
oilseed: sesame, til
ointment: balm, nard, ceroma, unguent
" **Biblical:** spikenard
" **wax:** cerate
Oise tributary: Aisne
Oisin's father: Finn
Oklahoma: (see special section)
" **people:** Sooners
old: senescent, aged, ogygian, stale, archaic, obsolete
" **age, pert. to:** gerontal, gerontic
" **study of old age:** geriatrics, nostology
" **Testament:**
" " **land of riches:** Ophir

" " **object:** urim
" " **people:** Phud, Phut
" " **writer:** Elohist
Old: Bailey: jail, goal
" **Faithful:** geyser
" **Gooseberry:** satan
" **Hickory:** Andrew Jackson
" **Noll:** Oliver Cromwell
" **Sod:** Erin
olea: olive
oleander: genus: nerium, shrub
olena: turmeric
oleoresin: balsam, anime, elemi, tolu
olinda bug: weevil
olive: drupe, tree, fruit
" **fly genus:** dacus
" **genus:** olea
" **inferior:** moron
" **stuffed:** pimola
" **wild:** oleaster
olive oil: comb. form: elaio
oliver: hammer
olla: jar, jug
olla-podrida: medley, hodge-podge, potpourri
oloroso: sherry
olp(h): bullfinch
Olympian: Zeus
" (Jupiter), Poseidon
" (Neptune), Hades
" (Pluto), Hestia
" (Vesta), Hera
" (Juno), Ares
" (Mars), Athena
" (Minerva), Apollo
" (Venus), Aphrodite
" (Mercury), Hermes
" (Diana), Artemis

" (Vulcan), Hephaestus
Olympic: cup bearer: Ganymede
Olympus: pert. to: godlike, celestial
" **region by:** Pieria
Oman: coin: gaj
Omar Khayyam's country: Iran (Persia)
omber card: basto
omega: last
omicron: little, short, tiny
" **ceti:** star, Mira
omission: neglect, oversight, default
" **mark of:** caret
" **of vowel:** elision
" **pretended:** paralepsis
omit: overlook, ignore
" **in pronounciation:** elide
omni: all, everywhere, omniscient
Omri's successor: Ahab
on: account of: for
" **and on:** tedious, forever
" **-the contrary:** rather
" **-the other hand:** but
" **time:** prompt
Ona: Fuegian
onager: ass
Onam's son: Jada
once: erst, quondam, anis (Scot.)
" **more:** echo, anew
oncorhynchus: genus: salmon
ondoyant: undy, wavy
one: after the other: seriatum
" **behind the other:** tandem

" **comb. form:** mon(o), uni, heno

" **footed:** uniped

" **hundred and forty four:** gross

" **hundred thousand:** lac

" **instructed in secret system:** epopt

" **million millions:** trillion

" **comb. form of trillion:** treg(a)

" **sided:** askew, unilateral

" **thousand:** mil

one and one-half: comb. form: sesqui

one's self: belief in: solipsism

O'Neill heroine: Anna

onion: boil, cepa, cibol, bulb, plant

" **bulb:** set

" **genus:** allium

" **small:** eschalot, scallion, shallot

onomatopoeic: imitative, echoic

on this side: cis

cont: camel

oopak: tea

oorial: sha, urial, sheep

opah: cravo, fish

opal: hyalite, resin, gem

" **fire:** girasol

open: public, ajar, liable, agape, evident, unclasp, artless

" **air:** alfresco

" **bursting:** dehiscence

" **country:** weald, wold

" **plain:** vega

opening: passage, eyelet, rima, stoma, slit, canal, aperture, vacancy, cave, introduction

" **in chess:** gambit

" **slitlike:** rima

" **small:** por

opera: aria: solo

" **Bellini:** NORMA

" **Bizet:** CARMEN

" **comic actor:** Buffo

" **Flotow:** MARTHA

" **Gounod:** FAUST

" **hat:** topper, gibus

" **Massenet:** MANON, THAIS, SAPPHO

" **Puccini:** BOHEME, TOSCA

" **Strauss:** SALOME, BAT

" **Verdi:** AIDA, OTHELLO, ERNANI

" **Wagner:** RIENZI, PARSIFAL

opinion: conclusion, estimate, idea, belief, view

" **expressed:** credo

opium: drug

" **seed:** maw

" **source:** poppy

oppidan urban, civic, townsman

Ops: consort: Saturn

" **daughter:** Ceres

" **festival:** opalia

" **son:** Zeus, Poseidon

optical: apparatus: lens, glass

" **illusion:** mirage

" **instru.:** alidade

oquassa: trout, fish

or: heraldry: gold, yellow

oracle: augur, seer, mentor,

prophet
" **Apollo's:** Delphic
" **pert. to:** pythonic
orange: bird: tanager
" **bowl site:** Miami
" **Chinese:** mandarin
" **genus:** citrus
" **heraldry:** tenne
" **kind of:** seville, navel, blood, osage
" **seed:** pip
" **seedless:** navel
" **-shaped:** oblate
orangewood: tree: osage
oratorio: Seasons, Messiah
" **coda in:** stretto
Oratory, Fathers of: founder: Neri
orbital point: apsis, apogee, nadir
orchid: Afr. genus: disa
" **appendage:** caudicle
" **edible root:** salep
" **genus:** disa, listera
" **male:** purple, cullion
" **part of:** anther
" **plant drug:** salep
" **tea:** faham
" **tuber:** salep
Orcus: Hades
order: form, genus, bid, ordain
" **connected:** seriatim
" **cosmic:** rita, tao
" **grammar:** taxis
" **law:** writ
" **writ:** precipe
orderliness: system
ordinary: soso, plain, lala
" **court of:** probate
ore: iron, tin, mineral, metal,

rock, coin
" **box:** flosh
" **deposit:** lode, mine
" **excavation:** stope
" **horizontal layer:** stope
" **iron pigment:** ocher
" **loading platform:** plat
" **receptacle:** mortar
" **vein:** lode, scrin
" **worthless:** matte, slag
Oregon: (see special section)
" **coin:** beaver
" **crab apple:** powitch
" **fabled monster:** Big Foot
    wind: chinook
Oreortyx genus: quail
Orestes: father: Agamemnon
" **mother:** Clytemnestra
" **sister:** Electra
" **wife:** Hermione
orf(e): ide, fish
organ: bristle-like: seta
" **elongated:** tentacle
" **footlike:** pes
" **of insect:** stinger
" **of motion:** muscle
" **respiratory:** lung
" **secreting:** gland
" **tactile:** feeler
organic: inherent, fundamental, structural
" **body:** zooid
" **compound:** amine, ketol
" **remains, without:** azoic
organism: monas, amoeba, plant, person
" **of certain plants:** spore
" **potential:** idorgan
" **swimming on sea:** nekton

organized body corps: army, navy, posse
Oriana's lover: Amadis
oribi: antelope
Orient, Oriental: Asian, Levantine, Eastern, bright, ortive, Asian, precious
  " **carpet:** Kali
  " **coin:** (see country involved)
  " **destiny:** Kismet
  " **dwelling:** dar
  " **kettledrum:** anacara
  " **laborer:** coolie
  " **market:** sook
  " **measure:** dra, para(h), (see country involved)
  " **mendicant priest:** fakir
  " **people, ancient:** Seres
  " **salute:** salaam
  " **ship:** dhow
  " **taxi:** ricksha(w)
  " **weight:** (see country involved)
origin on earth: epigene
oriole: bird, loriot, pirol
  " **genus:** oriolus
Orion: Rigel, constellation
  " **slayer:** Artemis
orison: prayer, speech
orlop: deck
ormer: abalone
ormolu: gilt, gold, alloy
ornament: decorate, bedizen, spangle, gutta, seme
  " **circular:** rosette
  " **raised:** boss, stud
Orozco specialty: mural
orp: weep, fret
Orpheus: birthplace: Pieria
  " **parent:** Apollo, Calliope

orthorhombic: mineral: iolite
ortolan: bunting, sora, bird
oscine bird: vireo, crow, tanager
osier: willow, wand, twig, rod, wicker
  " **band:** wicke(r)
Osiris: brother: Set(h)
  " **parent:** Geb, Nut
  " **son:** Anubis, Horus
  " **wife:** Isis
Osmanli: Turk
ossuary: tomb, grave
ostiole: stoma, os, aperture
ostracoderm: order: anaspida
ostrich: nandu
  " **feather:** boa, plume
  " **genus:** rhea, struthio
  " **like bird:** eme(u), ratite, rhea
otary: seal
Othello: moor
  " **character in play:** Cassio, Iago, Emilia, Bianca
  " **wife:** Desdemona
other: else, additional, more, former, left
  " **comb. form:** allo, heter(o)
others: residue, rest
  " **and:** et al(ii)
otherwise: or, else, alias
  " **in music:** ossia
otidium: ear, otocyst
otter: genus: lutra
  " **sea:** kalan
Ottoman: Turk
  " **court:** porte
  " **governor:** pasha
ouakari: monkey

ouch: brooch, bezel, exclamation

ouphe: goblin, elf

out: away, ex, end, begone, scram

" **of:** dehors

" **of date:** passe

" **prefix:** ec, ecto

" **of sorts:** cross

outas: clamor

outbreak: riot, ruckus, tumult

" **sudden:** spurt

outcast: exile, leper, pariah, Ishmael, castaway

" **Jap.:** rowin, eta

outer: foreign, external, utter

" **opposed to:** ental

outhouse: shed, privy

outlaw: tabu, taboo, ban

" **oriental:** dacoit, ronin

outlying: district: purlieu, environ, suburb

outmoded: dated, passe, obsolete

outre: strange, bizarre, extravagant

outrigger: proa, boat

outside: outer, alien, exterior

" **comb. form:** ecto

outward: ectad, outer, visible, formal

" **turn:** evert

ouzel: piet, thrush

oval: elliptic(al), oblong, ovoid

ovate: inversely: obovate

oven: kiln, oast, stove

" **annealing glass:** leer, lehr

" **goddess:** Fornax

" **mop:** scovel

over: excess, athwart, more, beyond, dead

" **and above:** atour, atop, best

" **prefix:** supra, sur, hyper, super

overcoat: ulster, capote, benny

" **close fitting:** surtout

" **loose:** raglan, paletot

" **seeveless:** inverness

overreach: strain, cozen, defraud

override: veto, nullify, abrogate

over-scrupulous: strict, prudish

overshoe: boot, arctic, rubber, galosh

oversprad: pall, fog, scatter

overtop: dwarf, excel, eclipse

Ovid: birthplace: Sulmo

" **burial place:** Tomi(s)

" **work:** Medea, Amores, Fasti, Tristia

ovule: egg, embryo, seed, germ, nit

" **outer   integument:** primine

ovum: spore, seed

" **comb. form:** ova

owal(l): bobo, owing, due, unpaid, indebted, obliged, payable, ascribable

owl: lulu, ullet, hawk, snowy, barred, gnome

" **and Pussycat author:** Lear

" **genus:** syrnium, strix, ninox

" **hoot of:** ululu

" **pert. to:** strigine

" **short-eared:** momo
" **S.A.:** utum
own: concede, possess, retain, divulge
" **comb. form:** idio
ox(en): steer, beeve, bullock, bison, kine, bull
" **cart:** ar(a)ba
" **comb. form:** bovi
" **extinct wild:** urus
" **grunting:**
" **India:** guar, gayal, zebu, yak
" **kind of:** neat, nowt
" **pair of:** yoke, span
" **stomach:** tripe
" **working:** av
oxalic acid salt: lemon
oxalis: oca, sorrel
oxeye: plover, daisy, camomile, fish, bird, flower
oxide: calx, rust

" **calcium:** lime
" **sodium:** soda
oxygen: allotropic: ozone
" **binary compound:** oxide
" **metal compound:** oxid(e)
" **radical:** oxyl
oyster: bivalve, mollusk
" **bed:** layer, stew, claire, bank
" **catcher:** tirma, bird
" **common family:** edulis
" **fish:** toad, tautog
" **genus:** ostrea
" **grass:** kelp
" **ova:** spawn
" **shell:** test, husk, shuck
" **spawn:** clutch, ova, spat
oysterfish: tautog, toad
Oz books author: Baum

P

P, letter: pee, pi
pa, pah: fort, papa, village
pac: boot
paca: labba, agouti, cavy, rodent
Pacific: island(s): Guam, Wake, Samoa, Fiji, Saipan, Tahiti, Okinawa, Upolu, Komodo, Truk, Uvea, Yap, Lifu, Ellice, Munga, Aru, Bali, Ducie, Rapa, Atoll
  " pine: hala, matsu
  " tree: ipil, taro, Kou
Pacific Ocean: discoverer: Balboa
  " shark: mako
  " stepping stones: Aleutians
pacifist: bolo, peacenik
  " colloq.: dove
pack: animal: ass, mule, burrow
  " horse: sumpter

packing: paper, straw, waste
  " box: crate
  " clay: lute
  " water-tight: gasket
  " plant: cannery
packsaddle: aparejo
Pacolet: dwarf, horse
Pactolian: golden
pad: mat, walk, stuff
  " of hay: wase
  " sl.: bed, apartment
  " with powder: sachet
paddlefish: spadefish
Paddy: Irishman, rice(field)
paddywack: rage, beating
Paderewski: Ignace, pianist
  " opera: Manru
padnag: horse
Padus: Po river
paean: hymn, song, ode, praise
pagan: heathen, paynim, ungodly

" **god:** Baal, idol
Paganini: Nicolo, violinist
page: call, child, servant, record
" **left hand:** verso
" **number:** folio
" **right hand:** recto
" **sl.:** buttons
" **title:** rubric
Pagliacci: character: Hedda,
Xonio, Canio
" **composer:** Leoncavallo
pagoda: ta(a), temple, tower,
coin
pagurian: crab
Pahlavi's realm: Iran
pain: ache, care, wound,
grieve
" **comb. form:** algia
" **dull:** ache
" **pert. to:** asonal
" **relayer:** nerve
paint: adorn, daub, stain,
color
" **comb. form:** picto
" **glossy:** enamel
" **first coat:** base, primer
" **in dots:** stipple
painting: canvas, oil, portrait,
stillife
" **collection of:** gallery
" **cult:** Dadaism
" **method:** grisaille
" **on dry plaster:** secco
" **style:** genre, impasto
" **wall:** mural
" **watercolor:** aquarelle
Pakistan, Pakistani: Pathan,
Sikh, Bengali
" **language:** Hindi, Punjabi, Bengali

" **pass:** Bolan
pal: cully, ally, chum
palace officer: paladin
Palamedes: enemy: Ulysses
" **war:** Trojan
palate: relish, taste
" **pert. to:** uranic
" **soft:** velum
pale: face: American, white-
man
" **yellow:** flaxen
Palestine: Israel, Canaan
" **animal:** daman
" **ancient Palestinian:**
Amorite
" **coin:** mil
" **conquerer:** Turk
" **part of:** Canaan
" **plain:** sharon
" **weight:** zuza
" **village:** bethel
palet: quoit
paletot: jacket, overcoat
palfrey: horse
paling: fencing
Pall Mall site: West End
palladium: symbol: Pd
Palladium of Rome: Ancile
Pallas: Athena
pallion: bit, nodule, piece
palm: tree, hand, steal, foist,
laurel, prize
" **Afr.:** doum, palmyra, raffia
" **Arizona:** date
" **Asia:** betel, nipa, areca
" **book:** taliera, tara
" **cabbage:** palmetto, saw
" **Ceylon:** talipot
" **dwarf fan genus:** sabal
" **edible fruit of:** nipa,

date, coconut
" **feather:** gomuti
" **Florida:** royal, palmetto
" **genus:** bacaba, areca, nipa, cocos, sabal, raphia
" **leaf:** frond, ol(l)a
" **lily:** ti, toi
" **mat:** petate, yapa
" **New Zeal.:** nikau
" **pith:** sago
" **reedlike stem:** rattan
" **sap:** toddy
" **spiny:** grugru
" **stem:** cane, rattan
" **wine:** toddy, sura
palmetto: saw
" **genus:** serenoa
palmyra tree: tala, talipot, brab
pampas: plains
" **cat:** pajero
Pan: Faunus
Panama, Panamanians: darien, hat
" **coin:** balboa
" **gulf:** Darien
" **locks:** Gatun
" **measure:** celemin
" **tree:** copa, yaya
Panama Canal: engineer: de Lesseps
" **lake:** Gatun
panax: herb
panda: wah, bearcat
Pandora: brother: Prometheus
" **daughter:** Pyrrha
" **husband:** Epimetheus
panfish: (king)crab, horseshoe
Pangim native: Goan

pangolin: anteater, manis
panpipe: syrinx
Pantagruel: giant
" **companion:** Panurge
" **father:** Gargantua
" **mother:** Badebec
pantalan: wharf
Panthea's husband: Abradatus
pantheon: temple, tomb
panther: cougar, leopard, pard, puma, cat
" **like animal:** ocelot
pants: jeans, slacks, trousers
" **leather:** chaps, chaparajos
papa: dad, paw, priest, potato
papal: apostolic, pontifical
" **book of edicts:** Decretal
" **cape or collar:** fanon
" **letter/seal:** bull
" **scarf or veil:** orale
papaya: pa(w)paw, fruit
" **genus:** carica
paper: essay, document, writing, theme
" **cloth like:** tapa, papyrus
" **cutter:** slitter
" **damaged:** retree
" **folded once:** folio
" **medicinal powders:** charta
" **pulp:** ulla
" **thin:** pelure
" **untrimmed edge:** deckle
paprika vitamen: citrin
par value: face, nominal
parable: fable, allegory, similitude
" **objective:** moral, prov-

erb

parabole: simile

paradigm: model, pattern, example

paradise: Eden, utopia, elysium

" **Buddhist:** Jodo, Gokuraku

" **Muslim:** Jenna

" **river:** Gihon

Paradise Lost angel: Ariel, Uriel

paragram: pun

Paraguay: coin: peso

" **Indian:** Guarani

" **tea:** mate, yerba

" **weight:** quintal

parallel: equal, correspond, analogous

" **render:** collimate

parallelogram: rhomb(us)

paralysis: stroke, palsy

" **comb. form:** plegy

paramo: plain

parang: knife

parapet: wall, rampart

" **part of:** crete

" **V-shaped:** redan

parasite: leech, sycophant, smut, fungus, louse

" **animal:** tick, mite, flea, cuckoo

" **fungus:** lichen

" **marine:** remora, sponge

" **plant:** thrips, aphid, entophyte

" **worm:** trichina

paravane: otter

Parcae: Fates

parcel out: mete, allot

parchment: forel, skin, vellum, paper

" **manuscript:** palimpsest

" **roll:** pell

pardon: spare, remit, forgive

" **general:** amnesty

parent: sire, pater, mater, source

" **undivided:** holethnos

parenthetical aside: er

pareu: skirt

parfleche: rawhide

parget: plaster

Paris: (city)

" **airport:** Orly

" **patron saint:** Genevieve

" **river:** Seine

" **Roman name:** Lutetia

" **subway:** metro

Paris: father: Priam

" **mother:** Hecuba

" **rival:** Romeo

" **victim of:** Achilles

" **wife:** Orenone

parliment member: lord

Parnassian: poet, butterfly

parrot: cockatoo, poll, kaka, corella, echo, mimic

" **Afr.:** joke

" **Brazil:** ara(ra), tiriba

" **gray:** jako

" **genus:** psittacus

" **green:** cagit

" **long-tailed:** macaw

" **Malay:** lory

" **Phillipine:** cagit

" **sheep-killing:** kea

" **small:** lorilet, parakeet

Parse, Parsee: Zoroastrian

" **holy book:** Avesta

" **priest:** Mobed

" **"Towers of Silence":**

Dakmas

parsley: lovage, plant, sanicle
"   **derivative:** apiol(e)
parsnip: plant
"   **water genus:** sium
parson bird: poe, tui, rook
part, parts: quota, dole, behalf, some
"   **basic:** core
"   **choice:** elite
"   **comb. form:** demi, hemi, meri, semi
"   **highest:** apex
"   **main:** body
"   **minor:** bit
"   **narrow:** neck
"   **root-like:** radicle
"   **small:** bit
"   **totality:** unity
"   **two:** binary
"   **-with:** lose, sell
partan: crab
Parthenon: temple
"   **designer:** Ictinus
"   **sculptor:** Phidias
"   **site:** Athens, Acropolis
Parthenope: siren
Parthenos: virgin
particle: granule, scintilla, atom, shred, iota, gen, speck, morsel
"   **atom:** proton, neutron
"   **cosmic:** meson
"   **electrified:** ion
parti-colored: pied, variegated
partisan: biased, devotee, pike
"   **comb. form:** crat
"   **unwavering:** zealot
partlet: hen, band, collar,

woman
partner: butty, mate, consort
"   **comedian's:** stooge
"   **paid:** gigolo
partridge: chukar, titar, yutu
"   **call:** juck, juke
"   **flock:** covey
"   **kind of:** grouse, quail, tinamou
"   **sand:** seesee
"   **young:** cheeper
partylike: gala
Pascal work: Pensees
Pasch(a): Easter, Passover
pasear: walk, promenade
pasha: dey, emir
Pasiphae's: daughter: Phaedra
"   **husband:** Minus
"   **son:** Minotaur
pasquinade: lampoon, squib, satire
pass: gap, col, pinch, strait, bygo, omit, expire, neglect
"   **Alpine:** col
"   **India mountain:** ghat
"   **in sports:** bye
"   **matador's:** faena
"   **off:** foist
"   **over:** omit
"   **through:** reeve
"   **up:** reject
"   **words about:** bandy
passage: route, duct, channel, sanction
"   **between two walls:** slype, arcade
"   **mine:** stope
"   **one end closed:** impasse, sac
passer of bad checks: kiter

passeriform bird: irena
Passover: Pasch(a), feast
  " **bread:** matzos, matzoth
  " **commencement evening:** Nisan
  " **first night of:** Seder
  " **pert. to:** Paschal
passus: canto
past: eld, ago, beyond, ancient, bygone
  " **master:** expert
  " **tense:** preterit(e)
paste: pap, hit, gem, stick
  " **rice:** ame
  " **jewelry:** strass
  " **mineral matter:** magma
Pasteur: Louis
  " **treatment of:** rabies
pasticcio: cento, pastiche, medley
pastoral: country, rustic, song, poem
  " **crook:** pedum, crosier
  " **pert. to:** agrestic, rural, bucolic, geoponic
  " **poem:** eclogue, idyl
  " **staff:** peda
pasture: agist, graze, lea, herbage
  " **grass:** grama, rye, clover
patagium: parachute
patand: base
paten: plate, disc
Pasternak novel: (Dr.) Zhivago
path: lane, orbit, footway, access
  " **math:** locus
Pathan: Moslem
pathos: suffering

  " **false:** bathos
  " **opposed to:** ethos
patois: argot, speech, lingo, cant, patter
patron: sponsor, saint, protector
  " **of animals:** Pan, Faunus
  " " **art:** Mascenas
  " " **beggers:** Giles
  " " **Broadway:** angel
  " " **children:** Nicholas
  " " **cripples:** Giles
  " " **England:** George
  " " **husbandry:** Grange
  " " **Ireland:** Patrick
  " " **lawyers:** Ives
  " " **literature:** Maecenas
  " " **musicians:** Cecilia
  " " **Russia:** Nicholas
  " " **sailors:** Elmo
  " " **Scotland:** Andrew
  " " **shoemakers:** Crispin
  " " **wine growers:** Vincent
patroon: tract, patron
  " **land:** manor
patsy: fallguy
Paul: associate: Titus
  " **birthplace:** Tarsus
  " **original name:** Saul
  " **place of conversion:** Damascus
Paul Bunyan: lumberjack
  " **ox:** Babe
paulownia tree: kiri
pavane: dance
pavis: protect, cover
Pavlova: Anna, ballet dancer
pavo: constellation, peacock
pawnbroker: money lender

" **shop:** spout
" **sl.:** uncle
pawpaw: papaya
pay: ante, stipend, wage, salary
" **attention:** heed, listen
" **back:** reimburse, refund
" **dirt:** ore, gold
" **penalty of:** aby
" **one's share:** ante
" **up:** pony
paynim: pagan, heathen
payola: bribe
Pb: lead
pea: legume, seed, gram
" **chick:** cicer, gram
" **India, split:** dal
" **soup:** fog
" **seeds:** palse
" **shaped:** pisiform
" **tree:** agati
" **vine:** earthpea
peabird: oriole
peace: pax, amity, calm, tranquillity
" **goddess:** Irene
" **pipe:** calumet
" **symbol of:** toga, olive, dove
peaceable: henotic, placid, serene
peach: Crawford, Elberta, Crosby, freestone, clingstone
" **blue:** paon
" **butterfly:** io
" **clingstone:** pavy
" **constellation:** pavo
" **female:** hen, peahen
" **genus:** pavo
" **heraldic:** pawn

" **like:** vain, pavonine, peag(e), tax, toll, wampum, pedage
" **origin:** almond
" **peacock:** mao, fowl
" **stone:** putamen, pit
peacoat: jacket
peacock: mao, pavo, bird
" **butterfly:** io
" **female:** peahen
" **fish:** wrasse
" **flower:** poinciana
" **like a:** vain
" **pert. to:** pavonine
" **tail spot:** eye
peag(e): tax, toll, beads
peak: climax, point, apex, Alp, zenith, crest
" **Eng.:** Scafell
" **ice:** serac
" **rocky:** Alp, crag
" **Rocky Mountain:** Pikes, Logan
" **snow-capped:** calotte
pear: melon, prickly
" **cider:** perry
" **late autumn:** Bosc
" **prickly:** Nopal, Tuna
" **genus:** opuntia
" **shaped:** bulbous, pyriform
" **stone:** pyrene
pearl: gem, margarite, onion
" **eye:** cataract
" **imitation:** olivet, seed
" **Harbor:** Oahu
" **of Antilles:** Cuba
" **of Orient:** Manila
" **opal:** cacholong
pearlwort: genus: sagina
pearmain: apple

Peary's discovery: North Pole

peasant: coolie, carl, boor, hind, rustic, swain, peon, tiller
  " **E. India:** ryot
  " **Egypt:** fellah
  " **Eng.:** churl
  " **Ireland:** kern(e)
  " **Scot.:** cotter

pease crow: tern

peat: fuel, turf
  " **bog:** moss
  " **cutter:** (Scot.) piner
  " **spade:** slane

pebble: scree
  " **fig-shaped:** sycite

pech: sign, pant, breath

pecht: fairy, pygmy, gnome

peck: dot, carp, hole, kiss
  " **at:** nag, tease

pectinoid bivalve: scallop

ped: basket, hamper

pedal digit: toe

pedestal: gaine, foot, support, leg, foundation
  " **part of:** plinth, dado, die, base
  " **projecting:** socle

pedometer: odograph

peduncle: stalk, stem, knot
  " **plant:** scape

peeper: frog, tom

peepshow: raree

Peeping Tom: voyeur
  " **lady he looked at:** Godiva

"Peer Gynt": author: Ibsen
  " **mother:** Ase
  " **suite author:** Grieg

peetweet: sandpiper

peg: dowel, tooth, bind, plug, reason, strike
  " **golfer's:** tee
  " **mountain climber's:** piton
  " **wood:** skeg, spill

Pegasus: horse
  " **rider:** Bellerophon
  " **source:** Medusa

pekan: weasel

pelagic: marine
  " **phenomenon:** tide

Pele: soccer star, Edson

Peleus: brother: Telamon
  " **father:** Aeacus
  " **son:** Achilles, Pelides
  " **wife:** Thetis

pelf: booty

pelham: bit

Pelias' nephew: Jason

pelicanlike bird: solan

pelmet: valance

Peloponnesus: city: Sparta
  " **river god:** Alpheus

Pelops: father: Tantalus
  " **son:** Atreus

pelota: jai alai
  " **basket/racket:** cesta
  " **court:** fronton

pelvic bone: ilium
  " **pert. to:** iliac

pen: stylus, confine, quill, hutch, enclosure, crib
  " **fish:** crawl
  " **point:** nib, neb
  " **sl.:** jail
  " **text:** ronde

pen name: see **pseudonym**

pendulum weight: bob

Penelope: weaver
  " **father:** Icarius

" **father-in-law:** Laertes
" **husband:** Odysseus, (Ulysses)
" **suitor:** Agelaus
penetralia: privacy, secret
penguin: auk, bird, Johnny
" **genus:** eudyptula
" **home:** rookery, pole
" **small:** Adelie
Penn: William, Quaker
penna: feather
pennant: banner, Jack, prize
" **pirates':** Roger
" **yacht:** burgee
Pennsylvania: (see special section)
" **sect:** Amish
Pentateuch: law, Bible, tora(h)
" **first book:** Genesis
Pentheus: grandfather: Cadmus
" **mother:** Agave
pentyl: amyl
penumbra: shadow
people(s): rabble, mob, mankind, clan, kin, populace, proletariat
" **ancient Asian:** Seres
" **group:** ethos
" **lowest order:** mob, rabble, canaille
" **pert. to:** demotic, ethnic
peplos: shawl, scarf
pepo: melon, squash, gourd
pepper: capsicum, condiment, spice, attack, pelt
" **betel:** itmo, ikmo
" **intoxicant:** kava
" **Java:** cubeb
" **picker:** Peter Piper

" **shrub:** kava
" **species:** betel, cayenne
Pepys: Samuel, diarist
pequod: whaler
" **captain of:** Ahab
per: by, each
" **annum:** annually, yearly
" **diem:** daily
" **se:** itself, directly
perch: sit, fish, roost
" **fish:** barse, okow, pope, mado
" **genus:** perca
" **like:** darter
Percheron: horse
Pere Goriot author: Balzac, Honore
peregrine: falcon, hawk, alien
perfect: utter, ideal, exact, model, holy
" **comb. form:** telev
" **realm:** nirvana
perforated: pierced, riddled
" **marker:** stencil
" **sphere:** bead
perfume: scent, odor, attar, redolence, bouquet
" **base:** musk
" **oriental:** myrrh
" **pad:** sachet
" **with burning spice:** cense
peri: elf, fairy, houri
" **cousin of:** nisse
periapt: amulet
Pericles' consort: Aspasia
period: end, point, stage, epoch, term, limit
" **brief:** spell
" **inactive:** lull
" **of extension:** grace

"   **of race's apex:** hemera
"   **seclusion:** retreat
"   **unbroken:** stretch
periwinkle: snail, mussel, myrtle
perkin: cider
permanent: abiding, constant, stable, persistent
"   **condition:** hexis, status
permit to travel: passport
pern: buzzard
pernio: chilblain
perpendicular: erect, sheer, plumb, upright
"   **geometry:** apothem
perplexed: asea, anxious, intricate
perquod: whereby
Perry Mason: creator: Gardner
"   **secretary:** Della Street
"   **T.V. actor:** Raymond Burr
perse: blue
Perse: daughter: Circe, Pasiphae
"   **father:** Oceanus
"   **husband:** Helios
"   **son:** Aeetes, Perses
Persephone:
"   **parent:** Demeter, Zeus
Perseus: father: Zues
"   **mother:** Danae
"   **star of:** Atik
"   **wife:** Andromeda
Persia, Persian: (see Iran)
persiennes: blinds
persimmon: chapote
"   **family:** ebony
person: one, chap, self
"   **beatified:** beatus

"   **cannonized:** saint
"   **charitable:** samaritan
"   **detested:** anathema
"   **disgruntled:** sorehead
"   **enterprising:** go-getter
"   **of bad luck:** jinx, jonah
"   **of distinction:** notable, star, VIP
"   **of good luck:** mascot
"   **left-handed:** portsider
"   **loud-voiced:** stentor
"   **timid:** milquetoast
"   **white:** ofay
personal: own
"   **comb. form:** idio
personification: embodiment
"   **of rumor:** Fama
"   **of truth:** Una
Peru, Peruvian: ancient: Inca
"   **bark:** cinchona
"   **coin:** dinero, libra, peseta, sol
"   **dance:** cueca
"   **goddess:** Mama
"   **llama:** alpaca, paco
"   **partridge:** yutu
"   **volcano:** (el) misti
"   **wind:** puna, sures
peruke: hair, wig
peshkash: tax, present, offering
peso: coin
"   **silver:** duro
pess: hassock
pestle: masher, grind, pound, pulverize
"   **vessel:** mortar
petal: ala(e), corolla
"   **without:** apetalous
petard: firecracker

petasus: cap, hat
Peter: Simon, Rock, Tsar
" **father of:** Jonas
Peter Pan: author: Barrie
" **dog:** Nana
" **pirate:** Smee
Petrarch's beloved: Laura
petrel: titi, bird
Petrograd: Leningrad
petroleum: oil
" **derivative:** naphtha, butane
petty: base, mean, minor, trivial
" **fault:** peccadillo
pewee: flycatcher
pewit: gull, lapwing
peyote: plant, mescal, cactus
Phaedo's school: Elian
Phaedra: father: Minos
" **husband:** Theseus
phalera: disk, boss, cameo
phantasm: ghost, specter, illusion
Phaon's consort: Sappho
Pharaoh: Rameses, ruler, King
" **ancestor:** Ra
" **chicken:** vulture
" **fig:** sycamore
" **mouse:** ichneumon
pheasant: cheer, monaul, fowl
" **Afr./Asia:** tragopan
" **Austral.:** leipoa
" **breeding place:** stew
" **brood:** nid(e)
" **finch:** waxbill
" **India:** monal
phenol: orcine, thymol
" **derivative:** salol, cresol

Phidias' statue: Athena
philabeg: kilt
Philippine, Filipino: Tagal, Atta
" **ant, white:** anai, anay
" **canoe:** vinta, banca
" **child:** bata
" **coconut meat:** copra
" **coin:** peso, conant
" **discoverer:** Magellan
" **farmer:** tao
" **food staple:** taro, saba
" **hemp:** abaca
" **house:** bahay
" **idol:** Anito
" **knife:** bolo, itac
" **liquor:** beno, pangasi
" **lizard:** ibid
" **measure:** apatan, chupa
" **native:** Ita, Moro, Aeta, Ata
" **nut:** pili
" **parrot:** cagit
" **plant:** alem
" **plum:** duhat, lanseh
" **rice:** paga
" **sash:** tapis
" **skirt:** saya
" **volcano:** Apo
" **water buffalo:** carabao
" **white man:** cachil
Philippine-Malayan: Italone
Philistine: hypocrite, barbarian
" **city:** Gath
" **foe:** Samson
" **giant:** Goliath
" **god:** Baal, Dagon
Philomela: nightingale
" **father:** Pandion
" **sister:** Procne

philosopher of Syracuse: Dion

philosophical: erudite, sapient, cool, rational, sedate
" **element:** rect
" **unit:** monad

philosophy: ancient: stoic, cynic
" **natural:** physics
" **school of:** Eleatic

phloem: bark, bast, tissue

phoca: seal

Phoebad: prophetess, seeress

Phoebe: Artemis, Diana, Selene, moon, peewee

Phoebus: Apollo, sol, sun

Phoenicia, Phoenician: anc. city/state: Tyre, Sidon
" **dialect:** Punic
" **god:** Baal
" **goddess:** Tanit(h), Astarte
" **king:** Agenor

phonetic: oral, vocal
" **sound:** palatal
" **system:** romic

photo: film, picture, likeness
" **copy:** stat
" **finish:** nose

photography: inventor: Talbot, Daguerre, Niepce

phratry: clan

Phrixos: father: Athamus
" **mother:** Nephele
" **sister:** Helle

Phrygian: god: Men, Attis, Atys
" **king:** Midas

physician(s): medic, curer, healer

" **comb. form:** iatro
" **pert. to:** iatric
" **symbol:** Caduceus

pi: mixture, jumble

pibroch: bagpipe, instrument

picador: jester, bullfighter, wit

Picasso: Pablo, painter
" **painting:** Gucenica

Piccadilly: London Street
" **-Circus:** London section

pick: elite, best, pike, call, glean
" **at:** nag
" **on:** tease, abuse
" **out:** select, choose

pickax(e): gurlet

pickling: herb: dill
" **solution:** brine, marinade, souse

picot: loop

picotee: carnation

Pickwick Papers author: Dickens, Charles

Picnic author: Inge, William

picture: image, scene, photo, reflect
" **border:** mat
" **composite:** montage
" **life:** still
" **long:** panel
" **painted on wall:** mural
" **puzzle:** rebus
" **stand:** easel

Picture of Dorian Gray author: Wilde, Oscar

pictograph: glyph

piebald: pintado, dappled, pied, mongrel, variegated

piece: coin, scrap, unit, detail, bit, shred, tune, repair
" **armor:** tane, tace, corse-

let
" **of eight:** peso, real
" **out:** eke
" **together:** patch
" **worker:** jobber
pieplant: rhubarb
pier: stilt, anta, berth, key, wharf, jetty
" **architectural:** anta
" **base:** socle
" **space:** slip
piet: magpie, ouzel
pig(s): hog, bacon, farrow, swine, pork, porker, mold, bar, ingot, slob, glutton
" **female:** sow, gilt
" **like animal:** peccary, aardvark
" **litter:** farrow
" **male:** boar, barrow
" **pickled feet of:** souse
" **young:** grice, shoat, elt
pigeon: dove, isabel, piper, cushat, carrier, fantail, jacobin, nun, trumpeter, turbit
" **Austral.:** wonga
" **call:** coo
" **carrier:** homer, homing
" **clay:** skeet, target
" **extinct:** dodo
" **genus:** columba, goura
" **hawk:** merlin
" **house:** cote, rook(ery)
" **pert. to:** peristeronic
" **variety:** nun, ruff, tumbler, pouter
" **young:** piper
pigment: color, stain, dye, tint, paint
" **black:** tar, soot
" **blue:** iolite, bice, smalt, azurite
" **board:** palette
" **brown:** bister, umber
" **lack of:** achrom(i)a
" **orange-red:** realgar
" **pale yellow:** etiolin
" **without:** albino, achromic
pignus: pawn, pledge
pigpen: sty, reeve, mess, piggery
pigtail: queue, braid, plait
pikelet: crumpet, pancake
Pilate: Pontius, procurator, Roman governor
" **wife:** Claudia
pilchard: fumado, salmon
" **young:** sardine
pile: pillar, accumulate, cock, gather, stack, money
" **driver:** ram, gin, beetle, fistuca
" **of hay:** rick, cock, stack
" **of stones:** scree, cairn
" **sl.:** fortune
pileus: (skull)cap
pilgrim: wayfarer, crusader
" **to Holy Land:** palmer
" **garb at Mecca:** ihram
Pilgrim's Progress author: Bunyan, Paul
" **character:** Demas
pilgrimage to Mecca: Hadj
pill bug: louse
pillar: support, beam, pier, column, shaft
" **pert. to:** stele, stelar
" **of ore:** jam
" **tapering:** obelisk
" **with figures:** osiride
Pillars of Hercules: Abila,

Calpe, Gibralter
pillbox: hat
pillow: covering tick
   "   **stuffing:** ceiba, kapok, eider
pilm: dust
pilot: flyer, lead, ace, conduct
   "   **bird:** plover
   "   **boat:** helmsman
   "   **cow:** pintano
   "   **fish:** remora, whitefish
   "   **seat:** cockpit
   "   **snake:** bull, copperhead
   "   **test:** solo
   "   **whale:** blackfish
Pima: cotton, Indian
pimola: olive
pimple scar: pock(mark)
pin: secure, fasten, bolt, nail
   "   **machine:** cotter
   "   **plant:** tacca
   "   **rifle:** tige
   "   **small:** peg, lill
   "   **wooden:** fid, peg, coag, dowel, coak
Pinafore authors: Gilbert & Sullivan
pincer(s): tong(s), plier(s)
   "   **claw:** chela
Pindaric form: ode
pine: ache, tree, hone
   "   **acid:** picnic
   "   **fruit:** cone
   "   **leaf:** needle
   "   **nut:** pinon
   "   **product:** resin, turpentine
pineapple: nana, pina, ananas
   "   **genus:** puya
   "   **segment:** pip

   "   **sl.:** bomb
   "   **weed:** marigold
pinion: wing, feather, quill, arm
pink: stab, scallop, flower, color
   "   **flower genus:** silene
   "   **pill:** "cure-all"
pinnacle: top, crest, apex, peak
   "   **glacial ice:** serac
   "   **rocky:** tor
Pinocchio author: Collodi, Lorenzini
pinochle term: meld, dix, kitty
pinpoint: dot, trifle, aim, fix
pintail: smee, duck
pinxter flower: azalea, honeysuckle
pip: ace, spot, seed, chirp
pipe: briar, reed, conduit, sound, oboe
   ·   **dream:** hope, illusion
   "   **flanged end:** taft
   "   **joint:** tee, ell
   "   **-like:** tubate
   "   **oriental:** nargileh, hooka(h)
   "   **pastoral:** reed
   "   **peace:** calumet
   "   **shepherd's:** oat, larigot
   "   **short:** dudeen
pipefish: earl, snacot, gar
pipit: titlark, wekeen
pippin: seed, apple
pirate: Kidd, Drake, Rogers, buccaneer, robber
   "   **flag:** Roger
   "   **gallows:** yardarm
   "   **literary:** plagiarist
   "   **state:** Tunisia

pirol: oriole
piscine: pool (Fr.), pond, basin
   "   **propeller:** fin
Pisgah: climber: Moses
   "   **summit:** Nebo
pishu: lynx
pismire: emmet, ant
pismo: clam
piste: path, spoor
pit: seed, fovea, dent, cavity, abyss, lacuna, crater
   "   **baking:** imu
   "   **bottomless:** abaddon
   "   **of theatre:** parquet
   "   **viper:** habu
pita: fiber, agave, bread
pitchblende derivative: radium, uranium
pitcher: crock, ewer, tosser, creamer
   "   **false move of: balk**
   "   **left-handed:** southpaw
   "   **motion:** windup
   "   **place:** mound
   "   **shaped:** urceolate
   "   **shaped vessel:** alguiere
pitchhole: cahut
pith: gist, nub, medulla, kernel, center, quintessence
   "   **helmet:** topi, topee
   "   **tree of Nile:** ambash, ambatch
pitman: miner, overseer (gambling)
pivot: wheel, turn, slew, timge
   "   **City:** Geelong
   "   **pin:** pintle, kingbolt
pixy: elf, goblin, sprite
Pizzaro: explorer
   "   **country:** Peru

place: set, put, region, lieu, bestow, deposit
   "   **apart:** enisle, separate
   "   **beneath:** infrapose
   "   **camping:** etape
   "   **comb. form:** topo, gea
   "   **intermediate:** limbo
   "   **of: nether darkness:** erebus
   "   "   **rapid growth:** hotbed
   "   "   **safety:** haven, refuge
   "   "   **torment:** gehenna
   "   **secret:** den
   "   **side by side:** collocate
   "   **snugly:** ensconce
   "   **storage:** depot
   "   **trial:** venue
plague: tease, harry, disease, epidemic, harass
   "   **carrier:** rat
   "   **-of:** locusts
   "   **pert. to:** loimic
plaice: flounder
plain: lowland, simple, frank, homely, distinct
   "   **Arctic:** tundra
   "   **Argentine:** pampa
   "   **Asia:** chol
   "   **elevated:** mesa
   "   **Eur.:** steppe
   "   **salt-covered:** salada
   "   **treeless:** savanna(h), veldt, pampa, llano, tundra, prairie
plaited: kilted, knitted, browden
   "   **rope:** sennit
   "   **trimming:** ruche
plane: level, grade, surface, flat, tool

" **chart:** mercator
" **curb elli**
" **inclined:** ramp, chute
" **on the same:** coplanar
planet: Earth, World, Star, Moon, Uranus, Neptune, Mars, Venus, Pluto, Saturn, Mercury, Jupiter
" **brightest:** Venus
" **nearest sun:** Mercury
" **red:** Mars
planetarium: orrery
plant(s): adapted to dryness: xerophyte, cactus
" **algae genus:** nostoc
" **Alpine:** edelweiss
" **ambrosia genus:** ragweed
" **ammoniac:** oshac
" **anise:** dill, cumin, anet
" **apoplexy:** esca
" **araceous:** cabbage, lily, taro, arum
" **aromatic:** anise, mint, nard, tansy, lavender, thyme, tarragon
" **arrowroot:** ararao, canna, tacca, pia, musa
" **Asiatic fiber:** ramie
" **Assam:** tea, tche
" **auricula:** primrose
" **Austral.: correa, alstonia**
" **bean family:** licorice
" **bitter:** rue
" " **leaves:** tansy
" " **vetch:** ers
" **bramble:** gorse, thorn, briar, furze
" **bud of:** cion
" **bulb:** camas(s),

quamash
" **burning bush:** wahoo
" **cactus:** cereus, dildo, mescal, saguaro
" **calyx leaf:** sepal
" **castor:** kiki
" **catnip family:** nep(eta)
" **cherry, laurel:** cerasus
" **Chinese:** ramie
" **chlorophyll lacking:** albino
" **climbing:** bine, vine, liana, ivy, philodendron
" **clover:** medic, alfalfa, lucern(e), melilot, alsike, trefoil
" **comb. form:** phyto
" **corn lily:** ixia
" **cutting:** slip
" **dill:** anet
" **disease:** blister, erinose, fungus, rot, gall, scale
" **dogwood:** cornus, osier, cornel, sumac
" **dwarf:** cum(m)in
" **everlasting:** orpine
" **flag, sweet:** calamus
" **flowerless:** fern, moss, lichen, acrogen
" **fragrant root:** orris
" **garlic, wild:** moly
" **hawthorne:** azarole, mayflower
" **healing:** sanicle
" **heather:** ling, besom, erica
" **honesty:** moonwort
" **indigo:** anil
" **iris family:** irid, orris, flag, lis
" **juice:** milk, sap, resin,

gum
" **life:** flora
" **male:** mas
" **medicinal:** arnica, senna, lobelia, tansy, jalap
" **Mex.:** datil, chia, salvia
" **mock orange:** syringa
" **mosslike:** hepatic
" **mustard family:** cress, alyssum
" **onionlike:** leek, chive, shallot
" **order:** ericales
" **part:** axil, stipel
" **perennial:** carex, sedum
" **pod:** boll
" **poisonous genus:** datura
" **rat poison:** oleander
" **root:** radix
" **roselike:** avens
" **seedless:** fern
" " **pert. to:** agamic
" **shoot:** sprig, stolon, rod
" **soap:** amole
" **S.Afr.:** aloe
" **starch-yielding:** pia, taro
" **stem:** bine, caulis, shaft
" " **joint:** node
" " **tissue:** pith
" **stawberry:** frasier
" **sweet flag:** calamus
" **tapioca:** cassava
" **taro root:** eddo(es)
" **tissue, relating to:** tapetal
" **trifoliate:** clover, shamrock
" **vinegar flavoring:** tarragon

" **wild growing:** agrestal
Plantagenets: Angevin
plantain: weed, banana, fleawort
" **eater:** touraco
" **spike:** chat
plantation: estate, farm, hacienda
" **cacti:** nopalry
" **coffee:** finca
" **Scarlett O'Hara's:** Tara
" **sugar:** trapiche
" **willow:** holt
plaster: daub, mortar, cover, compo
" **artist's:** gesso
" **coarse:** grout, stucco, parget
" **of Paris:** gesso, yeso, gypsum
" **support:** lath
" **tool:** spatula
" **wax:** cerate
plastered: (sl.) drunk
plasterer: mason
" **glue:** size
platanist: susu
platano: banana
plate: illustration, print, sheet, tile, plaque, dish
" **Eucharist:** paten
" **-horny:** scute
" **shaped like ship:** nef
" **thin:** lamella
" **throwing:** disc
platen: roller
platform: deck, map, floor, bench
" **floating:** raft
" **for execution:** scaffold
" **portable:** pallet

" **raised:** solea, dais, tribune, stand, podium
" **revolving:** turntable
platinum: comb. form: platin(o)
" **symbol:** Pt.
" **wire:** oese
Plato: idea: eidos
" **knowledge, highest:** noesis
" **school:** academe
" **work:** Grito, Meno, Phaedo, Republic
platonic philosophy follower: academist
platyfish: moonfish
platypus: duckbill
Plautus: forte: comedy
" **language:** Lat.
play: fun, act, drama, frolic, enact
" **around:** gad(about)
" **at love:** flirt
" **backer of:** angel
" **between acts:** intermission, interval
" **down:** minimize
" **just** " **first performance:** premiere, debut
" **silent:** pantomime
" **that folds:** turkey
" **the wrong card:** renege
playa: beach, basin, lake
playing cards: deck: 52, tarots
" **extra:** joker
" **hand:** deal
" **spot:** pip
" **shuffle:** riffle
" **suits:** spades, hearts, diamonds, clubs

playtime: recess
plea: nolo, request, alibi
" **to end:** abater
pleasure: gaiety, relish, mirth, joy
" **god of:** Bes
" **insensitivity to:** anhedonia
" **pert. to:** hedonic
" **seeker:** playboy/girl, sport
" **trip:** junket
" **voyage:** cruise
Pleiades: Atlantides
" **constellation:** Taurus
" **daughters of Atlas and Pleione:** Alcyone, Celaeno, Electra, Maia, Merope, Sterope, Asterope, Taygeta
" **father:** Allas
" **mother:** Pleione
plenty: ample, enough, opulence
" **goddess:** Ops
" **horn of:** cornucopia
plenum: plethora, space
" **opposed to:** vacuum
plexus: rete, network, tangle
plinth: socle, base, block
" **flat:** orlo
plot: cabal, map, design, connive
" **garden:** bed
" **ground:** lot, grave
" **play:** node
plouk: knob, pimple
plow: dig, till, furrow
" **blade or cutter:** share, colter, coulter
" **handle:** stilt
" **land:** arable

plug: stopper, boost, tampon, caulk
" **cock:** spigot
" **colloq.:** line, pitch
" **clay:** bod
" **in TV/radio:** commercial
" **wall:** outlet
" **water:** hydrant
plum: prune, damson, drupe, fruit, prize, lomboy
" **-colored:** puce
" **date:** sapote
" **dried:** prune
" **green:** Gage
" **wild:** sloe
plumber's tool: snake
plume: quill, egret, crest, preen
" **heron's:** aigret(te)
Plutarch's work: Lives, biography
Pluto: Orcas, Dis, planet, dog
" **kingdom of:** Hades
" **wife:** Persephone, Proserpina
Plutus: father: Jasion
" **mother:** Demeter
pneuma: soul, spirit, neume
pneumogastric nerve: vagus
Po: river: Padus
" **tributary:** Adda
" **tribesman:** Lombard
Pocahontas: father: Powhatan
" **husband:** Rolfe
pochard: duck, smee, fowl
pochette: violin, envelope, handbag
pod: sac, carob, pouch, shell
" **tree:** locust
podagra: gout

Poe: Allan Edgar, poetic
" **bird:** raven
" **character:** Pym
" **house:** Usher
" **poems:** Raven, Lenore, Ulalume
poem: rhyme, verse
" **bucolic:** eclogue
" **collection of:** sylra
" **division:** canto
" **eight-line:** triolet
" **sourteen-line:** sonnet
" **heroic:** epos, epic
" **love:** sonnet
" **mournful:** elegy
" **nonsensical:** limerick, doggerel
" **satirical:** iambic
" **six stanzas:** sestina
poetess: Sappho, Parker, Millay, Lowell, Plath, Jong
poetry: poesy, verse
" **god of:** Bragi
" **line of:** stich
" **muse of:** Calliope, Erato, Thalia
poets collectively: parnassus
Pogo's friend: Owl
poi: paste, food
" **source:** taro
point: dot, period, aim, object, prickle, barb, sharpen, needle, detail
" **curve:** node
" **highest:** apex, zenith, apogee
" **lowest:** nadir, perigee
" **pert. to:** focal, apical
" **strong:** forte
" **utmost:** extreme

pointed: aimed, leveled, brief, marked, concise, conical
" **as a leaf:** apiculate
" **end:** cusp, barb
" **missile:** dart, arrow
" **spike:** pike, goad, spear, arrow
" **tip:** apiculus
pointer: dog, rod, stick, hint
" **teacher's:** fescue, cue
poison: virus, bane, taint, corrupt
" **arrow:** inee, wagogo
" **comb. form:** toxic(o)
" **hemlock:** coni(i)ne
" **ivy genus:** rhus
" **tree:** upas
poisonous: fatal, lethal, malignant, noxious
" **fish (Jap.):** fugu
" **gas:** arsine, phosgene
" **herb:** henbane
" **izard:** gila
" **plant:** mandrake
" **weed:** loco
pokeweed: scoke, pocan, poke
Poland, Polish: Slav, Pole, Sarmatia
" **cake:** baba
" **coin:** ducat, grosz, zlot(y), abia
" **composer:** Chopin
" **dance:** polka
" **dynasty:** Piast
" **measure:** morg, mila, pret, cal
" **scientist:** Curie
" **weight:** lut
pole: sprit, rod, axis
" **negative:** cathode

" **to pole:** axial
" **positive:** anode
polecat: zoril, ferret, skunk
polishing: material: emery, rabat, sand, pumice
political: division: ward, hundred, county, state, shire, town, province, community
" **faction:** bloc, junta, party, clan
" **gathering:** rally
" **hack:** heeler
" **list:** slate
pollard: deer, goat
pollen: dust, flour, meal
" **bearing:** staminate, antheral
" **part:** anther
Pollux and Castor: Gemini, twins
" **father:** Zeus
" **mother:** Leda
polo: division of play: chuck(k)er
" **mount:** horse, pony
" **stick:** mallet
" **team:** four
" **Venetian traveler:** Marco
Polonius: daughter: Ophelia
" **servant:** Reynaldo
" **son:** Laertes
Polynesia, Polynesian: Maori, Kanaka, Malayan
" **apple:** kevi
" **banana:** fei
" **burial place:** ahu
" **butterfly:** io
" **dance:** siva
" **demon:** atua
" **fish:** aua

"   **garment:** pareu, malo
"   **god:** Oro, Maui, Atua
"   **goddess:** Pele
"   **oven or pit:** umu
"   **sky:** langi
"   **wages:** utu
"   **yam:** ube
Polyphemus: moth, cyclops
"   **captive:** Ulysses, Odysseus
Polyxena: father: Priam
"   **lover:** Achilles
"   **mother:** Hecuba
polyzoan: polyp, sea anemone, hydra
"   **skeleton:** coral
pomaceous fruit: apple
Pomp and Circumstance composer: Elgar
pompano: alewife, poppyfish
Pompeii: heroine: Ione
"   **scene of defeat:** Thapsus
Ponce de Leon's discovery: Florida
"   **searched for:** Fountain of Youth
Ponchielli opera: (la) Gioconda
pony: horse, glass, measure
"   **student's:** crib
pooka: goblin, specter
pool: cartel, game, pond, flash, kitty
"   **artificial:** tank
"   **mine:** sump
"   **triangle:** rack
"   **tree:** dilo, keena
"   **waterfall:** linn
poon tree: dilo
poor: needy, feeble, base, cheap, barren
"   **Clare:** nun, sister
"   **-house:** almshouse
"   **joe:** heron
"   **John:** cod, food
"   **player:** dub
"   **sl.:** lousy
"   **sport:** sorehead
pop: soda, burst, shoot, father
"   **art hero:** Andy Warhol
"   **the question:** propose
Pope: pontiff
"   **cathedral:** lateran
"   **crown:** tiara
"   **collar:** fanon, orale
"   **family name:** Leo, Pius, Urban, Adrian, Paul
"   **name of 12:** Pius
Pope: Alexander
"   **love of:** Gonne
popes, collectively: papacy
Popeye: sailor, comic strip
"   **sweetheart:** Olive (Oyl)
"   **rival:** Bruto
popinjay: fop, dandy, macaroni, parrot
poplar: alamo, aspen, tulip, lombardy
"   **balsam:** liar
"   **species:** bahan
"   **white:** abele
Poppaea: Sabina
"   **wife of:** Nero
poppy: opium
"   **genus:** papaver
"   **sap:** latex
"   **seed:** maw
population count: census
porbeagle: shark
porcelain: ceramics, china(ware)

"   **ingredient:** clay, kaolin
"   **types:** Sevres, Spoke, Limoges, Ming, Derby
porcupine: urson, rodent
"   **fish:** diodon
"   **spine:** quill
Portia: alias: Balthazar
"   **lover:** Bassanio
"   **maid:** Nerissa
Portugal, Portugese: boat: moleta
"   **coin:** escudo, conto, crown, dobra
"   **commune:** Braga
"   **folk tune:** fado
"   **lady:** Dona
"   **monetary unit:** escudo
"   **title:** Dom
"   **Saint:** Sao
"   **weight:** grao, libra, onca, marco
Poseidon: Neptune
"   **father:** Cronus
"   **mother:** Rhea
"   **scepter:** Trident
"   **wife:** Amphitrite
positive: certain, constant, dogmatic, explicit, photo
"   **not:** minus
"   **pole:** anode
"   **saying:** dictum
"   **sign:** plus
positivism: certainty, comtism
"   **founder:** Comte
possession: property, wealth
"   **assume again:** revest
"   **legal:** title, estate
posset: drink, pamper
post: mail, stake, inform
"   **airplane (race):** pylon

"   **boat (rope):** capstan
"   **doorway/window:** jamb(e)
"   **staircase:** newel
postea: entry, record
posterior: dorsal, rear, hinder
"   **opposed to:** anterior
postscript: codicil
pot: olla, bet, kitty, skillet, crock
"   **handle:** bool
"   **stand:** trivet
"   **wheel:** noria
potato: tuber, imo, spud
"   **bud:** eye
"   **disease:** pox, curl
"   **sweet:** yam, oca
"   **starch:** farina
potherb: chard, kale, wort, spinach
"   **pert. to:** olitory
potman: waiter
potpourri: medley, pasticcio, jumble, mishmash
pottery: ceramics, porcelain
"   **dish:** ramekin
"   **Hindu:** uda
"   **pert. to:** ceramic
"   **wheel:** disk, lathe, throw
poultry: foul
"   **breed:** Ancona, Dorking, Leghorn
"   **dealer:** eggler
"   **farm:** hennery
"   **yard:** barton
pour: rain, flow, stream, gush
"   **off:** decant
"   **to the gods:** libate
pout: moue, mope, sulk, pique
powder: talc, dust, pounce,

cosmetic
   " **case:** bandolier
   " **ground:** brag
   " **perfumed:** sachet
powdered: floury
   " **heraldry:** seme
power: vis, sway, control, vigor, ability
   " **comb. form:** dyna
   " **intellectual:** wit, genius
   " **lack:** atony
   " **natural:** odyl(e)
   " **third:** cube
   " **unit:** watt, volt
prad: horse
prairie: plain, steppe
   " **dog:** marmot
   " **hen:** grouse
   " **soil:** gumbo
   " **squirrel:** gopher
   " **vehicle:** schooner
   " **wolf:** coyote
praise: exalt, laud, kudos, bless, plaudit
   " **hunger for:** esurience
prandium: meal, dinner, repast
pray: beg, ask, invoke, request
   " **Yiddish:** daven
prayer: ave, bene, orison, vesper, matin
   " **beads:** rosary
   " **form:** litany
   " **nine day:** Novena
   " **short:** grace, benediction
   " **tower:** minaret
precept: act, code, canon, maxim, command, instruction, behest

precious: dear, costly, beloved, arrant
   " **sl.:** very
   " **stone:** topaz, ruby, gem, diamond
   " **stone cutter:** lapidary
precocious child: prodigy
predatory: bird: eagle, owl, vulture
   " **insect:** mantis
predicate: base
prefab: quonset (hut), nissen
prefatory note: foreword
prefix: before
   " **about:** peri
   " **across:** trans
   " **against:** anti
   " **backward:** retro
   " **bad:** mal
   " **before:** pre, ante
   " **between:** meta
   " **blood:** hemo
   " **both:** ambi
   " **distant:** tel(e)
   " **eight:** oct(o)
   " **equal:** iso
   " **false:** pseud(o)
   " **far:** tel(e)
   " **fire:** pyr(o)
   " **half:** semi, demi, hemi
   " **many:** mult(i)
   " **mountain:** oro
   " **outer:** exo, ect(o)
   " **over:** supra
   " **single:** mono
   " **thought:** ideo
   " **under:** sub
   " **with:** syn
   " **within:** endo
   " **wrong:** mis
prehistoric: comb. form:

pale(o)
" **human:** caveman
" **upright stone:** menhir
preliminary: prefactory
" **meeting:** caucus
" **race:** heat
" **statement:** preamble, foreword
premises, series of: sorites
preoccupation: with sex: erot(ic)ism
prepare: prime, train
" **copy:** edit
" **for action:** gird, unlimber
preposition: for, onto, into, unto, from, out, after
prepossession: bias
prerogative: right, privilege
" **king's:** regalia
preserve: cure, smoke, protect, pickle
" **by drying:** dessicate, dehydrate
" **game:** sanctuary
" **with salt:** corn
presidential: disapproval: veto
" **reception:** levee
prest: loan
Preston's milieu: Yukon
pretended courage: bravado, bluff
pretense: air, ruse, sham, claim
" **of virtue:** hypocrisy
pretentious: pompous
" **art:** Kitsch
pretext: for war: casus, belli
prevent: avert, deter, thwart, block
" **legally:** estop

preventative: court order: injunction
Priam: children: Cassandra, Paris, Creusa, Hector, Troilus
" **domain:** Troy
" **father:** Laomedon
" **wife:** Hecuba
price: charge, rate, cost, value, worth, fee
" **go down in:** bear
" **go up in:** bull
" **list:** catalog(ue)
prickly: thorny, burry, echinate, spiny
" **bush:** brier, rose
" **heat:** lichen, miliaria
" **shrub:** bramble
" **weed:** nettle
pride: vanity, conceit
" **disdainful:** hauteur
" **lion's:** litter, mane
" **ruffled:** pique
priest: clergyman, minister
" **assistant of:** acolyte
" **gift of:** mortuary
" **newly ordained:** neophyte
" **shaven head of:** tonsure
" **skullcap:** zucchetto
priests group of 20: fetial
primitive: crude, basic, ancient
" **comb. form:** pale(o)
" **fish:** coelancanth
prince: king, monarch, Raia, Principe, Ras
princeling: satrap
princess: Infanta
" **carried by bull:** Europa
principle: rule, maxim, theo-

rem, tenet
" **first:** rudiments
" **main:** keystone
print: **blurred/double:** mackle
" **in red letters:** rubricate
printer's: apprentice: devil
" **ink pad:** dabber
" **proof:** galley
" **roller:** bray
printing: edition
" **process:** offset
" **system for the blind:** braille
" **trial impression:** proof
Priscilla: husband: Alden
" **suitor:** (Miles) Standish
prison: jail, cage
" **cell:** hole
" **sl.:** stir, clink, jug, pen
" **guard: sl:** screw
" **underground:** dungeon
private: personal, secret, intimate
" **entrance:** postern
" **eye:** detective
" **information:** tip
" **remarks:** asides, ad libs
" **wrong:** tort
priveleges, equality of: isonomy
pro: for, professional
" **bono:** publico
" **tempore:** temporary
proceed: issue, advance
" **without power:** coast
process: course, outgrowth
" **of decline:** decadence
" **server:** sheriff
Procne: husband of: Tereus
" **parent of:** Pandion

" **transformation of:** swallow
prodrome: symptom
produced on earth's surface: epigene
producing: abundantly: feracious
professional: pro
" **non:** lay, amateur
profit: avail, gain, benefit
" **clear:** net, velvet
" **easy:** gravy
" **sudden, great:** killing
prog: plunder, forage
prohibit: forbid, ban, veto, taboo, enjoin
prohibitive price: dear, costly
projectile: bullet, rocket, missile
" **part of:** warhead, war nose
" **path of:** trajectory
prolonged dry weather: drought
Prometheus' boon to man: fire
prominence: between eyebrows: glabella
Promised Land: Canaan, Zion, Sion
promissory note: IOU
" **sl.:** marker
pronged thing: fork, antler, trident, rake
pronounce: declare, utter
" **indistinctly:** slur
pronunciamento: manifesto
proofreader's mark: dele, caret, stet
propeller: driver, rotor
" **driving force of:** thrust

"   **part of:** blade
proper: meet, suitable, prim
   " order: eutaxy
   " sl.: kosher
property: chattel, holdings, ownership
   " claim to: lien
   " reverted: escheat
   " willed to someone: legacy
prophesy: prediction, forecast
   " by lots: sortilege
prophets, book of the: Nebiim
proposed international language: ido, esperanto
Proserpina: Cora, Persephone
   " husband of: Pluto
   " mother of: Ceres
prosit: toast
Prospero's: slave: Caliban
   " sprite: Ariel
prosy: dull, jejune
protein: fibrin, albumin, globulin
   " egg yolk: vitellin
Protestant: Anglo-Saxon: wasp
protrusion of organ: hernia
Proust/novelist: Marcel
proverb: adage, parable, axiom, saying
proving directly: d(e)ictic
provisions: larder, groceries
   " search for: forage
prow: bow, nose
prowl: lurk, skulk
proximal: next, nearest
   " opposed to: distal

prude: prig
Prussian: Junker, German
psalm: hymn, introit, venite, laud
   " word: selah
pseudonym: pen, name, alias
   " Arouet: Voltaire
   " Austen: Dapsang
   " Bronte: (Currer) Bell
   " Clemens: (Mark) Twain
   " Dickens: Boz
   " Dudevant: (George) Sand
   " Lamb: Elia
   " Millay: (Nancy) Boyd
   " Porter: (O) Henry
   " Stein: (Alice) Toklas
   " Thibault: (Anatole) France
Psiloriti, Mount: Ida
   " location of: Crete
psoas: muscle, loin
Psyche: soul, mind
   " love of: Cupid
psyches, part of: ids, egos
Pt, in chemistry: platinum
pteropod: mollusk, clione
pterygoid: winglike
public: overt, community, common
   " auction: vendue
   " disclosure: expose
   " land: ager
   " opinion: consensus
Puccini, composer: Giacomo
   " heroine: Mimi, Tosca
   " opera: Tosca, Boheme, Manon Lescaut, Turandot
pucka: real, genuine, good
puddling tool: rabble

pudendum: vulva
puff: gust, whiff, breath
  "   **adder:** snake
  "   **bird:** barbet, monasa
  "   **of wind:** flatus
  "   **up:** bloat, swell
puffin: bird
puggree: scarf
pugh: bah, pish
pugnacious: combative, belli-cose
  "   **man (sl.):** bruiser
pukka: real, genuine
pulex: flea
pull: move, pluck, haul, tug
  "   **apart:** pan, rip
  "   **down:** reduce
  "   **off:** effect
  "   **sl.:** influence
  "   **up stake:** leave, depart
pulp: chyme, pap, pith
  "   **apple/fruit:** pomace
  "   **product:** paper
  "   **sl.:** magazine
pulse: beat, throb
  "   **beat absence:** acrotism
  "   **of the:** sphygmic
pulverizing device: spider
Punch: and   : Judy
  "   **and Judy character:** puppet
  "   **and Judy dog:** Toby
punchinello: clown, buffoon
punctuation   **mark:** (semi)colon, dash, period, comma, hyphen, brackets
Punic: citizen: Carthaginian
  "   **War battlesite:** Zama
punishment: penalty, rap
  "   **of:** penal, punitive
  "   **voluntary:** penance

Punjab: native: Jat, Sikh
punka(h): fan
punster: wag, wit
pupil: contraction of: myosis
  "   **organ with:** eye
purchase: or sale of office: barratry
purification: catharsis
  "   **by holy water:** baptism
purslane: weed
purulence: pus
push: impel, propel, shove, hustle
  "   **along:** plod
  "   **on:** proceed
  "   **over: sl.:** setup
pusher, sl.: commodity of: heroin, lsd, pot, marijuana
put: impel, set, place, state
  "   **aside:** discard
  "   **down:** crush, humble, record, quash
  "   **forth effort:** exert
  "   **forward:** present, propose
  "   **off:** delay, evade, divert
  "   **on:** clothe, don, (sl.) josh
  "   **on the block:** auction
  "   **out:** dismiss, evict, oust
  "   **side by side:** juxtapose
  "   **to work:** harness
  "   **up with:** bear
Putnam, Revolutionary general: Israel
putsch: rebellion, uprising
puttee: gaiter, putty
putting area: green
puttyroot: orchid
Putumayo river: Ica
puzzle: stump, nonplus, perplex, enigma

" **word:** logograph
pygarg: addax
Pygmalion: author: G.B. Shaw
" **statue:** Galatea
pygmy: antelope: oribi
pyralidid: moth
pyramid: builders: Egyptians
" **site of:** El Giza
Pyreness: goat: ibex
" **highest point:** Aneto

pyrexia: fever
pyrite: fool's gold
Pyrrhonism: skepticism
Pythagoras: birthplace: Samos
" **forte:** mathematics
Pythias: friend: Damon
pythoness: soothsayer
pyx: box, ciborium
pyxis: case, vase, box

Q

Q: cue, queue
" **Greek:** Kappa
Qara Qum's/Qatar's capital: Doha
q.e.d.: quod erat demonstrandum
qua: as, bird, heron
quack: faker, cry, fraud, crocus
" **crier:** duck
" **doctor's aide:** toady
" **mediane:** nostrum, herb
quad: campus, block, sibling, jail
quadra: plinth, fillet
quadragesimal: forty, Lenten
quadrangle: square, tetragon
quadrant: arc, fourth, instrument
" **graduated edge:** limb
quadrate: suit, ideal, balanced, square
quadriga: cart, chariot
quadrille: dance, cards

" **card:** matador
" **sight:** vane
quadrivium: part of: music, astronomy, geometry
quadroon: hybrid, mulatto
quadrumane: ape, chimpanzee, primate
quadruped: fourlegged, mammal
" **ex:** rhino, camel, tapir, donkey, zebra, ass, giraffe, hippo
quaere: question, inquiry
quaff: sip, drink, gulp
quag: quiver, quagmire, quake
quagga-like-animal: zebra, donkey
quaggy: soft, flabby, yielding, miry, boggy
quahaug, quahog: clam
" **young:** littleneck
quail: recoil, bird, wince, wilt, colin

273

"   **flock of:** bevy, covey

"   **young:**   cheeper, squealer

quaint: odd, crafty, singular, fanciful

"   **humor:** droll(ery)

quake: rese, shake, waver, vibrate

Quaker: Friend, broadbrim

"   **colonist:** Penn

"   **gray:** acier

"   **ladies:** flower, bluet

"   **midweek of A:** Wednesday

"   **founder:** George Fox

Quaker City: Philadelphia

quaking: trepid, shaky

"   **tree:** aspen, poplar

qualification: ability, requisite, modification, condition

qualified: eligible, able, competent

qualify: fit, pass, entitle, describe

qualifying word: adverb, adjective

quality: cost, sort, nature, caliber

"   **distinguishing:** trait

"   **of tone:** timbre, resonance

"   **poor/bad:** punk, bum

"   **special:** deluxe

qualm: pall, nausea, twinge, misgiving, compunction

qualmish: queer, queasy

quamash: prairie, ca(m)mas(s), lily

quandary: fix, pickle, dilemma, nonplus

quannet: file

quant: pole, punt, propel

quantity: dose, grist, portion, hoard, allowance

"   **fixed:** constant

"   **full:** complement

"   **indefinite:** some, any

large: slew, raft, bushel

"   **small:** lick, scantling

"   **per unit:** rate

"   **prescribed:** dose

"   **not prescribed:** scalar

Quantrill's men: raiders

quantum: unit, amount, portion

"   **of heat energy:** photon

quarantine: ban, exclude, isolate

"   **building/ship:** lazaretto

"   **signal:** yellow jack

quaranty: court

quarentene: rood, furlong

quark: caw, croak

quarl(e): brick, tile

quarrel: spat, pane, chisel, bicker, altercation

quarrelsome: hostile, petulant, bellicose, litigious

quarring tool: trepan, trapan

quarry: game, prey, chase, excavate

quarryman: stonecutter

quart: (see special section, metric)

"   **fourth, measure**

"   **four:** gallon

"   **one-eighth:** gill

"   **two:** flagon

quartan: fever, malaria

quarter: coin, allot, division, span, mercy, fourth, billet

"   **note:** crotchet

" **circle:** quadrant
" **phase:** diphase
" **round:** orolo
quartern: gill
quarters: camp, room, abode, shelter
" **nautical:** steerage, wardroom
" **winter:** hibernacle
" **women's:** harem
" **slang:** digs
quartz: sand, onyx, topaz, crystal, amethyst, flint, prase, silex
quartzite: sandstone, itabarite
quash: drop, void, annul, crush, cancel, suppress
" **legally:** abate
quasi: as if, seemingly
quat: boil, pimple, tetrad, satiate
quaternion: tetrad
" **turning factor:** versor
quatrain: poem, stanza
quay: pier, wharf, landing, levee
queach: fen, thicket, swamp, bog
quean: jade, hussy, wench, slut
Quebec: acre: arpent
" **patron saint:** Anne
" **peninsula:** Gaspe
" **vehicle:** caleche
quebrada: brook, gorge, ravine
Quechua: Inca(n), Peruvian, Indian
queen: monarch, regina, sovereign
" **Anne's lace:** carrot

" **beheaded:** Antoinette
" **fairy:** Mab, Una, Titania
" **legendary:** Dido
" **widowed:** dowager
Queen: of the: Adriatic: Venice
" " **Antilles:** Cuba
" " **Calydon:** Althea
" " **East:** Zenobia
" " **gods:** Juno, Sati, Hera
" " **Hearts:** Elizabeth
" " **Heaven:** Mary, Astarte
" " **Iceland:** Brunhilde
" " **Ithaca:** Penelope
" " **Isles:** Albion
" " **jungle:** Sheena
" " **Lydia:** Omphale
" " **Moslem:** begum
" " **Nile:** Cleopatra
" " **nymphs:** Mab
" " **Olympian:** Hera
" " **Palmyra:** Zenobia
" " **Roman gods:** Juno
" " **Sheba:** Balkis
" " **spades:** basta
" " **Thebes:** Jocasta
queen's: arm: musket
" **delight:** oil, herb, perennial
" **flower:** myrtle, bloodwood
Queen City: Cincinnati
queer: odd, weird, cranky, bizarre, singular
" **bird/person:** nut, crank
" **notion:** kink
" **sl.:** spoil, counterfeit
queest: ringdove
queet: coot

quelque chose: trifle

queme: snug, tidy, handy, quiet

quenelle: meatball

quercetin: dye, flavin(e)

quercitron: oak, dye

quercus genus: oaks

querida: (Sp.) lover, sweetheart, darling

querken: stifle, choke

querl: twist, coil

quern: mill, grinder

querulous: peevish, fretful, quizzical, complaining

question: ask, quiz, doubt, problem, issue, inquiry
   " **baffling:** poser
   " **denoting:** interrogational
   " **rhetorical:** eperotesis
   " **and answer teaching:** catechesis
   " **mark:** erotema, eroteme
   " **quetzal:** bird, trogon

queue: pigtail, braid, line
   " **torero's:** coleta

quey: heifer

quiaquia: scad, cigarfish

quica: opossum, sarigue

quick: fast, agile, snappy, pregnant
   " **assets:** cash
   " **bread:** muffins, biscuits
   " **in learning:** apt
   " **look:** glance, eyebeam
   " **tempered:** irascible
   " **witticism:** sally

quicker than: ere

quicklime: rusma

quicksand: flew, syrt(is), morass

quickset: hedge, thicket, slip

quicksilver: mercury, azoth

quid: cud, chew, trade, return
   " **pro quo:** substitute

quiddany: sirup, jelly

quiddit: subtlety

quidnunc: gossip, frump, busybody, snoop

quiet: calm, mum, allay, silent
   interval: lull
   secretly: clandestine

quietus: repose, death, mittimus

quiff: puff, girl

quill: pen, spine, remex, barrel
   " **feathers:** remiges, calami
   " **porcupine:** spine

quillai: soapbark

quillet: tube

quilt: eider, duvet, bedcover, pad, caddow

quilting party: bee

quince: bel, pome

quinine: Kina
   " **source:** cinchona
   " **water:** tonic

quinoa: seeds, pigweed

quinoline   **derivative:** analgen

quint: organ, stop

quip: mot, pun, jest, saying

quire: fold, paper, choir

quirk: kink, clock, twist, caprice

quirquincho: pichi, armadillo

quirt: whip, romal

quis: woodcock

quisling: rat, traitor, collaborator
   " **fifth columnist:** vidkun

quitch: weed, grass

quitclaim: release, acquit

quite: all, stark, wholly, entirely

  " **so:** exactly, precisely

quits: even

quittance: repay, reprisal, discharge

quiver: shake, nimble, tremble, vibrate

  " **content of:** arrows

quivering tree: aspen, palpitant

  " **leaf:** aspen

Quixote: giant: windmill

  " **horse:** Rosinante

  " **love:** Dulcinea

  " **squire/friend:** Sancho (Panza)

  " **title:** Don

quixotic: utopian, impractical, romantic, absurd

quiz: ask, joke, probe, exam(ination)

  " **kid:** prodigy

quizzing glass: eyeglass, monocle

quod: jug, jail, prison

quodlibet: medley, debate, subtlety

quoin: coin, corner, keystone, lock

quoit: disc, ring(er), throw

  " **pin:** hob

  " **target:** tee, peg

quomodo: means, manner

quondam: former, once, erstwhile, whilom

quonset hut: prefab

  " **British type:** Nissen

quop: throb

quorum: group, council, company, majority

quota: share, allotment, divide

quotation: cital, citation, excerpt

  " **ending speech/story/song:** tag

  " **mark:** guillemet (Fr.)

  " **opening chapter:** epigraph

  " **reader:** speculator, stockholder

quoth: spoke, said

quotha: indeed, forsooth

quotidian: daily, ordinary

quotient: result

quotity: group, collection

R

R, letter: Greek: rho
    " **in chemistry:** radical
    " **in mathematics:** ratio, radius
    " **pronunciation like I:** lallation
Ra: sun god
    " **crown of:** aten
    " **in chemistry:** radium
    " **symbol of:** sundisk
    " **wife of:** Mut
raad: catfish
rabato: ruff, collar
rabbi: teacher, Amora
    " **teachings:** Mishna(h)
rabbit: hare, rodent, cottontail
    " **breeding place:** warren
    " **ears:** antenna
    " **family:** leporid
    " **female:** doe
    " **fur:** lapin, con(e)y
    " **fur hat:** castor
    " **hunting dog:** harrier
    " **male:** buck
    " **pen:** hutch
    " **rock:** hyrax
    " **tail of:** scut
    " **variety:** lop
    " **young:** bunny
rabble: canaille
    " **rouser:** agitator
    " **the:** masses
Rabelais, Fr. satirist: Francois
Rabelaisian: earthy
RCA trademark: nipper
race: lineage, pedigree, stirps
    " **channel:** flume
    " **division:** negroid, caucasian, mongoloid
    " **engine:** rev
    " **of dwarfs:** nibelung
    " **pert. to:** ethnic
    " **prelims:** heats
    " **short:** dash, sprint
    " **start of:** breakaway
    " **water:** arroyo
    " **white:** caucasian

"   **yellow:** mongoloid
racecourse: track, turf, oval
"   **circuit:** lap
"   **comb form·** drome
"   **marker:** lane, pylon
"   **official:** starter
racehorse: disability: glanders, spavin, stringhalt
"   **enclosure/exercise area:** paddock
"   **kind of:** mudder, plater, trotter, pacer
"   **winless:** maiden
racer: hotrod, (black) snake, sprinter
"   **course of:** lane
racetrack: oval
"   **character:** dopester, tipster, tout
"   **cover:** tanbark
"   **fence:** rail
Rachel: father: Laban
"   **husband:** Jacob
"   **son:** Joseph, Benjamin
rachis: stem, spine, backbone
Rachmaninoff, composer/pianist: Sergei
Racine (Jean), Fr. poet: Baptiste
"   **masterpiece:** Phedre
racing: colors: silks
"   **program:** card, form
"   **scull:** wherry
rack: gin, grating, torture, stand, score
"   **corn:** crib
"   **display:** easel
"   **hat:** tree
"   **horse's:** pace, gait
racket: sl.: business, profes-

sion, line
"   **string:** catgut
raconteur: forte: stories, anecdotes
Radames' love: Aida
radar: device, for short: TFR
"   **image:** blip
"   **like device:** sonar
"   **screen flash:** blip
"   **sound:** racon, beep
"   **system:** shoran
radian: arc
radiant: bright, beaming, aglow
"   **comb. form:** heli(o)
radicel: root(let)
radio: wireless
"   **active shower:** fallout
"   **aerial:** antenna
"   **dash in:** dah
"   **frequency band:** channel
"   **interference:** static
"   **operator; amateur:** ham
"   **signal for aviators:** beam
"   **signoff:** roger
"   **tube:** grid
radioactive: matter: nobelium, carnotite, radon, niton
"   **particles:** geigers
radioactivity, measure of: curie
radium: discoverer: Curie, (Pierre, Marie)
"   **source of:** pitchblende, uranite
radix: base, root, radical, etymon
radon: niton
raft: balsa, lot, collection

"   **log:** catamaran
ragamuffin: tatterdemalion
raggee: grass, ragi
Raggedy doll: Anne, Andy
raglan: topcoat, overcoat
ragweed: ambrosia, cockle-bur
ragwort: jacoby, groundsel
raid: invade, foray, assault, sortie
"   **sl.:** pinch
rail: coot, sora, fence, bird, weka, heron, scoff
"   **bird like:** courlan
"   **kin of:** notornis
railing: fence, balustrade, parapet
railroad: rush, line, herd
"   **baggage car:** van
"   **bridge:** trestle
"   **center:** yard
"   **crossing:** gate
"   **engine serviceman:** hostler
"   **freight car:** gondola
"   **handcar:** velocipede
"   **line end:** terminus
"   **side track:** spur
"   **siding:** turn-out
"   **single track:** monorail
"   **stop for locomotives:** tank town
"   **supply car:** tender
"   **switch device:** frog, shunt
"   **tie:** sleeper, timber
rain: precipitation, shower
"   **briefly:** spit
"   **forest:** selva
"   **fine mist:** mizzle, serein
"   **formed by:** pluvial

"   **frozen:** sleet, hail
"   **gauge:** udometer
"   **mist:** scud
"   **sudden:** spate, brash
"   **tree:** zamia, saman
rainbow: arc(h), meteor, bow
"   **bridge:** bifrost
"   **goddess:** Iris
"   **color like:** pavonine
"   **trout:** steelhead
"   **pert. to:** iridal
rainmaker: sl.: lobbyist
raise: hoist, nurture, collect, erect
"   **in relief:** emboss
"   **nap:** tease(l)
"   **to third power:** cube
raisin: grape, sultana
"   **in pudding:** plum
raison   : d'etat, d'etre
rajah's wife: ranee, rani
ralline bird: rail
ram: pound, tup, sheep
"   **constellation:** Aries
"   **headed god:** Ammon
"   **horn:** shofar, shophar
"   **ship's:** beak
Ramadan, Ramazan: fasting
Rambouillet: (merino) sheep
ramekin/ramequin: dish
Rameses: pharaoh, monarch
"   **domain:** Egypt
ramie: fiber, hemp
ramjet: athodyd, engine
Ramona author: Jackson
rampaging person: amok, berserk, juramentado
Ramses' goddess: Anta
ramson: root, garlic
ramus: branch
rana: frog

range: row, rank, stove, Sierra, train, gamut
" **finder:** telemeter, stadia
" **of emotion:** gamut
" **of vision:** scan, eyesight, scope
" **Rocky Mountains:** Uinta, Teton
rani/ranee: Queen
" **husband of:** Raja(h)
Ranier's domain, Prince: Monaco
rank: eminence, position, grade, tier
" **and file:** soldiers, followers
" **having:** genetic
" **of lower:** puisne
ransom: person held for: hostage
ranunculaceous plant: peony, anemone, larkspur
ranunculus: buttercup, crowfoot
rapacious: greedy, avaricious, voracious
" **bird:** shrike
" **fish:** piranha
rape: ravish, pulp, cabbage, cole, fodder
" **soil/seed:** colza
rapid: swift, abrupt, ripple
" **comb. form:** tachy
" **fire:** staccato, fusillade
rapids: chute, dells, dalles
rappee: snuff
rapping: tattoo
rapscallion: rogue, rascal
raptorial bird: eagle, owl, hawk, falcon, vulture
rara avis: rarity, bird, oner

rarebit: rabbit
rareripe fruit: peach
rasher: ham, bacon
Rasmussen, Arctic explorer: Knud
rasorial: gallinaceous
" **bird:** hen, chicken
Raspe's character: Munchausen
Rasputin, Russian monk: Grigori
rasse: civet
rat: vermin, vole, rodent
" **domesticated:** guinea pig
" **genus:** mus
" **hair:** pad
" **kind of:** mole
" **poison:** ratsbane
" **rodent resembling:** mouse, hamster
" **sl.:** deserter, informer, stool pigeon
ratafia: liqueur, cooky, macaroon
rataplan: drumbeat
rate: ratio, class, esteem, scold
" **exchange:** agio
" **of mass to volume:** density
ratel: badger
ratfish: chimaera
rather than: ere
Ratibor river: Oder
ratio: quotient, proportion, cos, sine, pi
rational principle: logos
rations: food
" **bag:** haversack
ratite: emu, moa, ostrich

" **genus:** apteryx
ratoon: shoot, sprout
rats, of: murine
rattlepate: ass, fool
rattlesnake: viper, cascabel, sidewinder
" **bite:** rue
" **plantain:** orchid
" **rattleless:** copperhead
rattletrap: mouth, jalopy, rickety
raun: roe, spawn
raven: crow, corby, devour, prey
" **author:** Poe
" **cry of:** caw
" **genus:** corvus
" **like a:** corvine
" **of Odin:** Hugin
" **quote of:** nevermore
raw: sore, bleak, uncooked
" **cotton:** lint
" **material:** staple, stock, stuff
" **sl.:** unfair
rawhide: whip, parfleche
" **kind of:** shagreen
ray: beam, skate, trace, petal, sawfish
" **eagle:** obispo
" **fish:** dorn
" **kind of:** beta, gamma, laser
" **like part:** radius
rayon: acetate, ratine, viscose, jersey
" **corded/ribbed:** repp
" **sheer:** voile
" **twilled:** serge
razor: shave(r)
" **billed bird:** alca

" **clam:** solen
" **sharpen:** hone, strop
Rb, in chemistry: rubidium
re: anent, regarding, about
" **echoing:** reboant
reaction: reflex, tropism
read: peruse, pore, con, study
" **inability to:** alexia
" **metrically:** scan
" **superficially:** skim
reads alike forward or backward: palindrome
" **ex:** Madam I'm Adam
real: pucka, actual, coin
" **plural of:** reis
" **thing:** McCoy
real estate: claim: tax
" **pert. to:** predial
realism, opposite of: idealism
realistic: practical
" **opposed to:** visionary
ream: enlarge
reamer: borer, broach, drift
reaper: mower
" **Grim:** death
rear: build, ramp, breed, nurse, aft
" **horse's:** pesade, stend
" **young bird:** fledge
rearrange: permute
reason: sanity, argue, justify, logos, motive
" **against:** oppugn
" **deprive of:** dement
" **for being:** end, raison d'etre
" **pert. to:** noetic
" **with:** rightly
reasoning: logic
" **basis:** premise

"   **correct:** logical
"   **false:** idolism, sophism
"   **faulty:** paralogism, syllogism
"   **subtle, difficult:** metaphysics
reata: noose, lasso
Rebecca, Rebekah:
"   **brother:** Laban
"   **diminutive of:** Reba, Becky
"   **father:** Bethuel
"   **husband:** Isaac
"   **mother:** Milcah
"   **sister:** Laban
"   **son:** Esau, Jacob
rebel: angel: Belial
rebus: puzzle, riddle
recede: draw back, ebb
receiver: recipient, treasurer
"   **stolen goods:** fence
"   **trust property:** bailee, trustee
recent: current
"   **comb. form:** neo
receptacle: vessel, bin, box, basin
"   **flower:** torus
"   **holy water:** font, stoup
Recife: Pernambuco
reciprocal: repay, return
"   **comb. form:** allelo
recite: narrate, relate
"   **loudly:** declaim
"   **mechanically:** patter
"   **monotonously:** chant, drone
reck: heed
reckless: madcap, wanton, wild, rash
reclaimed land: polder

reconnaisance: survey
record: tab, dope, file, register
"   **copy of:** estreat
"   **formal:** minutes, document
"   **historical:** annals
"   **personal:** diary, dossier
"   **police:** blotter
"   **ship:** log
records: place for public: archives
recovery in law: trover
recrement: waste, dross
rectifier: adjuster
"   **tube:** diode
recto: opposed to: verso
recurring period: cycle
red: color, radical
"   **and blue color:** purple
"   **ape:** orangutan
"   **arsenic:** realgar
"   **breast:** robin, sandpiper
"   **cedar:** juniper, savin(e)
"   **corpuscle deficiency:** anemia
"   **corundum:** ruby
"   **deep:** ruby, garnet
"   **deer:** staggart, spay
"   **Desert:** Nefud
"   **eyed fish:** carp, rudd
"   **fir:** pine, spruce, Douglas
"   **gum:** eucalyptus, strophulus
"   **in heraldry:** gules
"   **inscribed in:** rubric
"   **lead:** minium
"   **letter:** memorable
"   **pigment:** chica, roset
"   **squirrel:** chickaree

" **star:** Mars, Antares

" **viper:** copperhead

Red: Cross, founder: Barton (Clara)

" " **concern:** disaster, calamity

" **Planet:** Mars

" **Sea:** Erythrean

" " **Kingdom:** Yemen

" **Square, landmark:** Kremlin

redd: tidy-up

Redeemer: Jesus Christ, Savior, Goel

Redemptorist founder: Liguori

redfin: carp, fish

redhead: duck, woodpecker, carrot top

" **kin of:** pochard, widgeon

redmouth: grunt, fish

redness: excessive: erythrism

" **of skin:** rubefaction

redowa-like dance: waltz, polka

redundancy: nimiety, pleonasm, tautology

reduplicate: in botany: valvate

redwood: sequoia

reed: oat, grass

" **bird:** bobolink

" **instrument with:** oboe, clarinet, organ, saxaphone, bassoon

" **loom:** sley

" **poetic:** arrow

" **weaver's:** sley

reef: coral: cay, key

" **mining:** vein, lode

reel: for thread: filature

" **of cocoon silk:** filature

refer: assign, allude, point

" **to:** vide

referendum: plebiscite

refine: polish, purify, improve

" **by distillation:** rectify

" **by melting:** smelt

" **vessel used:** cupel

reflet: luster

reformer: moralist, Riis

" **religious:** Luther

refuse: naysay, nill, reject, ejecta

" **consent to:** veto

" **metal:** scum, dross

" **table:** ort, scrap

" **wine:** lees

Regan: father: Lear

" **sister:** Goneril, Cordelia

regent: interrex

" **of the sun:** Uriel

regicide's victim: King

regiment: order, cadre

" **flag:** pennon

" **member:** grenadier

Regin: son of: Sigurd, Siegfried

region: zone, realm, locale

" **comb. form:** nesia

" **pert. to:** areal

" **upper:** ether

" **warm:** tropics

" **woodless:** plain

register: cash: damper

" **legal:** docket

regma: schizocarp, maple

regulating box: rheostat

rehearsal: training, practice

" **kind of:** dryrun

rehoboam: hat, bowl

Rehoboam: father: Solomon
" **son:** Abijah
reign: rule, govern, prevail
" **of a family:** dynasty
" **pert. to:** regnal
reindeer: caribou
" **genus:** rangifer
" **man:** Lapp
rejoinder: answer, reply
related: germane, akin, allied
" **by blood:** sib, kin(dred)
" **on father's side:** agnate
" **on mother's side:** enate
relationship: sympathetic: rapport
relative amount: ratio
relatives: kinfolk
" **favoritism to:** nepotism
release: free, untie, undo, liberate, exempt
" **claim:** remise, waiver
" **mass of ice:** calve
relic: curio, souvenir
" **sacred:** halidom
" **cabinet:** etager(e)
religious: pious, devout, monk, nun
" **beggar:** fakir
" **belief:** creed
" **devotion:** novena
" **expedition:** crusade
" **image:** icon
" **journey:** pilgrimage
" **offering:** oblation, sacrifice
" **order:** Jesuit, Templar, Dominican, Marist, Franciscan
" **reformer:** Huss, Luther
" **saying:** logia
" **vigil:** watch

relish: condiment, gusto, enjoy, radish, chutney, sapor, curry, mustard
" **fish egg:** caviar
" **jelled:** aspic
relying on experience: empiracal
remain: stay, last, endure, tarry
" **balanced:** librate
" **firm:** stand (pat)
" **undecided:** pend, hang fire
remark: word, note, barb, aside
" **correct: (sl.):** mouthful
" **embarrassing:** faux pas, boner
" **indirect:** innuendo
" **witty:** bon mot, sally, quip
Rembrandt: Dut. painter: (Van) Rijn
" **work:** Titus
remedy: cure, heal, antidote
" **cure-all:** elixir, panacea
" **quack:** nostrum, placebo
" **soothing:** balm
remex: oarsman, feather, quill
remo(u)lade: sauce, dressing
remora: clog, pega, fish, delay
remote: aloof, alien, vague
" **goal:** thule
" **most:** ultima
remove: oust, expel, eject
" **from grave:** disinter
" **from office:** depose, oust
" **impurities:** refine
" **in law:** eloin

" **water:** dehydrate
Remus: brother/slayer: Romulus
" **father:** Mars
" **foster-mother:** wolf
" **mother:** Rhea
Renard: fox
Renoir: painter: Pierre Auguste, Fr.
rensselaerite: talc
rep: fabric, cloth
repair: fix, mend, remedy
" **hole/tear:** darn
repartee: retort, mot, rejoinder
" **engage in:** fence
" **skilled at:** witty
repast: meal, refection, treat
" **pert. to:** prandial
repeat: mus.: bis
" **performance:** encore
" **sign:** (mus.) segno
repeating rifle inventor: Mauser
repertoire/repertory: stock
repetition: recitation, copy, recurrence
" **in music:** reprise
" **mechanical:** rote
" **of performance:** encore, replay
" **of sound:** echo
repine: complain, fret, grouse
replica: facsimile, copy, carbon
repondez s'il vous plait: RSVP
report: rumor, denounce, account, broadcast, hansard
" **concern of:** scoop, data
" **false:** slander, canard

" **routine of:** legwork
repository: safe, confidant, sepulcher
representation: image, allegory, mimesis
" **of heavenly bodies:** orrery
" **ridiculous:** travesty
reprisal: quittance, vengeance
reproduce asexually: clone
reproductive cell: gamete, gonad
" **organ:** testis, ovary
reptile: saurian, lizard, alligator, lacert(il)ian
" **age:** Mesozoic
" **carnivorous:** tuatara
" **extinct:** pterosaur
" **footless:** snake, apod
" **fossil:** stegosaurus
" **mythical:** salamander
" **Nile:** croc
" **pert. to:** saurian
" **scale:** scutum, platelet
" **study of:** herpetology
republic: democracy
" **author:** Plato
" **of letters:** literati
" **imaginary:** Oceania
Republican: Whig
" **mascot:** elephant
" **Party:** GOP
" **recalcitrant:** mugwump
repute: odor, esteem
request: formal: rogation
requiem: hymn, dirge, mass
requiescat in : pace
reredos: partition, screen
reremouse: bat
res: thing, point

research: study
  " **center:** lab(oratory)
reseau: network
reseda: mignonette
resemblance: sl.: ringer
reservation: in law: saying, salvo
reserves: National Guard
  " **armed forces:** militia
reservoir: store, supply, cistern
  " **overflow of:** spilth
residence: abode, domicile, biding
  " **rural:** bower
  " **stately:** mansion
residential street: terrace
resin, rosin: shellac(k), pitch, amber, alkyd
  " **aromatic:** copaiba
  " **cathartic:** scammony
  " **fossil:** amber
  " **gum:** myrrh, resinoid, copal, mastic
  " **incense:** sandarac, myrrh
  " **perfume making:** benzoin
  " **purified:** shellac
  " **solvent for:** ether
  " **synthetic:** bakelite, silicone
  " **thermoplastic:** saran
  " **varnish:** anime
resinous tree: fir, pine, balsam
resort: recourse, spa
  " **Riviera:** Cannes
  " **place frequented:** haunt
Respighi, composer: Ottorino

respiration: breathing
  " **comb. form:** spiro
  " **difficult:** dyspn(o)ea
  " **organ of:** lung
  " **normal:** eupnoea
rest: seat, recline, sleep, repose
  " **sl.:** breather, break
  " **midday:** siesta
  " **reading:** caesura
restaurant: diner, cabaret, eatery, bistro
  " **bench:** banquette
  " **compartment:** booth
restive: balky, unruly, fretful
restorative: anodyne, salutary
restore: printer's mark: stet
  " **to health:** recuperate
result in: cause
resurrection: revival, rebirth
  " **experienced by:** Jesus, Lazarus
resuscitation: anabiosis
ret: soak, damp, macerate
retable: shelf, gradin
retainers, body of: retinue
retaining wall: revetment
retch: vomit, gag, keck
rete/reticulum: network, plexus
retem: juniper
retepore: mullusk
retiarius: gladiator
retort: repartee, riposte, quip, sally
retraction: palinode
retreat: asylum, nest, sanctum, lair, pullout
  " **kind of:** convent, monastery, hermitage

" **shaded:** bower
" **signal:** chamade
" **underground:** cave, abri
retribution goddess: Ate
retributive justice: nemesis
return: in kind: reciprocate
" **of the Native author:** Hardy
Reuben: brother: Joseph
" **father:** Jacob
" **mother:** Leah
Reuel's father: Essau
reunion: get-together
" **with Brahma:** Nirvana
reus: defendant
reveille: call, signal, rouse, dian(a)
revelations: Apocalypse
revelry: festivity, saturnalia
" **cry:** evoe
revenue: income
" **bishop's:** annat
reverence: awe, worship, adoration
" **gesture:** genuflection, kneeling
" **lacking:** impious
revers: lapel
reversion: return
" **of property:** escheat
" **to type:** atavism
review: report, inspect, critique
" **adverse:** pan
" **enthusiastic:** rave
" **one who does:** critic
revivalist: evangelist
revolting: offensive, loathsome, horrid
revolution: gyre
" **fighter:** minuteman

" **general of the:** Gates, Arnold, Greene, Lincoln
revolutionist: anarch, reb(el)
revolutions per minute: RPM, revs
revolving part: rotor, rotator
Reynard: fox
rezai: coverlet
Rh factor: rhesus
Rhea: ostrich, Ops
" **husband of:** Cronus
" **father of:** Uranus
" **child of:** Zeus, Hades, Hera, Hestia
rhesus: macaque, monkey
rhetorical: florid
" **device:** orator
rheumatism: of back/loins: lumbago
" **remedy:** salol
" **weed:** pipsissewa
Rhine: Rijn, river
" **city on the:** Mannheim
" **magic hoard:** Rheingold
" **nymph:** Lorelei, Lurlei
" **pert. to:** Rhenish
" **wine:** Hock, Moselle
rhino(ceros): abada, money, cash
" **black:** borele
" **cousin of:** tapir
" **beetle:** uany
" **bird:** beefeater
" **one-horned:** badak
" **two-horned:** keitloa
rhizoid: rootlike
rhizopod: testacean
rhoda: rose
Rhode Island: (see special section)
" **founder:** (Roger) Wil-

liams
Rhodes: Rodi
" **ancient wonder:** Colossus
Rhodesia: language: Bantu, Shona
" **tribe:** Ilas
rhomb, rhomboid: parallelogram, lozenge
Rhone tributary: Isere, Saone
rhubarb: hassle, pieplant
" **genus:** rheum
rhus tree: sumac(h)
rhythmic: metrical
" **rise and fall:** heave
" **accent:** ictus
riata: lasso, rope
rib: vein, kid, wife, tease
" **in architecture:** lierne
" **leaf:** nervure
" **pert. to:** costal
ribaldry: japery
ribbon: decoration, braid, strip, bow
" **badge:** cordon
" **binding:** lisere
" **decorative:** riband
" **document/seal:** label
" **fish:** cutlass
" **knot:** cockade
" **like part:** t(a)enia
" **paper:** ticker tape
" **trimming:** galloon
ribs: having: costate
" **without:** decostate
rice: grass, cereal, grain
" **dish, spicy/meat:** pilau
" **field:** paddy
" **husk:** bran
" **paste:** ame

" **wine:** sake
rice rail: sora
Richard I: of England: Lionheart, Coeur de Lion
rich man: nabob, plutocrat, Midas, Cropsus
Richelieu: Cardinal
" **successor:** Mazarin
riches: demon of: Mammon
" **region of:** Eldorado
" **worship of:** plutomania
ricin: protein
rick: heap, scold, stack, jingle
Rickenbacker: Amer. flying ace: Eddie
ricksha(w): jinrikisha, samlor
rictus: mask, gape
riddle: enigma, sieve, puzzle, conundrum
" **picture:** rebus
ridge: ruga, wale, crest, cuesta, aas, seam
" **cloth:** wale
" **glacial:** osar, drumlin, esker
" **pert. to:** cardinal
" **sand:** dune, dene
" **skin:** welt
ridicule: gibe, jeer, mock, roast
" **deity:** Momus
" **object of:** laughingstock
riding: outfit: habit
" **pants:** jodhpurs
" **school:** manege
" **shoe:** solleret
" **whip:** crop, quirt
rifle: carbine, pillage, rob, repeater
" **ball:** minie
" **chamber:** magazine

"   **pin:** tige
"   **person/man:** jager
Riga: balsam
"   **Gulf island:** Oesel
"   **native:** Latvian
right: title, correct, license, fit
"   **comb. form:** rect(i)
"   **hand:** dextra
"   **legal:** title, droit
"   **of way:** easement
"   **sl.:** roger
"   **to mail free:** frank
"   **turn:** gee
"   **word:** mot juste
rights: equality of: isonomy
"   **relating to:** jural
Rigoletto: composer: Verdi
"   **heroine:** Gilda
rigor: fury, harshess
"   **companion of:** mortis
Riis, social reformer: Jacob
Rijn: Rhine
Rilke, Ger. poet: Rainer
rim: lip, brink, orle, margin
"   **cap's projecting:** visor
"   **pipe:** flange
"   **roof's:** eave
"   **wheel:** felly, felloe
Rinaldo's steed: Bayard
ring: knell, rim, arena
"   **comb. form:** gyro
"   **of chain:** link
"   **of guards:** cordon
"   **of light:** halo
"   **of rope:** grommet
"   **of rubber:** gasket
"   **pert. to:** annular
ringing: clam, bright, resonant
"   **sound in ear:** tinnitus
rings: interlocking: gimmal

"   **series:** coil
Rio   : Bravo, Grande
"   **de**   : Oro, Janiero
Rip van Winkle author: Irving
ris de veau: sweetbread
rise: stand, aspire, rebel, flow
"   **again:** resurrect
"   **and float in the air:** levitate
"   **and fall:** heave
rissole: meatball
Ritter: knight
Ritz, Swiss hotelman: Cesar
river: arm: estuary
"   **bank:** ripa, levee
"   **barge:** gondola
"   **"beautiful":** Ohio
"   **bend:** oxbow
"   **blue, poet:** Danube
"   **bottom:** bed
"   **comb. form:** potamo
"   **current:** rapids, eddy
"   **crossed by Caesar:** Rubicon
"   **dam:** weir
"   **edge:** bank, levee
"   **island:** holm
"   **log run:** sluiceway
"   **myth:** Styx
"   **nymph:** naiad
"   **of oblivion:** Lethe
"   **of Sorrows:** Acheron
"   **outlet:** bayou
"   **rapid:** sault
"   **winding of:** ess
Rivera, Mex. painter: Diego
Riviera: beach: (Fr.) plage
"   **resort:** Cannes
rizzom: ear, stalk, straw
Rn, in chemistry: radon

road: freeway, expressway
    ‘‘ **bend:** hairpin
    ‘‘ **charge:** toll
    ‘‘ **edge:** shoulder
    ‘‘ **map abbrev.:** rte
    ‘‘ **military:** agger
    ‘‘ **runner:** cock, bird, cuckoo
    ‘‘ **surface:** tar, macadam
roadster: horse, bicycle
    ‘‘ **seat:** rumble
roan: horse, bay
roaring: brisk, noisy
    ‘‘ **game:** curling
    ‘‘ **Meg:** cannon
roast: brown, broil, pan, criticize
    ‘‘ **meat:** kabobs
    ‘‘ **prepare:** truss
    ‘‘ **stick:** skewer
rob: plunder, flay, reave
    ‘‘ **a truck/airplane:** hijack
    ‘‘ **Roy:** canoe, drink
    ‘‘ **sl.:** cop
robber: thief, bandido, brigand
    ‘‘ **cattle:** rustler
    ‘‘ **den of:** hideout
    ‘‘ **sea:** corsair, pirate
robe: toga, gown, vestment
    ‘‘ **bishop's:** chimer, chimar
    ‘‘ **long-sleeved:** caftan, kaftan
    ‘‘ **loose:** simar
    ‘‘ **monk's:** frock
Robin, Hood: outlaw
    ‘‘ **chaplain:** Friar Tuck
    ‘‘ **companion:** Will (Scarlet)
    ‘‘ **sweetheart:** (Maid) Mar-

ian
    ‘‘ **weapon:** longbow
Robinson Crusoe: author: Defoe
    ‘‘ **man:** Friday
roc: bird, simurg
    ‘‘ **passenger of the:** Sin(d)bad
rock: shake, stone, candy
    ‘‘ **boring tool:** trepon
    ‘‘ **black:** basalt
    ‘‘ **carving:** petroglyph
    ‘‘ **comb. form:** saxi, petr(o), lith(o)
    ‘‘ **crushed:** ballast
    ‘‘ **ejected by volcano:** lapillus
    ‘‘ **growths on:** lichen
    ‘‘ **molten:** magma
    ‘‘ **myth:** Scylla
    ‘‘ **pert. to:** petric
    ‘‘ **suffix:** ite, yte
    ‘‘ **volcanic:** lava, latite, perlite
rocket: asroc, projectile
    ‘‘ **firing platform:** launching pad
    ‘‘ **load:** warhead
Rocky Mountain: goat: antelope
    ‘‘ **peak:** Pikes, Logan
    ‘‘ **range:** Teton, Wasatch
    ‘‘ **sheep:** bighorn
    ‘‘ **wind:** chinook
Rockne, football coach: Knute
    ‘‘ **school:** Notre Dame
rocks: of the oldest: archean
    ‘‘ **sl.:** money, gem, diamond
    ‘‘ **study of:** petrology,

lithology

rocky: shaky, craggy, dizzy
" **cliff:** scar
" **hill:** tor
" **mountain   sheep:** bighorn

rod: pole, toggle, wand, perch, pistol
" **billiards:** cue
" **divination:** dowsing
" **sl.:** gat
" **square:** perch

rodent: jap, paca, mouse, gerbil, mole
" **genus:** mus
" **jumping:** jerboa
" **pert. to:** rosorial
" **water:** beaver, muskrat

Rodin, Fr. sculptor: Auguste
" **famous work:** Thinker

roe: milt, ova, spawn, coral, (fish) eggs, caviar

Roentgen: see **X-ray**

rogan: bowl

roger: OK, over

roi: King (Fr.)
" **heir:** Dauphin
" **realm:** France
" **wife:** Reine

Roland: emperor: Charlemagne
" **enemy:** Gano
" **friend:** Oliver
" **horse:** Veillantif
" **love:** Aude
" **sword:** Durendal

roll: brioche, elapse, catalog(ue), cake, drumbeat, peal, list, wrap, enfold, register, lurch
" **along:** trundle

" **back:** reduce
" **hard:** bagel
" **in:** wallow
" **of cloth:** bolt
" **of coins:** rouleau
" **of hair:** bun, chignon
" **of paper:** web, bolt
" **parchment:** scroll
" **sl.:** rob, money, wad

Rollo: Viking

rom: gypsy, buzz

Rome, Roman: Eternal City, Latin, Italian
" **Abode of gods:** Olympus
" **adviser to king:** Egeria
" **amphitheater:** colosseum
" **agreement:** pacta
" **assembly:** forum, comitia
" **bathhouses:** thermae
" **Caesar's title:** imperator
" **cap:** pileus
" **chariot:** essed
" **circus arena:** hippodrome
" **circus fighter:** gladiator
" **citadel:** arx
" **coin:** aes, denarius, semis
" **commoner:** plebeian
" **concert hall:** odeum
" **court:** atrium
" **date:** nones, ides
" **emperor:** Titus, Nerva, Otho, Hadrian, Galba, Probus, Carus, Otto, Trajan, Caligula
" **empire founder:** Augustus

" **farewell:** addio
" **fiddler:** Nero
" **first emperor of:** Augustus
" **founder of:** Romulus
" **games:** ludi
" **general:** Titus, Scipio, Marius, Lucullus, Cassius, Agricola, Sulla, Drusus, Agrippa
" **god:**
" " **fire:** Vulcan
" " **gates:** Janus
" " **herds:** Pan
" " **household:** Lar, Penates
" " **night:** Somnus
" " **pastoral:** Faunus
" " **sea:** Neptune
" " **sleep:** Morpheus
" " **sun:** Sol
" " **underworld:** Dis, Orcus
" " **wine:** Bacchus
" " **woods:** Sylvanus
" **goddess:** dea
" " **beauty:** Venus
" " **dawn:** Aurora
" " **earth:** Terra
" " **fertility:** Fauna
" " **fire:** Vesta
" " **flowers:** Flora
" " **fruits:** Pomona
" " **hope:** Spes
" " **hunting:** Diana
" " **love:** Venus
" " **marriage:** Juno
" " **moon:** Luna
" " **night:** Nox
" " **sea:** Mare
" " **underworld:** Proserpina
" " **war/wisdom:** Minerva
" **headband:** vitta
" **helmet:** galea
" **highway:** iter, via
" **hill of:** Palatine, Capitoline
" **jar:** amphora
" **law:** lex
" **meal:** cena, gena
" **monster, myth:** Typhon, Lamia
" **name:** nomen
" **noble:** patrician
" **orator:** Cato, Cicero, Caesar
" **people:** Sabines
" **philosopher:** Seneca
" **poet:** Juvenal, Lucretius, Virgil, Lucan, Ovid
" **pound:** libra
" **river:** Tiber, Lethe
" **soothsayer:** Haruspex
" **tablet:** tessera
" **theater's stage:** proscenium
" **urn:** capanna
" **vase:** pyxis
" **writing tablet:** diptych
Romeo: lover
" **and Juliet character:** Tybalt, Paris, Mercutio, Capulet, Montague
" **father of:** Montague
" **rival of:** Paris
Romulus: Quirinus
" **brother:** Remus
" **father:** Mars
" **mother:** Rhea
rondure: circle, sphere

ronin: outcast, outlaw
roof: gambrel, top, shelter
"   **arched:** vault
"   **border:** eave
"   **comb. form:** stego
"   **covering:** shingle, slate, thatch
"   **drain:** gutter
"   **opening:** skylight, scuttle
"   **point (finial):** epi
"   **rounded:** cupola, dome
"   **slate:** rag
"   **sloped:** leanto, shed
"   **two-sloped:** mansard
"   **window:** dormer
"   **without:** homeless, hypethral
rookery: tenement, building
"   **inhabitant:** penquin
room: sala, cell, closet, quarter, space
"   **band, ornamental:** frieze
"   **conversation:** locutory, exedra
"   **harem:** ada, oda
"   **hot bath:** caldarium
"   **inner:** ben
"   **private:** boudoir
"   **storage:** shed, attic
rooming house: kip
roorback: lie, libel, hoax
roose: praise, extol
Roosevelt: see special section
"   **F.D.R.'s dog:** Fala
" "   **mother:** Sara
rooster: bantam, chanticleer
"   **castrated:** capon
"   **comb. of:** caruncle

"   **young:** cockerel
root: origin, core, cheer, plug
"   **aromatic:** ginseng, orrice
"   **comb. form:** rhiz(o)
"   **dried:** rhatany
"   **edible:** taro, radish, potato, cassava
"   **growth:** tubercle
"   **pert. to:** radicle
"   **outer layer:** exoderm
"   **shoot:** sucker, tiller
"   **starch:** arum
"   **substance:** zedoary
"   **word:** etymon
rope: cord, lasso, cable, tie
"   **and pulley block:** tackle
"   **cattle catcher's:** bola
"   **dancer/walker:** funambulist
"   **fiber:** hemp, jute, sisal
"   **guiding:** dragline
"   **holder:** becket
"   **in:** lure, entice
"   **knotted at end:** colt
"   **ship's:** shroud, vang, tye
"   **wire:** cable
rorqual: finback, whale, razorback
rosaceous: rosy, blushing
"   **plant:** strawberry, agrimony
rosary: chaplet, beads
rose: flower, perfume, damask
"   **Bowl:** arena
" "   **site:** Calif., Pasadena
"   **city:** Portland
"   **extract:** attar
"   **of Sharon:** althea

" **petal oil:** attar
" **under the:** sub rosa
" **wild:** brier, eglantine
rosebush fruit: hip
rosette: cockade
Rosinante: horse, jade, steed
" **master:** Quixote
ross: bark, peel, waste
Rossini: opera: Otello, Barber of Seville, William Tell
rot: decay, putrefy, decompose, spoil, ret
" **grass:** flukewort
" **sl.:** bosh, nonsense, rubbish
rotch(e): guillemot, dovekey
rote: routine, custom, system
" **by:** memory
rotten: foul, fetid, carrion, corrupt, evil
" **comb. form:** sapr(o)
rottenstone: Tripoli
rough: crude, agrestic, coarse, jagged
" **and-tumble fight:** brawl, melee
" **cloth:** terry, shag
" **comb. form:** trachy
" **edged:** erose
" **skin:** shagreen
rouky: misty, foggy
roulette: epicycloid
" **man:** croupier
" **term:** noir (black), rouge (red), manque, bas, passe
round: course, circular, plump
" **clam:** quahog
" **make:** circinate
" **protuberance:** umbo, knob
" **robin:** contest, letter

" **Table knight:** Lancelot, Bors, Kay, Balan, Geraint, Galahad, Tristan, Percival, Parsifal
" **trip:** excursion
roundabout: indirect
" **expression:** ambage
" **way:** detour
roundhead: Swede, Puritan
roundworm: ascarid, parasite
Rousseau hero: Emile
route: gest, trail, direction
" **circuitous:** detour
" **straight:** beeline
routine: regular, rota, humdrum
" **task:** chore
rove: roam, gad, card
" **for adventure:** errant
" **for plunder:** maraud, forage
row: oar, file, fuss, tier
" **of cut grass:** swath
" **of planted seeds:** drill
rowan tree: ash, sorb
rowen: grass, hay, aftermath, field
Roy Rogers: horse: Trigger
" **wife:** Dale
royal: noble, august
" **agaric:** mushroom
" **color:** purple
" **crown:** tiara, coronet
" **house:** Tudor, Windsor, Stuart, Hapsburg
" **initials:** HRH
" **rock snake:** python
" **standard:** emblem
royalty: symbol of: ermine
rub: wipe, stroke, polish, obstacle

" **down:** comb, curry, massage

" **elbows:** fraternize

" **out:** erase, kill

"Rubaiyat" author: Omar (Khayyam)

rubber: masseur, eraser, ebonite

" **boot:** wader

" **City:** Akron

" **product basis:** latex

" **roller:** squeegee

" **tree:** ule, seringa

rube: rustic, yokel, bumpkin

rubella: rash, measles

Rubicon: he crossed the: Caesar

ruche: frill, trimming

rudd: carp, fish, vireo

rudder: helm

" **guide:** steer

" **handle:** wheel, tiller

" **part:** yoke

ruff: bird, fish, trump, ruffle, disorder

" **female:** ree, reeve

ruffle, at the neck: ruche, jabot

ruga: fold, crease, wrinkle

rugby: football

" **formation:** scrum

" **score:** try

rule: norm, canon, order, theorem

" **Brittannia composer:** Arne

" **out:** bar, forbid

" **over:** manage

" **pert. to:** rutic

ruler: Emir, Monarch, Potentate, Czar

" **absolute:** Shah, tyrant, despot

" **family:** dynasty

" **one of three:** triumvir

" **one of two:** duarch

" **wife of:** rani, tzarina

rules of: conduct: code

" **Order author:** Robert

" **infraction:** foul

Rumania, Rumanian: Magyar

" **coin:** leu, ley, ban

" **composer:** Enesco

" **folk dance:** Hora

rumble: growl, uproar

" **seat:** dickey

rumbo: grog

rumen: cud, paunch

ruminant: chewing, meditative

" **female:** doe, cow, ewe, nanny

" **genus:** bos, capra

" **male:** ram, bill, buck

" **type:** ox, yak, goat, bison, camel, steer, alpaca, buffalo, giraffe

rummer: cup, glass

rummy: gin, odd, strange, sot, game

" **s/:** sot, drunk

Rumpelstiltskin: dwarf

run: sprint, incur, leak, publish, smuggle

" **across:** meet

" **aground:** founder

" **away:** abscond, flee

" **cricket:** bye

" **down:** summary, outline

" **of-the-mill:** so-so, ordinary

" **off:** print
" **out:** expel, spill
" **over:** exceed
" **through:** practice, examine
" **up:** enlarge, increase
runcible spoon: fork
rundlet: cask, tun
rune: magic, secret
runic alphabet: futhark
running: linear, contest, successive
" **birch:** snowberry
" **board:** footboard
" **knot:** noose
" **toad:** natterjack
Russia, Russian: Rossiya, Muscovy
" **alcoholic drink:** kvass, vodka
" **assembly:** rada
" **calendar:** Julian
" **carriage:** troika, dros(h)ky
" **chalet:** dacha
" **citadel/gov't:** Kremlin
" **coin:** ruble, kope(c)k
" **commune:** kolhoz
" **community:** mir
" **cossack:** Tatar
" **dance:** ziganka
" **dramatist:** Gogol
" **empress:** Tsarina
" **exile's place:** Siberia
" **farmer:** kulak, Ivan
" **fish:** beluga
" **founder of:** Ivan
" **guitar:** balalaika
" **horse team:** troika
" **house:** dacha
" **ibex:** tek

" **measure:** verst, archine, lof
" **"mother of cities":** Kiev
" **museum:** Hermitage
" **no:** nyet
" **news agency:** Tass, Novosti
" **novelist:** Tolstoi, Gorki
" **peasant:** kulak, muzjik
" **peninsula:** Crimea
" **poet:** Pushkin
" **revolutionary leader:** Lenin, Trotsky
" **ruling family:** Romanov
" **satellite:** sputnik
" **scarf:** babushka
" **saint:** Olga
" **soup:** borsch
" **spa:** Ems
" **teapot/urn:** samovar
" **weight:** dola, pood, pud
" **windstorm:** buran
" **wolfhound:** alan, Borzoi
" **yes:** da
rust: oxide, fungus, corrode
" **on bronze:** patina
" **plant:** ferrugo
rustler: thief
" **object of:** cattle
Rustum: father: Zal
" **son:** Sohrab
rutabaga: turnip, Swede
Ruth: husband of: Boaz
" **mother-in-law:** Naomi
" **sister of:** Eileen
" **son of:** Obed
Ruthenia, Ruthenian: Russia, Ukranian
rye: gypsy, grass, cereal, whiskey
" **disease:** ergot, blackrust

`` **grass:** darnel
ryke: (Scot.) reach

ryot: peasant, tenant
Ryukyu island: Okinawa

S

S-curve: ogee, ess
  "   letter: ess
  "   mark: pothook
  "   shaped: sigmoid, sigmate, ess
Sa, in chemistry: samarium
Saarinen, architect: Eero
Sabaist's object of worship: stars
sabalo: milkfish
Sabine goddess: Vacuna
sable: fur, dark, sobol, lemming
  "   genus: mustela
  "   imitation: kolinsky
  "   pert. to: zibel(l)ine
sabot: shoe
sac: Indian, pouch, bursa
  "   SAC: Strategic Air Command
Sacar's son: Ahiam
sacerdotal: priestly, hieratic
sachem: chief, Sagamore
sackcloth: symbol of: penitence, mourning
sack fiber: gunny, burlap
sacred: holy, divine, pious
  "   bean: lotus
  "   beetle: scarab
  "   bird: ibis
  "   bull: apis, hapi
  "   city: Mecca, Jerusalem
  "   comb. form: hiero, hagi(o)
  "   cow: untouchable
  "   fig tree: pipal
  "   fountain: Hippocrene
  "   literature: Veda
  "   opposed to: secular, profane
  "   most: sacrosant
  "   plant: ragtree
  "   scriptures: Koran, Bible
  "   song: motet, psalm
  "   wine vessel: ama
  "   word: om, logos
sacrifice: oblation
  "   burning place: pile

" **by killing:** immolate
" **human:** suttee
sacrificial: animal: lamb
" **fire:** igni
" **rite:** libation
sacristy, pert. to: vestral
sad: trist, lugubrious, blue
" **comb. form:** tragi
saddle: load, encumber, seat
" **bag:** alforja
" **blanket:** tilpah
" **cloth:** panel, manta
" **footrest:** stirrup
" **front part:** pommel
" **girth:** cinch
" **pack:** aparejo
" **part:** cantle, latigo, pad
" **rock:** oyster
" **sl.:** pigskin
" **stirrup:** gambado
Sadducee: opposed to: Pharisee
safe: vault, siker, coffer, untouched
" **cracker:** yegg(man), peteman
" **place:** haven, port
safety: security
" **device:** Mae West, armor, valve
" **lamp:** davy
" **pin:** fibula
" **zone:** island
saga: epic, edda, Iliad
sagamore: sachem, chief
sage: seer, herb, prudent
" **cheese:** cheddar
" **cock:** grouse
" **of Chelsea:** Thomas Carlyle
" " **Concord:** Ralph

Waldo Emerson
" " **Ferney:** Voltaire
" " **Monticello:** Thomas Jefferson
Sagitta: arrow, keystone, constellation
saguaro: cactus
Sahara: desert, wasteland, arid
" **fertile area:** Fezzan
" **people:** Nomads, Arabs
" **wind:** leste
saic: ketch
sail: glide, float, cruise, lug, jigger
" **boats:** schooner, galleon, frigate, ketch, sloop, yawl
" **close to wind:** luff
" **haul up:** trice
" **hoist:** clue-up
" **kind of:** jib, main, royal, lateen
" **pert. to:** velic
" **poetic:** sheet
" **rope:** halyard, tye
sailor's: bad luck: Johah, Jonas
" **call:** ahoy
" **carving:** scrimshaw
" **dish:** scouse
" **drink:** grog
" **hat:** sou(th)wester
" **patron saint:** Elmo
" **patroness:** Eulalia
" **rebellion:** mutiny
" **underwear:** skivy
" **yes:** aye
saint: sacred, canonize, holy
" **Andrew's cross:** saltier
" **Anthony's fire:** erysipe-

las
" **Barbabas's prayer:** Ave Maria
" **declare person a:** canonize
" **Francis' birthplace:** Assisi
" **homage to a:** dulia
" **tomb of:** shrine
" **Vitus' dance:** chorea
saker: falcon
Sakti: Maya
salaam: obeisance, greeting, bow
Saladin's foes: Crusaders
Salammbo author: Flaubert
Salem: witchcraft trial judge: Sewall
salep: tuber
" **source:** orchid
salicaceous tree: poplar, willow
salient: point: feature, detail
salix: genus, willows
salmacis: nymph
salmon: mort, jack, quinnat, sprod, coho, holia, chinuck
" **eggs:** roe
" **female:** raun, baggit
" **male:** cock, kipper
" **one year old:** bluecap
" **red:** sockeye
" **salted/smoked:** lox
" **silver:** coho
" **trap:** slap
" **young:** smolt, parr, grilse, samlet
Salome: father: Herod(ias)
" **grandfather:** Herod
" **known for:** dance of Seven Veils

salt: sal, humor, sailor, season
" **acid:** oleate
" **bed:** vat
" **deposit:** lick
" **marsh:** salina
" **pert. to:** saline
" **pork:** sowbelly
" **rock:** halite
" **water:** brine
salted: corned
saltpeter: niter, nitre
saltwort: barilla, kali
Salus: Hygeia
" **concern of:** health
salute: greet, bow, hail
" **flag:** dip
" **gun:** salvo
salvation: rescue, preservation
" **Army founder:** Booth
" **pert. to:** soterical
samaj: church
samara: key fruit, chat
" **tree bearing:** ash, elm
Samaritan god: Tartak
same: ditto, alike, equal
" **comb. form:** homo, iso
Samhain Eve: Halloween
Samoa, Samoan: Polynesian
" **bird:** iao
" **cloth:** tapa
" **council:** fono
" **loincloth:** lava-lava
" **maiden:** taupo
" **mollusk:** asi
" **owl:** Lulu
" **warrior:** toa
sampan: boat
" **derivative:** sam three
" " **pan** wood

Samson: betrayed by: Deliah
  " **deathplace:** Gaza
  " **vulnerability:** hair
Samuel: mentor: Eli
  " **mother:** Hannah
  " **son:** Abiah
  " **victim:** Agag
San: saint
  " **Antonio shrine:** Alamo
  " **Simeon:** Hearst castle
Sancho Panza's: master: (Don) Quixote
  " **mule:** Dapple
sanctuary: refuge, bema, asylum, grit
sand: polish, smooth, beach
  " **bank:** cay, shoal
  " **bar:** spit, shelf, reef
  " **dollar:** sea urchin
  " **dune:** towan
  " **flea:** chigger
  " **hill:** dune, dene
  " **lily:** soaproot
  " **sl.:** grit, courage
  " **snake:** eryx
sandal: winged: talaria
  " **wooden:** patten
  " **woven:** huarache
sandalwood: incense, algum
  " **island:** Sumba
Sandburg: poet: Carl
sandpiper: bird, ruff, stilt, teeter
  " **female:** reeve
  " **relative:** plover
sandstone: medina, berea, paar, arkose
  " **block:** sarsen
  " **pert. to:** arenilitic
Sandwich: island: Hawaii

sanforize: preshrink
sang froid: composure, cool, poise
Sangraal: (Holy) Grail
sans: (Fr.) without
  " **pareil:** peerless
  " **souci:** gay, castle
  " **Souci site:** Potsdam
Sanskrit: Vedic, Indic
  " **dialect:** pali
  " **god:** Indra, Vayu
  " **epic character:** Sita
  " **soul:** atman
Santa Claus' reindeer: Comet, Cupid, Vixen, Dancer, Donner, Dasher, Blitzen, Prancer
santon: hermit, monk
sap: trench, fluid, fool, dig
  " **dried:** gum
  " **tree:** latex, milk, balata
sapajou: capuchin, grison, monkey
sapodilla: sapota, plum, acana, bustic, marmalade
Sapphira's weakness: lying
Sappho: consort: Phaon
  " **home:** Lesbos
  " **work:** poetry
sapsago: cheese
sapsucker: woodpecker
Saracen: Arab, Moslem, Moor
  " **foe of:** Crusader
  " **leader:** Saladin
Sarah: husband: Abraham
  " **slave:** Hagar
  " **son:** Isaac
sardine: pilchard, herring, lour
Sardinia, Sardinian: coin: carline

" **language:** Catalan
" **ruling house:** Savoy
sark: chemise, shirt
sarmentose plant: strawberry
sarong: pareus, comboy
" **made famous by:** Dorothy Lamour
Sarpedon's parent: Zeus, Europa
sasin: buck, antelope
sassaby: antelope
Sassenach: Saxon, Lowlander
Satan: devil, Lucifer, Mephisto, Abaddon
" **cohort:** Azazel
" **son:** Imp
Satchmo: Armstrong, Louis; trumpet player
satellite: follower, planet, Sputnik, Explorer, Pioneer
" **path:** orbit
" **shadow:** umbra
" **weather:** Tiros
satin pod: honesty
satirize: expose, attack, denounce
" **in verse:** berime
satisfactory: enough, pat
" **sl.:** jake, cool
Saturday: Sabbath
" **pert. to:** sabbatine
Saturn: Cronus, planet
" **in alchemy:** lead
" **wife of:** Ops
saturniid: moth
satyr: deity, lecher, Silenus, faun
" **god attended by:** Bacchus

" **staff of:** Thyrsus
sauce: dressing, chili, mornay, curry, flavor
" **thickener:** roux
" **type:** Bordelaise, Hollandaise, Bernaise
Saudi Arabia: desert: Red, Nefud
" **inhabitant:** Bedouin
" **monetary unit:** riyal
Saul: concubine: Rizpah
" **daughter:** Michal
" **father:** Kish
" **kingdom:** Israel
" **son:** Jonathan
" **successor:** David
saunter: lag, idle
" **across street:** jaywalk
saurian: lizard, dinosaur, reptile
sausage: casing: bung
" **-shaped:** allantoid
Savage Island: Niue
savin(e): juniper
savoir-faire: tact, diplomacy
saw: cut, motto, maxim, rede
" **blade:** web
" **comb. form:** serri
" **cut of:** kerf
" **toothed:** serrate
sawbuck: sl.: ten(spot)
sawdust: coom, scobs
sawing frame: horse
Saxon: English
" **king:** Harold
" **lady:** Godiva
sayings: attributed to Jesus: logia
" **collection of:** ana
" **distinguishing:** shibboleth

Sb in chemistry: stibium, antimony

scads: lots, oodles, many

scale: climb, clamber, gamut, falke
" **animal:** squama
" **charges:** tariff
" **comb. form:** lepid(o) scutum
" **measuring:** vernier
" **notes:** do, re, me, fa, sol, la, ti

scallop: badge, mollusk, quin, crena

scalp: cheat, skin
" **disease:** scall, favus
" **tumor:** wen

scaly: scurfy, scabby, mangy, base, mean
" **comb. form:** lepid(o)

scampi: prawn

scandent plant: vine

Scandinavia, Scandinavian: Lapp, Dane, Swede, Nordic, Finn, squarehead
" **coin:** ore
" **country:** Norway, Sweden, Denmark, Iceland
" **explorer:** Eric
" **folklore being:** troll
" **giantess:** Urth, Wyrd
" **god:** Thor, Loki, Alfadir
" **heaven: myth:** Asgard, Asgarth
" **inlet:** fiord, fjord
" **measure:** alen
" **plateau:** fjeld
" **weight:** lod

scar: mar, blemish, wound
" **pert. to:** uloid
" **tissue:** keloid, adhesions

Scaramouche: rascal, braggart
" **author:** Sabatini

scarecrow: malkin, straw man, bugaboo

scarf: ascot, kerchief, sash, foulard
" **clerical:** tippet, stole
" **head:** babushka (Rus.)
" **sun helmet:** puggry

scarlet: red, lewd
" **bird:** tanager

Scarlett O'Hara: home: Tara
" **husband:** Rhett Butler

scatter: litter, sprinkle, strew, dispel, disperse
" **by blowing:** winnow
" **for lost scent:** cast

scent: smell, track, clue, odor
" **kitchen:** nidor, aroma
" **left by animal:** drag
" **of wine:** bouquet

schelm: rascal, rogue

schemer: artist

Schicklgruber's son: Hitler (Adolph)

schistosome: fluke

schizocarp: fruit

schmaltz: corn, sentimentality

schnapps: gin, spirits

scholar: savant, pupil, classicist, pundit
" **day:** extern
" **inferior:** pedant
" **literary:** harmonist
" **Moslem:** Ulem

scholarly: paper: thesis
" **people:** literati

school: teach, academy, ecole, academe, lyceum
" **banner:** pennant

"   **boy, new:** scum
"   **of birds:** pod
"   **of fish:** shoal
"   **of whales:** pod, gam
"   **riding:** manege
school: teach, train, ecole (Fr.), cult, pod, cultivate
"   **grounds:** campus
"   **of fish:** shoal
"   "   **whales:** gam
"   **pert. to:** academic
schoolmaster's rod: ferule
Schubert: composer: Franz
"   **classic:** Ave Maria
sciatic area: hip
science: art, skill
"   **comb. form:** techno
"   **of:**
"   "   **boxing:** fisticuffs
"   "   **causes:** etiology
"   "   **human behavior:** psychology
"   "   **law making:** nomology
"   "   **motion:** kinetics, dynamics
"   "   **origins:** etiology
"   "   **plants:** botany
"   "   **words:** semantics
"   **principle:** logic
scilicet: to wit, namely
Scipio: victim of: Hannibal, Carthage
sciurine animal: squirrel, marmot
scombroid fish: mackerel, tuna, bonito
scop: bard, poet
Scorpio: brightest star: Antares
Scotland, Scottish: Caledo-

nian, kiltie, Pict, Gael
"   **ago:** syne
"   **bagpipe music:** pibroch, coronach
"   **bank:** brae
"   **beggar:** randy
"   **biscuit:** scone
"   **boy:** loon
"   **breeches:** trews
"   **brook:** sike
"   **burn:** stream
"   **cap:** Glengarry, Tam O'Shanter
"   **cat:** malkin
"   **charm:** cantrip
"   **chest:** kist
"   **chief:** thane
"   **child:** bairn, wean
"   **clan chief:** thane
"   **coin:** baubee, demy, lion
"   **cup:** tass
"   **devil:** deil, mohound
"   **dish:** haggis
"   **dog:** sealyham
"   **fellow:** carl(e)
"   **girl:** cummer, lassie, quean
"   **go:** gae, gang
"   **good:** gude
"   **hawk:** allan
"   **Highlander:** Gael, Celt
"   **hill:** dod(d), inch
"   **hill(side):** brae
"   **kilt:** filibeg
"   **kiss:** pree
"   **lake:** lin, loch, katrine
"   **little:** sma
"   **lowlander:** Sassenach
"   **Lowlands:** Lallan
"   **measure:** cran
"   **men's undergarment:**

trews
- " **money:** siller
- " **more:** mair
- " **musical instrument:** bagpipe
- " **national emblem:** thistle
- " **negative, no:** dinna, nae
- " **New Year's Eve:** Hogmanay
- " **one:** ane, yin
- " **peasant:** cotter, crofter
- " **pig:** grice
- " **pipe:** cutty
- " **plaid:** maud, tartan
- " **poet:** Burns, Edina, Hogg, Dunbar
- " **prefix to names:** Mac
- " **pronunciation:** burr
- " **rock:** skerry
- " **servant:** gilly, gillie
- " **shirt:** sark
- " **since:** syne
- " **sister:** titty
- " **skirt:** kilt
- " **spirit:** banshee
- " **sweetheart:** Jo(e)
- " **tartan pattern:** sett, plaid
- " **tobacco pouch:** spleuchan
- " **topper/hat:** tam
- " **town:** bur(g)h
- " **true:** leal
- " **uncle:** eam, (y)eme
- " **village:** rew
- " **wear under kilts:** trews
- " **weight:** trone
- " **woman:** cummer, randy, carline
- " **woman, unmarried:** quean

Scourge of God: Attila
scrambled: pied
scrap: tatter, ort, shred, morsel
- " **glass:** cullet
scrape: claw, grit, difficulty, hoe
- " **bottom:** dredge, sour
- " **ground in golf:** sclaff
scraps: literary: ana
scratching ground for food: rasorial
screen: partition, pavis, shield, sift, shroud, seclude
- " **altar:** reredos
- " **bulletproof:** mant(e)let
- " **chimney:** bonnet
- " **material for:** vetiver
- " **mesh:** sieve
screw: miser, salary, turn, twist
- " **thread:** helix
- " **-like:** spiral
scriptural: Biblical
- " **analysis:** exegesis
- " **interpreter:** exegete
- " **part:** lesson
- " **Moslem:** Alcoran
- " **occult:** cabala
scrivello: tusk
scrod: codfish
scroll: list, roll
- " **shaped:** turbinate
- " **tablet like:** cartouch(e)
- " **Hebrew:** mezuza(h)
- " **writing:** makimono
Scrooge: miser
scrupulous to excess: prudish, finicky
sculpin: bullhead, sea raven, hardhead

scullery, contents of: pots, pans

sculptor: carver

  " **framework of:** armature

  " **tool of:** chisel, graver, caliper

  " **work: pert. to:** glyphic

scye: armhole

Scylla: rock

  " **father:** Nisus

  " **whirlpool opposite:** charybdis

  " **lover:** Minos

scyphozoan: jellyfish

scythe: bea, sickle

  " **bearer:** death

  " **cut, one stroke:** swath

  " **handle:** nib, snead

sea: wave, swell, ocean, deep, mer (Fr.)

  " **anemone:** polyp, actinia

  " **bat:** devilfish

  " **bird:** gull, albatross, gannet, skua

  " **born goddess:** Aphrodite

  " **borne:** afloat

  " **calf:** seal

  " **cow:** manatee, walrus

  " **creature, legendary:** mermaid, merman

  " **devil:** angelfish, octopus

  " **dog:** tar, sailor

  " **foam:** spume, meerschaum

  " **god:** Ler, Neptune, Nereus, Triton, Poseidon, Aegir, Proteus

  " **grave:** locker

  " **marker:** dan, buoy

  " **mile:** naut, knot

  " **nettle:** medusa, jellyfish, acaleph

  " **of the:** pelagic, naval, marine

  " **pen:** polyp

  " **poetic:** foam

  " **prefix:** mari

  " **serpent:** Elops

  " **surface movement:** lipper

  " **swell:** surf

  " **urchin:** echinus, echinoid

  " **wall:** jetty, breakwater

  " **with many islands:** archipelago

  " **worthy:** stanch

seal: initial, stamp, close, signet

  " **bottle/tube:** capsule

  " **letter:** cachet

  " **off:** trap

  " **Pope's:** bull

  " **wax:** lac

sealed completely: hermetic

seals: carnivore

  " **breeding place:** rookery

  " **flock:** pod

  " **limb:** flipper

  " **pelt:** sculp

  " **pert. to:** phocine

  " **young:** pup, harp, calf

seamen's chapel: Bethel

seance: sitting

  " **leader:** medium, spiritualist

  " **writing device:** ouija

search: quest, probe, forage

  " **for food:** forage

  " **for Holy Grail:** quest

  " **for talent:** scout

"   **party:** posse
"   **a person:** frisk
"   **thoroughly:** comb
seasickness: mal de mer
seaside strip: boardwalk
seasons: Horae
"   **goddess:** Dike, Horae, Eirene
seat: bishop's: Metropolis
"   **church:** pew, sedilia
"   **coach:** dicky
"   **of judgement:** tribunal
"   **on camel/elephant:** howdah, houdah
"   **tier of:** gradin
seaweed: tangle, sargasso, varec, kelp
"   **extract:** agar
"   **genus:** alaria
"   **purple:** sion
"   **red:** dulse
"   **study:** algology
seaworm: lurg, sao
second: aid, moment, abet
"   **childhood:** dotage, senility
"   **growth crop:** rowen
"   **lieutenant: sl.:** shavetail
"   **self:** alter ego
"   **story man:** burglar
"   **team:** scrub
secret: hidden, arcane, covert, cryptic
"   **agent:** spy, saboteur
"   **meeting:** conclave
"   **place:** hideout, sanctum
"   **remedy:** elixir
"   **society:** camorra, mafia, Ku Klux, Poro
"   **writing:** code
secundine: afterbirth

security: pledge, surety
"   **for payment:** lien, bond, collateral
Seder: event: Exodus
seed: sow, germ, bean
"   **bearing organ:** pistil
"   **bud:** plumule
"   **case:** pod, bur(r), cypsela
"   **comb. form:** sperm, spermat(o)
"   **immature:** ovule
"   **organ:** pistil
"   **oyster:** spat
"   **pod:** cypsela
"   **without:** agamous
seeds: comb. form: carpo
"   **row of planted:** drill
"   **study:** carpology
seeled bird: hawk, falcon
segment: body: somatone
"   **-shaped:** toric
sego: plant, lily
seidel: mug
seize for debt: attach, distrain
Sekhet's husband: Ptah
Selassie, Emperor: Haile
self: ego
"   **comb. form:** auto
"   **confidence:** panache, aplomb
"   **cremation:** suttee
"   **defense art:** jujutsu, karate, judo
"   **destruction:** suicide, immolation
"   **esteem:** pride, vanity
"   **evident:** axiomatic, obvious
"   **important:** pompous

" **love:** narc(iss)ism
" **pert. to:** personal
" **reproach:** remorse
" **respect:** pride
" **righteous:** pharisaical
" **worship:** autolatry
sell over official price: scalp
seme: dotted
Semele: husband: Zeus
" **father:** Cadmus
" **son:** Dionysus, Bacchus
" **sister:** Ino
Seminole chief: Osceola
Semite: Jew, Arab, Assyrian, Babylonian, Phoenician
" **god:** Hadad, Baal, Shamash
send: dispatch, forward
" **back:** return, remit
" **flying:** rout
" **for:** summon
" **forth:** emit
" **out:** deport, exile
" **packing:** dismiss
" **up:** (sl.) jail
Senegal: gazelle: korin
seneschal: major domo, kay
sense: meaning, perceive, sight
" **and Sensibility author:** Austen
" **of sight:** optic
" **of smell:** olfaction
" **of taste:** gustation
sensitivity: erethism
" **plant:** mimosa
sentence: one word: monepic
" **construction:** syntax
" **part:** object, subject, predicate

" **types:** simple, complex, compound
sentinel: guard, picket
" **mounted:** lookout
sepal: leaf
separate: secede, alienate, part, split
" **forcibly:** wrench, rend
" **into parts:** dismember
" **prefix:** dis
Sephardim: Jews
" **original country:** Spain, Portugal
" **dialect:** Ladino
sepoy: policeman
seppuku: harakiri, suicide
September 13, Roman calendar: Ides
seraglio: harem, zenana
Serb, Serbia: Slav
" **coin:** dinar
" **comb. form:** Serbo
" **measure:** ralo
sere: dried, dry, wax, threadbare
serein: rain, mist
serf: slave, helot
" **female:** neif
" **liberate a:** manumit
series: set, sequence, chain
" **of columns:** colonnade
" **of six:** hexad
sermon: discourse, lecture
" **subject:** text
serow: jagia, antelope
serpent: reptile, entwine
" **comb. form:** ophi(o)
" **nine headed:** hydra
" **pert. to:** anguine
" **worship:** ophism
serranoid fish: redhind, ca-

brilla
servant: salve, ancillary, hind, menial
  " **boy:** page, gossoon
  " **garment:** livery
  " **feudal:** sergeant
  " **pert. to:** famulary
  " **retired:** emeritus
serving: portion
  " **boy:** knave
  " **man:** potman
  " **stand:** dumbwaiter
serviette: napkin
sesame seed: gingili
set: batch, seat, fix, rigid
  " **afloat:** launch
  " **aside:** reject
  " **down (as a fact):** posit
  " **firmly:** infix
  " **in motion:** activate
  " **of nine:** ennead
  " **of rules:** code
  " **on fire:** kindle
  " **sail:** cast off
  " **up:** erect, exalt
  " **upon:** browden
Set: god, deity, Seth
  " **brother:** Osiris
  " **father:** Geb
  " **mother:** Nut
  " **victim:** Osiris
seta: bristle
Seth: brother: Cain, Abel
  " **parents:** Adam, Eve
  " **son:** Enos
settle: on land illegally: (sl.): squat
  " **strike:** mediate
seven: heptad, sept, zeta
  " **comb. form:** hept(a)
  " **days:** hebdomad

  " **deadly sins:** lust, envy, pride, anger, sloth, gluttony, covetousness
  " **Hills of Rome:** Caelian, Esquiline, Palatine, Aventine, Quirinal, Viminal, Capitoline
  " **Wonders of the World:** COLOSSUS, PYRAMIDS, MAUSOLEUM, SPHINX, PHAROS, PHIDIAS, EPHESUS
seventeen year locust: cicada
Seward's "folly": Alaska
sewer opening: manhole
sewing: machine inventor: Howe
sex: gender
  " **comb. form:** geno
  " **hormone:** steroid
sexes, common to both: epicene
shade: umbra, trace, color, blind
  " **blue:** Alice
  " **light:** pastel
  " **lines:** hatch
  " **of difference:** nuance
  " **of meaning:** nuance
shades, the: Hades
shadow: dog, omen, vestige, shade
  " **astronomer's:** umbra
  " **man without:** Ascian
  " **of death:** Sheol
  " **outline:** silhouette
  " **without:** Ascian
Shadrach: fellow captives: Meshach, Abednego
  " **persecutor:** Nebuchad-

nezzar
shagbark: walnut, hickory
Shaker founder: Lee
Shakespeare, William:
" **actors:** Booth, Barry-more, Geilgud, Olivier
" **home:** Avon
" **plays:** Hamlet, MacBeth, Lear, Caesar, Othello, Twelfth Night, Temptest
shako: decoration: pompom
" **cap:** headdress
shakti: Devi, power, force
shallop: dinghy, boat
shallot: bulb, onion
" **kin:** leek
shamal: wind
Shamash: sun God
" **consort:** Ai; Aya
" **worship center:** Larsa, Sippar
Shamo: Gobi
shandrydan: chaise, cart
Shrangri-la: utopia, paradise
shank: leg, shaft
" **pert. to:** crural
" **in botany:** footstalk
sharecropper: metayer
shark: swindler, man-eater
" **blue pointer:** mako
" **loan:** usurer
" **nurse:** gata
" **small:** tope, lamia, sharklet
" **young:** puppy
sharp: acute, clear, vitriolic, clever
" **sl.:** adept, expert
" **comb. form:** acet(o), oxy
" **cry:** yelp

" **edged/witted:** keen
" **eyed one:** eagle, lynx
" **reply:** retort
" **taste:** tart, tang
Shasta: volcano, daisy
shavetail: mule, lieutenant
Shavian forte: wit
shaw: grove, wood
Shawnee Indian chief: Te-cumseh
shearing machine: cropper
sheatfish: catfish, wels
Sheba: Saba
" **queen of:** Balkis
shedding of skin: ecdysis
Sheean, writer: Vincent
sheep: bleater, karakul, sha, urial, merino
" **castrated:** wether
" **coat:** fleece
" **dog:** collie
" **female:** ewe
" **flock:** fold, dryband
" **genus:** ovis, bos
" **kept together:** fold
" **pert. to:** ovine
" **male:** ram, tup, wether
" **mark:** brand
" **pen:** fold, kraal
" **skin dealer:** fellmonger
" **wool:** fleece
" **young:** hog, (y)eanling, lamb, teg
shekel: money
shell: cover, mollusk, car-tridge, shuck
" **abalone:** ormer
" **boat:** hull
" **casing:** gaine
" **corn:** husk
" **defective:** dud

" **enclosed in a:** obtected
" **hole:** crater
" **large:** conch
" **money:** cowrie, peag(e), se(a)wan, wampum
Shelley, poet: Percy, Ariel
" **poem:** Adonais
shelter: haven, retreat
" **dove's:** cote
" **hillside:** abri
" **overhanging:** canopy
" **soldier's:** (pup)tent
Shem: father: Noah
" **son:** Lud, Aram, Asshur
Sheol: Hades, grave, hell
shepherd: lead, tend
" **concern of:** sheep
" **clock:** salsify
" **god of:** Pan, Faunus
" **pert. to:** pastoral, bucolic
" **staff of:** crook, kent, peda
shepherdess: bergere, Amaryllis
Sheridan play: Rivals
Sherlock Holmes:
" **creator of:** Doyle
" **friend:** Watson
Sherwood Forest hero: Robin Hood
Shetland Island: inlet: voe
" **measure:** ure
" **tax:** scat
shibboleth: slogan, password, test word
shield: armor, defend, cover, ecu (Fr.)
" **arm:** buckler
" **Athena's/Zeus':** (A)egis
" **bearer:** escudero
" **center point:** fess

" **large:** pavis
" **Roman:** testudo
" **shaped:** scutate, clypeate
" **strap:** enarme
shillelagh: cudgel, club
shin: kick, shank, tibia
" **pert. to:** cnemial
Shinto: Sintu
" **deity:** Kami
" **temple:** Sha
" **temple gate:** Torii
ship: vessel, embark
" **ancient:** galleon
" **bow flag:** jack
" **breadth:** beam
" **capacity:** tonnage
" **carpenter:** chips
" **chains:** tyes
" **crew member:** hand, mate, yeoman, stoker
" **forward part:** bow, prow, stem
" **group of:** fleet
" **hospital:** sick bay
" **jail:** brig, hulk
" **left-side:** port, larboard
" **load:** bulk, cargo
" **mythical:** Argo
" **not seagoing:** hulk
" **path of:** lane
" **poetic:** keel, bark
" **rear of:** aft
" **record:** log
" **sink a:** scuttle
" **tender:** pinnace, cockboat
" **torpedoed May 1915:** Lusitania
" **water in the hold:** bilge
" **window:** porthole

" **windless:** becalmed
shipwrecked: goods: flotsam, jetsam
" **person:** castaway
shirt: chemise, skivvy, polo
" **collar stiffener:** stay
" **front ornament:** stud
" **sleeve button:** cufflink
shock: absorber: snubber
" **mental:** trauma
" **to reality:** sober
shoe: footwear
" **baby:** bootee
" **canvas:** sneaker
" **flap:** tongue
" **form/model:** last, tree
" **maker:** cordwainer
" **mender:** cobbler
" **mule's:** planch
" **part:** (in)sole, rand, heel
" **winged:** talaria
" **wooden:** sabot
shoelace: lachet
" **tip:** aiglet
shoemaker: cobbler, farrier
" **apprentice:** snob
" **patron saint:** Crispin
" **tool:** butt, els(h)in
shoot: dart, throw, fire, chit
" **firearm:** fire
" **from cover:** snipe, ambush
" **objective:** target
shore: coast, beach, rivage
" **pert. to:** littoral
" **poetic:** strand
short: brief, abrupt, scant, concise
" **comb. form:** brachy, brevi
" **lived:** ephemeral

" **of:** lacking
" **ride:** spin
" **sighted:** myopic
" **sl.:** shy
" **story:** conte
" **tail:** scut
shortchange: cheat
shorthand: Gregg, Pitman, stenotype
" **character:** pot, hook
" **sign:** phonogram
Shostakovich, composer: Dmitri
shou: deer
shoulder: carry, push, epaul
" **comb. form:** omo
" **muscle:** deltoid
" **of the:** scapular
" **pack:** knapsack
" **pert. to:** alar, humeral
" **to shoulder:** serried
show: evince, display, guide, expose
" **anger:** fume
" **in:** usher
" **off:** parade, flaunt
" **of water:** aquacade
shower: spray, bestow, party
" **fall in a:** cascade
" **meteor:** Leonid
showman, famous: Ziegfeld, Barnum, Ringling, Carroll, Rose
shrew: vixen, scold
" **long-tailed:** sorex
" **pert. to:** soricine
" **name of Shakespeare's:** Kate
" **sister of Shakespeare's Kate:** Bianca
shrimp: crustacean, kid,

shaver
" **covering:** mail
Shrove Tuesday: Mardi Gras
shrub: bush, plant
" **bean family:** ulex
" **berry:** currant
" **bushy:** cade, tod
" **climbing:** clematis, liana
" **dwarfed:** bonsai
" **fence:** hedge (row)
" **genus:** olea, spirea, erica
" **holly family:** ilex
" **rubber source:** guayule
" **tea family:** camellia
shut: close, bar
" **eye; sl.:** sleep
" **in:** invalid, confine
" **out:** exclude, ban
" **up:** immure, closet
Shylock: usurer, money-lender
" **daughter:** Jessica
" **friend:** Tubal
siamang: gibbon
Siamese (see Thailand)
Sibelius: composer: Jean
" **work:** Finlandia
Siberia, Siberian: Vogul, Samoyed(e)
" **antelope:** saiga
" **fish:** nelma
" **forests:** Taiga, Urman
" **fur:** calabar
" **ibex:** tek
" **leopard:** ounce
" **wasteland/plain:** Steppe
" **wild cat:** manul
" **windstorm:** buran
sic: thus, so much, attack

Sicily, Sicilian: Trinacrian
" **god:** Adranus
" **inhabitant, legendary:** Cyclops
" **landmark:** Etna
" **measure:** salma, caffiso
" **secret society:** Mafia
" **volcano:** Etna
" **wine:** Marsala
Siddhartha: Buddha
side: aspect, facet
" **by side:** abreast
" **interest:** hobby
" **kick:** alter ego, pal
" **pain:** stitch
" **pert. to:** lateral
" **step:** avoid, dodge
" **view:** profile
sideboard: credenza, buffet
sidero, as comb. form: iron, star
sideways: indirect, askance, lateral
" **move:** sidle
" **walker:** crab
Siegfried: mother: Sieglind
" **slayer:** Hagen
" **sword:** Balmung
" **vulnerable place:** shoulder
sierelike: cribrate
sigmoid: ess
Sigmund: father: Volsung
" **son:** Sigurd
" **sword:** Gram
" **wife:** Hiordis
sign(s): token, indication, symptom, mark
" **affirmative:** nod
" **away:** convey
" **in magic:** sigil

"   **omission:** caret
"   **pert. to:** semic
"   **Zodiac:**   Aquarius, Pisces, Aries, Taurus, Gemini, Cancer, Leo, Virgo, Libra, Scorpio, Capricorn, Sagittarius
signal: token, alarm, warn
"   **actor's:** cue
"   **distress:** mayday, SOS
"   **eye:** wink
"   **Indian:** smoke
"   **seance:** tap
"   **system:** code
Sigard: father: Sigmund
"   **foster father:** Regin
"   **horse:** Grani
"   **slayer:** Hogni
"   **wife:** Gudrun
Silas Marner: author: Eliot
silence, goddess of: Angerona
Silenus: deity, satyr
"   **foster son of:** Bacchus
silk: tulle, foulard, pekin
"   **cocoon:** bave
"   **for mourning:** almas
"   **hat:** topper
"   **like:** sericeous
"   **raw:** grege
"   **rough:** rajah
"   **source of:** eria, cocoon
"   **unspun:** sleave
"   **weight:** pari
"   **yarn:** tram
"   **yarn size:** denier
silkworm: tusser, bombyx, eri(a)
"   **covering:** cocoon
"   **food:** mulberry
"   **not:** calcino

silver: coin, siller, sycee
"   **comb. form:** argyro
"   **containing:** lunar
"   **fluoride:** tachiol
"   **lace:** filigree
"   **in alchemy:** luna
"   **unminted:** sycee, bullion
"   **symbol:** Ag
"   **-tongued:** eloquent
silverware decoration: gadroon
Simenon: author: Georges
"   **detective/novel:** Maigret
Simeon: father: Jacob
"   **mother:** Leah
similar: akin, like, such
"   **comb. form:** homeo
simnel: biscuit, fruitcake
simoleon: dollar
sin, canonical: heresy, idolatry
Sinai mountain: Horeb
Sinbad the   : sailor
"   **bird:** roc
since: ago, hence, inasmuch as, before now
Singapore: founder: Raffles
"   **old name:** Temasek
single: individual, sole, unwed
"   **comb. form:** mono, uni, haplo
"   **file:** tandem
"   **handed:** unaided
"   **thing:** unit
singular: opposed to: plural
sinister: opposed to: dexter
sipping tube: straw
siren, of the Nile: Cleopatra
Sisera: enemy: Barak

"   **slayer:** Jael
sister: pert. to: soral
"   **Superior:** abbess
"   **younger:** cadette (Fr.)
Sistine Chapel: features: frescoes
"   **Madonna**   **painter:** Raphael
Sitting Bull's antagonist: Custer
"   **tribe:** Sioux
Sitwell: poet: Edith, Osbert
six: hexad, sestet
"   **comb. form:** hexa
"   **pert. to:** senary
size: anea, mass, stiffen, cover
"   **book page:** duodecimo
"   **indefinite:** nth
"   **yarn:** lea, dernier, forty
skate: glide, fish, shoe
"   **blade:** runner
"   **order:** raja
"   **place:** rink
skein: hank, mesh
"   **of yarn:** hasp
skerry: reef
ski: race: slalom
"   **run:** schuss
skill: talent, prowess, finesse
"   **comb. form:** techno
skin: coat, shell, strip
"   **comb. form:** dermat(o), derm(o), derma
"   **dark:** melanic
"   **deeper layer:** cutis
"   **design on:** tattoo
"   **diver's aid:** scuba
"   **flaw:** wrinkle
"   **Latin:** cutis
"   **oil:** sebum

"   **opening:** pore
"   **person with abnormal white:** albino
"   **pert. to:** cutaneous, dermal
"   **shed:** molt
"   **sl.:** cheat, swindle, defraud
"   **without:** apellous
skirt: periphery, border, petticoat
"   **armor:** tasse
"   **ballet dancer's:** tutu
"   **divided:** culotte
"   **sl.:** woman, girl
"   **steel:** lamboys
"   **triangular part:** gore
skull: head, sconce
"   **part**   **of:**   cranium, bregma, calvaria
"   **pert. to:** cranial
"   **soft spot:** fontanel
skull cap: beanie
"   **Arabian:** chechia
"   **cardinal's:** berrettino
"   **clergy's:** callot(te)
"   **felt:** pileus
"   **Hebrew:** yarmulke
slang: cant, argot, patois, lingo
"   **suffix:** eroo
slant: tilt, incline, slope, angle
"   **comb. form:** clino
"   **line:** solidus
slapdash: offhand
slave: servant, helot, serf, vassal
"   **Biblical:** Hagar
"   **block:** catasta
"   **dealin:** mango
"   **driver:** taskmaster

" **liberate:** manumit
" **educated:** hetaera
" **traveling group:** coffle
sleep: repose, slumber
" **comb. form:** hypno
" **deep:** stupor
" **god of:** Somnus, Hypnus, Morpheus
" **inability to:** insomnia
" **lightly:** doze
" **pert. to:** somnial
" **short:** (cat)nap, siesta, snooze
Sleepy Hollow author: Irving
sleeve hole: scye
slice: of bacon: rasher
" **of meat:** collop
slightest: least
" **amount:** grain
" **sound:** peep
slingshot: catapult
" **killer with:** David
slip: mistake, lapse, boner
" **away:** elapse
" **back:** relapse
" **by:** pass
" **knot:** noose
" **up:** error
slogan: catchword, motto, phrase
slope: slant, grade, splay
" **comb. form:** clino
slot: aperture, groove, track
" **machine coin:** slug
" **machine windfall:** jackpot
sloth: laziness, inertia
" **three-toed:** ai
" **two-toed:** unau
slow: comb. form: brady
" **in music:** lento, tardo,

largo, andante
" **leak:** drip
" **train:** local
" **-witted:** dull
slug: snail, strike, loiter
" **genus:** limax, elysia
" **pert. to:** limacine
" **sea:** trepang
sly: cagy, foxy, shrewd
" **look:** leer, ogle
" **remark:** (sl.) catty
small: low, trivial, minuscule, bantam
" **allowance:** pittance
" **amount:** drop
" **animal:** runt
" **bite:** nip
" **car:** compact
" **coin:** mite
" **comb. form:** micr(o), steno, lepto
" **fry:** tot
" **hollow:** areola
" **piece:** snip(pet)
" **portion:** modicum
" **prefix:** micro
" **quantity:** spot, iota, bit
" **talk:** chitchat
smartly dressed: natty, dapper
smell: scent, flavor
" **comb. form:** osmo
" **loss of:** anosmia
" **offensive:** stench, fetor
" **pert. to:** olfactory
" **pleasant:** aroma
" **stale:** musty
smelling salts: inhalant, hartshorn
smew: duck, merganser
smile: grin, beam, simper

" **Mona Lisa's:** enigmatic, cryptic

smoke: fragrance: incense
" **-jack:** funnel
" **out:** flush
" **screen:** camouflage

smolt: salmon, clear, smooth

smooth: serene, oily, slick, soft
" **comb. form:** lio
" **feathers:** preen
" **over:** gloss
" **tongued:** glib, oily
" **with rock:** pumice

smuggled: goods: contraband
" **whiskey:** moonshine

snail: escargot, mollusk
" **genus:** nerita, oleacina
" **shell:** periwinkle, caracole

snake: reptile, serpent
" **comb. form:** ophi(o)
" **charmer's flute:** pungi
" **crusher:** boa, python
" **deity:** zombi
" **haired woman:** Medusa, Gorgon
" **horned:** cerastes
" **marine:** chital
" **sea:** kerril
" **skin shedding:** ecdysis
" **study of:** ophiology

snapdragon: figwort

snark: boojum

snee: dirk

snickersnee: knife

snit: tizzy

snook: robalo

snow: firn, sleet
" **living in:** neval

" **of:** nival
" **on a glacier:** neve
" **sl.:** heroin, cocaine, opium
" **slide, mass:** avalanche
" **White's friends:** dwarfs

snowdrop: anemone

snub: ignore, retort, check
" **nose(d):** pug

so: ergo, sic, very
" **be it:** amen, altercate
" **Big author:** Ferber
" **Big heroine:** Selina
" **far:** thus
" **so:** average

soak: saturate, wet, steep
" **in brine/vinegar:** marinate
" **sl.:** hit, pawn
" **up:** sorb

soap: detergent, cleanser
" **foam:** suds
" **ingredient:** lye
" **material:** tallow
" **opera:** melodrama
" **pharmaceutical:** sapo
" **plant:** amole
" **sl.:** money

soccer: football
" **player, famed:** Pele

social: party, convivial
" **affair:** soiree, ball
" **asset:** tact, grace
" **climber:** upstart
" **CONTRACT author:** Rousseau
" **error:** faux pas
" **finesse:** tact
" **insect:** bee
" **outcast:** pariah, leper
" **men only:** smoker, stag

" **register:** Bluebook
" **system:** regime
society: company, association
" **comb. form:** socio
" **entrance into:** debut
" **for animals** SPCA
" **Island:** Tahiti
" **of Friends:** Quakers
" **of Friends founder:** Fox
sockeye: salmon
Socrates: biographer: Plato
" **dialogue:** Meno, Phaedo, Apologia
" **disciple:** Plato
" **wife:** Xanthippe
sodium: natrium
" **carbonate:** trona
" **chlorate:** NaClo
" **comb. form:** natro
" **nitrate:** saltpeter, caliche
Sodom's neighbor: Gomorrah
soft: velvety, mild, gentle
" **and limp:** flabby
" **and sweet:** dulcet
" **feathers:** down, eider
" **job:** sinecure, snap
" **mass:** pulp
" **pedal:** play down
" **soap:** flatter, blarney
soil: defile, sod, earth, dirty
" **comb. form:** geo, agro
" **goddess:** Demeter
" **orangic:** humus
" **poetic:** glebe
" **unfruitful:** barren
sola: alone
solan goose: gannet
solar: room, tropic, story, heliacal

" **diety:** Shu
" **disk:** aton
" **streak:** facula
" **system model:** orrery
" **system part:** planet
soldier: warrior
" **fellow:** buddy
" **killed/wounded:** casualty
" **of fortune:** adventurer
" **old:** vet(eran)
" **sl.:** doughboy, sadsack
" **vacation:** pass, leave, furlough
Soldiers Three author: Kipling
sole: fish, foot, only, solitary
" **foot's:** plantar, vola, pelma
" **part:** shank
" **pert. to:** plantar
solid: firm, cubic, sphere
" **comb. form:** stereo
" **ground:** terra firma
" **six-sided:** cube
solidum: dado, sum
solitary: monk, hermit, recluse, alone
" **comb. form:** eremo
Solomon: sage, king, wise man
" **ally:** Hiram
" **father:** David
" **gold from:** Ophir
" **mother:** Bathsheba
" **sayings of:** maxims, proverbs
" **temple:** shamir
solus: alone
some: any, about, part
" **time:** later, one day

something: easy: pie
　" **imagined:** figment
　" **notable/outstanding:**
daisy
somewhat: rather, aliquid
　" **suffix:** ish
son: heir, progeny
　" **favorite:** Benjamin
　" **of: prefix:** Fitz, Mac
　" **of God:** Savior
　" **pert. to:** filial
　" **roi's:** Dauphin
　" **Scot.:** Mac
song: baby's: lullaby
　" **comb. form:** malaco
　" **evening:** vespers
　" **folk:** ballad
　" **identification:** theme
　" **improvisation:** vamp
　" **last words:** tag
　" **love:** serenade
　" **morning:** matin
of Solomon/of Songs: canticles
　" **operatic:** aria
　" **pert. to:** melic
　" **poetic:** rune
　" **prefix:** melo
　" **sacred:** motet, psalm, hymn
　" **words of:** lyrics
songs, anthology of: garland
sonnet: verse, poem, song
　" **last six lines:** sestet
soogan: rope, blanket
soosoo: dolphin
soothsaying: augury
Sophocles play: Oedipus
Sorb: Slav, apple
　" **descendants:** Wends
sorceress: Circe, Gorgon,
witch
sore: tender, pustule, touchy, lesion
　" **dressing:** patch, gauze
　" **mustard application on:** poultice
soricine animal: shrew
sorrel: plant, horse
　" **wood:** oca
sort: ilk, sift, part, genus
　" **of:** somewhat
sotol, plant like: yucca
sotto: below, under
soucar: banker, straight
soul: embodiment, spirit
　" **dead person's:** manes
　" **personified:** psyche
　" **without:** brute
sound: noise, safe, stable, valid, audio
　" **comb. form:** phon(o)
　" **dull:** thud
　" **gleeful:** chortle
　" **gutteral:** grunt, grate
　" **harsh:** jar, rasp
　" **lung:** rale
　" **mournful:** knell
　" **of contentment:** purr
　" **of laughter:** peal
　" **of yearning:** sigh
　" **off:** speak
　" **pert. to:** tonal
　" **science of:** acoustic(s)
　" **thin, sharp:** squeak
　" **unit of measurement:** mach, decibel
　" **voiceless:** cedilla
　" **whispering:** susurrus
　" **without:** silent, mute
Sousa: John Phillip
　" **employment:** Marine

" **soubriquet:** march king

South African: Boer, Afrikaner

" **assembly:** raad
" **aunt:** tanta
" **beverage:** mate
" **bushman:** Qung
" **Dutch:** Boer, Taal
" **foreigner:** uitlander
" **monetary unit:** rand
" **monkey:** vervet
" **mulatto:** griqua
" **plain:** veldt
" **policy:** apartheid
" **tribal council:** Indaba
" **spirit:** tikolosh
" **stream:** aar
" **warrior:** impi
" **whip:** sjambok

South American: Latin

" **animal:** vicuna, alpaca, llama
" **bird:** agami, rhea, jacu, topaz, guan
" **coin:** condor
" **dance:** beguine, samba, tango
" **duck:** pato
" **hat:** jipijapa
" **herdsman:** llanero
" **Ind. hut:** toldo
" **liquor:** chicha
" **lizard:** teju, coati
" **measure:** vara
" **mountains:** Andes
" **ostrich:** ehea
" **parrot:** macaw
" **palm:** grugru, ita
" **rabbit:** tapeti
" **serpent:** aboma
" **strait:** Magellan

" **tree:** carob, balsa, mora
" **weapon:** bola
" **wind:** pampero
" **vulture:** condor

South Carolina: (see special section)

" **native:** weasel

South Dakota: (see special section)

South Pole explorer: Amundsen

South Sea: canoe: proa, prau

" **garment:** sarong
" **island drink/shrub:** kava(kava)
" **loincloth:** lava-lava
" **native:** Polynesian, Kanaka, Balinese, Samoan, Tahitian

South wind: notus, auster

southern: austral

" **Cross:** crux
" **France:** midi
" **States:** Dixie

sow: pig, sluice, plant, scatter, broadcast

" **young:** gilt

sowens: porridge

Soviet: (see Russian)

soy bean: soja

space: gap, rank, void, extent, duration

" **agency: abbr.:** NASA
" **beacon:** pulsar, quasar
" **between eyes:** lore
" **craft capsule:** Specs
" **craft part:** module
" **craft to moon:** Apollo
" **craft to Venus:** Mariner
" **dog:** Streika

" **filler:** shim
" **in biology:** lacuna
" **monkey:** Enos
" **pert. to:** spatial
" **ship blister:** module
" **small:** areda
" **void:** chasm
" **wall:** niche
spade: dig, graft, shovel
" **kind of:** scavel
" **plasterer's:** server
" **sharp:** spud
Spanish, Spain: Espana, Iberia, Hesperia
" **afternoon:** tarde
" **article:** el, las, la, los, un, una
" **as:** como
" **aunt:** tia
" **baby:** nina, nena
" **bayonet:** yucca
" **bear:** oso
" **berry, dried:** pasa
" **blanket,** poncho, serape, manta
" **boy:** nino
" **cape:** Trafalgar
" **chaperon:** duen(n)a
" **cheer:** ole, bravo
" **club(house):** casino
" **coin:** doubloon, centavo, peseta, peso, dobla
" **composer:** (de)Falla
" **council:** junta
" **cup:** taza
" **cupid:**   Amorino, Amoretto
" **dance:** flamenco, tango, jota, carioca, bolero
" **dear:** caro
" **dish:**   olla,   bacalao,
paella
" **farm:** hacienda, ranco, granja
" **forest:** monte
" **friend:** amigo
" **game:** pelota, jai alai
" **girl:** nina, chica
" **god of love:** Amadis
" **grape:** malaga
" **gypsy dance:** flamenco
" **half-breed:** ladino
" **hall:** sala
" **hat:** sombrero
" **hill:** alto, alcor
" **holiday/feast:** fiesta
" **hour:** hora
" **house:** casa
" **jail:** calabozo
" **landmark:** alhambra, escorial
" **little:** poco
" **Madrid   boulevard:** Prado
" **man:** hombre
" **measure:**   vara,   linea, cantara
" **mother:** madre
" **none/nothing:** nada
" **painter:**   Dali,   Picasso, Miro, Goya
" **park:** alameda
" **police:** rurale
" **prefix:** hispano
" **rabbi:** Maimonides
" **ruling house:** Bourbon
" **sherry:** Jerez
" **street:** calle
" **sweet:** dulce
" **thank you:** gracias
" **tomorrow:** manana
" **uncle:** tio

"   **weapon:** bola, arma

"   **weight:** peso, carga, marco, tonelada

"   **woman:** mujer, senora

spark: woo, court, particle, kindle

"   **gives off:** ignescent

"   **stream:** arc

sparoid fish: porgy

sparrowgrass: asparagus

sparse: scanty, meager

"   **opposed to:** dense, crowded

Sparta, Spartan: Lacedaemon, hardy, warlike

"   **festival:** Carneia

"   **king:** Tyndareus, Leonidas

"   **magistrate:** ephor

"   **queen:** Leda

"   **serf/slave:** helot

spasm: throe, fit, kink

"   **muscle:** crick, cramp

"   **of pain:** throe

"   **series of:** clonos

"   **twitch:** tic

Spassky, chess champ: Boris

spatterdash: legging

spatterdock: lily

spavined: lame

spayed hen: foulard

speak: utter, carp, declare

"   **against:** oppose

"   **angrily:** snarl

"   **at length:** expatiate

"   **comb. form:** lalo

"   **imperfectly:** lisp, stutter

"   **inability to:** alalia

"   **irreverently:** blaspheme

"   **of:** mention

"   **offhand:** extemporize

"   **pert. to:** oratorical

"   **slowly:** drawl

"   **unable to:** dumb, mute

"   **under the breath:** mutter

speaker: annoys a: heckler

"   **loud: stentor**

"   **many languages** polyglot

spear: pierce, dart, harpoon

"   **body of:** shaft

"   **Neptune's:** trident

"   **point:** pike

"   **-shaped:** hastate

"   **three-pronged:** trident, leister

spearfish: marlin

specialist: city planning: urbanist

"   **money matters:** economist

specie: coin, money

"   **factory:** mint

speculation: vision, surmise

"   **reckless:** flyer, flier

speech: tongue, utterance, lip, sermon, oration

"   **abusive:** tirade

"   **art:** oratory, rhetoric

"   **blunder:** solecism

"   **comb. form:** log(o)

"   **defect:** stammer, dysphonia, impediment

"   **expert:** phonetist

"   **farewell:** valedictory

"   **figure of:** simile, metaphor

"   **formal:** address, oration

"   **goddess:** Vac

"   **incoherent:** gibberish,

jargon
" **peculiar:** idiom
" **sl.:** spiel
" **surplusage:** padding
" **without:** silent, mute, aphasic
" **world language:** esperanto
speed: velocity, rev, rate
" **full:** amain
" **measuring device:** tachometer
" **of sound:** mach
" **writing:** shorthand
spelean: cave-like
spell, in another alphabet: transliterate
spelunk: den, lair, cavern
spence: larder, pantry
spend, the summer: (a)estivate
sperm: semen, seed
" **whale:** cachalot
spheroid, example of a: earth, ball
sphinx: moth, monster
" **head of:** ram, hawk
" **land of:** Egypt
" **mother:** Echidna
" **query of:** riddle
spider: mite, trivet, skillet, arachnid
" **comb. form:** arachn(o)
" **girl turned into:** Arachne
" **monkey:** ateles, quata
" **nest of:** nidus
" **trap of:** web
" **venomous:** black widow, tarantula
" **web-spinning organ:**

spinneret
spike: prong, antler, secure, nail
" **like:** spinate
" **mountain climber's:** piton
Spillane's hero: Hammer
spinal: rachidian, balas
" **column:** spine
" **column, having:** vertebrate
" **cord:** myelon
" **layer:** dura
spiral: helical, helix
" **comb. form:** helico
" **like a:** spiroid
" **motion:** gyre
spirit: air: Ariel
" **evil:** Ate, Ker, Lilith
" **female:** banshee
" **fire:** Agni
" **good:** genie
" **of censure:** Momus
" **of people:** ethos
spirits: mood, liquor
" **night-walking:** lemures
" **of the dead:** manes
" **of wine:** alcohol
spiritual: apathy: acedia
" **opposed to:** corporeal
spiritus frumenti: whiskey
spiteful: vindictive, malicious, snide
" **woman:** cat
split: divide, cleave, rift, schism
" **capable of being:** fissile
" **open:** dehisce, break
" **pea:** dal
" **sl.:** leave
spoil, eggs: addle

spoilsport: wet-blanket
spokes: radii
spoon: -fed: pampered
  " **large:** ladle
  " **shaped:** spatulate
spoor: trail, track, scent
Sporades island: Samos
sportsman's vest: tattersall
spot: blemish, fleck
  " **sl.:** jam, trouble
  " **playing card:** pip
spotted fever: typhus
spout: nozzle, stream, gush
  " **sl.:** pawn(shop)
  " **steam:** jet
  " **whale's:** blowhole
spread: oleo, unfold, extend, scatter, feast, stretch
  " **as plaster:** teer
  " **sl.:** meal
  " **false rumors:** asperse
  " **grass:** ted, tedder
  " **here and there:** strew, scatter
  " **rapidly:** mushroom
  " **thick:** slather
  " **thin:** bray
spring: leap, bound, source, season
  " **abruptly:** bolt
  " **Apollo's:** Castalia
  " **back:** rebound
  " **Biblical:** Ain
  " **deposit:** trona
  " **festival:** Mayday
  " **holiday:** Easter
  " **mineral:** spa
  " **of:** fontal
  " **pert. to:** vernal
  " **poet's:** Castalia
  " **poetic:** font

  " **sl.:** free, release
  " **up:** arise
sprinkling: aspersion
  " **with holy water:** asperges
sprit: spar, boom, pole, dart
sprout: son, bud, shout, growth
  " **comb. form:** blast(o)
spruce: trig, trim, conifer
  " **sl.:** spiffy, natty
  " **up:** titivate
spud: potato
  " **tool like:** spade, chisel
spurt: jet, gush, stream
  " **of energy:** lick
Spyri's heroine: Heidi
square: plaza, settle, fair, quadrate, tally
  " **column:** pilaster
  " **dance:** hoedown, reel, quadrille, lanc(i)ers
  " **dance need:** caller
  " **public:** plaza
  " **root of nine:** three
  " **shooter:** fair dealer
  " **sl:** hick
squeeze: hug, wring, crowd, neck
  " **the chin:** chuck
squid: mollusk, cuttlefish
  " **arm of:** tentacle
  " **pen:** quill
  " **secretion:** ink
  " **shell of:** pen
squirrel: rodent, woodchuck, pentail, xerus
  " **burrowing:** gopher
  " **flying:** assapan
  " **genus:** sciurus
  " **nest:** drey, dray

" **skin:** vair, calabar
sri: holy, fortunate, lakshmi
St.: (see **Saint**)
stabile: stationary
" **opposed to:** labile
stables, royal: mews
staccato: opposed to: legato
stacte: spice
staff: truncheon, rod, wand, retinue, cane
" **bearer:** verger
" **bishop's:** crosier
" **in music:** stave
" **mountain climber's:** alpenstock
" **of life:** bread
" **shepherd's:** crook
" **symbol:** clef
" **winged:** Caduceus
stag: hart, pollard, informer
" **horn:** rial, bezantler
" **horn's tine:** brocket
stage: dock, present, dais, show
" **curtain:** backdrop
" **front:** apron, orchestra
" **hand:** grip, callboy
" **overact on:** ham
" **pert. to:** scenic
" **prop:** curtain, drop, footlights
" **side scene:** coulisse
" **sl.:** legit
" **whisper:** aside
staggered arrangement: zigzag
Stagirite: Aristotle
staining art: marbling
stair: step, stile
" **face:** riser
" **post:** newel

" **series:** flight
staircase: perron, gri(e)ce
" **bend:** ramp
" **guard:** handrail
" **post:** baluster, newel
" **ship's:** companionway
" **spiral:** caracole
stalk: filament, stem, culm
" **having a:** petiolate
" **without:** sessile
stamping: ground: haunt, hangout
" **plate:** die
stamp(s): beat, mark, tool, impress, postage
" **collecting:** philately
" **fencing:** appel
" **substitute for:** indicia
stand: position, attitude, stall, face, resist, halt, view
" **against:** oppose
" **artist's:** easel
" **by:** maintain
" **conductor's:** podium
" **cup's:** zarf
" **high:** tower
" **in:** substitute
" **orator's:** soapbox
" **small:** taboret
" **three-legged:** trivet, tripod
" **two-legged:** bipod
standard bearer: gonfalonier
stang: pain
stanza: verse, envoi, strophe
" **eight-line:** triolet
" **four-line:** tetrastich, quatrain
" **seven-line:** heptastich
" **six-line:** sextain, hexastich

star: sun, planet, excel, leading
" **brightest:** Cor, Lucida, Sirius
" **cluster:** milky way, asterism, galaxy
" **comb. form:** astro, sider(o)
" **exploding:** nova
" **fallen:** alga
" **five-pointed:** pentacle
" **pert. to a:** sidereal
" **poetic:** lamp
" **shooting:** meteor
" **spangled, in heraldry:** seme
" **worshiper:** sabaist
starch: carbohydrate, amylum, amidine
" **comb. form:** amyl
" **source:** taro, cassava, arum
starling: pastor, mino, trout, enclosure
starnose: mole
Star-Spangled Banner author: Francis Scott Key
state (see special section): condition, etat, declare, mood
" **ideal:** Utopia
" **of affairs:** case
" **of balance:** equipoise
" **of excitement:** ferment
" **of mind:** morale, mood
" **of suspended animation:** anabiosis
" **pert. to:** federal
" **under foreign control:** protectorate
statement: bill, remark, mani-

festo, report
" **assumed correct:** premise
" **authoritative:** dictum
" **defamatory:** libel
" **mathematical:** theorem
" **self-contradictory:** paradox
statue: carving, effigy, figurine
" **base of:** pedestal
" **gigantic:** colossus
" **of Liberty poetess:** Lazarus
" **of Liberty sculptor:** Bartholdi
" **that came to life:** Galatea
" **weeping:** Niobe
staying power: stamina
staylace: a(i)glet
steady: firm, stable, constant, staid, calm
" **opposed to:** astatic, jerky, unstable
stealer of cattle: rustler
steel: toughen, metal, inure
" **poetic:** sword, dagger
" **process:** Bessemer
" **with inlaid gold:** damask
steeper: teapot, cistern
stegomyia: mosquito
steinkirk: cravat
stem: petiole, pedicel, peduncle, arise
" **comb. form:** caul(o)
" **covering:** ocrea
" **of arrow:** stele
" **pert. to:** cauline
" **rootlike:** rhizome

" **underground:** corm, tuber

steno: comb. form for: thin, narrow, small

step: gait, tread, pace, stair, dance
" **dance:** pas
" **down:** resign, abdicate
" **heavily:** trample, plod
" **in:** intervene
" **lightly:** trip
" **softly:** pad, tiptoe

stepmother, of /like a: novercal

steps, outdoor: perron, stile

sternum: breastbone
" **attachment:** rib

Stevenson: author: Robert Louis
" **statesman:** Adlai

stick: wand, rod, adhere, pierce, cling, ferule
" **bamboo:** lathi
" **celery:** stalk
" **insect:** emesa
" **match:** linstock
" **pointer:** fescue
" **up for:** defend

stiff: bum, hard, proper, exacting
" **-necked:** stubborn
" **sl.:** corpse

stilton: cheese

stimulant: bracer, tonic, beverage
" **in coffee:** caffein
" **in tea:** thein

sting: bite, smart, nettle, cheat
" **sl.:** dupe, cheat, shaft

stinging: caustic, nippy, irritating
" **ant:** kelep
" **sensation:** urtication
" **taste:** pungent

stirk: heifer, bullock, cow

stirrup: footrest, gambado, support
" **bone:** stapes
" **cup:** toast, drink
" **straps:** chapelet

stitch: sew, ache, tack, baste
" **bird:** ihi

stocking: hose
" **bishop's:** caliga, bushkin
" **foot only:** ped
" **footless:** hushion
" **soleless:** traheen

stoic: impassive, spartan
" **philosopher:** Seneca

Stoic School founder: Zeno

Stokowski, conductor: Leopold

stomach: abdomen, appetite, desire, gut, bear
" **ache:** colic
" **animal's:** paunch
" **bird's:** crop, craw
" **comb. form:** gastro
" **opening:** pylorus
" **pert. to:** gastric
" **washing out of:** lavage

stone: rock, pelt, dentrite, pebble
" **abrasive:** emery
" **Age human:** caveman
" **Age period:** eolithic, neolithic
" **broke:** penniless
" **carved:** cameo
" **carver:** graver

" **change into:** petrify
" **comb. form:** lith(o), petr(o), lite, lyte
" **cutter:** mason
" **cutter's chisel:** drove
" **druid:** sarsen
" **engraving:** intaglio
" **measure:** perch
" **particles:** grit
" **pert. to:** lithoid(al)
" **pile:** talus
" **philosopher's:** elixir, carmut
" **prefix:** litho
" **sharpening:** hone, whet
" **tablet:** stele
" **uncut:** naif
" **woman turned to:** Niobe
"Stonewall — ," general: Jackson
stooge: foil
stop: block, close, end, arrest, check
" **hole:** plug
" **legally:** estop
" **nautical:** avast
" **short:** balk
" **temporarily:** pause
" **watch:** timer
store: fund, save, amass, garner
" **cargo:** steve
" **hidden:** cache
" **military:** PX, canteen
" **sl.:** stash
stork's bill: geranium
storm: assault, expugn, rage, gust, wind
" **god:** Zu, Rudra
" **sand:** tebbad

" **snow:** buran
story: lie, myth, legend, tier
" **animal:** fable
" **continued:** serial
" **exaggerated:** yarn
" **exclusive:** scoop, beat
" **false:** canard, fable
" **heroic:** saga
" **part of:** passus
" **short:** conte, parable
" **sl.:** fib
" **teller:** raconteur
" **with moral lesson:** allegory, parable
stoss: opposed to: alee
stot: ox, bull, steer, stagger, bounce
Stowe: author: Harriet Beecher
" **character:** Topsy, Eva, Legree
Stradivarius, "Strad": violin
straight: erect, pure, unmixed
" **comb. form:** rect(i), euthy
" **edge:** ruler, liner
" **-faced:** deadpan
" **man:** foil, stooge
" **out:** direct
" **route:** beeline
strain: air, tax, force, melody
" **blood:** breed, stock, lineage
" **comb. form:** tono
" **great:** stress
strait: Malacca, Magellan, isthmus, Gibralter, narrow, channel
" **laced:** priggish, stuffy
strange: odd, alien, quaint, uncommon

"   comb. form: xen(o)

strap: belt, girth, secure, tie, whip

"   falcon's: jess

"   for leading animal: halter

"   shaped: ligulate, lorate

straphanger: standee

Stravinsky: composer: Igor

"   work: Firebird, Rites of Spring, Petrouchka

straw: culm, stalk, stem, fodder, trifle

"   bale of: truss

"   bed: pallet

"   bunch of: wisp, whisk

"   color: flaxen

"   cover plant: mulch

"   in the wind: omen, sign

"   stack: mow, rick

"   vote: poll

"   weaving: rafia

strawberry: fraise, runner

"   bush: wahoo

stream: flow, pour, creek, arroyo

"   dry bed: arroyo

"   of lava: coulee

"   swift, violent: torrent

"   underground: aar

street: calle, road, avenue, via, lane, dead end, one-way, easy, main

strength: brawn, power, might

"   deprive of: unnerve, weaken

"   diminish: dilute

"   liquor: proof

"   poet: puissance

"   regain: rally

streptomycin: discoverer: Waksman

stretched: out: prolate

"   tight: taut

"   to dry: tentered

stretching muscle: tensor

strife: feud, combat, quarrel

"   civil: stasis

strigil: fluting

strike: smite, hit, attack, buffet

"   and rebound: carom

"   breaker: fink, scab

"   demonstrater: picket

"   dumb: amaze, astound

"   kind of: sit-in, hunger

"   out: fan, cancel

"   series of: pelt

string: cord, line, lace, josh, twine

"   of beads: rosary

"   of horses (racing): stable

"   quartet   instruments: viola, violin, cello

"   up: hang, lynch

stringed   instrument: lyre, zither, harp, koto, banjo, ukalele

strip: undress, bare, divest

"   of land: neck

"   of leaves: defoliate

"   of tree trunk: flitch

"   tease dancer: ecdysiast

striped: striate, zonate, bandy

"   lengthwise: vittate

stroke: blow, caress, shot

"   brilliant: coup, ace

"   cutting: chop, slice

"   end-like: coup de grace

"   lucky: fluke, coup

" **oblique:** bricole
" **of luck:** windfall
Stromboli: island, volcano
strong: intense, virile, robust, firm
" **arm man (sl.):** bouncer, goon
" **current:** undertow, riptide
" **man:** Atlas, Samson
" **muscled:** brawny
" **point:** forte
" **scented:** olid
strudel: pastry
strummer: guitarist
struthious bird: theal, emu, ostrich, rhea
student: disciple, pupil
" **Annapolis:** midshipman
" **fellow:** classmate
" **former:** dropout
" **girl:** co-ed
" **in charge:** monitor
" **initiate:** haze
" **military school:** cadet
" **West Point:** cadet
studies: academic: arts, sciences, humanities
" **self-chosen:** electives
" **series:** course
study: closely: pore, examine
" **course:** seminar
" **hard:** bone(up)
" **of: animals:** zoography
" " **bees:** apiology
" " **fingerprints:** dactylography
" " **flowers:** anthoecology
" " **horses:** hippology

" " **insects:** entomology
" " **mountains:** orology
" " **population:** larithmics
" " **wine:** enology
" " **words:** etymology
stumbling block: obstacle, hindrance
stumps: legs
stunted: person: runt
" **tree:** scrag, bonsai
stupa: mound, tower
stupid, to be rendered: hebetate
stupor: coma, trance, lethargy
" **comb. form:** narco
" **pert. to:** carotic
sturgeon: gray/white: beluga
" **roe:** caviar
" **small:** sterlet
Stygian: infernal, gloomy
style: needle, manner, mode, brand, technique
" **art:** genre
" **out of:** dated, passe
" **painting:** genre, dada, cubism
" **show off:** ostentatious
" **with:** gusto
stylized flower: (fleur) de lis
Styx: river, Lethe, nymph
" **ferryman of:** Charon
" **locale:** Hades
subject: text, liable, theme, servant
" **change to another:** metastasis
" **main:** motif
" **point:** moot

"   **to change:** mutable
"   **to dislike:** aversion
"   **to mistakes:** erratic
"   **to 3rd degree:** sweat
submerged continent: Atlantis
subscription to newspaper: Fr. abonnement
subsequently: later, afterward
substance: core, mass, spirit, essence
"   **animal:** gelatin
"   **dissolving:** resolvent
"   **expansive:** gas
"   **rubber-ish:** gutta
"   **simple:** element
"   **transparent:** celluloid
"   **white:** alba
substitute, temporary: stopgap
subway: tube, metro, tunnel
"   **entrance:** turnstile, kiosk
succory: chicory
succubus: demoness
such: sic (Lat.), similar, kind
suckfish: remora, lamprey
Sudan, Sudanese: Mossi, Fulah, Haussa
"   **antelope:** oterop
"   **language:** Toshi, Mandingo
"   **sultanate:** Wadai
"   **weapon:** trumbash
Suez Canal builder: Lesseps
suffering: loss, agony, distress
"   **comb. form:** path(o)
"   **person involved in:** victim, martyr
suffix: postfix

"   **adj.:** ent, ial, ish, ist, ous
"   **comparative:** ier, ior
"   **diminutive:** ule, ette
"   **lacking:** less
"   **superlative:** est
sugar: alcohol: sorbitol
"   **burnt:** caramel
"   **cane:** sucrose
"   **comb. form:** racchar(o)
"   **crude:** gur
"   **lump:** cube
"   **milk:** lactose
"   **sl.:** money
"   **source of:** cane, maple, beet
su-: generis, juris
suit: kind, cards, dress, match
"   **of armor:** panoply
"   **of mail:** armor
"   **playing card:** spades, hearts, diamonds, clubs
"   **tarot card:** swords, wands, cups, pentacles
"   **to a   :** tee
Sullivan's collaborator: Gilbert
Sumatra: animal: balu, orang
"   **deer:** napu
"   **language:** Nias
"   **measure:** paal
summer: ete (Fr.)
"   **beverage:** ade
"   **pert. to:** (a)estival
"   **theater:** stock
summon: call, subpoena, rouse
"   **by calling name:** page
"   **by magic:** conjure
"   **roll call:** muster
"   **to a meeting:** convoke
"   **to court:** sist, cite

sumpter: packhorse, mule
sun: sol, bask, bleach
  " **comb. form:** heli(o)
  " **darkening of the:** eclipse
  " **dog:** parhelion
  " **god:** (see god, goddess)
  " **greatest distance from:** apsis
  " **halo of:** corona
  " **pert. to:** solar, heliacal
  " **poetic:** Phoebus, lamp
  " **point farthest from:** aphelion
  " **shadow:** umbra
  " **worship:** heliolatry
Sunday: following Easter: Low, Quasimodo
  " **mid-Lent:** Laetare
  " **pert. to:** dominical
  " **special:** Easter, Palm
sundial: horologe
  " **pointer:** gnomon
sundog: parhelion
sunfish: bream, roach, bluegill, cichlid
  " **genus:** mola
sunflower maid: Clytie
sunset, occuring at: acronical
superabundance: plethora
superficial: shallow, cursory
  " **polish:** veneer
superhumeral: amice
superlative: acme, ultra
  " **absolute:** elative
  " **suffix:** est
supersonic noise: boom
supine: opposed to: prone
supplement: add
  " **in law:** codicil

support: buttress, uphold, abet, second
  " **chief:** mainstay
  " **idea/cause:** espouse
  " **main:** pillar
suppository: pessary
suppress news story: kill
supreme being: monad, Allah
Supreme Court nickname: 9 old men
surcoat: jupon, cloak
sure: confident, secure, stable
  " **thing: sl.:** cinch, in the bag
surface: exterior, facet, area
  " **antique:** patina
  " **flat:** plane
  " **front:** obverse
  " **main:** airfoil
  " **pert. to:** facial
  " **slanting:** cant
  " **toward:** ectad
surfbird: plover
surgical: compress: stupe
  " **instrument:** trepan, scalpel
  " **operation: comb. form:** tomy
  " **sewing:** suture
  " **thread:** seton, catgut
Suribachi: site of: Iwo Jima
Surinam: hut: benab
  " **toad:** pipa(l)
  " **tree:** balata
surmounting: atop
surplice: cotta, ephod
surrealist: Dali, Salvadore
surrender: yield, cede, resign
  " **conditionally:** capitulate

"   **sign of:** white flag
surtout: (over)coat
surveying: instrument: level, stadia, caliper
"   **nail:** spad
susceptible, to error: fallible
suslik: squirrel, sisel, gopher
suspension: delay, stoppage
"   **of court sentence:** probation
"   **of hostilities:** truce
"   **of proceedings:** adjournment, recess
Susskind, (TV): David
susu: dolphin
swag: pit, list, spoil, swing
"   **sl.:** loot, plunder
swallowwort: celandine
swamp: slough, fen, morass, flood
"   **fever:** malaria
"   **pert. to:** paludal
"   **trees:** mangrove
"   **vapor:** miasm(a)
swan: declare, elk, surprise
"   **constellation:** cygnus
"   **female:** pen
"   **genus:** olor
"   **male:** cob
"   **river:** Avon
"   **young:** cygnet
Swann's Way author: Proust, Marcel
swaraj: home rule
swarmer: bee, locust, ant, insect
swat: clout, hit
"   **king of:** (Babe) Ruth
swear: vow, curse, pledge
"   **falsely:** perjure
"   **off:** renounce

"   **to secrecy:** tile
"   **word:** profanity
sweat: egesta, ooze, exude
"   **causing:** hidrotic
Sweden, Swedish: Sverige
"   **coin:** krona, ore, crown
"   **dance:** polska
"   **measure:** stang
"   **"nightingale":** (Jenny) Lind
"   **noble title:** graf
"   **parliament:** Riksdag
"   **prize:** Nobel
"   **tribe:** Geatas
"   **writer:** Strindberg
sweet: pleasant, candy, honey
"   **and soft:** dolce
"   **clover:** melilot
"   **drink:** nectar
"   **flag:** calamus
"   **smelling:** olent
"   **sounding:** melodic, dulcet
sweetbread: ris de veau
sweetfish: ayu
sweetheart: Jill, valentine, beau
"   **Scot.:** jo
"   **sl.:** steady
sweetsop: ates
swelling: edema, puff, bulge
"   **armpit/groin:** bubo
"   **comb. form:** c(o)ele
"   **foot:** chilblain
"   **pert. to:** nodal, edematose
swellfish: puffer
sweven: vision, dream
swift: rapid, lizard, fleet
"   **comb. form:** tachy

Swift's: "flying island": Laputa

" **hero:** Gulliver

" **lady friend:** Stella (fictional)

" **pen name:** Drapier

swile: seal

swimmer, of English Channel: Ederle, Gertrude

swimming: natant, vertigo, flooded

" **pool:** tank, natatorium

" **stroke/style:** crawl, butterfly, breast

" **suit:** bikini, maillot, tank

swine: hog, sow, pig, boar

" **female:** sow, gilt

" **flesh:** pork

" **genus:** sus

" **litter of:** farrow

" **male:** boar

" **pert. to:** porcine

" **young:** porker, piglet, shoat

switchman: shunter

Swiss, Switzerland: Helvetia, Suisse

" **ax:** piolet

" **card game:** jass

" **cottage:** chalet

" **designer:** Corbusier

" **Family Robinson author:** Wyss

" **food:** bernerplatte

" **herdsman:** senn

" **hero:** William Tell

" **lake:** Zug, Neuchatel, Lucerne, Geneva

" **measure:** elle, im(m)i

" **money:** batz

" **mountain:** Jungfrau

" **painter:** Klee

" **pert. to:** Alpen

" **plant:** edelweiss

" **psychologist:** Jung

" **song:** yodel

" **wind:** bise

swivet, in a: agog

sword: rapier, cutlas(s), falchion

" **belt:** baldric

" **handle:** hilt, haft

" **Highlander's:** claymore

" **knob:** pommel

" **legendary:** Excalibur, Balmung

" **poetic:** steel

" **shaped:** ensate, ensiform, xiphoid

" **short:** dirk

" **Siegfried's:** Balmung

" **St. George's:** Ascalon

" **two-edged:** pata

swordfish: dorado, aus, espada

" **saw of:** serra

syagush: caracal

sycamine: mulberry

syce: groom

syconium: fig

sycosis victim: beard

Syleus' slayer: Hercules

syllable: added: prefix

" **deletion:** apocope

" **last:** ultima

" **next to last:** penult

" **short:** breve

" **stressed:** arsis

sylvan: rustic, woody

" **diety:** satyr, Pan, Faun(us)

symbol: emblem, token

"   **bad luck:** opal
"   **British:** John Bull, lion
"   **bondage:** yoke
"   **death:** cross bones
"   **grief:** rue
"   **immortality:** ph(o)enix
"   **peace:** dove
"   **phallic:** linga(m)
"   **purity:** lily
"   **saintliness:** halo
"   **strength:** Atlas, sinew
"   **sun:** aten
"   **universe:** mandalga
"   **wisdom:** owl
sympathetic: humane, piteous
"   **response:** echo
symphony: form: sonata
"   **division of:** movement
"   **of Beethoven for Napoleon:** Eroica
symptoms: continuing: syndrome
"   **pert. to:** semiology, semiotic
synagogue: shul, temple
"   **officer:** parnas
"   **platform:** almemar
"   **singer:** cantor
syne: ago, since
synthetic: artificial, sham

"   **silk:** rayon, nylon
Syracuse, founder: Archias
Syrian, Syria: Saracen, Hittite, Levantine
"   **bishop:** abba
"   **buried city:** Dura
"   **goat:** angora
"   **goddess:** Ashtoreth
"   **peasant:** fellah
"   **religious   follower:** Druse
"   **script:** serta
"   **seaport:** Tripoli
"   **weight:** cola
"   **wind:** simoon
syringa: shrub, lilac
syrinx: panpipe, nymph
syrphus fly: gnat
system: method, order, circle, theory
"   **betting:** parimutuel
"   **of rules:** code
"   **of weights:** troy
"   **of worship:** cult
"   **orderly:** cosmos
systematic: orderly
"   **arrangement:** schema
systematics: taxonomy
syzygy: dipody
szopelka: oboe

T

T: letter, tee
" **shaped:** tau
ta, (Ch.): tantalum
taa: pagoda
Taal: Afrikaans
tab: flap, pan, check, tongue
" **shoe:** latchet, aiglet
" **sl.:** record
tabanid: horsefly
tabard: gown, mantle, cape
tabby cloth: moire, moreen
tabby moth genus: Aglossa
taberna: tavern, booth, tent, shop
table: food, rota, canon, list, postpone
" **calculating:** abacus
" **centerpiece:** epergne
" **communion:** altar
" **linen:** napery
" **philosopher:** deipnosophist
" **three-legged:** tripod, trivet

" **workman's:** siege
tableland: mesa, plain, plateau
" **Central Asia:** pamirs
" **S. Afr.:** karoo
tablet: pill, troche, lozenge, plaque
" **stone:** stele, slab
" **symbolic:** pax
tabor: drum, camp, timbrel
tachina: fly
tack: annex, jibe, laveer, join
" **glazier's:** brad
tael, 1/10th: mace
taffeta: samite, gaudy, florid
taffy: blarney, candy, flattery, Welshman
tag: flap, frazzle, label, append
" **metal:** a(i)glet
Tagalog: (see **Philippines**), Malayan
" **mother:** ina
" **peasant:** tao

" **wine:** alac
Tahiti, Tahitian: Polynesian
" **apple:** hevi
" **canoe:** pahi
" **capital:** Papeete
" **centipede:** veri
" **god:** Taaroa
" **robe:** maro
Tai, Thai: Siamese
" **race:** Lao
taiga: forests
tail: follow, dog, scut, shadow
" **boar's:** wreath
" **comb. form:** uro
" **coin's:** verso
" **furry:** scut
" **having a:** caudate
" **pert. to:** caudal
" **short:** scut, bun
" **without:** acaudal
" **amphibial family:** rani-
dae, frog, tenrec
tailleurs: amphibian, anura,
frogs
tailor: sartor, fit, fashion
" **iron:** goose
" **lapboard:** panel
" **work of:** sartorial
Taiwan: Formosa
" **deer:** sika
" **tea:** oolong
Taj Mahal: builder: Jahan
" **site:** Agra
tajo: trench
take: bag, nab, usurp, embez-
zle, swallow, grasp, capture
" **advantage of:** abuse,
misuse
" **away:** wrest, heave,
adeem
" **back:** recant, retract, re-

turn
" **off:** doff, flight, ape, burlesque
" **possession:** seize, escheat
" **sl.:** trick, cheat
" **shape:** form
" **shelter:** nestle
" **some of:** partake
" **to court:** sue
" **turns:** alternate
" **umbrage:** resent
" **up weapons:** arm
" **without authority:** usurp
takin: gazelle
talapoin: monk(ey), guenon
talaria: location of: ankles
" **of Hermes:** wings, san-
dals
talc: agalite, steatite, powder,
soapstone
tale: yarn, myth, fiction, recital, narrative
" **adventure:** gest(e)
" **bearer:** gossip, blabber,
quidnunc
" **medieval:** lai
" **Norse:** saga
" **of sorrow:** Jeremiad
" **traditional:** saga
Tale of Two Cities: author:
Dickens
" **hero:** Carton
" **heroine:** Lucie
taliera: palm, tara
talipot: palm
talisman: charm, fetish, amulet, phylactery
" **beetle:** scarab
" **ic:** magical
" **stone:** agate

talk: prate, spiel, lecture, discourse
" back: sass
" freely: descant
" glib: patter
" light: banter
" sales: spiel
" sl.: lip
" wildly: rave
tall: chest: highboy
" tale: yarn
tallow: suet, grease, sevum
" pert. to: stearic
" product: soap, candle
" sediment: greaves
" tree: cera, roka
Talmud: commentary: Gemara
" parts in: Gemara, Mishnah
" title: Abba
Talos' slayer: Daedalus
tamarack: tree, larch
tamarau: buffalo, carabo
Tamil: Dravidian
" caste member: Vellala
"Taming of the Shrew" character: Katharina (Kate), Bianca, Petruchio, Baptista, Sly, Gremio, Tranio
Tammuz's love: Ishtar
tanager: bird, lindo, habia, yeni
" genus: piranga
Tanganyika: Zanzibar
" mountain: Kilimanjaro
Tangier measure: kula, mudd
Tanis: Zoan
tank: vat, vehicle
" rainwater: cistern

" weapon: bazooka
tankard: vessel, hanap, facer
tanner's gum: kino
" shrub: sumac(h)
" solution: bate, amaltas
" substance: splate
Tanoan: Indian, Isleta
" See "Indian(s), Pueblo"
Tantalus' daughter: Niobe
" father: Zeus
" punishment: hunger, thirst
" son: Pelops
tantivy: rapid, haste(n)
Taoism, right conduct: te
tape: braided: inkle
" needle: bodkin
tapered: terete
tapering: spired, conical, fusiform
" piece: shim
tapestry: arras, tapis, fabric
" comb.: reed
" kind: Bruges, Gobelin
" warp thread: lisse
tapeworm: cestode, entozoan
" genus: taenia
tapioca like food: salep
" source: cassava
tapir: anta, seladang
" pride of: snout
tappet: cam
tar: pitch, sailor, salt
" mineral: brea, pitch, maltha
" product of: creosol
taradiddle: lie, fib
Taranaki volcano: Egmont
tarboosh: fez, turban
tare: weed, plant, vetch
targe: shield

target: mark, butt, aim
" 　**center:** eye, blank
" 　**easy:** sitting duck
" 　**of blame:** scapegoat
Tarheel: Carolinian
Tarkington: novelist, Booth
taro: plant, gabi, koko
" 　**dish (paste):** poi
" 　**root(s):** eddo(es)
" 　**W. Indies:** tania
tarpon: fish, elops, sabalo
" 　**genus:** elops
" 　**related to:** chiro
tarsus: ankle, hock, shank
Tartar: Turk, Hu, Tatar
" 　**dynasty:** Wei, Kin
" 　**horseman:** cossack
" 　**king:** Khan
" 　**nobleman:** murza
tartar: argol, calculus
Tartarus: Hades
Tartuffe: comedy, hypocrite
" 　**author:** Moliere
Tarzan: mate: Jane
" 　**monkey:** Cheeta
task: job, stint, duty, metier
" 　**punishing:** pensum
" 　**routine:** chore
" 　**take to:** lecture, scold
Tasmania: cape: Grim
" 　**devil:** Dasgure
tass: cup, goblet
tassel: thrum, tag, cordelle
taste: sup, sapor, relish, palate, liking
" 　**absence of:** ageus(t)ia
" 　**delighting the:** friand
" 　**Fr.:** soupcon
" 　**strong:** tang
tatterdemalion: ragamuffin
tattersall: checkered

tattler: blab, gossip, quidnunc
tau: ankh, crux, tace
taurine: bovine, bull, Taurus
taurotragus: eland, oreas
tautog: chub, blackfish
taw: tan, harden, marble
tax: levy, duty, excise, stent, custom
" 　**assess on default:** doomage
" 　**church:** tithe
" 　**feudal:** tallage
" 　**on hides:** hidage
" 　**salt:** gabelle
taxite: lava
taxus genus: yew
Taygeta: star, pleiad
tazza: bowl, vase, cup
tea: Asia: cha, oolong, hyson, congo(u)
" 　**black:** pekoe
" 　**bowl:** chawan
" 　**box:** caddy
" 　**Brazil holly:** mate, yerba
" 　**caffein in:** thein(e)
" 　**cake:** scone
" 　**China:** hyson, congo(u), oopak, oolong
" 　**drug in:** thein(e)
" 　**extract:** adenine
" 　**genus:** thea
" 　**plant:** kat, thea
" 　**table:** teapoy
" 　**urn:** samovar
" 　**weak:** blash
teacher: pedagog(us), docent, pundit, scribe
" 　**Jewish:** rab(bi)
" 　**Moslem:** alim, mulla(h)
" 　**pointer of:** fescue
" 　**Rus.:** starets

" **unattached:** docent
teaching: of a fable: moral
" " **pert. to:** pedagogic
teakettle: suke, suky
teal: fowl, duck
tear: rive, part, binge, drop, bead, slit
" **heraldry:** larme
" **sl.:** spree
" **up by roots:** pluck, assart, arache
" **ful:** moist, maudlin
" **pert. to:** lacrimal
teardrop design: larme
tearful mother: Niobe
teasel: herb, plant, boneset, comb
teck: cravat
ted: spread, scatter, toad
teeth: cavity tissue: pulp
" **decay of:** caries
" **deposit on:** tartar
" **double:** grinders, molars
" **grinding of:** bruxism
" **hard tissue:** dentine
" **having all alike:** isodont
" **long-pointed:** tusks, fangs
" **sockets:** alveoli
" **without:** edentulous, edentated
teetotum: toy, top
teg: doe, fleece, woman
tegua: sandal
tegula: alula, tile
tegument: skin, cortex, coat
tela: membrane, tissue, web
telamon: atlas, pilaster, column
Telamon's brother: Peleus
" **companion:** Hercules

" **son:** Ajax
telecost fish: eel, apoda
telegraph: instrument, part of: key, tapper, anvil
" **inventor:** Morse
" **signal:** dot, dash
Telemachus: father: Ulysses, Odysseus
" **mother:** Penelope
telephone: inventor: Bell
" **receiver:** cymaphen
telephotographic lens: adon
Telephus' mother: Auge
telescope site: Palomar
television: TV, tube, telly, video
" **award:** Emmy
" **cable:** coaxial
" **camera platform:** dolly
" **interference:** snow
" **lens:** zoom
Tell's home: Uri
telluride: hessite, altaite
telson: segment, somite
" **of king crab:** pleon
tempera painting: secco
Tempest characters: Ariel, Caliban, Prospero, Miranda
Templar: knight, crusader
temple: huaca, tabernacle
" **basin:** laver
" **builder, early Jewish:** Micah
" **chief chamber:** naos, cella
" **Chinese:** pagoda, taa
" **gateway:** torii
" **inner:** cella
" **pert. to:** hieron
" **portico:** narthex
" **Shinto:** sha

" **vestibule:** pronaos
tempo: time, pulse, beat
" **pert. to:** agogic
" **rapid:** presto
" **slow:** lento
" **very slow:** grave
tempus: time
ten: decad(e)
" **acres:** decare
" **century note:** grand
" **decibels:** bel
" **gallon hat:** sombrero
" **prefix:** dec(a), deka
" **square chains:** acre
" **thousand:** grand, myriad
tenacious: animal: bulldog, pitbull
" **person:** shadowy follower, tail
tenant: lessee, renter
" **farm:** croft
" **feudal:** vassal, leud(e), socager
" **neglect to pay rent:** cesser
" **tribute, F.:** cens
tending toward an end: telic
tendon: thew, sinew
" **broad, flat:** aponeurosis
" **comb. form:** teno
tendril: stipule, shoot, cirrus
Tennessee: (see special section)
" **old name:** Franklin
Tennyson: heroine: Maud, Enid, Elaine
" **heroine's home:** Astolat
" **subject: "In Memoriam":** Hallam
tenon: tooth, tusk, coo, dovetail

tense, grammar: present, future, past, perfect
" **opposite of:** slack, loose
" **past:** preterite
tensile: ductile, plastic
tent: lodge, canopy, probe
" **circular:** yurt
" **covering:** fly, tilt
" **dweller:** nomad, Arab, Kedar, Scenite
" **India:** pawl
" **large field:** marquee
" **maker:** Omar
" **surgical:** plug
tentacle: palp, tendril, feeler
" **without:** acerous
tenth, comb. form: deci
" **muse:** Sappho
" **part:** tithe
tenure of land: socage
teocalli: temple
tera: church, monastery
Terah: father: Nahor
" **son:** Abraham
teraph: idol, image
terbium symbol: TB
terebinth: teil, tree, turpentine
teredo: borer, (ship)worm
Tereus: son: Itylus
" **wife:** Procne
tergal: back, dorsal, aboral
tergum: back
term: period, boundary, rhema, state
" **in office:** tenure
" **math:** sine, cosine
" **of life:** age, sands
termagant: shrew, vixen, virago, scold
terminal: depot, final, end, pole

" **negative:** cathode
" **of a leaf:** apiculus
" **positive:** anode
termite: anal, anay, ant
tern: fowl, starn, noddy, pirr
" **genus:** anous, sterna
" **Hawaii:** noio
terpene: nerol
" **derivative:** camphor
Terpsichore: muse
" **concern:** dancing
terra: (firma) earth
" **cotta:** clay
terrace: dais, plateau, street
" **in series:** parterre
" **wall:** podium
terrapin: emyd, tortoise, turtle
" **order:** chelonia
" **red-billed:** slider
terret: ring
terrine: stew
territory: domain, region
" **division of:** amt
terry: loop
tertiary period: pliocene, neocene
tesselate: tile, mosaic
test: prove, check
" **flight:** trial run
" **operation:** shakedown
" **ore:** assay
" **paper:** litmus
" **series:** gantlet
testa: shell
teston: coin
Tethys' brother: Cronus
" **father:** Uranus
" **husband:** Oceanus
tetrachord: music: meson, nete
tetrad: four, quadrivalent

tetter: fret, herpes, lichen, eczema, psoriasis
Teutonic, anc. tribe: Ubi(i)
" **barbarian:** Goth
" **letter:** rune
" **people:** Gepidae
Texas: see special section
" **shrine:** Alamo
" **tree:** pecan
textile: fabric, fiber, cloth
" **dealer:** mercer
" **worker:** Reeder
Thackeray: character: Esmond, Becky (Sharp), Amelia
" **tale country:** Paflagonia
Thai, Thailand: Siam, Shaw, Lao
" **coin:** fuang, att, bhat, tical, bia, catty
" **demon:** nat
" **dress:** panung
" **garment:** panung
" **measure:** sesti, sok, cohi, niou, tanan
" **temple:** wat
" **twins:** Chang, Eng
" **weight:** catty, bat, fuang
thais: courtesan, opera
" **composer:** Massenet
thalassic: marine, oceanic, neritic, pelagic
thalia: muse
" **concern:** poetry, comedy
" **sisters:** Clio, Graces, Charities
" **slayer:** Erato
Thames: landmark: Eton, bridge
Thanatos, mother: Nyx

" **personified:** Death
thankless person: ingrate
that: which, who, so, what, as, because
" **is:** id est, ie
" " **-to say:** namely
" **not:** lest
thatch: grass: neti
" **palm:** nipa
" **peg:** scob
" **support:** wattle
thaumaturgy: magic
" **work:** miracle
the: (Fr.) la, le, les
" (Ger.) der, die, das
" (It.) il, la, le, egli, ella
" (Sp.) el, la, las, los
" **same:** ditto, idem
theater, theatre: legit, stage, drama, opera, cinema
" **award:** Tony
" **box:** loge
" **classic:** lyceum
" **floor:** pit
" **full:** SRO
" **Gr.:** odeon
" **-in-the-round:** arena
" **part of:** scena, stage
theban, Thebes: blind soothsayer of: Tiresias
" **deity:** Mut, Amon
" **founder:** Cadmus
" **king:** Creon, Oedipus, Laius, Lycus
" **one of the 7 against:** Tydeus
" **poet:** Pindar
" **statute:** Memnon
" **wicked queen:** Dirce
theca: cell, sac, capsule
theme: literary: motif

" **mus.:** tema
" **title:** lemma
Themis: goddess
" **concern:** law, justice, harmony
" **father:** Uranus
" **holds:** scale
" **mother:** Gaea
theorbo: lute
theoretical: academic
" **opposed to:** applied, practical
theory: of Darwin: evolution
" **of Einstein:** relativity
" **of Newton:** gravity
there: that, thence, yon(der), thither, at
therefore: then, so, hence, ergo, accordingly, consequently
thersitical: abusive, scurrilous
thesaurus: cyclopedia, lexicon
" **compiler:** Roget
Theseus': father: Aegeus
" **mother:** Aethra
" **victim:** Minotaur
" **wife:** Phaedra
thesis: essay, article, dissertation
" **opposed to:** arsis
thespis forte: tragedy
Thetis': husband: Peleus
" **son:** Achilles
thick: dull, crass, fat, compact
" **as thieves:** close
" **headed:** dense
" **slice:** slab
" **soup:** puree
thief: gonof, stealer, larcener

" **cattle:** rustler
" **compulsive:** kleptomaniac
" **literary:** lifter, plagiarist
" **sells loot to:** fence
thigh: ham, coxa, meros
" **bone:** femur
" **comb. form:** mer(o)
" **part:** flank
" **pert. to:** crural
" **of the:** femoral
thill: shaft, plank, thwart
thimble: sput, ring, bushing
" **machine:** sleeve
" **rigger:** cheat, swindler
thimblerig: shell game
thin: lean, slim, meager, sparse, flimsy, subtle, lanky
" **coat/layer:** film, veneer
" **comb. form:** steno
" **disk:** wafer
" **glue:** size
" **out:** peter
" **paper:** tissue
" **plate:** leaf, wedge
" **scale:** flake, lamina
" **-skinned:** touchy, sensitive
thing: idea, item, cause, being, object, article, affair, happening
" **accomplished:** deed, acta
" **added:** insertion, appendix
" **aforesaid:** ditto
" **an easy:** cinch
" **complete unto itself:** unity
" **cursed:** anathema
" **extra:** bonus

" **following:** sequel
" **found:** trove
" **indefinite:** so and so, nondescript
" **ineffectual:** dud
" **in law:** res
" **invariable:** constant
" **of remembrance:** token
" **out of place:** estray
" **precious:** relic, curio
" **reasoned:** noumena
" **sensed:** phenomena
" **to be done:** chore, agenda
" **unusual:** freak, oddity
" **valueless:** trifle, picayune, nihil
things: goods, effects, belongings
" **done:** res gestae
" **edible:** esculents
" **forbidden:** vetanda
" **for sale:** wares, services
" **hidden:** penetralia
" **holy:** hagia
" **linked by nature:** cognates
" **movables:** chattels
" **worth remembering:** memorabilia
think: alike: agree
" **logically:** reason
" **out:** plan
" **over:** brood
Thinker sculptor: Rodin
thinness: tenuity, rarity
third: day: tertian
" **in music:** tierce
" **power:** cube
" **row:** cee
this: hoc, here

"   **minute:** pronto, now

"   **one:** haec

Thisbe's love: Pyramus **this-**
tle: burr, cosmos, arnica

"   **genus:** layia

"   **-like plants:** carlina, artichoke

thistledown: tufts, pappus

tho: still

thole: fulcrum, oarlock, bear,
peg, allow

Thomas' opera: Mignon

thong: knout, strap, romal

"   **shaped:** lorate

Thor: Sisech

"   **concern:** thunder

"   **father:** Odin

"   **stepson:** Ull

"   **weapon:** hammer

"   **wife:** Sif

thorax: insect's: trunk

thorn: briar, spine, prickle,
trouble

"   **apple:** meter, datura

"   **back:** ray, skate, fish

"   **comb. form:** spini

"   **like:** spina(te)

thoroughwort: plant, boneset

thought: idea, belief, opinion

"   **continuous:** meditation

"   **force:** phrenism

"   **to transfer:** telepathy

thousand: mil(le)

"   **comb. form:** milli, kilo

"   **headed snake:**
S(h)esha

"   **sl.:** (dollars) grand

"   **years:** millennium, chiliad

thread: lisle, cord

"   **ball:** clew, clue

"   **comb. form:** nema,
mit(o)

"   **cross:** woof, reticle

"   **guiding:** clew

"   **lengthwise:** warp

"   **like:** nemaline, linear, fi-
lar

"   **linen:** inkle

"   **shoe latchet:** lingel,
lingle, lace

"   **silk:** tram

"   **worm:** filaria, nematode

three: trio

"   **dimensional:** solid

"   **fold:** ternal, ternate

"   **group of:** trio, tern, triad

"   **in one:** triune, oil

"   **of a kind:** leash

"   **prefix:** ter, tri(o)

"   **toed bird:** stilt

"   **toed sloth:** ai

three: B's (mus.): Bach,
Brahms, Beethoven

"   **Graces:** Aglaia, Thalia,
Euphrosyne

"   **Holy:** (mus.) Weber, We-
bern, Schoenberg

"   **Kingdoms:** Wu, Shu,
Wei

"   **Musketeers:** Athos,
Aramis, Porthos

"   **R's:** reading, (w)riting,
(a)rithmetic

"   **Wise Men:** Gaspar, Mel-
chior, Balthasar

thrice prefix: ter, tri

throat: gorge, gullet, trachea,
pharynx, passage

"   **comb. form:** lemo

"   **covering:** barb

"   **part:** glottis

" **pert. to:** gular, jugular, esophageal
" **upper:** gula
through, thru: by, via, among, finished
" **comb. form:** di(a)
throughout: about, perfect, during
" **comb. form:** per
throw: hurl, dash, toss, flury
" **away:** discard
" **back:** revert
" **down:** fling
" **over:** jilt
" **overboard:** jettison
" **stones at:** lapidate
" **up:** puke, spew
" **water on:** douse
thrum: tassel, drum, waste, recite
thrush: ouzel, robin, missel, bird
" **disease:** aphtha, soor
" **genus:** turdus
" **ground:** pitta
" **Hawaii:** omao
" **India:** shama
thuja: pine, cedar
Thule: part of: Iceland, Norway
thulium, symbol: TM
thumb: digit, handle, phalanx
" **pert. to:** thenar
thunder: Fulminate, rage, peal, bronte
" **comb. form:** bront(o)
" **god:** Thor, Zeus
" **storm of Cuba:** bayamo
" " **of West Indies:** houvari
" **witch:** baba

thunderfish: raad, loach
thurible: censer
Thursday: god of: Thor
" **Holy:** Skire
thus: hence, sic, so, yet, ergo, consequently
" **Latin:** ita, sic
Thyestes: brother: Atreus
" **father:** Pelops
" **son:** Aegisthus
thylacine: yabbi, tiger
thyroid: growth / enlargement: goiter
Tibet, Tibetan: Sitsang, Tangut
" **animal:** panda
" **antelope:** goa, sus
" **banner:** tanka
" **coin:** tanga
" **deer:** shou
" **kingdom:** Nepal
" **lama:** Dalai
" **leopard:** ounce
" **monk/priest:** lama
" **ox:** yak
" **religion:** Bon
tibia: shin, bone, cnemis
" **pert. to:** cnemial
tick: mite, insect, tap
" **fowl:** argas
" **genus:** argas, cimex, ixodes, ixodidae
" **sheep:** ked
ticket: sl.: ducat
" **stub:** rain check
tidal: flow: ebb, bore, estuary
" **wave:** eagre
tide: flow, current, befall
" **low, lowest of high, pert. to:** neap
tidy: prim, spruce

" **make:** redo
tie: join, equal, cement
" **down:** restrain
" **fast:** belay
" **tightly:** bind
" **up:** moor, delay
tiffin: tea, lunch, repast
tiger: cat, feline, shir
" **family:** felidae
" **young:** cub, whelp
tight: -fisted: stingy
" **-lipped:** secretive
" **place:** fix, jam, spot
" **sl.:** tipsy
" **-wad:** miser, piker
til: plant, sesame
tile: curved: pantile
" **large:** slab
" **pattern:** mosaic
" **pert. to:** tegular
" **roofing:** pantile
tillage: culture
" **fit for:** arable
timber: log, bitt, wood, fuel
" **crack:** anemosis
" **defect:** conk
" **grooved:** coulisse
" **peg:** coak
" **rot:** doat
" **tree:** yew
" **wolf:** lobo
time: period, epoch, tempo, beat
" **before:** eve
" **being:** nonce
" **comb. form:** chron(o)
" **division:** eon, year, hour
" **error in order of:** anachronism
" **fast:** Lent, DST
" **past:** ago, yore

" **pert. to:** eral
" **piece:** clock, horologue, sundial
" " **water:** clepsydra
" **to come:** tabor
Timor coin: avo
tin: metal, preserve, coat
" **box:** trummel
" **fish:** torpedo
" **foil for mirrors:** tain
" **pert. to:** stannic
" **symbol:** SN
tinamou: yutu, bird
tinean: moth
tined, three: tridentate
tintinnabulum: bell, rhyme
tip: off: warn, hint
" **over:** upset
" **pen's:** neb, nib
tippet: amice, scarf, muffler, cape, fur
Tiresias: seer, soothsayer
" **blinded by:** Athena
" **home:** Thebes
tissue: fat, bast, fabric, meat
" **comb. form:** hist(o)
" **connecting:** tendon, stroma
" **decay:** caries, atrophy
" **hardening:** sclerosis
" **pert. to:** telar
" **weblike:** tela, plexus
Titan: Oceanus, Atlas, Rhea, Creus, giant
" **female:** Rhea, Dione
" **father:** Uranus
" **mother:** Ge, Gaia
Titania: queen, fairy
" **husband:** Oberon
titanium, principal ore: ilmenite

tithe: tax
  " **pert. to:** decimal
titi: monkey
titivate: tidy, spruce
titlark: bird, pipit
title: (see under specific country) record, assign, notice, appelation, placard
  " **ecclesiastic:** dom, fra, abba
  " **feminine:** dame, hanum, milady
  " **personage:** peer, noble
  " **pert. to:** titular
titmouse: bird, nun, yaup, tomtit
tittup: prance, caper
Titus Andronicus: daughter: Lavinia
  " **queen:** Tamora
Tivoli's anc. Roman name: Tibur
tmesis: diacope
to: be: Fr. etre; Lat. esse
  " **each his own:** suum cique
  " **the point:** ad rem
  " **wit:** namely, scilicet, viz
toa: warrior
toad: pipa, bufonid, frog
  " **fish:** sa(r)po
  " **genus:** bufo, hyla
  " **largest:** agua
  " **order of:** anura
  " **tongueless genus:** aglossa
  " **tree:** hyla
tobacco: caporal, latakia, uppowoc, capa, vuelta, knaster, burley, plant
  " **ash:** dottle, dottel

  " **coarse:** caporal
  " **kiln:** oast
  " **left in pipe:** dottel
  " **low grade:** shag
  " **plant, heart of leaf:** ratoon
  " **pouch:** doss
  " **shreds:** shag
  " **smoke hater:** misocapnist
Tobacco Road: author: Caldwell, Erskine
  " **character:** Pearl, Jeeter
Tobias: father: Tobit
  " **wife:** Sara
today: pert. to: diurnal
tode: sled, haul, boat
toe: digit, obey, phalanx
  " **comb. form:** dactyl
  " **great:** hallux
  " **pert. to:** digital
  " **small:** minimus
together: mass, union, (con)jointly, mutually, accompanying
  " **prefix:** con, com, syn
toilet case: etui, etwee
token: proof, gift, signal
  " **affection:** amoret, keepsake
  " **victory:** palm
Toltec, anc. capital: Tula
tolypeutine: apar, armadillo
Tom: of Lincoln: bell
  " **Thumb:** dwarf
  " **Tulliver's river:** Floss
Tom Sawyer: aunt: Polly
  " **author:** Twain, Mark
  " **brother:** Sid
  " **girl:** Becky
  " **pal:** Huckleberry Finn

tomb: crypt, catacomb, mastaba
" **for bones of dead:** ossuary
" **Moslem:** tabut
" **saints:** shrine
tomboy: girl, hoyden, romp
tomcat: gib
tone(s): key, sound, energy, feel, color, attitude
" **artificial unit:** nil
" **down:** mute
" **lack of:** atony, mute
" **rhythmical:** cadence
" **series:** octave
tongue: dialect, flap, prate, lorriker
" **bone:** hyoid
" **comb. form:** glosso
" **disease:** agrom
" **fish:** sole
" **like process:** ligula
" **pert. to:** lingual
" **tip:** corona
" **wagon's:** neap, pole
tonsil: gland, amygdala
" **inflammation:** quinsy
too: bad: alas
" **late:** tardy
" **much:** nimiety
" **soon:** premature
tool(s): pawn, puppet, implement, gadget
" **ability to use:** chrestic
" **bookbinder's:** gouge
" **cleaving:** frow, hatchet
" **cutting:** die, adz(e), razor
" **edge:** bit
" **engraver's:** burin
" **flat:** spatula

" **kit:** etui, chest
" **marble worker's:** fraise
" **mining:** gad, pick
" **theft of:** ratten
tooth: tusk, cog, fang
" **canine:** cuspid
" **cavity:** caries
" **comb. form:** odonto
" **grinding surface:** mensa
" **having but one:** monodont
" **less:** edentate, edentulous
" **molar:** wang
" **part of:** dentine, root, cusp, trigon
" **projecting:** snag, buck
" **pulp:** nerve
" **sockets:** alveoli
top: apex, excel, toy
" **hat:** gibus
" **ornament:** epi, finial
" **spin with fingers:** teetotum
topaz sign of: fidelity
tope: rig, wren, stupa, boat
topi: helmet, cap
topic of discourse: theme
tops: best, aces, A-one
" **opposed to:** (sl.) pits
tor: crag, peak, pinnacle
tora: tetel, antelope, law
toril: gateway
tormina: colic, pains
torpedo: fish: ray
" **sl.:** gunman
tortoise: emyd, turtle, terrapin
" **genus:** emys
" **marsh:** gopher
" **pert. to:** chelonian

" **shell:** carapace
torture device: rack
tosspot: sot, drunkard
tota: grivet, monkey
totem post: xat
toto: baby
toucan: toco, bird, aracari
touch: abut, shave, contact, vein
" **comb. form:** tac
" **examine by:** palpate
" **-hole:** vent
" **organ for:** palp, antenna, feeler
" **pert. to:** haptic, tactile
" **-stone:** test, basanite, criterion
" **-wood:** punk, tinder, amadou
" " **pert. to:** agaric
Toulouse: Lautrec, painter
toupee: peruke, wig
" **sl.:** rug
tour de force: feat
towai: tree, kamahi
tower: spire, babel, minaret, soar
" **Buddhist:** tope
" **glacial ice:** serac
" **India:** minar(et)
" **medieval:** donjon
" **pyramidal:** sikhra, sik(h)ara
" **small:** turret
" **small round:** rondel
" **Spain:** atalaya
" **spirical:** cupola, steeple
towhee: bird, finch, chewink
town: map: plat
" **pert. to:** civic, urban, oppidan

" **small:** whistle-stop
" **street:** maindrag
toxin: venom, poison
" **alkaloid:** venom, brucin
" **protein:** abrin
toxophilite: Eros, Cupid, archer
toy: flirt, plaything, trinket
" **bear:** teddy
" **stilt-like:** pogostick
" **stringed:** yoyo
trabea: toga
trachyte: domite
track: animal: pug, mark, spoor
" **deer:** slot, spoor
" **railroad:** siding
" **ship's:** wake
tractor: bulldozer, caterpillar
" **and trailer:** semi
trade: job, swap, (Fr.) metier, barter, craft
" **agreement/assoc.:** cartel
" **-man:** (sl.) huckster
" **-mark:** brand
" **unlawful:** contraband
" **wind:** monsoon
tragacanth: gum, shrub, tree
tragedy Muse: Melpomene
tragopan: fowl, pheasant
trail: blazer: pioneer
" **marker:** cairn
train: series, teach, aim, cortege
" **fast:** limited
" **overhead:** el(evated)
" **slow:** local
" **underground:** tube, subway, metro
transfer: cede, grant, shift

" **design:** decal
" **legal:** deed, lease
transparent: lucid, diaphanous, obvious
" **comb. form:** hyal(o)
" **mineral:** mica, quartz
" **not:** opaque
trappist: monk, merton
trapshooting: skeet
" **target:** (clay) pigeon
travel: mush, trip, wend
" **pert. to:** viatic
traverse: cross, range, refute
" **rear:** parados
trawl: net, fish, troll
treacle: molasses, syrup, remedy
treat: badly: scorn, abuse
" **lightly:** palter
" **tenderly:** pet, TLC
treatise: thesis, discourse, book
" **elementary:** primer, grammar, donet
" **on fruit trees:** pomona
" **preface to:** isagoge
tree: timber, boscage, forest
" **Abyssinia, dried flower:** cusso
" **acacia:** siris, babul, cooba(h)
" " **Australia:** myall
" **alder:** arn
" " **genus:** alnus
" **algarroba:** carob, calden
" **allspice:** pimento
" **apple:** shea, sorb
" " **genus:** malus
" **babul:** garad
" **bark:** tan, crut
" **bay:** laurel

" **bee:** linden
" **beech:** buck, fagus, myrtle
" " **Chile:** roble
" **birch:** betula
" **black gum:** nyssa, tupelo
" " **haw:** sloe
" **branches:** ranage
" **Buddhist sacred:** pipal
" **cabbage:** angelin, (yaba)
" **candlenut:** ama, kukul, bankul
" **Ceylon:** tala
" **coffee:** chicot
" **comb. form:** dendri(o)
" **coral:** dapdap
" **cottonwood:** alamo
" **custard:** atta, sweetsom
" **dead:** rampick, rampike
" **devil:** dita
" **dogwood genus:** cornus
" **drupe bearing:** bito
" **dwarf:** arbuscle, bush
" **elm genus:** ulmus, celtis
" **eucalyptus:** gum, yate
" **evergreen:** fir, yew, pine, holm, holly, olive
" " **N. Zealand:** tarata
" **fabaceous:** agati
" **fir:** balsam
" **fir genus:** abies
" **forgetfulness:** lotus
" **gingerbread:** dum, doom
" **glasswort:** jume, kali
" **grove:** tope
" **Guinee:** akee
" **hickory species:** pecan,

carya
"   **honeyberry:** genip
"   **light wood:** balsa
"   **lime:** bass, teil
"   **live oak:** encina
"   **locust:** kowhai, courbaril
"   "   **pod:** carob
"   **loquat:** biwa
"   **maple genus:** acer
"   **moss:** lichen, usnea
"   **moth:** egger
"   **oil:** ebo(e), poon, tung, mahwa
"   **olive genus:** olea
"   **papaya:** carica, pawpaw
"   **pea:** agati
"   **pear:** pyrus, seckel
"   "   **prickly:** nopal
"   **pert. to:** arboreal
"   **pine:** ocate
"   **plum genus:** prunus
"   "   **wild:** sloe
"   **poisonous:** upas, hemlock, bunk, sassy
"   **poplar:** aspen, abele, alamo
"   **rain:** zaman, genisaro
"   **rowan:** ash, sorb
"   **rows of:** stich
"   **rubber:** para, ule, caucho
"   **sandalwood:** algum
"   **sassafras:** ague
"   **science of:** silvics
"   **shea:** karite
"   **stately:** palm
"   **swamp:** alder
"   **taxus genus:** yew
"   **toad genus:** hyla
"   **trunk:** bole, caber
"   **willow:** osier

"   "   **genus:** itea
trees, to clear of: assart
trefoil: clover, arch, medic, plant
trelliswork: pergola
trench: embankment: parados
"   **knife:** bayonet
tres: chic, bien, very
trial: test, cross, doom, bout
"   **inconclusive:** mistrial
"   **pert. to:** empiric
"   **severe:** ordeal
"   **site:** venue
triangle: trigon(e), trinity
"   **draw circle in:** escribe
"   **heraldry:** giron
"   **insert:** gore
"   **shaped:** deltoid, scalene
"   **side:** leg
tribe: clan, sept
"   **emblem:** (Indian) totem
"   **head:** chief
"   **New Zealand:** ati
"   **Roman:** Sabine, Etruscan, Latin
trichord: lyre
tricks: device: gimmick
"   **play mean on:** shab
"   **win all:** capot
Trieste: measure: orna, orne
trifle: dally, palter, bit, flirt
"   **insignificant:** fico
trifoliate: three-leaved
"   **plant:** clover, shamrock
triglyphs, space between: metope
trigo: wheat
trigonometric figure: co(sine)
Trilby: author: duMaurier

"   **character:** Svengali
trillion: comb. form: trega
Trinidad: fish: guppy
"   **music:** calypso
"   **tree:** mora
trio: fictional: Musketeers
"   **myth:** furies, fates, graces
"   **one of a:** hope, faith, charity
"   "   Tom, Dick, Harry
"   "   Athos, Porthos, Aramis
triplet(s): tercet, siblings
"   **one of:** trine
Tripoli: coin: piastre
"   **measure:** dra(a)
"   **ruler:** dey
trippet: cam
triptych: (writing) tablet, panel
"   **wing:** volet
trismus: lockjaw, tetanus
Tristam, Tristan: beloved: Isolt, Isolde
"   **uncle:** Mark
"   **villain:** Melot
trite expression: cliche, bromide
triton: eft, newt
trivet: tripod, stand, stool, knife
trochilus: scotia, warbler, hummingbird
trochlea: pully
"Troilus and Cressida" character: Hector, Ajax, Nestor, Paris, Helen
"   **father of:** Priam
"   **mother of:** Hercuba
Trojan: Ilian, Darden

"   **country:** Troy
"   **epic:** Iliad
"   **hero:** Hector, Aeneas
"   **horse builder:** Epeus
"   **King:** Priam
"   **war cause:** Helen
"   **warrior:** Agenor
trombone: sackbut
"   **mouthpiece:** bocal
"   **part:** slide
trona: urao
troops: army, battery
"   **group:** band, brigade
"   **quarters:** barracks, etape
"   **reserve:** echelon
tropical: hot, torrid
"   **disease:** malaria, beri-beri, yaws
"   **fish:** opah
"   **herb:** loofa
"   **tree:** palm, guara, balsa
tropo: comb. form: turn
Tros' son: Ilus
trotyl: TNT
trough: hod, channel, conduit, basin
"   **inclined:** chute
"   **mining:** sluice
Troy: Ilium, Ilion, Troas
"   **defender:** Aeneas
"   **founder:** Ilus
"   **Greek general:** Agamemnon
"   **king:** Priam, Paris
"   **myth.:** Tros
"   **pert. to:** Iliac
truck: van, lorry, wagon, dolly
"   **trailer:** semi
truffle: fungus, mushroom, earthnut

trumpet: horn, bugle, clarion
  " **bell of:** codon
  " **belt:** baldric
  " **blare:** tantara
  " **call:** sennet
  " **caller:** Gabriel
  " **mouth:** codon
  " **muffler:** mute
  " **shell:** triton
trumpet-creeper: plant, tecoma
trumpeter: bird, fish, agami
  " **perch:** mado
trunk: stem, coffer, caber, torso
  " **animal's:** soma, snout
  " **tree:** burl
trusty: convict
truth: drug: pentothal
  " **goddess:** Maat
  " **personification:** Una
  " **self-evident:** axiom
tsamba: barley, flour
tsetse fly: mau, kivu, muscid
  " **disease caused by:** encephalitis, nagana
  " **genus:** glossina
tsine: ox, banteng
tub: vat, firkin, skeel, bath
  " **-handled:** cowl
  " **wooden:** soe
tuba mouthpiece: bocal
Tubal: father: Japheth
  " **grandfather:** Noah
tuber: potato, eddo, jalap, truffle
  " **orchid:** salep
Tuesday: god: Tyr, Tiu
  " **Shrove:** Mardi Gras
tuft: wisp, crest, tussock
  " **bird's head:** cop

  " **botany:** coma
  " **feathers:** alula
  " **-hunter:** snob
  " **pert. to:** comal
Tuileries: palace, gardens
tule: bulrush
  " **genus:** scirpus
  " **root:** wapatoo
tumbleweed: pigweed, bugseed, amaranth
tumor: swelling, keloid, moro, yaw
  " **comb. form:** coele
  " **fleshy:** sarcoma
  " **glandular:** adenoma
  " **small:** wen, papilla
  " **suffix:** oma
tun: vat, cask, drink
  " **half:** pipe
  " **shell /fossil:** dolite
tung oil product: varnish
tungsten: wolfram
  " **ore:** cal
Tunis, Tunisia: cape: bon
  " **measure:** cafiz, zah
  " **money:** dinar
  " **ruler:** dey, pasha
  " **weight:** rotl, artel, kantar
tup: ram, sheep, mallet
tupelo: gum, tree, nyssa
tur: goat, pea
turban: fez, pata, mandil, cap
  " **cloth:** lungi
  " **flower:** tulip
turbot: flatfish
turdine bird: thrush
  " **pert. to:** turdidae
turkey: buzzard: vulture
  " **male:** tom
  " **sl.:** failure
  " **trot:** dance

" **wild:** bustard
" **young:** po(u)lt
Turkey, Turkish, Turk: Ottoman, Osmanli, Tartar, Porte
" **boat:** mahone
" **cap:** fez, calpac
" **cape:** Baba baba
" **carpet:** Smyrna
" **coin:** para, lira, asper,
beshlik, iklik
" **fermented drink:** boza,
airan
" **garment:** colman
" **harem:** serai
" " **ladies of:** kadein
" **measure:** kilo, almud,
parmack
" **name:** Ali
" **non-moslem:** raia
" **palace:** serai
" **peasant:** raya
" **pipe:** chibouk
" **prayer rug:** melas
" **rug:** konia
" **sword:** yataghan
" **weight:** chequi, roti,
maund, mane, cantar
turn: aside: divert, swerve
" **frontward:** obvert
" **inside out:** evert, invert
" **left:** haw, port
" **out of course:** veer,
deviate
" **over:** keel, spill
" **right:** gee, starboard
" **to side:** splay
turnip: nape, swede, rutabaga
" **shaped:** napiform
" **wild:** rape, navew
turnstone: plover, redleg, bird

turpentine: thus, oleoresin
" **resin:** alk, pitch, galipot
" **tree:** tarata, pine
turtle: terrapin, cooter, jurara
" **back:** carapace
" **fresh-water:** emyd
" **genus:** emys, chelone
" **giant:** arrau
" **marine:** caretta
" **snapping:** torup
Tuscany: city: Pisa
" **island:** Elba
" **river:** Arno
tut: rebuke, hush, King
tutta: all, whole
tuyere: nozzle, pipe, tew
twelfth part: uncia
twenty: score, corge, kappa
" **comb. form:** icosa
" **pert. to:** icosian
" **years:** vicennial
twice: bi(s), doubly
" **prefix:** di, dis
twilight: dusk, evening, obscure
" **pert. to:** crepuscular
twin: dual, pair, counterpart
" **one:** gemel
" **Siamese:** Eng, Chang
" **stars:** Castor, Pollux,
gemini
twist: warp, dance, whirl,
gnarl, contort
" **inward:** intort
" **to and fro:** wrench, wrig-
gle
twisted: tortile, (a)wry, cam,
complex
" **cord:** torsade
" **spirally:** torse
two: and 1/2 inches: nail

"   **-bit:** (sl.) cheap
"   **celled:** bolocular
"   **colors:** dichromic
"   **consisting of:** bivalent, dyad
"   **edged:** ancipital
"   **-faced:** false
"   "   **god:** Janus
"   **fingered:** bidigitate
"   **fold:** dual
"   **footed:** biped
"   **forked:** bifurcated
"   **handed:** bimanual, am-bidextrous
"   "   **animals:** bimana
"   **headed:** ancipital
"   **of a kind:** brace
"   **-pronged:** bident
"   **-sided:** bilateral, hypo-critical
"   **-spot:** deuce
"   **-time:** cheat
Tyche: goddess, fortuna
tylopod: camel

type: genre, sort, pattern, model
"   **face:** kern, runic
"   **kind:** elite, pica, ionic, ronde, pearl, agate, minion
"   **metal piece:** quad
"   **part of:** nick, face, foot
"   **script:** ronde
"   **set:** font
"   **slanted:** italic
"   **style:** caslon, ionic, runic, script
"   **tray:** galley
typewriter: roller: platen
"   **type:** pica, elite
typographical error: erratum
Tyr: Zeus, Jupiter, Tiu
"   **parent of:** Odin
tyre: milk, curds, wine
Tyre: king: Hiram, Belus
"   **prince:** Pericles
"   **princess:** Dido
tzigane: gypsy

U

U: letter: eu
  " **shaped bone:** hyoid
  " **turn:** hairpin
uang: beetle
Ubangi tributary: Uele
ubermensch: overman, su-
perman
uberous: abundant, fruitful
uca: crab
Ucayali tributary: Apurimac
udder: part: teat, nipple
  " **product:** milk
Uganda: capital: Kampala,
Entebbe
  " **cattle:** ankoli
  " **kingdom:** Buganda
ughten: dusk, dawn, twilight
ugly: duckling (arc.): swan
  " **sight:** eyesore
  " **symbol:** toad
Ugrian: Avar
uhlan: soldier, lancer, German
uintaite: asphalt

uitlander: foreigner
ukase: decree
Ukraine, Ukrainian:
  " **assembly:** rada
  " **coin:** grivna, schagiv
  " **dance:** gopak
  " **holy city:** Kiev
  " **native:** cossack
  " **seaport:** Odessa
Ulalume author: Poe
Ulan Bator: Khoto, Urga
ulcer: sore, canker, noma
  " **kind of:** peptic
ule: caucho
  " **fluid:** latex
ulema: mufti
ulmus: elm
ulna: bone, cubitus
  " **end of:** ancon
Ulster: (over)coat
  " **lake:** Erne
ult: ultimo, ultimate
Ultima Shule: Ireland
ultra: beyond, radical, ex-

treme
" **modern:** avant garde
" **nationalist:** chauvinist
ultramarine: pigment
ulu: knife
Ulysses: Odysseus
" **author:** Joyce
" **character:** Bloom, Molly
" **country of:** Ithaca
" **dog:** Argos
" **enchantress of:** Circe
" **enemy:** Poseidon
" **father:** Laertes
" **friend:** Mentor
" **mother:** Anticlea
" **plant:** moly
" **name given to Cyclops:**
Noman
" **son:** Telemachus
" **voyage:** odyssey
" **wife:** Penelope
umbelliferous plant: carrot,
parsley
umber: pigment, shade
" **bird:** umbrette
umbo: knob, boss, beak
umbra: shade, ghost, fish,
shadow
umbrella: chatta, gamp,
cover, parasol, screen
" **cloth:** gloria
" **like flower:** umbel
" **like fungus:** mushroom
" **like thing:** canopy
" **of leaves:** talipot
" **part:** rib
" **tree:** magnolia
Umbria: town: Assisi
" **river:** Tevere
umiak: canoe, kayak, boat
umlaut: dieresis

" **in linguistics:** mutation
UN: Agency, WHO, UNESCO,
UNRRA, GATT, ICAO,
FAO, IDA
una: catboat
unaccented: atonic, lene,
stressless
" **vowel sound:** schwa
unaging: eternal
Unalaskan: Aleut
unalloyed: pure, genuine
unanimous opinion: consensus
unanimously: una voce
unau: sloth
unbleached: ecru, blae
" **fabric:** beige
unbeliever: pagan, heretic,
atheist, agnostic, infidel
unborn: in uterus: fetus
unbosom: tell, reveal
unbranched antler: dag
unbranded cow: maverick
unburnt brick: adobe
unbury: exhume
uncanonical: apocryphal
unchaste: wanton
uncia: inch, coin, ounce,
twelfth
unciform: hook-shaped
uncle: nunks, oom, eam, unk,
(sl.) pawnbroker
" **cry:** yield, surrender
" **pert. to:** avuncular
Uncle: American: Sam
" **Remus:** author, Harris
" " rabbit, Brer
" **Tom:** Cabin author,
Stowe
" " characters: Eva, El-
iza, Topsy, Legree

unco: news, weird, great, notable, very

uncoined metal: bullion

unconfirmed news: rumor, gossip, hearsay

unconscious: inanimate, mindless, torpid

" **render:** stun

" **sl.:** blotto, out

" **state:** narcosis, swoon, apsychia, coma(tose)

unconventional one: rebel, Bohemian

unction: oil, unguent, ointment

" **give extreme:** anele

und so weiter: etc., et cetera

unde, in heraldry: wavy

under: obligation: indebted, bound

" **par:** sick, ill, term (golf)

" **prefix:** sub, hyp

underage: minor, immature

underbrush: thicket, covert, abature

undercroft: crypt

underground: hidden, secret

" **being:** dwarf, gnome, troll

" **burial place:** crypt, catacomb

" **drain:** sewer

" **fighter:** partisan, maquis

" **fungus:** truffle, earthnut, tuckahoe

" **passage:** tunnel

" **railway:** tube, subway, metro

" **worker:** sandhog

underlying principle: elixir

underpinning, sl.: legs

undersea boat: u-boat, submarine

" **eye:** periscope

undershirt: skivvy, jersey, singlet

understanding: nous, sense, accord

" **between nations:** entente

understatement: litotes

undertaking: guarantee, venture

" **written:** cautio(nes)

undertow: riptide, vortex, eddy

underwater: submarine

" **apparatus:** scuba, snorkel, caisson

" **captain:** Nemo

" **explorer:** Picard

" **ledge:** reef

" **missile:** torpedo

" **plant:** benthos

" **prefix:** hyp(o)

" **sound detector:** sonar, sofar

" **swimmer:** frogman

underworld: **boatman:** Charon

" **deity:** Bran, Pluto, Osiris, Dispater

" **goddess:** Trivia, Hecate, Belili

" **king:** Yama

" **pert. to:** chtonic

" **queen:** Hel

" **river:** Styx, Lethe, Acheron

" **watchdog:** Cerberus

undeveloped: latent

" **quality:** potential

undine: nymph, sylph, seamaid

undressed skin: pelt, kip

Undset: Sigrid (Nor. novelist)

undulant fever: brucellosis

undulating object: worn, snake, wave, ripple

uneasy: restive, stiff, fidgety
 " **feeling:** malaise

unequal: uneven, irregular, impar
 " **angled:** scalene
 " **comb. form:** aniso
 " **condition:** odds

uneven: erose, rough, spotty, varying
 " **condition:** asperity
 " **contest:** lopsided

unexamined: aprivri

unexpressed: tacit

unfading flower: amaranth, everlasting

unfermented grapejuice: stum

unfledged: callow
 " **bird:** eyas, nestling

ungodly: impious, dreadful, sinful

ungual growth: claw, hoof, nail, talon

unicellular: animal: amoeba, protozoan
 " **plant:** spore

unicorn: lin, reem, monocero
 " **fish:** unie, filefish
 " **whale:** narwhal

uniform: even, outfit, level, steady
 " **cord:** aiguillette
 " **in color:** flot, flat
 " **servant's:** livery

" **shoulder ornament:** epaulet(te)

uninflected: aptotic

unio: mussel

union: merger, coalition, fuision, alliance
 " **business:** syndicate, cartel
 " **"jack":** flag
 " **member:** cardholder
 " **merchants:** hanse
 " **trade:** guild

unison: harmony, concord
 " **sing/utter in:** chorus

unit: item, piece, one
 " **caloric:** therm
 " **electrical:** watt, volt
 " **of** " **resistance to:** ohm
 " **of energy:** erg, joule
 " **of light:** lux, lumen
 " **of pressure:** barad
 " **of value:** point
 " **wire:** mil

United States: (see **America**)
 " Presidents & Indians (see special section)

univalve: snail, mollusk

universe: of the: cosmic

university: grounds: campus
 " **officials:** bursar, dean, regent
 " **professorship:** chair, tenure

unknown: obscure, unco
 " **person:** John/Jane Doe

unlawful: illegal, illicit
 " **goods:** contraband
 " **to distill:** bootleg (liquor)
 " **to hunt:** poach(ing)
 " **to import:** smuggle

" **to intrude:** trespass
" **underage:** minor
unleavened: azymous
unmarried: in-law: sole
unpopularity: odium
unreasoning devotion: fetish
unredeemed territory: irredenta
unrelated: fremd
unscrupulous person: swindler, cheat
untamed state: ferity
untanned hide: kip, pelt
untidy person: slob, pig, sloven
" **place:** pigsty
until: up to, till, unto, before, pending
unto: until, till
untouchable: leper, brahman
untreated: raw, virgin
unvarying sound: drone, monotone
unvoiced: muted, surd
unwonted: rare
unwritten: blank
" **but understood:** tacit
" **law:** custom, tradition
up: over, aloft, above
" **and coming:** promising
" **and moving:** astir
" **in arms:** irate, angry, miffed
" **in the air:** a-sea, unsettled
" **prefix:** ana
" **-to-the-minute:** redhot
Updike (John) novels: Couples, Centaur, (Rabbit) Redux
upholstery stuffing: flock

upon: over, atop, up and over
" **prefix:** ep(i)
upper: berth, ramp, bunk, superior
" **air:** ozone, ether
" **case:** capital
" **crust:** elite
" **limit:** ceiling
" **lips:** flews
upright: just, good, piano, honest
" **comb. form:** ortho
" **support:** stud, jamb
upscuddle: quarrel
Uracus: asp, cobra
Urania: muse, Aphrodite
" **pert. to:** celestial
" **son:** Hymen
" **sphere:** astronomy
Uranus: children: Cyclops, Titan, Rhea, Saturn, Cronus, Furies
" **discoverer:** Hebschel
" **moon:** Ariel, Oberon, Umbriel, Titania
" **mother/wife:** Gaia, Gaea, Ge
" **satellite:** Ariel
urane: rat, curare
urban: civic, oppidan
" **division:** ward
urease: enzyme
uredo: hives, urticaria
Urfa: Edessa
Uriah: Heep
" **wife:** Bathsheba
urial, ooriah: sha, sheep
Uriel: angel, archangel
Urim's partner: Thummim
Uris, Leon novels: Exodus, QBVII

urisk: brownie
urn: Kist, bury, jar, container
   " **figurative:** grave
   " **for bones:** ossuary
   " **for tea:** samovar
   " **shaped:** urceolate
Urne-Buriall: (author) Browne
urodela: salamander, newts
Ursa: Bear
   " **pert. to:** ursine
Urth: Norn
urticaria: uredo, hives
urubu: vulture
Uruguay: coin: peso, cente-simo
   " **cowboy:** gaucho
   " **discoverer:** Diaz
   " **language:** Spanish
   " **measure:** vara, cuadra, suete
   " **weight:** quintal
urus: ox, tur, aurochs
us: (Fr.) nous, (Ger.) uns
use: try, employ, function, value
   " **as example:** cite
   " **divining rod:** dowse
   " **efforts:** strive, exert
   " **over again:** secondhand

   " **to be of:** avail
   " **up:** eat, tire, expend, de-plete
   " **wastefully:** fritter, squander
Uspallata Pass: cite: Andes
usquebaugh: whiskey
U.S.S.R. (see Russia)
usury: gombeen
Utah: (see special section)
   " **natives:** Mormons
Uther's son: Arthur
Utopia, Utopian: ideal, edenic
   " **author:** More
   " **Harrington's:** Oceana
   " **imaginary:** Shangri-La
Uttar Pradesh capital: Lucknow
   " **part of:** Oudh
utterance: expression, aside, ditty
   " **soft:** murmur, whisper
   " **voiceless:** surd, spirate
utu: reward
uva: grape, fruit
uxorial: wifely
Uzbek: capital: Tashkent
   " **city:** Khiva

V

V: letter/shaped, vee
　" **shaped piece:** pie, wedge
　" **symbol:** victory
vaca: cow
vacation: place: spa, beach, resort
　" **person:** tourist, camper
vaccination: inventor: Jenner
vaccine: serum
　" **discover/polio:** Salk, Jonas
vacuum: void
　" **opposite of:** plenum
　" **pump:** pulsometer
　" **tube:** diode, tetrode
vade mecum: manual, hardbook
vadium: bail, pledge, pawn
vagabond: vag, drifter, rove, scamp, rascal
vagrant: rover, tramp, nomadic, hobo, caird

　" **lives in:** skid row, Bowery
vail: tip, use, doff, yield, decline, submit
vain: idle, flory, silly, trivial, ineffectual
　" **bird:** peacock
　" **boasting:** fanfaronade
　" **manners:** airs
　" **person:** fop, dandy, coxcomb
　" **to do in   :** wild goose chase, futile
vainglorious: boastful, proud
vair: fur
Vaishnavas: diety: Vishnu
　" **priest:** gusain
vakass: amice
valance: curtain, pelmet, drapery
valediction: adieu, address, farewell
Valence's river: Rhone
valentine: card, lover, sweet-

heart
" **derivation:** (myth.) Pan, Faunus
" **feast of:** Lupercalia
valerian: drug, plant, hemlock
Valetta: capital of: Malta
" **native:** Maltese
" **without:** rivers or lakes
valetudinarian: sickly, invalid
valgus: knock-kneed
Valhalla: maiden: Valkyrie
" **palace of:** Odin (Wotan)
Vali's mother: Rind(r)
valid: just, true, legal, robust, cogent
" **opposite of:** void, null
valise: grip, case, bag
Valkyrie: Brunnhilde
" **love of:** Sigard
vallancy: wig
vallation: wall, rampart
valley: brae, cove, dale, glen, basin
" **between volcanic cones:** atrio
" **deep:** canyon
" **entrance to:** jaws
" **moon:** rill(e)
valor: arete, virtue, bounty
valse: waltz, triste
valuable discovery: find
" " **lucky:** serendipity
value: prize, worth, admire, rate, cheap
" **equal:** parity
" **highly:** cherish
" **mean:** average
" **more:** prefer
" **net:** reserve
" **of little:** trifle
" **reduction:** depreciation

valve: spigot, plug, tap, poppet
" **engine:** choke, throttle
" **heart:** mitral
" **sliding:** piston
vamoose: lam, scat, scram, depart
vampire: siren, corpse, lamia, bat
" **famous:** Dracula
van: wagon, lorry, fourgon, shovel
" **man:** mover, hauler
Vance: Philo, sleuth
Van Gogh: Vincent, painter
" **town:** Arles
vandal: hun, plunderer
" **act of:** mar, deface
Vandyke: beard, goatee, collar, artist
vane: arm, blade, weathercock, feather
" **feather:** web, vexillum
vanguard: front, avantgarde
vanilla: orchid, flavoring
" **substance:** coumarin
vanity: (see **vain**) falsity, conceit, pride
" **case:** etui
" **symbol:** peacock
Vanity Fair character: Amelia, Becky
vantage: fee, profit, gain
" **point:** coign
vapor: reek, bray, cloud, fancy, steam
" **aircraft's:** contrail
" **comb. form:** atm(o)
" **frozen:** hail, sleet, frost
" **in air:** fog, mist
" **mass:** wrack

" **measuring device:** tonometer

vaporizer: etna, steamer

vaquero: cowboy, herdsman

Varangian: Scandinavian

varec: kelp, seaweed

variation: change, mutation

" **slight:** shade, nuance

varicella: chicken pox

varicolored: mottled, varied, rainbow

varicose: swollen, dilated, varix

" **pert. to:** veins

varied: daedal

variegated: menald, dappled, pied, flecked, speckled

variety show: vaudeville

variola: cowpox, smallpox, horsepox

" **scar:** pockmark

variole: foreola

varlet: page, gippo, menial, rascal

varnish ingredient: resin, copal, lac, dammar

varsity: team

" **eight member:** stroke

" **of:** junior, senior

varus: bowlegged

vas: duct, vessel, pledge

vase: tazza, echew, urn, amphora, crater, potiche

" **handle:** ansa

" **support:** pedestal

vassal: esne, serf, slave, subject

" **pert. to:** feudal

" **tax paid:** tribute

vat for bleaching: keir

vatic: prophetic, inspired, oracular

Vatican: art gallery: Belvedere

" **chapel:** Sistine

" **chapel ceiling artist:** Michelangelo

" **guard's nationality:** Swiss

" **official:** datary

Vaud: Canton

" **capital of:** Lausanne

vault: leap, cope, dome, bound

" **burial:** crypt, tomb

" **underground:** dungeon

veal: meat, calf, (Fr.) gigot, & veau

" **cutlet:** schnitzel

" **stew:** goulash

vector: host, carrier

" **opposite of:** scalar

Vedic: Sanskrit, Pali

" **artisans of gods:** Ribhus

" **cosmic order:** Rita

" **fire god:** Agni

" **god:** Aditya

" **goddess:** Ushas

" **sky serpent:** ahi

" **sun god:** Savitar

" **text:** Sakha

vee: fin, fiver

veery: thrush

vega: meadow, tract

Vega: star, Lyra

vegetable: plant, legume

" **basket:** scuttle

" **carbonized:** lignite

" **caterpillar:** aweto

" **dealer:** huckster, greengrocer

" **decayed:** duff, humus
" **ferment:** yeast
" **green:** sabzi
" **growing art:** horticulture
" **pear:** chayote
" **pod:** hull, peasecod
" **poison:** abrin
" **sponge:** loofa(h)
" **stunted:** scrub
" **variety:** cabbage, lettuce, tomato, beet, okra, bean, corn, squash, spinach, cucumber, eggplant, artichoke, rhubarb
vegetation: growth, verdure
" **floating:** sadd
" **god:** Attis, Esus
vehicle: armored: half-truck
" **army:** tank, jeep
" **child's:** pram, walker, scooter
" **covered:** sedan, caravan
" **display/parade:** float
" **snow:** plow, sled
" **two-wheeled:** sulky, tonga
veil: mask, hide, cloak, screen, shroud
" **having a:** velate
" **head:** caul
" **in botany:** velum
" **papal:** orale
vein: bed, mood, seam, vessel, tenor
" **arrangement of:** neuration
" **enlarged:** varix
" **fluid:** ic(h)or
" **inflammation:** phlebitis
" **leaf:** rib

" **mine/mining:** lode, reef
" **pert. to:** venous, veinal
" **rich ore:** bonanza
" **small:** venule
" **throat:** jugular
veining: marbling
veinstone: matrix, gangue
velamen: membrane
velar: guttural, palatal
veld(t): grassland, meadow
vellum: parchment
velocity: rate, speed, pace, rapidity
" **instrument:** cinemograph
" **measuring device:** tachometer
velum: soft palate, membrane
velvet: profit, drink, birodo (Jap.), surplus
" **fabric like:** velure, panne
" **knife:** trevet
" **-breast:** merganser
vendace: whitefish
vendor: seller, butcher, peddler
" **route:** walk
veneration: homage, reverence, awe, fear
" **of saints & angels:** dulia
Veneto: via, street
Venezuela, Venezuelan:
" **coin:** real, medio, bolivar
" **dam:** Guri
" **discoverer:** Columbus
" **fiber:** erizo
" **fish:** guppy
" **god:** Tsuma
" **language:** Pume, Span-

ish
- " **measure:** milla, fanega, (wgt.) bag, libra
- " **patriot:** Bolivar
- " **snake:** lora
- " **tree:** balata

vengeance: god: Alastor, Erinys
- " **goddess:** Ara, Ate, Nemesis

venial: trivial, pardonable, insignificant
- " **opposite of:** mortal

Venice, Venetian: barge: bucentaur
- " **beach:** Lido
- " **boat:** gondola
- " **boatman:** gondolier
- " **bridge:** Rialto
- " **canals:** Rii
- " **coin:** bezzo, ducat, sequin
- " **gondolier's song:** barcarole
- " **magistrate:** doge
- " **river:** Brenta
- " **traveler:** Marco Polo
- " **Little Venice:** Venezuela
- " **Venice of the North:** Stockholm

venireman: juror

vennel: lane, sewer, alley

Venite: psalm, canticle

vent: exit, hole, outlet, flue
- " **tailor's:** slit
- " **whale's:** blowhole, spiracle

ventage: (finger)hole

venter: womb, belly

ventral: sternal, abdominal
- " **opposite of:** dorsal

ventriloquist's medium: puppet, dummy

Venus: planet, Vesper
- " **as morning star:** Lucifer
- " **beloved:** Adonis
- " **flytrap:** plant, dionaea
- " **girdle:** cestus
- " **island:** Melos
- " **planet:** Vesper
- " **poet.:** Hesperus
- " **mother:** Dione
- " **son:** Cupid
- " **tree sacred to:** myrtle

verandah: piazza, balcony, loggia
- " **Southern:** gallery

verb: action
- " **as a noun:** gerund
- " **auxiliary:** had, has, was, may, will, might, shall, would
- " **form:** tense
- " **suffix:** le, ire, ise, esce
- " **table:** paradigm
- " **taken from:** rhematic
- " **tense:** aorist

verbal: oral, spoken
- " **attack:** diatribe, tirade
- " **thrust:** (sl.) dig
- " **word for word:** literal, verbatim

verdant: green, fresh, raw, innocent

Verdi: Guiseppe, composer
- " **character:** Radames, Amneris
- " **opera:** Aida, Otello, Rigoletto, Traviata

verdigris: aerugo, patina, rust

verdin: bird, titmouse

verecund: shy, modest, bashful

verein: society, organization

verger: dean, official, garden

Vergil: see **Virgil**

verily: yea, amen, certes, parde, really

verjuice: acidity, sourness

vermiform: long, thin, slender, wormlike

  " **process:** appendix

vermin: filth, rodents, lice, rats, mice

Vermont: (see special section)

  " **mountain range:** Taconic

Verne: Jules, author

  " **character:** Nemo

  " **submarine:** Nautilus

verneuk: swindle, cheat

veronal: barbital

verrel: ferrule

verruca: wart

versant: slope

verse: meter, revolve, stichos, rune, poem, line, stanza

  " **accented:** arsis

  " **Bible:** text

  " **foot:** iamb

  " **form:** couplet, sonnet

  " **half line:** hemistich

  " **pert. to:** poetic

  " **set to music:** lyric(s)

  " **stress:** ictus

verse-maker: meterist

verset: prelude

verso: vo

  " **opposite of:** recto, obverse

versus: against, con, vs.

vertebra: axis, spondy

  " **comb. form:** spondyl(o)

  " **body of:** centrum

  " **top:** atlas

vertebrae: spine

vertebral bone: coccyx, sacrum

vertebrate: ray, fish, reptile

  " **class:** aves

  " **division:** somite

  " **feathered:** bird

verticil: whorl

Vertumnus' wife: Pomona

vervet: monkey

very: so, too, molto (It.), tres (Fr.), quite, real

  " **comb. form:** eri

  " **new:** redhot

  " **well:** first rate

vesica: bladder, vessel

vesicate: blister

vesicle: cell, cyst, cavity, bulla, sac

  " **air:** aerocyst

vespa: wasp

Vesper: star, Venus, Hesperus

vespertilione: bat

vessel: utensil, craft, duct, cask

  " **anatomical:** vein, artery

  " **comb. form:** vaso

  " **drinking:** flask, stein

  " **having more than one:** vascular

  " **oil:** cruet

  " **sacred:** pyx, ama

  " **wooden:** skeel, piggin

vesta: match

Vesta: Itestia

vestal: pure, chaste, virgin, nun

  " **virgin:** tuccia

vestiture: dress, garb
vestment: gown, dress, robe, garment
   " **clerical:** alb, amice, cope, fanon, miter
   " **pert. to:** vestiary
Vesuvius, Vesuvian: volcano, volcanic, fusee, match
   " **city destroyed by:** Pompeii
vetch: ers, tare, weed, fetch
veteran: vet, old, trouper, seasoned
   " **of battles:** warhorse
veterinarian: leech, doctor, furrier
vetiver: bena, grass, cuscus
veto: forbid, overrule
   " **sl.:** kibosh, nix
vettura: couch, carriage
veuve: bird, whydah
vex: rile, irk, nettle, cark, gall, roil, acerbate, tew, miff
vexed: grieved, sorry
vexillum: flag, banner, web
viand: food, fare, edible, dish
   " **choice:** cate
viaticum: money, supplies, Eucharist
viator: traveler, wayfarer
Viaud's pen name: Loti
vibration: thrill, tremor, tremolo, quivar
   " **check:** damp
   " **point without:** node
vibrissa: whiskers
vicar: priest, proxy, deputy
   " **assistant:** curate
   " **of Christ:** Pope
Vicar of Wakefield author: Goldsmith
vice: sin, fault, taint, defect
   " **president:** (see special section), Veep
   " **versa:** conversely
vicenary number: twenty
viceroy: nabob, exerch, satrap, butterfly
   " **wife of:** vicereine
vicious: lewd, vile, faulty, mean, unruly
   " **act:** outrage
victim: prey, dupe, goat, sucker, quarry
   " **accident:** casualty
   " **list:** toll
victoria: queen, empress, carriage, waterlily
   " **goddess:** Nike
victory: success, triumph, win, supremacy
   " **author of:** Conrad; heroine, Lena
   " **celebration of:** epinician
   " **crown of:** bay, laurel, anadem
   " **easy:** runaway
   " **goddess:** Athena, Nike
   " **kind of:** landslide, rout
   " **memorial:** trophy, spoils, arch
   " **ruinous:** Pyrrhic
   " **symbol:** palm, laurel
   " **victualler:** innkeeper, caterer
videlicet: viz, namely
Vienna: Wien
   " **palace:** Schonbrunn
   " **park:** Prater
   " **Woods composer:** Strauss

Vietnam (North): capital: Hanoi
  " **coin:** dong
  " **gulf:** Tonkin
  " **native:** meo
Vietnam (South): capital: Saigon
  " **coin:** piastre
  " **guerrillas:** vietcong
  " **river:** Mekong
view: aim, goal, scene, slant, opinion, survey
  " **extended:** panorama
  " **mental:** envision
  " **obstruct:** hide
  " **open:** bare
vigilant person: Argus
vigilantes: posse
vigneron: winegrower
vignettist: artist, painter, author, writer
vigor: snap, dash, force, energy
  " **drain of:** sap, enervate
  " **loss of:** sag, fail, pine, decline
  " **pinnacle of:** heyday
  " **with great:** amain
Viking: rover, pirate, Norseman, Scandinavian
  " **famous:** Olaf, Eric, Rollo
  " **poet:** Skald
vilaget: region, division, eyalet
  " **subdivision:** sanjak
villa: aldea, house, dacha (Rus.)
Villa: Pancho, Mexican, leader
villatic: rural, rustic
villein: serf, churl, tenant, cottier
villian: rogue, knave, felon, churl
  " **fictional:** Legree, Iago
  " **movie:** heavy
  " **myth.:** dragon, giant, ogre
  " **nemesis:** hero
Villon: (Fr.) poet, Francois
vimen: shoot
vin: wine
vina: instrument
vinaceous fruit: grape
Vinci's patron: Sforza
vincible: conquerable, beatable
vincit omnia   : veritas
vindication: apology
vine: creeper, odal, betel, wisteria, hop
  " **coil:** tendril
  " **comb. form:** viti
  " **covered with:** ivied, lianaed
  " **fruit bearing:** grape, cupseed
  " **parasite:** aphis
  " **twining:** bine
  " **woody:** smilax
vinegar: acid, eisel, alegar
  " **bottle:** cruet, castor
  " **change to:** acetify
  " **dregs:** mother
  " **pert. to:** acetic
  " **pickling:** marinade
  " **spice:** tarragon
vinegarroon: scorpion
vineyard: clos, cru
  " **protector:** Priapus
vinous: winy
vintage: yield, crop, choice,

model
vintner: merchant
" **assistant:** gourmet, taster
viol: gigue, rebec(k), sarinda
viola: alto, (de) gamba, violet, pansy
Viola's brother: Sebastian
violate: break, infract, rape, defoul, deseerate
" **trust:** betray
violation: sentence structure: anacoluthon
violent: acute, fiery, rabid, stormy, intense
" **anger:** fury
" **blow:** bash
" **contact:** collision, impact
violet: mauve, blaver, purple, flaver
" **blue:** indigo
" **perfume:** irone
" **root:** orrisroot
" **tip:** butterfly
violin: kit, fiddle
" **border:** purfling
" **bow:** arco; (knob) nut
" **city:** Cremona
" **forerunner:** rabab
" **part:** peg, hole, neck, string, scroll, eclisse
" **rare:** Amati, Strad, Guarnerius
" **small:** kit
" **stroke:** upbow
violin-shaped: waisted
violinist: (first) concertmaster
" **comic:** Benny, Jack
" **fabled:** Nero
" **famous:** Auer, Elman, Stern, Ricci, Kreisler,

Ysage, Menuhin, Perlman, Heifetz
V.I.P.: notable, very important person, bigshot, celebrity
viper: asp, adder, snake, fer-de-lance
" **genus:** echis
" **horned:** cerastes
vir: green
virelay: poem, verse
vireo: grasset, greenlet, red-eye, songbird
virgate: twiggy
Virgil: birthplace: Mantua
" **family name:** Maro
" **friend:** Maecenas
" **hero:** Aeneas
" **language:** Latin
" **queen:** Dido
" **work:** Aeneid, epic
virgin: new, pure, modest, chaste
" **queen:** Elizabeth
" **the:** Mary
" **unblemished:** camilla
" **vestal:** Rhea
virgin's-bower: clematis
Virgin Island: discoverer: Columbus
" **coin:** bit, franc, daler
Virgin Mary: flower: marigold
" **image:** Pieta
" **mother:** Anne
virginal: spinet, virgin, harpsi-chord, pure, maidenly
Virginia: (see special section)
" **aristocrats:** FFV
" **creeper:** ivy
" **dance:** reel
" **settlement:** Jamestown
" **signature:** R. Lee

Virgo: virgin, constellation
   " **star:** spica
virgularian: searod
viridian: pigment
viridity: youth, greenness
virl: ferrule
virtu: curio, rarity, bibelot, antique
virtue: merit, excellence, bounty, quality, chastity
   " **cardinal:** hope, faith, charity, justice, prudence, temperance
   " **paragon of:** saint
vis: force, power, rigor, visual, strength
   " **-a-vis:** sofa, seat, face-to-face, opposite
viscount: peer, deputy, sheriff
   " **heir of:** master
vise: clamp, dial
   " **part:** jaw
Vishnu: the Preserver
   " **bearer:** Garuda
   " **consort:** Sri, Lakshmi
   " **incarnation:** Rama, Krishna
   " **serpent:** Naga
visible: evident, obvious
   " **to naked eye:** macroscopic
Visigoth: Teuton
   " **King:** Alaric
vision: fancy, dream, image, sight
   " **comb. form:** opto
   " **defect:** myopia
   " **double:** diplopia
   " **illusory:** mirage
   " **instrument:** retina

   " **lacking:** purblind
   " **pert. to:** optical, visual, ocular
   " **scope:** scan
visionary: airy, laputan, fey, idealist
   " **pert. to:** Quixote, quixotic
visit: sojourn, stay, haunt, inspection
   " **kind of:** social, professional, official
   " **short:** call, drop by
visne: jury, hood, neighbor
vison: mink
Vistula River: Wisla
   " **tributary:** Bug, San
vita: life
Vita Nuova author: Dante
vital: basic, fatal, viable, essential
   " **fluid:** blood, sap, lymph
   " **organ:** liver, lung, heart
   " **principle:** soul
   " **statistics:** age, race, size, gender, measurements
vitalize: animate
vitals: viscera
vitellus: yolk
vitrics: glassware
vitrify: glaze, bake
vitrine: showcase
vitriol: sory, acid, caustic
vitta: ribbon, headband
vittle: food
vituline animal: calf
viva: cheer, acclaim, **voce:** orally
vivandier: sutler
vivarium: box, zoo, hothouse

vive: brisk, lively
" **-le:** roi
vixen: nag, fox, shrew, scold, woman
viz: namely, to-wit, videlict
vizard: visor, mask, guise
vizcacha: rodent
Vladimir, Illich Ulianov: Lenin
vocabulary: argot, slang, lexicon, words, diction
" **of a:** lexical
vocabulist: lexicographer
vocal: oral, vowel, unwritten, sung
" **chords:** larynx
" **composition:** song
" **solo:** (mus.) aria
vocalist: alto, basso, tenor, soprano, singer, coloratura
vocalization: melismatics
voe: inlet, bay, creek
vogie: vain, proud, merry
vogue: fad, ton, cut, mode, style
" **in:** prevailing, au courant (Fr.)
voice: say, vox, emit, wish, utter
" **box:** larynx
" **handicap:** lisp, stutter
" **loss:** aphonia, anaudia
" **loud:** foghorn, megalophonic
" **natural singing:** dipetto
" **part:** glottis
" **pert. to:** phonetic, vocal
" **practice:** solfeggio
" **principle:** cantus
" **quality:** timbre
" **quiet:** sotto

" **stop:** affricate
" **stress:** arsis
voiced: sonant, vibrant
" **stop:** media
voiceless: mum, mute, surd, flated, silent
" **sound sign:** cedilla
voices, for all: tutti
void: free, null, egest, empty, vacuum
" **of infinite space:** inane
voila: lo, behold
voile: ninon, fabric
voiture: carriage, wagon, auto
volary: cage, aviary
volcano: activity: belching, eruption
" **ash:** tuff
" **cinder:** scoria
" **crater:** maar
" **earth:** trass
" **kind:** active, dormant
" **matter:** aa, oo, tufa, lava
" **mud:** salse
" **opening:** fumarole, mouth, crater
" **slag:** scoria, cinder
" **steam:** stufa
" **well known:** Apo, Etna, Pelee, Shasta, Taal, Vesuvius, Fuji, Asama
vole: rodent, mouse, rat, craber
Volga: Rha
" **figure:** boatman
" **tributary:** Kama
volk: people, nation
volplane: coast, glide
Volsunga Saga: dragon: Fafnir

" **dwarf:** nibelung
" **hero:** Sigurd
" **king:** Atli
Voltaire: character: Pangloss
" **estate:** Ferney
" **novel:** Candide, Zadig
" **true name:** Arouet
volume: bulk, book, mass, cubage, strength
" **large:** tome
" **measure:** stereometer
" **of sound unit:** decibel
Volund's brother: Egil(l)
volunteer: offer, enlist, proffer
" **opposite of:** draftee
vomica: pus
vomit: spew, disgorge, reject
" **act of:** emesis
" **effort:** retch
voodoo: obi, beah, fetish, sorcerer
" **charm:** mojo
" **deity:** zombie
vorago: gulf, abyss
vortex: eddy, gyre, apex, whirl
votary: zealot, fan, nun, monk, devotee
vote: elect, assign, choice, grant, declare
" **counting/survey:** poll
" **group:** bloc
" **kind of:** straw, proxy, secret, write-in ballot, voice
" **of assent:** yea, aye, nod, placet
" **of dissent:** nay
" **receptacle:** situla(e)
" **right to:** suffrage, franchise
" **solicitation of:** lobby

voter: poller, balloter, constituent
" **body of:** electorate
" **illegal:** repeater, underage
voucher: chit, debenture, credential
voussoir: wedge, keystone
" **projection:** ear
voust: boast
vow: oath, promise, bind, wish, swear
" **by these:** nun, monk, witness, celibate, votary
" **dedicated by:** votive
vowel: vocal, letter
" **change sound:** umlaut
" **contraction:** crasis, diphthong, syneresis
" **omission:** aphesis
" **slurring:** elision
" **sound:** labial, palatal, dental
" **unaspirated:** lene
vox: voice
voyage: trip, journey, passage
" **act of:** asea
" **one who:** traveler, boatman, sailor, trapper
" **pleasure:** cruise
voyeur: peeping Tom
vraic: seaweed
vrouw: frau, frow, woman, housewife
vs.: versus
vug, vugh: hollow, cavity
Vulcan: (black)smith, Hephaestus
" **consort:** Venus, Maia
" **epithet:** Mulciber

" **son:** Cacus
" **workshop:** Etna
vulcanite: rubber, ebonite
vulcanize: cure
vulgar: randy, gross, crude, lewd, common, plebeian
Vulgate: author/translator: Jerome
vulnerable point: Achilles heel
Vulpecula: constellation, little fox
vulpine: foxy, clever, artful, cunning, alopecoid
vult: mien, aspect, expression
vulture: condor, urubu, arend, atrata, griph(e), lammergeier
" **food:** carrion
" **genus:** gyps
" **hawk like:** caracara
vum: vow

W

W: Ar.: waw
  " **in chemistry:** tungsten
  " **old English:** wen
waag: monkey, grivet
Wabash River city: Terre Haute
  " **tributary:** Tippecanoe
wabeno: shaman
wachna: cod
wad: cram, lump, pledget, dossil
  " **of paper money:** roll
Wadai Museum: Maba
wadding material: cotton, hemp, kapok
waddy: cane, club, beat, cowboy
wadi, wady: oasis, river, channel, ravine
wading bird: ibis
wadset: pawn, pledge
wafer: cracker, snap, disk
  " **container for:** pyx, pix
waff: gust, flap, odor, paltry

waffie: tramp, vagrant
wagang: death, departure
wage: hire, stipend, salary, utu, incur
  " **boost:** raise
  " **deduct from:** dock
  " **insurance:** chomage
  " **war:** levy
wagger: dog, pipit
waggery: joke, foolery, jest
waggly: unsteady
Wagner: Richard
  " **father-in-law:** Liszt
  " **wife:** Cosima
Wagnerian earth goddess: Erda
wagon: trailer, dray, cart, tumbrel
  " **ammunitions:** caisson
  " **baggage:** fourgon
  " **driver:** carter
  " **horse:** poler
  " **oriental:** araba
  " **police:** black maria,

paddy
" **prairie:** schooner
" **track:** rut
" **yoke:** inspan
wagoner: auriga
wagon-lit: sleeper
wagonload: fother
wagtail: lark, pipit, bird
wah: panda
wahine: wife, woman
wahoo: elm, peto, fish, non-sense
Wailing Wall chore: prayer, lamentation
" **site:** Jerusalem
wain: fetch, cart, convey, wagon
wainscot: lining, partition, ceiling
waist: blouse, bodice
" **circumference:** girth
" **of dress:** taille
waistcoat: benjy, gilet, fecket, jerkin, oest
" **unlined:** singlet
waiting line: queue, cue
waka: canoe
Wakashan: Nootka
Walden author: Thoreau
Waldensian: Leonist
Wales: Cymru
" **city:** Swansea
" **dog:** corgi
" **emblem:** leek
" **musical   instrument:** pibcorn
" **patron saint:** David
" **poet:** Thomas
" **poet. name:** Cambria
walk: tramp, plod, tread, hike, hoof, alley, stoa

" **a beat:** patrol
" **about:** ambulate
" **beach:** esplanade
" **covered:** arcade, stoa
" **inability:** abasia
" **kind of:** waddle, limp, strut
" **on stilts:** trampolio
" **to and fro:** pace
walk-out: strike
walk out on: desert, abandon
walking: ambulant, gradient
" **adapted for:** gressorial
" **like a bear:** plantigrade
" **meter:** pedometer
" **papers:** dismissal
" **shoes:** balmoral
" **stick:** cane, malaga, staff
wall: parapet, barrier
" **band:** cordon
" **border:** dado
" **bracket:** sconce
" **dividing:** septum
" **-ed town:** burg
" **end of:** anta
" **eyed fish:** pike, dory
" **garden:** haha
" **lizard:** gecko
" **opening:** bay, scuttle
" **pert. to:** mural
" **sea:** mole, pier
walla(h): owner, fellow, servant, agent
wallaba tree: apa
wallaby: kangaroo
wallflower: heartsease
wallowish: flat, insipid
wallpaper measure: bolt
wally: fine, sturdy, robust, first-rate

walnut: bannut
  " **skin:** zest
Walpurgis Night revelers: witches
walrus: seal, seacow, tusker
  " **herd:** pod
  " **male:** bull
  " **order:** bruta
  " **tooth:** tusk
walt: unsteady
waltz king: Strauss
wambly: shaky, faint
wame: belly
wampish: swing, fluctuate
wamus: jacket, cardigan, doublet
wand: scepter, baton, pointer
  " **shaped like a:** virgate
wanderer: vag, Arab, nomad, truant, pilgrim, waif
  " **religious:** palmer
wandering: vagrant, erratic, odyssey
  " **aimlessly:** gad, stray, traipse
  " **beggar:** rogue
  " **student/minstrel:** goliard
  " **tribe:** gypsy
wandering Jew: ivy, plant, zebrina
Wandering Jew author: Sue
wanderoo: monkey, langur, macaque
wandle: lithe, agile, supple
wane: ebb, lack, abate, peter, dwindle
  " **opposed to:** wax
wang: ruler, prince, king
wanga: spell, voodoo, charm
wanhap: mishap, misfortune

wanigan: ark
wanion: curse, plague
wanted man: outlaw, desperado, escapee
wanton: lewd, unchaste, tart
  " **destroyer:** vandal
wantwit: fool
wanty: rope, tie, girth
wapiti: deer, elk, stag
war: strife, conflict
  " **acquisitions:** spoils
  " **agreement:** truce, cartel
  " **and Peace: author:** Tolstoi
  " " **heroine:** Natasha
  " **cause:** casus belli
  " **dance:** pyrrhic
  " **games:** maneuvers
  " **god:** Mars, Ares, Irra, Tyr
  " **holy:** crusade, johad
  " **pert. to:** martial
War and Peace author: Tolstoi, Tolstoy
warbird: tanager, aviator
warbler: songster, trochilus, beccafico, pipit, wren, thrush
ward: part of a: precinct
  " **politician:** heeler
  " **pert. to:** pupillary
  " **off:** fend, avert
wardship: custody
warehouse: depot, bodega, etape
  " **candles:** chandlery
  " **fee:** storage
  " **platform:** pallet
  " **weapons:** arsenal
war hawk: jingo
warhead: missile: payload

war-horse: leader, charger, partisan, steed
warkloom: tool, utensil
warm: heat, ardent
" **baths/springs:** thermae
" **compress:** stupe
warmonger: militarist, jingo
warmth: zeal, ardor, elan
" **increasing:** calescent
" **pert. to:** thermal
warning: alarm, omen, knell, caveat
" **in law:** caveat
" **signal:** hiss, siren, tocsin
warp: abb, hit, bias, expel, deform, pervert
" **thread for loom:** stamen
warragal: horse, dingo
warrant: plevin, voucher, order
" **convict's:** mittimus
" **officer:** bosun
warren: hutch, rabbitry, tenement
warrior: soldier, jingo, singh, toa, impi
" **arena:** gladiator
" **female:** Amazon
" **Trojan:** Hector, Agenor
warship: cruiser, destroyer, frigate, flattop
" **boat on:** dinghy, launch
" **deck, lowest:** orlop
" **fleet of:** armada
" **pert. to:** naval
" **prison:** brig
" **tower:** turret
warts, covered with: verrucose
wash: silt, clean, drift, scour, pan

" **away:** purge, erode
" **out:** elute, flush, fail
" **up:** finish, discard
washbowl, church: lavabo
wase: wisp, bundle, pad
washer: clove, rove
washing: lavation, ablution
" **board:** dolly
" **chemical:** eluate
" **out (organ):** lavage
Washington, D.C.: capital
" **art gallery:** Freer, Cocoran, Mellon, National
" **educator:** Booker T.
" **original   planner:** L'Enfant
" **Moscow   telephone:** hotline
Washington (state): (see special section)
" **fort:** Lewis
" **volcano:** Rainier
" **wind:** chinook
wasp: yellow jacket, hornet, digger
" **genus of:** sphex
" **nest:** vespiary
wassail: orgy, lark, revel, drink, carouse
Wasserman: test subject: syphillis
waste: ruin, leftover, ocean, fritter
" **allowance:** tret
" **away:** rot, decay, emaciate
" **drain:** sewer
" **glass:** cullet
" **metal:** slag, dross
" **product:** run-off
wasting: tabes, cachexia

wat: temple
watch: tend, sentry, eye, vigil, timepiece
  " **chain:** fob
  " **covering:** crystal
  " **duty:** vigil, patrol
  " **maker:** horologist
  " **men (myth.):** Argus, Talos, Heimdall
  " **part:** dial, detent, stud, stem, pallet
  " **sl.:** ticker
  " **time:** horologe
watchdog: guardian
  " **Hel's:** Garm(r)
  " **underworld:** Cerberus
watchtower: garret, beacon, bantayan
watchworks: movement
  " **arrangement:** caliper
water: aqua, dilute, irrigate
  " **baptismal:** laver
  " **bearer, astonomy:** Aquarius
  " **carrier bird:** albatross
  " **channel:** flume, sluice, gully
  " **chestnut:** ling, caltrap
  " **clock:** clepsydra
  " **comb. form:** hydr(o)
  " **conduit:** aqueduct
  " **corral:** crawl
  " **cress:** potherb, mustard
  " **excursion:** cruise
  " **fairy:** nix
  " **gum:** tupelo
  " **hen:** coot
  " **ice:** sherbet
  " **jug:** ewer, olla
  " **nymph:** naiad, oceanid
  " **of:** aqueous

  " **raising device:** noria, tabut
  " **science of:** hydrology
  " **snake:** moccasin
  " **source, power:** white coal
  " **sports:** aquatics
  " **spring:** lymph
  " **storage:** tank, reservoir, cistern
  " **tube:** hose
  " **vessel:** lota
  " **without:** dry, arid, parched
watercress: brooklime
watered: moire
waterfowl: loon, diver
Watergate judge: Sirica
watertight box: caisson, cofferdam
waters: primeval: Apsu
waterwheel: noria, sakia
watery: thin, serous, soggy
  " **discharge:** rheum
  " **grave:** sea
wattle: flog, beat, twig, cooba, fence, acacia, lappet
wawl, waul: squall, howl
waugh: stale, weak, insipid
Waugh, novelist: Evelyn
wave: flap, flutter, surf, crimp, marcel
  " **comb. form:** ondo
  " **large:** swell, roller, decuman
  " **little:** ripple
  " **tidal:** bore, eagre
  " **to and fro:** wag, flap
  " **top of:** crest, whitecap
wavering sound: tremolo
wax: grow, paraffin, cere

" **artist:** Tussaud
" **comb. form:** cer(o)
" **covered with:** cerated
" **pert. to:** ceral
" **match:** vesta
" **myrtle:** bayberry
" **source:** carnauba
" **used on skis:** klister
waxbill: astrild
waxwing: cedarbird
waxy substance: cutin, sub-erin
way: mode, street, method, habit, cost
" **give:** yield
" **of walking/running:** gait
" **station town:** whistle stop
" **open:** pioneer
" **out:** egress
waybill: manifest
waymark: ahu, arrow, milestone
weaken: dilute, sap, flag
" **morally:** vitiate
" **spirit:** demoralize
weakfish: acoupa, totuava
weakling: sissy, softie, puler
weakness: defect, fetish, liking, frailty
" **bodily/organic:** atony
" **moral:** frailty
weal: mark, ridge, choice, wealth, pomp, stripe
wealth: dhan, good, assets, opulence
" **comb. form:** pluto
" **god:** Plutus
" **income from:** usance
" **person of:** nabob, pluto-

crat, Midas, Croesus
weanie: baby
weaponry: ordnance
weapons, sl.: hardware
wearisome: boring, tedious, toilsome
" **grow:** pall, bore
Weary Willie: tramp, shirker, feather bedder
weasand: windpipe, trachea, esophagus
weasel: stoat, ermine, sable, ferret, cane, vare
" **cat:** linsang
" **-like:** musteline
weather: sky, season, survive
" **indicator:** barometer
" **item:** moisture, temperature
" **satellite:** Tiros
" **study:** meteorology
weathercock: fane, vane
weaver's tool: loom, sley, reed
weaverbird: taha, baya
weaving: frame: loom, cylinder
" **goddess:** Ergane
" **material:** yarn, fiber, reed, wicker
web: net(work), tissue, snare
" **feather's:** vexillum
" **footed/toed:** palmate
" **like membrane:** tela
" **pert. to:** retiary
webbing: binding
Weber opera: Oberon
wedding: splice, nuptials
" **canopy:** chupa, huppah
" **proclamation:** banns
wedge: cotter, key, jam, shim,

cleat
" **shaped:** cuneiform, sphenoid
Wednesday: god: Odin
" **source:** Woden
" **special:** Ash
weed: band, loco, milk, cockle, rid, dock, dandelion
" **killer:** herbicide
" **mourning:** crape, weeder
" **noxious:** tare
" **poison(ous):** hemlock, darnel, loco
" **roadside:** dogfennel
" **sl.:** cigar, tobacco
" **tool:** hoe, spud
week: hebdomad
weekday: feria
weeks: (two) fortnight
weel: pit, cave
ween: hope, fancy, expect, think
weeping goddess: Niobe
" **philosopher:** Heraclitus
weet: wet, wit, know
weevil: beetle, borer, boll, kis, lota
" **larva:** grugru
" **wing cover:** shard
weft: film, yarn, shoot, web
weighing machine: scale, trone, steelyard
weight: load, stress, burden, value
" **allowance:** tret, tare
" **balloon's/stabilizer:** ballast
" **diamond:** carat
" **for wool:** tod
" **leaden:** plumb
" **lifting machine:** crane

" **pert. to:** baric
" **science:** metrology
" **sl.:** heft
weir: dam, bank, levee, garth, barrier
wejack: weasel, pekan
weka: rail, bird
welding: gas: acetylene
" **material:** solder, thermït
welfare: sele, weal, prosperity
" **goddess:** Salus
welkin: sky, heaven
well: hale, fit, spring, expertly
" **bred:** genteel
" **comb. form:** bene
" **feeling:** euphoria
" **grounded:** informed
" **lining:** stean, steen
" **made:** affabrous
" **nigh:** almost, nearly
" **pit:** sump
" **prefix:** eu
" **to-do (sl.):** loaded
" **versed:** erudite
" **worn:** overused, trite
Welland: river, city, canal
wellaway: alas, regret, woe
wellhead: spring, fountain, source
Wellington's soubriquet: Old Nosy, Ironduke
wellspring: fountainhead
Welsh, Welshman: (see **Wales**) Celt(ic), Cambrian, Taffy
" **cheese dish:** rabbit, rarebit
" **dog:** corgi
" **god of sea:** Dylan
" **onion:** cibol
" **sl.:** cheat, swindle
wem: scar, spot, flaw, stain

wen: cyst, mole, tumor, talpa
Wend: Sorb, Slav
Wendy's brother: Peter
  "   **dog:** Nana
wenzel: jack, knave
werewolf: loup-garou
wergild: cro, eric
Wesley (John), follower: Methodist
Wessex King: Ini, Ine
West: frontier, Occident
West Indies: bird: tody, limpkin, courlan
  "   **coin:** pistareen
  "   **fish:** pega, testar, bacalao
  "   **lizard:** arbalo, galliwasp
  "   **magic:** obi
  "   **music:** calypso
  "   **patois:** gumbo
  "   **pert. to:** Antillean
  "   **shrub:** anil, cascarilla
  "   **tree:** calaba, balata, bonace
  "   **"white man":** buckra
  "   **volcano:** Pelee
West Point: island: Iona
  "   **mascot:** mule
  "   **student:** cadet, plebe
West Virginia: (see special section)
Western treaty alliance: NATO
Westminster: clock: Big Ben
  "   **landmark:** Abbey
  "   **rite:** coronation
  "   **street:** Whitehall
West wind: zephyr
  "   **of the:** favonian
wet: all (sl.): wrong, mistaken
  "   **blanket:** killjoy, spoilsport
  "   **comb. form:** hygro
  "   **flax:** ret
  "   **plaster painting:** fresco
  "   **-one's whistle:** drink, imbibe
weta: insect
wetback: peon, bracero
  "   **nationality:** Mexican
wetbird: chaffinch
whale: thrash, whip, cetacean, finback
  "   **Arctic/tusked:** narwhal
  "   **biggest:** blue
  "   **constellation:** Cetus
  "   **cry:** fall
  "   **dolphin:** orca
  "   **fat:** blubber
  "   **female:** cow
  "   **food:** brit
  "   **male:** bull
  "   **Melville's:** Moby Dick
  "   **pert. to:** cetic
  "   **school of:** gam, pod
  "   **skin:** muktuk
  "   **sound:** bark, squeal, mew, whine
  "   **spear:** harpoon
  "   **sperm:** cachalot
  "   **tail part:** fluke
  "   **young:** calf
whaling: huge, whopping
  "   **cask:** rier, cardel
  "   **profit:** lay
  "   **ship:** whaler, Pequod
whammy: jinx, evil eye
whample: blow, stroke
whangee: bamboo, cane
wharf: dock, pier, quai, quay
  "   **fish:** cunner
  "   **space:** quayage

"   **worker:** stevedore
whatnot: etagere, cabinet
whaup: fuss, outcry
wheal: mark, stripe, postule
wheat: durum, corn, cereal, spelt
"   **beer:** weiss
"   **cracked/hulled:** groats
"   **duck:** widgeon, baldpate
"   **ground:** flour, meal
"   **louse:** aphid
"   **meal:** semolina
"   **smut:** bunt, colbrand
wheatbird: lark
wheatear: bird, chickell, gorsehatch
wheel: rotate, pulley, pivot, helm
"   **center of:** hub, nave
"   **horse:** poler
"   **like:** trochal
"   **little:** caster
"   **part:** hub, axle, spoke, rim, hob, cam, felly, tire
"   **shaped:** rotate, rotiform
"   **spindle:** axle, arbor
"   **tooth:** sprocket
"   **water:** noria
wheezy breather: asthmatic
whelk: acne, snail, pimple
whemmel: upset, tumble, confusion
when: while, whereas, moment, time, as
where: whither
whereas: while, since
wherefrom: whence
whereness: ubiety
wherret: hit, slap, box
wherry: boat, scull, vehicle, barge

whether: if
whewl: cry, whine, howl
whey of milk: serum
which: who, that, whom
which was to be shown: QED
whicker: neigh, whinny
whid: fib, lie, frisk, wold
whiffet: dog, puff
whig: jog, whey, beverage
Whig, opposed to: Tory
"   **poet:** Og, Shadwell
while: as, yet, until, albeit, occupy
whilly: gall, cajole
whilom: formerly, once, erst
whinchat: gorsechat
whinnock: whimper
whinyard sword
whip: whale, flay, lash, flog, scourge, flail
"   **Biblical:** scorpion
"   **leather:** knout, kurbash
"   **riding:** crop, quirt
whipcord: catgut
whippersnapper: upstart, squirt
whippoorwill: goatsucker
"   **feathers:** vibrissa
whirlbone: patella, kneepan
whirling man: dervish
"   **on toes:** pirouette
"   **wind:** cyclone, tornado
whirlpool: eddy, vortex, maelstrom
whirlwind: oe, maelstrom, cyclone
whisht: hush, silence
whiskers: beard, sideburns
"   **cat's:** vibrissa
"   **chin:** goatee

" **side:** chops, mutton

whiskey: rye, corn, poteen, rotgut, moonshine, bus-thead

" **maker:** distiller

" **punch:** facer

whiskin: bowl

whist: game, mute, cards, hush

" **declaration:** misere

" **dummy:** mort

" **hand:** tenace

whistle: hiss, pipe, toot, siren

" **-duck:** goldeneye

" **-pig:** woodchuck

" **-wing:** goldeneye

whit: jot, atom, iota, speck, doit

white: snowy, ashen, pale

" **alkali:** soda ash

" **animal:** albino

" **ant:** anai, termite

" **cedar:** arborvitae

" **cliffs' site:** Dover

" **clouds:** cerri

" **comb. form:** leuk(o)

" **crow:** vulture

" **eye:** songbird

" **feather:** fear, cowardice

" **fish:** atinga, cisco, beluga

" **flag:** surrender

" **Friar:** Alsatian, Carmelite

" **gentian:** feverroot

" **gum:** eucalyptus

" **horse nettle:** trompillo

" **House designer:** Hoban

" **jade:** alabaster

" **lead:** ceruse

" **magic:** theurgy

" **man:** buckra

" **Monk:** Cistercian

" **mule:** gin, moonshine

" **nun:** smew

" **plantain:** pussytoes

" **poplar:** aspen, abele

" **pudding:** sausage

" **Rose house:** York

" **sl.:** honest, fair

" **Sunday:** Whitsunday

" **turning:** albescant

" **walnut:** syxamore

" **whale:** beluga

whitebelly: grouse, pigeon

whiteboy: pet, favorite

whitefish: cisco

whitewash: defeat, parget, blanch

whiteweed: daisy

whitewing: sail, sweeper

whiting: fish, chalk

whitlow: sore, felon

whitster: bleacher

whitten: rowan

Whitman, poet: Walt(er)

Whitney, cotton gin inventor: Eli

Whitsunday: pentecost

Whitsuntide: pinkster

whittling refuse: shavings

who: (L) quo, (Ger.) Wer, (Sc.) wha

who goes there: challenge, qui va la

whole: intact, entire, uncut, toto

" **comb. form:** holo

" **number:** integer

wholesale: gross

" **opposed to:** retail

wholly: quite, algates

" **comb. form:** toto

whooper: swan
whorl: spire
   " **fingerprint:** ridge
whyo: robber, footpad
wicked city: Babylon, Sodom, Gomorrah
wicker: twig, withe, osier
   " **basket:** pannier, hamper, core
   " **cradle:** bassinet
   " **hut:** jacal
wickiup: shelter, hut
widdrim: fury, madness, confusion
widdy: noose, widow, halter, rope
widespread: prevalent
   " **disease:** epidemic
   " **fear:** panic
widgeon: duck, goose, simpleton
   " **genus:** mareca
widow: relict, widdy
   " **in cards:** skat
   " **monkey:** titi
   " **right:** dower
   " **suicide:** suttee
widowhood: viduage
wife: spouse, helpmate
   " **bequest to:** dos
   " **common-law:** mistress
   " **dowry of:** dot
   " **knight's:** dame
   " **pert. to:** uxorial
wig: gizz, caxon, jasey, caxon, peruke, spencer
   " **repair:** careen
wigwag: signal
wild: primitive, licentious, stormy, gaga, savage, fierce
   " **apple:** crab, creeper

   " **ass:** onager
   " **banana:** pawpaw
   " **Bill:** Hickok
   " **carrot:** hilltrot
   " **cattle:** banteng
   " **cry:** evoe, shriek, screech
   " **dog:** dingo
   " **Duck: author:** Ibsen
   " **goat:** ibex
   " **goose:** greylag, Jacobite
   " **guess:** stab
   " **hog:** boar
   " **horse:** mustang
   " **life:** game
   " **plum:** sloe
   " **revelry:** orgy
   " **sage:** claru
   " **state of being:** ferity
wildebeast: gnu
wildfowl: quail, goose, duck, partridge
   " **flight:** skein
wildlife preserve: sanctuary, wetland
Wilkes Island: Ashi
will: volition, desire, power
   " **addition to:** codicil
   " **exercise of the:** volition
   " **handwritten:** holograph
   " **having made a:** testate
   " **having no:** intestate
   " **power, loss of:** abulia
Willard, boxing champion: Jess
   " **temperance leader:** Frances
William II's home: Doorn
William Tell: canton: Uri
   " **composer:** Rossini
   " **hero:** Egil

William the Conqueror: burial place: Caen
willies: creeps, jitters
Willkie, presidential candidate: Wendell
" **dream of:** one world
willow: osier, sallow, salix, iva, itea
" **basket:** prickle
" **herb:** rosebay
" **of the:** salicaceous
" **shoot:** wand
" **wren:** chiffchaff
willy: trap, basket, willow
Wilson's thrush: veery
Wimbledon event: tennis
" **location:** England
wimick: cry
wimple: fold, turn, veil, ripple
win: pot, earn, attain, defeat, entice
" **all tricks:** slam, thirteen
" **back:** recover
" **over:** persuade
wince: crab, reel, start, recoil
Winchester: rifle
wind: gale, hint, blast, duster
" **away from:** alee
" **comb. form:** anemo
" **dry:** foehn
" **east:** eurus
" **equatorial:** trade
" **god:** Adda, Vayu, Eolus
" **Indian Ocean:** monsoon
" **myth.:** Sansar
" **north:** boreas, aquilo
" **science of:** anemology
" **side away from:** lee
" **side toward:** weather
" **of the:** salicaceous
" **shoot:** wand

" **wren:** chiffchaff
willy: trap, basket, willow
Wilson's thrush: veery
Wimbledon event: tennis
" **location:** England
wimick: cry
wimple: fold, turn, veil, ripple
win: pot, earn, attain, defeat, entice
" **all tricks:** slam, thirteen
" **back:** recover
" **over:** persuade
wince: crab, reel, start, recoil
Winchester: rifle
wind: gale, hint, blast, duster
" **away from:** alee
" **comb. form:** anemo
" **dry:** foehn
" **east:** eurus
" **equatorial:** trade
" **god:** Adda, Vayu, Eolus
" **Indian Ocean:** monsoon
" **myth.:** Sansar
" **north:** boreas, aquilo
" **science of:** anemology
" **side away from:** lee
" **side toward:** weather
" **south:** auster
" **warm:** foehn
" **west:** zephyr(us), favonian
winder pear: warden
windflower: anemone
winding staircase: caracole
windmill fighter: (Don) Quixote
" **part:** vane
" **pump:** gin
window: bay: oriel
" **dressing:** trim
" **frame:** casement

`"` **part:** pane, sill, sash, lintel, jamb(e), grill(e), grating
`"` **pert. to:** fenestral
`"` **trellised:** lattice
Windward Island: Grenda
Windy City: Chicago
wine: age of: vintage
`"` **bottle:** decanter, magnum
`"` **comb. form:** bini, oeno
`"` **distillate:** brandy, cognac
`"` **dry:** sec, brut
`"` **flavor:** mull
`"` **fragrance:** bouquet
`"` **god:** Bacchus
`"` **of:** vinous, vinic
`"` **Rhine:** hock, moselle
`"` **sauterne:** yquem
`"` **study of:** oenology
wine and dine: fete
wineskin: askos
wing: pinna, pennon
`"` **comb. form:** ptero
`"` **cover:** elytrum, shard
`"` **feather:** pinion
`"` **in anatomy:** ala
`"` **length:** span
`"` **of building:** ell, alette, annex
`"` **pert. to:** alar
`"` **shaped:** alar(y), aliform
`"` **without:** apteral, apterous
`"` `"` **bird:** emu, kiwi, apteryx
winged: alate, pennate, feathered, flew, alar
`"` **being:** angel, seraph(im), amor
`"` **figure:** Icarus

`"` **goddess:** Nike
`"` **fruit:** samara
`"` **hat:** petasos
`"` **hat/sandals**
`"` **wearer:** Mercury, Hermes
`"` **heraldry:** aile
`"` **horse:** Pegasus
`"` **monster: myth:** harpy
`"` **staff:** caduceus
`"` **two:** dipteral
`"` **without:** apteral
wingless locust: weta
winks, forty: nap, doze
winner: victor, reaper
`"` **longshot/surprise:** sleeper
Winnie the Pooh: author: Milne
`"` **character:** Roo, Owl, Piglet, Tigger
winning: lottery combination: tern
`"` **winnings: sl.:** velvet
winter: season, hibernate
`"` **cap:** tuque
`"` **pert. to:** hiemal, brumal, hibernal
`"` **solstice festival:** saturnalia
winterbloom: azalea
wintergreen: pipsissewa
winy: drunken
wire: brush: card
`"` **coil/spiral:** spring
`"` **cutting tool:** pliers
`"` **light bulb:** filament
`"` **measure:** mil, stone
wirepuller: puppeteer
wirework: filagree
wireworm: millipede

wis: deem, know, suppose

Wisconsin: (see special section)
  "   **state animal:** badger
  "   **state fish:** musky

wisdom: sapience, learning, lore
  "   **god of:** Nebo, Ganesa
  "   **goddess of:** Minerva
  "   **symbol of:** owl
  "   **universal:** pansophy

wisdom tooth: molar

wise: informed, sage, deep, erudite
  "   **adviser:** mentor
  "   **and pithy:** gnomic
  "   **infinitely:** omniscient
  "   **men, Bib.:** magi
  "   **saying:** saw, adage, maxim
  "   **sl.:** fresh, savvy

wiseacre: dunce, wisenheimer, prophet

wish: mood of expression: optative

wishbone: furculum

wisht: dismal, eerie, uncanny

wishy-washy: pale, weak, watery, trashy

wist: know

wistaria: fuji, bush, violet

wit: wag, mind, sense, irony
  "   **lively:** esprit (Fr.)
  "   **lowest form of:** pun
  "   **sting of:** barb

witch: baba, wizard, hex, sorceress, siren, hellcat, hag
  "   **cat:** grimalkin
  "   **city:** Salem
  "   **folklore:** Lilith
  "   **Homer's:** Circe
  "   **male:** warlock
  "   **Shakespeare's:** Duessa

witchcraft: sorcery, sortilege, cunning
  "   **goddess:** Hecate, Obeah

witches' broom: hexenbesen

witch hazel: tree, astringent, hornbeam

with: (It.) con, (Lat.) cum, (Ger.) mit, (Fr.) avec, near, along, among
  "   **cruel tendencies:** sadistic
  "   **force:** (mus.) con brio
  "   **prefix:** col, com, cyn, pro, syn

withering away: tabescent

within: inside, inner, ben
  "   **comb. form:** ent(o), eso
  "   **prefix:** intra

without: lacking, bereft, sans, sine
  "   **comb. form:** ecto
  "   **feet:** apod
  "   **life:** azoic
  "   **prefix:** se, ect
  "   **sound:** mute, silent
  "   **this:** sine hoc

witness: attest, testify, see, onlooker
  "   **perjured:** strawman
  "   **place in court:** stand

Witt's planetoid: Eros

witticism: gag, quip, pun, (bon) mot

wittol: fool, cuckold

witty: jocose, droll, salty
  "   **exchange:** repartee
  "   **poem:** epigram
  "   **reply:** sally, retort

wivern: dragon
wizard of Menlo: Edison
woad: dye, pastel, mustard
Woden: Odin, Othin
woe: tale of: jeremiad, lamentation
wolaba: kangaroo
wold: lea, plain, (Ger.) woods
wolf: lupus, philanderer
  " **female:** bitch
  " **male:** dog
  " **pert. to:** lupine
  " **young:** whelp
Wolfe, fiction detective: Nero
wolfhound: borzoi, alan
wolfsbane: aconite, monkshood
Wolsey's brithplace: Ipswich
wolverine: carcajou
  " **genus:** gulo
woman: bad-tempered: shrew, bitch, vixen
  " **beautiful:** belle, siren, Venus
  " **Brit. sl.:** bird
  " **chaste:** virgin, vestal
  " **childless:** nullifara
  " **comb. form:** gyn
  " **domineering:** battle-ax
  " **dowdy:** frump
  " **fairest:** Helen
  " **graceful:** sylph
  " **hater:** misogynist
  " **head and shoulder covering:** nubia
  " **homosexual:** Lesbian
  " **killing:** femicide
  " **old, unmarried:** spinster
  " **origin of:** rib
  " **pert.:** minx, hussy, tart

  " **popular:** belle
  " **repulsive:** Gorgon
  " **riding costume:** habit, Joseph
  " **shameless:** Jezebel
  " **sl.:** skirt, broad, tit, babe
  " **spiteful:** cat
  " **spy:** Mata Hari
  " **work of a:** distaff
wombat: badger, marsupial
won: win, live, dwell, abide
wonder boy: prodigy
wonder of the world: Pharos, Colossus, pyramids
wong: field, meadow
wonky: off, shaky, tottering
wood: grove, forest, lumber
  " **alcohol:** methanol
  " **anemone:** thimbleweed
  " **bits:** kindling
  " **block:** nog, sprag
  " **charred:** bray
  " **comb. form:** lign(o), xyl(o), hyl(o), ligni
  " **cutter:** ripsaw
  " **eater:** termite, anay
  " **flat piece:** splat
  " **groove:** chamfer
  " **hard:** locust, hickory, ebony, mahogany
  " **inlaid:** buhl
  " **knot:** knar
  " **layer:** veneer
  " **light:** balsa
  " **measure:** cord, foot
  " **of:** ligneous, xyloid
  " **pussy:** skunk
  " **shoe:** clog, sabot, patten
  " **stork:** ibis
  " **strip:** slat, batten
woodbine: honeysuckle, ivy

woodchuck: marmot, groundhog

wooded: sylvan
" **area:** weald, boondocks
" **hill:** holt

wooden: stiff, dull, stolid
" **bench:** settle
" **bowl:** kitty, mazer
" **bucket:** cannikin
" **limb:** peg leg
" **shoe:** clog, geta, sabot

woodland: burned: brulee
" **clearing:** glade
" **deity:** Pan, faun, satyr, Silenus, Diana
" **landscape:** boscage

woodpecker: flicker, sapsucker, popinjay
" **genus:** yunx, picus
" **type:** hairy, imperial, pileated

woods: forest
" **love of:** nemophily
" **pert. to:** nemoral, sylvan

woody: bosky, xyloid, ligneous
" **fiber:** hemp, xylem, bast

woof: cloth, fabric, filling, abb

wool: fleece, angora, alpaca, pile
" **bearing:** laniferous
" **blemish:** mote
" **cluster:** nep
" **comb. form:** lani
" **covered with:** lanate, floccose
" **dryer:** fugal
" **fiber:** noil, sliver, pile
" **goat's:** cashmere
" **lock of:** tag
" **measure:** heer

" **particles:** down
" **sheep:** merino
" **spinning machine:** throstle
" **twisted:** rove
" **weight:** tod

woolen cloth: worsted, jersey, tartan, melton, doeskin

woolfell: pelt

woolly haired people: Ulotrichi

word: pledge, remark, parole, talk
" **action:** verb
" **appropirate:** mot juste
" **battle:** logomachy
" **change in a:** metaplasm
" **final:** amen, ultimatum
" **four-letter:** tetragram
" **hard to pronounce:** jawbreaker
" **long, sl.:** mouthful
" **of mouth:** oral
" **of opposite meaning:** antonym
" **of similar meaning:** synonym
" **same pronunciation, different meaning:** homonym, homophone
" **same spelling, different meaning:** homograph, heteronym
" **symbol:** logogram

word-for-word: verbatim, literally, exactly

Word of God: Logos

word puzzle: rebus, charade, acrostic, crossword, anagram

wordy: prolix, verbose

work: job, labor, effort
" **amount of:** load
" **at:** ply:
" **avoid:** shirk
" **bag:** kit
" **book:** manual
" **box:** etui, (tool) kit
" **hard:** toil, sweat
" **life:** career
" **of wonder:** miracle
" **pants:** levis
" **suitable:** metier
" **trainee:** apprentice
worker: employe(e), laborer
" **agricultural:** farmer, Okie
" **coal mine:** collier
" **farm:** hand, peon
" **skilled:** artisan, craftsman
" **transient:** floater, hobo
" **white collar:** clerk
works: oeuvres
world: earth, cosmos, universe, realm
" **bearer of the:** Atlas
" **out of this:** outre
" **pert. to:** terrestrial, temporal, mundane
" **wide:** global, universal, ecumenic
worm: ess, nematode, wretch, grub, bob
" **bloodsucking:** leech
" **comb. form:** vermi
" **feeler of a:** palp(us)
" **flat:** trematode, fluke
" **genus:** nereis
" **larva:** maggot, caterpillar
" **out:** extract
" **round:** ascarid

" **sand:** nemertean
" **sea:** sao
" **shaped:** vermiform
worn: tattered, shabby, jaded
" **by friction:** attrite
" **clothes:** rags
" **out:** spent, exhausted, seedy
worricow: devil, bugaboo
worse: pejority
worship: comb. form: latry
" **of all gods:** pantheism
" **of idols:** idolism
" **of saints:** hagiolatry
" **of stars:** sabaism
" **pert. to:** liturgic
" **system of:** cult, fetish
wort: herb, fleabane
worth: price, value, merit
" **having:** asset, desirable
" **of little:** trifle
worthless: fellow: bum, idler
" **ideas:** bilge
" **scrap:** ort
" **thing:** tripe, chip
wound: gore, sting, harm, trauma
" **in heraldry:** vuln
woven: double: two-ply
" **with raised design:** broche
wowf: wild, crazed
wowser: prude
wrap: cover, swathe, pelisse
" **around:** loincloth, sarong
" **in burial cloth:** cere
" **snugly:** tuck
" **up:** enfold, envelop
wrapper: fardel, galabeah
wrasse: cunner, fishes, ballan

wreath: lei, garland, anadem
  " **bridal:** spirea
  " **heraldry:** torse
  " **victor's:** laurel, crown
wreckage: flotsam, jetsam
wrestling: hold: scissors, (head)lock, (half) nelson
  " **oriental:** sumo
  " **score:** fall
  " **throw:** hipe
Wright, airplane inventor: Orville, Wilbur
wrinkled: rugate, crepey
  " **without:** erugate, smooth
wristbone: carpal(e), trapezoid
writ: warrant, process, document, breve
  " **of execution:** outre
  " **to serve in court:** subpoena, summons, venire
writer: author, scribe, amanuensis
  " **inferior:** hack
  " **play:** dramatist
  " **verse:** poet, rhymer
writing: comb. form: log(ue)
  " **mark:** character
  " **pretentious:** kitsch

  " **secret:** code, cipher
  " **senseless:** balderdash
  " **sentimental:** slush
writings: literature
  " **collection of:** papers
  " **unpublished:** remains
wrong: evil, abuse, incorrect, erroneous
  " **act:** misdeed
  " **civil:** tort
  " **name:** misnomer
  " **prefix:** mis, mal
wryneck: loxia, woodpecker, (snake)bird, torticollis
  " **genus:** jynx
Wurttemberg: city: Ulm, Stuttgart
  " **measure:** imi
  " **river:** Danube
Wuthering Heights author: Bronte
Wycliffe disciple: Hus(s), Lollard
wynd: haw, alley, court, lane, close
Wyoming: (see special section)
  " **cavern:** Shoshone
  " **mountain:** Teton, Moran
wyvern: dragon

X

X: ten, mark, signature
" **Greek:** xi
" **latter:** ex
" **marker, usually:** illiterate
" **marks the-:** spot
" **shaped:** ex
Xanadu's river: Alph
xanthic: yellow
Xanthippe: husband: Socrates
" **prototype:** nagger, shrew, termagant, virago
xanthous: Mongolian, yellow
Xavier, Sp. Jesuit, saint: Francis
Xe: in chemistry: xenon
xebec: ship, vessel, boat
" **common users:** corsairs
xema: gull
xenagogue: guide
xenagogy: guidebook
xenium: gift, present
xeno: guest

" **as prefix:** strange, foreign
xenodochy: hospitality
xenogamy: fertilization
xenon: Xe
Xenophon: teacher: Socrates
" **work:** Anabasis
Xenophanean: eleatic
Xeres: Jerez, sherry, wine
" **bridge site:** Abydos
xerophilous plant: cactus, xerophyte
" **animal:** camel
xerotic: dry, sec
xerus: squirrel
Xerxes I: parents of: Darius, Atossa
" **wife:** Esther
Xhosa, Xosa: tribe, language, Bantu
xiphoid: ensiform, swordshaped
xiphosuran: arachnid, king

crab

X-ray: inventor: Roentgen

" **measuring device:** quantimeter

" **science:** rontgenology, roentgenlogy

" **source:** target

" **type:** grenzray

X-shaped: cruciate

Xtian: Christian

xylan: pentosan

xylem: wood, hadrome

xylo: comb. form: wood

xylograph: print, engraving, impression

xyloid: woody, ligneous

xylonite: celluloid

xylophone: saron, gender, gambang, marimba, gigelira, sticcado, gamelan

xylophone-like instrument: marimba, saron

xylotomous insect: termite, anay

xyrid: iris

xyst: portico, walk

xyster: (bone) scraper

xystus, xystos: stoa, porch, terrace, portico

Y

Y: in mathematics: ordinate
    " **letter:** wye
    " **men:** elis
yabber: talk, jabber, chatter, language
yabby(ie): crayfish
yacht: boat, race, craft, sonder
    " **club president:** commodore
    " **flag:** burgee
    " **racing:** sonderclass
    " **sail:** spinnaker
    " **tender:** dinghy
Yadkin: peedee, river
yaff: yap, yelp, bark
yaffle: armful, handful, woodpecker
yager: rifleman
yahoo: lout, brute, savage, bumpkin
    " **creator:** Swift
Yahwe(h): God, Jehovah
yak: ox, zobo, sarlak, buffalo
    " **cross bred:** yakalo, yakattalo
    " **found in:** Tibet
yakamik: trumpeter
yaki: cayman
yakka: work, labor
yaksha: god, ogre, jinn, demon, angel, dryad, gnome, spirit, fairy
Yakut/Yakutsk River: Lena
Yale: university, Eli, lock
    " **bowl sound:** boola-boola
    " **Mr.:** (Elihu) Root
Yalta: native: crimean
yam: ube, ubi, hoi, tuqui, igname, boniata, cush-cush, sweetpotato
Yamashita, Jap. general: Tomoyuki
    " **sobriquet:** tiger
yamen: office, mansion, headquarters
    " **resident:** mandarin

yammadji: native, blackfellow
yamp: tuber
yang: cry, honk
yang-kin: dulcimer
Yangtze River city: Wuhu, Nanking
yank: pull, jerk, hoick
yannigan: scrub
yap: apt, cur, yelp, bark, active, bumpkin
   "   **sl.:** rowdy, hoodlum, greenhorn
Yap Island money: fei, stone
yapp: binding
yardland: virgate
yarm: wail, whine, scream
yarn: abb, eis, tale, crewel, genappe
   "   **ball:** clew
   "   **count:** typp
   "   **holder:** cop
   "   **reel:** pirn
   "   **spindle:** hasp
   "   **waste:** thrum
yarr: spuvrey
yarrow: herb, milfoil
yashmak: veil
yataghan: saber, knife
yaud: mare, jade
yauld: mare, sharp, healthy
yaupon: holly, cassena
   "   **use:** tea
yaw: turn, veer, deviate, tumor
yawp: bay, yap, call, complain
yaws: frambesia
   "   **cause of:** spirochete
yclept: called, named, known (as)
yeanling: kid, lamb, newborn
year: Lat. annus, age, time

book: almanac, annal
   divisions: ¼ trimester (calendar)
   "   ½ semester (academic)
   "   ⅓ trimester (academic)
   types: leap, lunar, fiscal, solar, calendar
yearling: colt, leveret
years, 1000: chiliad
yeast: bee, rise, froth, ferment
   "   **brewer's:** barm
   "   **enzyme:** zymase
yegg: thief, beggar, burglar
yellow: mean, sere, blake, fallow
   alloy: brass
   copper ore: chalcopyrite
   jacket: wasp, eucalypt
   mustard: charlock
   pigment: etiolin, orpiment
   star: sneezeweed
yeme: care, heed, regard, observe
Yemen: Arab, Arabian
   "   **seaport:** Mocha, Mukha
   "   **town:** Sana, Damar
   "   **sect:** Zaidi
   "   **seat of government:** Taiz
yenite: livaite
yeoman: clerk, retainer, assistant
   "   **of guard:** exon
   "   **ly:** sturdy, faithful
yes: yep, yea(h), agree
   "   **Ger.:** ja
   "   **Fr.:** oui
   "   **Russ.:** da
   "   **Sp. & It.:** si
   "   **opposite of:** nope
   "   **man:** sycophant

yeso: gypsum
yeti: monster, snowman
yew: tree, conifer
   " **genus:** taxus
   " **fruit:** berry, cone
Yiddish: Jewish, language
   " **synagogue:** shul
   " **pray:** daven
   " **authority:** maven
yill: ale
Ymir: giant
   " **slayer:** Ve, Odin, Vili
yin: one, feminine, negative
yirr: snarl, growl
yogi: sakir, yogin, ascetic, swami
yoke: wed, pair, pillory, harness
   " **bar, S. Afr.:** skey
   " **comb. form:** zygo
yoked: conjugate
yokel: oaf, clod, rube, gullible, hayseed
yoking: bout, contest
yolk: essence, vitellus
yore: eld, longago, formerly
young: fry, tyro, tender, junior
   " **animal:** cub, joey, chick, tadpole

   " **hare:** leveret
   " **herring:** brit
   " **branch:** shoot
   " **kangaroo:** joey
   " **squab:** piper
younker: knight, nobleman
youth: bud, hoyden, adolescent, minor
   " **goddess of:** Hebe
   " **myth.:** Etana, Adonis, Apollo, Icarus
   " **shelter:** hostel
yowl, yowt: cry, wail, yell
yperite: mustard gas
   " **used in battle:** Ypres
Yucatan: people: Maya(n)
   " **tree:** yaxche
   " **city:** Usmal
yucca: lily, flat, pita
   " **fiber:** isote
   " **plant like:** sotol
Yugoslavia: people: Serb, Croat
   " **coin:** para, dinar
   " **region:** Banat, Bosnia
   " **weight:** oka(e), tovar, dramm
yummy: tasty, delectable

Z

zac: goat, ibex
zacate: hay, grass, forage
Zacch(a)eus: pure, innocent
zachun: oil, bito
zadok: just, righteous
Zagreb(ab): City in Yugoslavia
Zagreus: Dionysus
zaguan: gate, entrance, entranceway
Zambales: (Malay)
" capital: Iba
" language: Tino
Zamboanga: chief city of Mindanao
Zamindar: chief/overseer: mirdha, mirdaha
zampogha: bagpipe, panpipe
zanja: canal, ditch, gully, arrow
zanni, zanny: clown, dolt, simpleton, dotty, buffoon, merry-andrew
Zanzibar island: Pemba

" sultan: sayid
Zarathustra: see Zoroaster
zarf: stand, cupholder
Zealand Island: fiord: isse
zealot: bigot, votary, partisan
Zebedee's son: John, James
zebra: dauw
" extinct: Quagga
" wood: araroba, naked-wood, marblewood
zecchin(o): coin, sequin
zenana: harem, seraglio
" factotum: eunuch
" resident: odalisk(que), concubine
zeno: follower: stoic, cynic
" philosophy: stoicism
zephyr: breeze, wind, aura
Zerulah's son: Abishai
zest: brio, tang, gusto, piquancy
" ful: sapid, racy, pungent
Zeus: Jupiter
" attendant of: Nike

405

" **beloved to:** Io, Europa, Leda

" **breastplate of:** (A)egis

" **brother of:** Hades, Poseidon

" **changed her to stone:** Niobe

" **daughter of:** Irene, Hebe, Ate, Kore, Athena(e), Artemis, Astraea, Despoina, Aphrodite, Persephone, Proserpina, Perephassa

" **disguise of:** swan

" **Egyptian's:** ammon

" **epithet:** soter, ammon, Alastor

" **festival:** nemean

" **gift to Minos:** talos

" **lover of:** Demeter, Juno, Ceres, Latona, Callisto, Themis, Aegle, Leda, Europa, Alceme, Aegina, Eorynome, Antiope

" **messenger of:** Iris, Hermes

" **monster killed by:** Typhoeus

" **nurse:** Cynosura

" **nurse of:** goat

" **oracle:** Dodona

" **parent of:** Rhea, Cronus, Kronos

" **punishment to mankind of:** Pandora

" **sister of:** Hera

" **son of:** Gad, Ares, Arcas, Argus, Minos, Aeacus, Apollo, Hermes, Tityus, Perseus, Dardano, Dionysos(sus), Heracles, Herakies, Hercules, Tanta-

lus, Hephaestus, Sarpedon, Amphion

" **surname of:** Alastor

" **victim of:** Idas

" **wife of:** Hera, Danae, Metis, Semele

ziarat, ziara: tomb, shrine

Zilpah's son: Gad, Asher

zimarra: cloak, cassock, soutane

zimb: bug, fly, insect

zinc: spelter, adamine, tutenag

" **alloy:** bidri, oroide, tombak(ach)

" **blend:** sphalerite

" **carbonate:** calamine, smithsonite

" **ingots:** spelter

" **ore:** blende

" **oxide:** tutty

" **silicate:** calamine

zingara(o): gypsy

zingel: perch, fish

Zion: hill, heaven, Jew

" **Zionism founder:** Herzl

Zipangu: Cipango, Japan

" **namer of:** (Marco) Polo

zizany: tares, cockle, weed

zizith: fringes, tassles

zloty: money of Poland

Zoan: tanis

Zobeide's sister: Amina

zodiac: girdle, circle

zombi(e): cocktail, snake, python

" **subject of:** corpse

zone: area, belt, cincture

" **geological succession:** assise

" **marked by:** zonate

zooid: coral, polypite, hydranth

zoom: chandelle

zoophyte: coral, sponge, retepore

zoril(a): weasel, polecat, mariput

Zoroaster: Zarathustra
" **birthplace:** Azerbaijan
" **demon:** Deva
" **evil spirit:** Ahriman
" **supreme deity:** Ormazd
" **teaching:** Humata
" **trian:** Parsi, gheber, yema
" **works:** (Zend) Avesta

Zug: canton

zuisin: baldpate, widgeon, duck

zules: rook

Zulu: Matabele, Rantu, Kaffir, island
" **capital:** Eshowe
" **headman:** Induna
" **language:** Bantu
" **native:** (Philippines) Muslim, Moro, Badjao
" **spear:** assagai, assegai
" **warriors:** impi

zygodactl bird: parrot

zygoma: bone

zygote: oosperm

zymase: enzyme

zymogen activating substance: kinase

zymone: gluten

zythepsary: brewer

SPECIAL SECTION

What to find there:

1—Alphabets: Greek, Hebrew, Arabic

2—Calendar and Holidays: Jewish

3—Foreign Days of the Week, Months, Numbers: French, Italian, Spanish, German

4—Indians: American and other countries

5—Presidents: Vice-Presidents, Secretaries of State, Wives (including their maiden names)

6—States: Motto, Nickname, Flower, Tree

ALPHABETS

GREEK	HEBREW	ARABIC
alpha	aleph	alif
beta	beth	ba
gamma	gimel	ta
delta	daleth	tha
epsilon	he	jim
zeta	vav	ha
eta	zayin	kha
theta	cheth	dal
iota	teth	dhal
kappa	yodh	ra
lambda	kaph	zay
mu	lamedh	sin
nu	mem	shin
xi	nun	sad
omicron	samekh	dad
pi	ayin	ta
rho	pe	za
sigma	sadie	ayn
tau	koph	ghayn
upsilon	resh	fa
phi	shin	gaf
chi	sin	kaf
psi	tav	lam
omega		mim
		nun
		hah
		waw
		ya

JEWISH CALENDAR

Tishrei
Cheshvan
Kislev
Tevet
Shevat
Adar or Veadar
Nissan
Iyar
Sivan
Tammuz
Ab or Av
Elul

JEWISH HOLIDAYS

Rosh Hashana, Rosh Hashona
Yom Kippur
Sukkos, Succos, Sukkoth
Shemini Atzereth
Simhath Torah
Hanukkah, Chanukah
Purim
Pesah, Pesach, Passover
Lag b'Omer
Shevouth
Tishah b'ab or bov

Days of the Week

French	Italian	Spanish	German
Sun. dimanche	domenica	domingo	Sonntag
Mon. lundi	lunedi	lunes	Montag
Tues. mardi	martedi	martes	Dienstag
Wed. mercredi	mercoledi	miercoles	Mittwoch
Thurs. jeudi	giovedi	jueves	Donnerstag
Fri. vendredi	venerdi	viernes	Freitag
Sat. samedi	sabato	sabado	Sonnabend

Months

French	Italian	Spanish	German
Jan. janvier	gennaio	enero	Januar
Feb. fevrier	febbraio	febrero	Februar
Mar. mars	marzo	marzo	Marz
Apr. avril	aprile	abril	April
May mai	maggio	mayo	Mai
June juin	giugno	junio	Juni
July juillet	luglio	julio	Juli
Aug. aout	agosto	agosto	August
Sept. septembre	settembre	se(p)tiembre	September
Oct. octobre	ottobre	octubre	Oktober
Nov. novembre	novembre	noviembre	November
Dec. decembre	dicembre	diciembre	Dezember

Numbers

1- un	uno	uno	eins
2- deux	due	dos	zwei
3- trois	tre	tres	drei
4- quatre	quattro	cuatro	vier
5- cinq	cinque	cinco	funf
6- six	sei	seis	sechs
7- sept	sette	siete	sieben
8- huit	otto	ocho	acht
9- neuf	nove	nueve	neun
10- dix	dieci	diez	zehn
20- vingt	venti	veinte	zwanzig
30- trente	trenta	treinta	dreissig
40- quarante	quaranta	cuarenta	vierzig
50- cinquante	cinquanta	cincuenta	funfzig
60- soixante	sessanta	sesenta	sechzig
70- soixante-dix	settanta	setenta	siebzig
80- quatre-vingt	ottanta	ochenta	achtzig
90- quatre-vingt dix	novanta	noventa	neunzig
100- cent	cento	cien	hundert
1000- mille	mille	mil	tausend

INDIAN TRIBES

ALASKA: Aleut, Sitka

ALEUTIAN: Attu

ALGONQUIN: Abnaki, Arapaho, Blackfoot, Cheyenne, Cree, Delaware, Fox, Illinois, Lenape, Massachuset, Miami, Micmac, Mohican, Montagnais, Ojibway, Ottawa, Piegan, Sac, Sauk, Shawnee, Sokoki, Wea

AMAZON: Apcoa, Mua

AMERICAN: Abenaki, Abnaki, Aht, Algonquin, Amerind, Apache, Apalachee, Apalachi, Arapaho, Bank, Caddo, Cherokee, Chickasaw, Chippewa, Choctaw, Comanche, Coree, Cree, Creek, Dakota, Dene, Erie, Hitchiti, Hopi, Huron, Ioni, Iowa, Iroquis, Kania, Kansa, Kansas, Kaw, Keres, Keresan, Kickapoo, Kiowa, Lenape, Miami, Mohave, Mojave, Muskhogean, Narraganset, Navaho, Navajo, Nootka, Omaha, Oneida, Onondaga, Osage, Oto, Otoe, Ottawa, Paiute, Pawnee, Pima, Piute, Pokonchi, Red, Redman, Redskin, Sac, Sagamore, Sambos, Seminole, Seneca, Shoshone, Sioux, Siwash, Tana, Taos, Tinne, Ute, Winnebago, Yuma, Zuni

APACHE: Lipan

ARAUCANIAN: Auca

ARAWAK: Araua, Campa, Ineri

ARAWAKAN: Guana

ARIKARA: Ree

ARIZONA: Apache, Hano, Hopi, Moki, Moqui, Navaho, Navajo, Pima, Tewa, Yuma

ATHAPASCAN: Apache, Dene, Hoopa, Hupa, Lipan, Navaho, Navajo, Taku, Tinne, Tinneh

AYMARA:	Colla
BOLIVIA:	Aymara, Chiriguano, Cholo, Ite, Iten, Leca, Mojo, Moxo, Uran, Uro, Uru
BRAZIL:	Acroa, Andoa, Araua, Bravo, Came, Carib, Diau, Ge, Guana, Maku, Mura, Puri, Puru, Siusi, Tariana, Tupi, Yao, Zaparo
BRITISH COLUMBIA:	Gitksan
CADDOAN:	Adai, Andarko, Arikara, Arikaree, Bidai, Caddo, Eyeish, Hainai, Ioni, Machitoch, Pawnee, Ree, Waco
CALGARY:	Sarsi
CALIFORNIA:	Hupa, Koso, Maidu, Mono, Nozi, Pomo, Salina, Seri, Tatu, Yana, Yanan
CANADA:	Aht, Athabasca, Athabascan, Cree, Dene, Niska, Sanetch, Sarcee, Taku, Tinne, Tinneh
CARIB:	Trio, Yao
CARIBAN:	Akawais, Aparais, Arara, Arecunas, Bakairis, Caribs, Chaymas, Cumanagotos, Macusis, Maquiritares, Oyanas, Tamanacos, Trios, Woyaways, Yaos, Yauapery
CAROLINA:	Catawba
CHACO:	Toba
CHILE:	Auca
COLORADO:	Ute
COLUMBIA:	Boro, Duit, Choco, Muso, Muzo, Tama, Tapa
COPEHAN:	Wintun

415

COSTA RICA:	Boto, Voto
COWICHAN INDIANS:	Nanaimo
DAKOTAS:	Arikara, Mandan, Ree, Santee, Sioux, Teton
DELAWARE:	Lenape
ECUADOR:	Andoa, Ardan, Cara
ESKIMO:	Aleut, Atka
FLORIDA:	Calusa
FUEGIAN:	Alikuluf, Ona, Yahgan
GREAT LAKES:	Erie, Huron
GUATEMALA:	Chol, Itza, Ixil, Ixli, Kiche, Mam, Maya, Pipil, Ulva, Voto
HONDURAS:	Paya
HOPI:	Moki, Moqui
IOWA:	Fox, Sac, Sauk
INDIANA:	Miami, Wea
IROQUOIS:	Cayuga, Erie, Hochelaga, Huron, Mohawk, Oneida, Seneca, Wyandot
JALISCO:	Cora
KERESAN:	Acoma, Sia
KUSAN:	Coos
LESSER ANTILLES:	Ineri

MANITOBA:	Cree
MAYAN:	Chol, Mam
MEXICO:	Aztec, Chol, Cora, Mam, Maya, Mixe, Otomi, Pima, Pime, Seri, Seria, Teca, Teco, Toltec, Wabi
MIAMI:	Wea
MISSISSIPPI:	Biloxi, Tiou
MISSOURI:	Osage
MONTANA:	Crow, Hohe
MUSKOHEGAN:	Choctaw, Creek, Hitchiti, Seminole, Yamasi
NEBRASKA:	Kiowa, Omaha, Otoe
NEVADA:	Digger, Paiute
NEW MEXICO:	Acoma, Keres, Pecos, Piro, Sia, Tano, Taos, Tewa, Zuni
NEW YORK:	Erie, Oneida, Seneca, Tuscarora
NICARAGUA:	Mixe, Rama, Ulva
NORTH CAROLINA:	Buffalo, Coree
NORTHWEST:	Cree
OKLAHOMA:	Caddo, Cherokee, Choctaw, Creek, Kansa, Kiowa, Loup, Osage, Oto, Otoe, Pawnee, Ponca, Quapaw
OREGON:	Chinook, Coos, Kusan, Modoc

ORINOCO

VALLEY: Guahiribo

PANAMA: Cueva, Cuna, Guaymi, Guaymie

PANAMINT: Koso

PARAGUAY: Guayaqui

PARU RIVER: Araquaju

PAYAGUAS: Agas

PEBAN: Yagua

PERU: Ande, Anti, Aymara, Boros, Campa, Cana, Carib, Chanca, Chimu, Cholo, Colan, Inca, Inka, Jibaro, Jiyaro, Kechua, Lama, Lamano, Panos, Peba, Pesa, Piba, Piroc, Quechau, Quichu, Yunca, Yuru

PERU SOUTH: Cana, Chanca, Colla

PIMAN: Cora, Jova, Mayo, Opata, Pima, Xova, Yaki, Yaqui

PLATTE RIVER: Pawnee

PLAINS: Cree, Crow, Kiowa, Osage, Pawnee, Ponca, Teton

PUEBLO: Hopi, Keres, Moki, Moqui, Piro, Tano, Taos, Zuni

QUAPAW: Ozark

QUECHUAN: Inca

418

RIO GRANDE:	Tano, Tao
SACRAMENTO	
VALLEY:	Yana
SALISHAN:	Atnah, Lummi, Tulalip
SHOSHONE:	Comanche, Hopi, Koso, Moki, Mono, Moque, Otoe, Paiute, Piute, Uinta, Utah, Ute
SIOUX:	Biloxi, Catawba, Crow, Dakota, Hidata, Iowa, Kansa, Kaw, Mandan, Omaha, Osage, Oto, Otoe, Ponca, Saponi, Tutelo
SONORA:	Jova, Pimi, Seri
SOUTH	
AMERICAN:	Arawak, Aztec, Carib, Ges, Inca, Ineri, Lule, Moxo, Ona, Pano, Piro, Toba, Yao
SOUTH	
CAROLINA:	Catawba
TACANAN:	Cavina
TANOAN:	Tewa
TAPUYAN:	Acroa, Ge, Ges, Ghes
TEXAS:	Lipan
TIERRA	
DEL FUEGO:	Agni, Ona
TLINGIT:	Auk, Sitka
TUPIAN:	Anta

419

UCHEAN:	Uchee, Yuchi
UTAH:	Paiute, Piute, Ute
VANCOUVER	
ISLAND:	Aht, Ehatisaht
VENEZUELA:	Carib, Guarauno, Timote, Timotex
VIRGINIA:	Algonquin, Powhatan
WAKASHAN:	Nootka
WASHINGTON:	Aht, Callam, Hoh, Lummmi, Makah
WESTERN:	Kaw, Seri
WISCONSIN:	Sac
WYOMING:	Crow, Kiowa
XINGU RIVER:	Aneto
YUCATAN:	Maya
YUKIAN:	Huchnom, Tatu, Wappo, Yuki
YUKON:	Taku
YUNCAN:	Chimu
ZUNI LAND:	Cibola

PRESIDENTS OF THE UNITED STATES

President Wife	Vice President	Secretary of State
1. George Washington Martha Dandridge Custis	John Adams	Jefferson, Randolph, Pickering
2. John Adams Abigail Smith	Thomas Jefferson	Pickering, Marshall
3. Thomas Jefferson Martha Wayles Skelton	Aaron Burr George Clinton	Madison
4. James Madison Dorothy (Dolly) Payne Todd	George Clinton Elbridge Gerry	Smith, Monroe
5. James Monroe Elizabeth Kortwright	Daniel D. Tompkins	John Quincy Adams
6. John Quincy Adams Louisa Catherine Johnson	John C. Calhoun	Clay
7. Andrew Jackson Rachel Donelson Robards	John C. Calhoun Martin Van Buren	Van Buren, Livingston, McLane, Forsyth
8. Martin Van Buren Hannah Hoes	Richard M. Johnson	Forsyth
9. William Henry Harrison Anna Symmes	John Tyler	Daniel Webster
10. John Tyler Letitia Christian, Julia Gardiner		Webster, Upshur, Calhoun

#	President / Spouse	Vice President	Secretary of State
11.	James Knox Polk / Sarah Childress	George M. Dallas	Calhoun, Buchanan
12.	Zachary Taylor / Margaret Smith	Millard Fillmore	Buchanan, Clayton
13.	Millard Fillmore / Abigail Powers / Caroline Carmichael McIntosh		Clayton, Webster, Everett
14.	Franklin Pierce / Jane Means Appleton	William R. King	Marcy
15.	James Buchanan	John C. Breckinridge	Marcy, Cass, Black
16.	Abraham Lincoln / Mary Todd	Hannibal Hamlin / Andrew Johnson	Black, Seward
17.	Andrew Johnson / Eliza McCardle		Seward, Washburne
18.	Ulysses Simpson Grant / Julia Dent	Schuyler Colfax / Henry Wilson	Washburne, Fish
19.	Rutherford Birchard Hayes / Lucy Ware Webb	William A. Wheeler	Fish, Evarts
20.	James Abram Garfield / Lucretia Rudolph	Chester A. Arthur	Evarts, Blaine
21.	Chester Alan Arthur / Ellen Lewis Herndon		Blaine, Frelinghuysen
22.	Grover Cleveland / Frances Folsom	Thomas A. Hendricks	Frelinghuysen, Bayard

23.	Benjamin Harrison Caroline Lavinia Scott Mary Scott Lord Dimmock	Levi P. Morton	Bayard, Blaine, Foster
24.	Grover Cleveland Frances Folsom	Adlai E. Stevenson	Gresham, Olney
25.	William McKinley Ida Saxton	Garret A. Hobart Theodore Roosevelt	Olney, Sherman, Day, Hay
26.	Theodore Roosevelt Alice Hathaway Lee Edith Kermit Carow	Charles W. Fairbanks	Hay, Root, Bacon
27.	William Howard Taft Helen Herron	James S. Sherman	Bacon, Knox
28.	Woodrow Wilson Ellen Louise Axon Edith Bolling Galt	Thomas R. Marshall	Knox, Bryan, Lansing, Colby
29.	Warren Gamaliel Harding Florence Kling De Wolfe	Calvin Coolidge	Hughes
30.	Calvin Coolidge Grace Anna Goodhue	Charles G. Dawes	Hughes, Kellogg
31.	Herbert Clark Hoover Lou Henry	Charles Curtis	Kellogg, Stimson
32.	Franklin Delano Roosevelt Anna Eleanor Roosevelt	John Nance Garner Henry A. Wallace Harry S Truman	Hull, Stettinius

33.	Harry S Truman Elizabeth (Bess) Virginia Wallace	Alben W. Barkley	Stettinius, Byrnes, Marshall, Acheson
34.	Dwight David Eisenhower Mamie Geneva Dowd	Richard M. Nixon	Dulles, Herter
35.	John Fitzgerald Kennedy Jacqueline Lee Bouvier	Lyndon B. Johnson	Rusk
36.	Lyndon Baines Johnson Claudia (Lady Bird) Alta Taylor	Hubert H. Humphrey	Rusk
37.	Richard Milhous Nixon Thelma Patricia Ryan	Spiro Agnew Gerald R. Ford	Rogers, Kissinger
38.	Gerald Rudolph Ford Eliabeth (Betty) Bloomer Warren	Nelson A. Rockefeller	Kissinger
39.	Jimmy (James Earl) Carter Rosalynn Smith	Walter F. Mondale	Vance

ALABAMA

State Nickname(s)   Heart of Dixie, Cotton State
    Yellowhammer State

State Motto   We Dare Defend Our Rights
State Flower   Camellia
State Tree   Southern Pine
State Bird   Yellowhammer

ALASKA

State Nickname(s)   The Great Land
State Motto   North to the Future
State Flower   Forget-me-not
State Tree   Sitka Spruce
State Bird   Willow Ptarmigan

ARIZONA

State Nickname(s)   Grand Canyon State, Apache
    State, Sunset Land

State Motto   God Enriches (Ditat Deus)
State Flower   Saguaro (Giant Cactus)
State Tree   Paloverde
State Bird   Cactus Wren

ARKANSAS

State Nickname(s)	Land of Opportunity, Wonder, Bear State, Bowie State
State Motto	Let the People Rule (Regnat Populus)
State Flower	Apple Blossom
State Tree	Shortleaf Pine
State Bird	Mockingbird

CALIFORNIA

State Nickname(s)	Golden State
State Motto	I Have Found It (Eureka)
State Flower	Golden Poppy
State Tree	Redwood
State Bird	Valley Quail

COLORADO

State Nickname(s)	Centennial State, Rover State
State Motto	Nothing Without The Diety (Nil Sine Numine)
State Flower	Columbine
State Tree	Colorado Blue Spruce
State Bird	Lark Bunting

CONNECTICUT

State Nickname(s)	Constitution State, Nutmeg State, Blue Law State
State Motto	He Who Transplanted, Sustains (Qui Transtulit, Sustinet)
State Flower	Mountain Laurel
State Tree	White Oak
State Bird	American Robin

DELAWARE

State Nickname(s)	First State, Diamond State, Blue Hen State
State Motto	Liberty and Independence
State Flower	Peach Blossom
State Tree	American Holly
State Bird	Blue Hen Chicken

FLORIDA

State Nickname(s)	Sunshine State
State Motto	In God We Trust
State Flower	Orange Blossom
State Tree	Sabal Palm
State Bird	Mockingbird

GEORGIA

State Nickname(s)	Empire State of the South, Peach State
State Motto	Wisdom, Justice, Moderation
State Flower	Cherokee Rose
State Tree	Live Oak
State Bird	Brown Thrasher

HAWAII

State Nickname(s)	Aloha State
State Motto	The Life of the Land Is Perpetuated In Righteousness
State Flower	Hibiscus
State Tree	Kukui (Candlenut)
State Bird	Nene (Hawaiian Goose)

IDAHO

State Nickname(s)	Gem State, Potato State
State Motto	It Is Forever (Esto Perpetua)
State Flower	Lewis Mock Orange (Syringa)
State Tree	Western White Pine
State Bird	Mountain Bluebird

ILLINOIS

State Nickname(s)	Prairie State, Land of Lincoln
	The Inland Empire
State Motto	State Sovereignty. National Union
State Flower	Native Violet
State Tree	Bur Oak
State Bird	Cardinal

INDIANA

State Nickname(s)	Hoosier State
State Motto	Cross-roads of America
State Flower	Peony
State Tree	Tulip (Yellow Poplar)
State Bird	Cardinal

IOWA

State Nickname(s)	Hawkeye State
State Motto	Our Liberties We Prize, and
	Our Rights We Will Maintain
State Flower	Wild Rose
State Tree	Oak
State Bird	Eastern Goldfinch

KANSAS

State Nickname(s)	Sunflower State, Jayhawker State
State Motto	To The Stars Through Difficulties (Ad Astra per Aspera)
State Flower	Sunflower
State Tree	Cottonwood
State Bird	Western Meadow Lark

KENTUCKY

State Nickname(s)	Blue Grass State, Corncracker State
State Motto	United We Stand, Divided We Fall
State Flower	Goldenrod
State Tree	Tulip Poplar
State Bird	Cardinal

LOUISIANA

State Nickname(s)	Pelican State, Creole State, Sugar State
State Motto	Union, Justice and Confidence
State Flower	Magnolia
State Tree	Bald Cypress
State Bird	Brown Pelican

MAINE

State Nickname(s) Pine Tree State
State Motto I Guide (Dirigo)
State Flower White Pine Cone and
Tassel
State Tree White Pine
State Bird Chickadee

MARYLAND

State Nickname(s) Old Line State, Free State
State Motto Manly Deeds, Womanly Words
(Fatti Maschi, Parole Femina)
and
With The Shield of Thy Good Will
(Scuto Bonae, Volintatis Tuae
Coronasti Nos)
State Flower Blackeyed Susan
State Tree White Oak
State Bird Baltimore Oriole

MASSACHUSETTS

State Nickname(s)	Bay State, Old Colony State
State Motto	By The Sword We Seek Peace But Peace Only Under Liberty (Ense Petit Placidam Sub Libertate Quietem)
State Flower	Mayflower
State Tree	American Elm
State Bird	Chickadee

MICHIGAN

State Nickname(s)	Wolverine State, Great Lake State
State Motto	If You Seek A Pleasant Peninsula Look About You (Si Quaerie Peninsulam Anoenam Circumspice)
State Flower	Apple Blossom
State Tree	White Poplar
State Bird	Robin

MINNESOTA

State Nickname(s)	North Star State, Gopher State
State Motto	The Star of the North (L'Etoile du Nord)
State Flower	Pink and White Lady's-Slipper
State Tree	Red (Norway) Pine
State Bird	Common Loon

MISSISSIPPI

State Nickname(s)	Magnolia State
State Motto	By Valor and Arms (Virtute et Armis)
State Flower	Magnolia
State Tree	Magnolia
State Bird	Mockingbird

MISSOURI

State Nickname(s)	Show Me State
State Motto	Let The Welfare of the People Be The Supreme Law (Salus Populi Suprema Lex Esto)
State Flower	Hawthorn
State Tree	Flowering Dogwood
State Bird	Eastern Bluebird

MONTANA
State Nickname(s)   Mountain State, Treasure State,
                        Bonanza State, The Big Sky Country
State Motto   Gold and Silver (Oro y Plata)
State Flower   Bitterroot
State Tree   Ponderosa Pine
State Bird   Western Meadowlark

NEBRASKA
State Nickname(s)   Cornhusker State, Beef State,
                        Antelope Blackwater State
State Motto   Equality Before The Law
State Flower   Goldenrod
State Tree   American Elm
State Bird   Western Meadowlark

NEVADA
State Nickname(s)   Silver State, Sagebrush State,
                        Battle Born State
State Motto   All For Our Country
State Flower   Sagebrush
State Tree   Single-leaf Pinon
State Bird   Mountain Bluebird

434

NEW HAMPSHIRE

State Nickname(s)	Granite State
State Motto	Live Free or Die
State Flower	Purple Lilac
State Tree	Paper (White) Birch
State Bird	Purple Finch

NEW JERSEY

State Nickname(s)	Garden State
State Motto	Liberty and Prosperity
State Flower	Purple Violet
State Tree	Red Oak
State Bird	Eastern Goldfinch

NEW MEXICO

State Nickname(s)	Land of Enchantment
State Motto	It Grows As It Goes (Crescit Eundo)
State Flower	Yucca
State Tree	Pinon (Nut Pine)
State Bird	Road Runner

NEW YORK

State Nickname(s)	Empire State
State Motto	Ever Upward (Excelsior)
State Flower	Rose
State Tree	Sugar Maple
State Bird	Bluebird

NORTH CAROLINA

State Nickname(s)	Tar Heel State, Old North State
State Motto	To Be, Rather Than To Seem (Esse Quam Videri)
State Flower	Dogwood
State Tree	Pine
State Bird	Cardinal

NORTH DAKOTA

State Nickname(s)	Flickertail State, Sioux State
State Motto	Liberty and Union, Now and Forever, One and Inseparable
State Flower	Wild Prairie Rose
State Tree	American Elm
State Bird	Western Meadowlark

OHIO
State Nickname(s)   Buckeye State
State Motto   With God All Things Are Possible
State Flower   Scarlet Carnation
State Tree   Buckeye
State Bird   Cardinal

OKLAHOMA
State Nickname(s)   Sooner State
State Motto   Labor Conquers All Things
                     (Labor Omnia Vincit)
State Flower   Mistletoe
State Tree   Redbud
State Bird   Scissortailed Flycatcher

OREGON
State Nickname(s)   Beaver State
State Motto   The Union
State Flower   Oregon Grape
State Tree   Douglas Fir
State Bird   Western Meadowlark

PENNSYLVANIA
State Nickname(s) Keystone State
State Motto Virtue, Liberty and Independence
State Flower Mountain Laurel
State Tree Hemlock
State Bird Ruffed Grouse

RHODE ISLAND
State Nickname(s) Little Rhody, Ocean State
State Motto Hope
State Flower Violet
State Tree Red Maple
State Bird Rhode Island Red (hen)

SOUTH CAROLINA
State Nickname(s) Palmetto State
State Motto Prepared In Mind and Resources
(Animis Opibusque Parati)
and
While I Breathe I Hope
(Dum Spiro, Spero)
State Flower Yellow Jessamine
State Tree Palmetto
State Bird Carolina Wren

SOUTH DAKOTA
State Nickname(s)   Coyote State, Sunshine State, Blizzard State

State Motto   Under God The People Rule
State Flower   Pasqueflower
State Tree   Black Hills Spruce
State Bird   Ringnecked Pheasant

TENNESSEE
State Nickname(s)   Volunteer State, Big Bend State
State Motto   Agriculture and Commerce and America At Its Best

State Flower   Iris
State Tree   Tulip Poplar
State Bird   Mockingbird

TEXAS
State Nickname(s)   Lone Star State
State Motto   Friendship
State Flower   Bluebonnet
State Tree   Pecan
State Bird   Mockingbird

UTAH

State Nickname(s)	Beehive State
State Motto	Industry
State Flower	Sego Lily
State Tree	Blue Spruce
State Bird	Seagull (California Seagull)

VERMONT

State Nickname(s)	Green Mountain State
State Motto	Freedom and Unity
State Flower	Red Clover
State Tree	Sugar Maple
State Bird	Hermit Thrush

VIRGINIA

State Nickname(s)	Old Dominion State
State Motto	Thus Ever To Tyrants (Sic Semper Tyrannis)
State Flower	Flowering American Dogwood
State Tree	Flowering American Dogwood
State Bird	Cardinal

WASHINGTON

State Nickname(s)	Evergreen State
State Motto	By and By (Alki)
State Flower	Western Rhododenron
State Tree	Western Hemlock
State Bird	Willow Goldfinch

WEST VIRGINIA

State Nickname(s)	Mountain State, Panhandle State
State Motto	Mountaineers Are Always Free (Montani Semper Liberi)
State Flower	Big Rosebay Rhododendron
State Tree	Sugar Maple
State Bird	Robin

WISCONSIN

State Nickname(s)	Badger State
State Motto	Forward
State Flower	Butterfly Wood Violet
State Tree	Sugar Maple
State Bird	Robin

WYOMING

State Nickname(s)	Equality State
State Motto	Equal Rights
State Flower	Indian Paintbrush
State Tree	Cottonwood
State Bird	Western Meadowlark

DISTRICT OF COLUMBIA

State Nickname(s)	(no nickname)
State Motto	Justice To All (Justita Omnibus)
State Flower	American Beauty Rose
State Tree	Scarlet Oak
State Bird	Wood Thrush